#중학기본영문법
#내가바로문법강자

바로 문장 쓰는 문법

바로 시리즈 검토에 도움을 주신 분들

홍정환 선생님(영어의 힘)
박용철 선생님(PK대치스마트에듀)
원영아 선생님(멘토영어)
원지윤 선생님(아잉카영어)
이성형 선생님(해윰학원)
김란숙 선생님(샘앤아이영어)
이차은 선생님(BOB영어)
박주경 선생님(PK대치스마트에듀)
주은숙 선생님(원클래스 학원)
김도희 선생님(원클래스 학원)
Kyle 선생님(한스터디)
윤지원 선생님(고려학원)
김현욱 선생님(동광학원)
이형언 선생님(훈성학원)
박은영 선생님(PK대치스마트에듀)
김지혜 선생님(Epic English)
박지혜 선생님(다이나믹 학원)
이민정 선생님(BMA 어학원)
채효석 선생님(빅터 아카데미)

원어민 검토

Stephanie Berry, Matthew D. Gunderman

Chunjae Makes Chunjae

[바로 문장 쓰는 문법] LEVEL 3

기획총괄 남보라
편집개발 김미혜, 신현겸
디자인총괄 김희정
표지디자인 윤순미, 안채리
내지디자인 디자인뮤제오
제작 황성진, 조규영

발행일 2022년 5월 15일 2판 2022년 5월 15일 1쇄
발행인 (주)천재교육
주소 서울시 금천구 가산로9길 54
신고번호 제2001-000018호
고객센터 1577-0902
교재 내용문의 (02)3282-8834

※ 정답 분실 시에는 천재교육 교재 홈페이지에서 내려받으세요.

쓰기가 쉬워지는 중학 기본 영문법

바로 문장 쓰는 문법

LEVEL 3

CONTENTS

중학교 교과서 문법 연계표 3학년

단원	천재(이재영)	천재(정사열)	동아(윤정미)	동아(이병민)	미래엔(최연희)	능률(김성곤)	비상(김진완)
1	• 관계대명사 what [32] • 5형식(지각동사+목적어+동사원형) [2]	• 간접의문문 [38] • 계속적 용법의 관계대명사 [34]	• 접속사 if, whether [38] • to부정사 형용사적 용법 [11]	• It ~ for ... to부정사 [10] • 관계대명사 what [32]	• 관계대명사 what [32] • 접속사 although [39]	• 현재완료진행 [6] • 관계대명사 what [32]	• 관계대명사 what [32] • 관계부사 [33]
2	• 명사를 수식하는 분사 [19] • 접속사 since, though [39]	• 과거완료 [5] • 비교급 강조 [42]	• 5형식(사역동사+목적어+동사원형) [2] • so that(목적) [39]	• 부분을 나타내는 표현 • 조동사가 있는 수동태 [25]	• It ~ that 강조구문 [53] • 계속적 용법의 관계대명사 [34]	• 계속적 용법의 관계대명사 [34] • 명사를 수식하는 분사 [19]	• to부정사의 의미상 주어 [10] • 현재완료진행 [6]
3	• 현재완료진행 [6] • so ~ that [39]	• enough+to부정사 [13] • not only *A* but also *B* [37]	• 계속적 용법의 관계대명사 [34] • 가주어 It ~ that	• 5형식(사역동사+목적어+동사원형) [2] • It ~ that 강조구문 [53]	• 명사를 수식하는 분사 [19] • 강조의 do [53]	• 과거완료 [5] • 부사절을 이끄는 접속사 [39]	• 접속사 if, whether [38] • 과거완료 [5]
4	• 관계부사 [33] • 접속사 if, whether [38]	• 분사구문 [21, 22] • 관계대명사 what [32]	• 현재완료진행 [6] • 의문사+to부정사 [9]	• The+비교급, the+비교급 [42] • 접속사 since [39]	• 간접의문문 [38] • 과거완료 [5]	• 접속사 if, whether [38] • 조동사가 있는 수동태 [25]	• 명사를 수식하는 분사 [19] • 가목적어(it) ~ to부정사 [10]
5	• 과거완료 [5] • It ~ that 강조구문 [53]	• 가정법 과거 [45] • 관계대명사 whose [31]	• 명사를 수식하는 분사 [19] • 원급 비교 [41]	• 가정법 과거 [45] • 의문사+to부정사 [9]	• 분사구문 [21, 22] • not only *A* but also *B* [37]	• to부정사의 의미상 주어 [10] • 관계부사 [33]	• 분사구문 [21, 22] • so that(목적) [39]
6	• It ~ for ... to부정사 [10] • 가정법 과거 [45]	• The+비교급, the+비교급 [42] • It ~ that 강조구문 [53]	• 과거완료 [5] • 관계대명사 what [32]	• so that(목적) [39] • enough+to부정사 [13]	• 관계부사 [33] • 접속부사 however, thus [40]	• The+비교급, the+비교급 [42] • 분사구문 [21, 22]	• It ~ that 강조구문 [53] • 5형식(사역동사+목적어+과거분사) [2]
7	• 분사구문 [21, 22] • 조동사가 있는 수동태 [25]	• 간접화법 [51, 52] • 명사절을 이끄는 접속사 if [38]	• 분사구문 [21, 22] • 접속사 as [39]	• 관계대명사 whose [31] • 접속사 while [39]	• 관계대명사 whose [31] • 가정법 과거 [45]	• 가정법 과거 [45] • so that(목적) [39]	• 접속사 as [39] • 부분을 나타내는 표현
8	• 조동사+have+p.p. [8] • 계속적 용법의 관계대명사 [34]	• 부정대명사 • 5형식(동사+목적어+to부정사) [1]	• It ~ for ... to부정사 [10] • 가정법 과거 [45]	• 분사구문 [21, 22] • 과거완료 [5]			• 가정법 과거 [45] • with+(대)명사+분사 [24]
9							

YBM(박준언)	YBM(송미정)	지학사(민찬규)	능률(양현권)	금성(최인철)	다락원(강용순)
• 강조의 do 53 • 관계대명사 what 32	• too ~ to부정사 13 • to부정사의 부정 9	• 관계대명사 what 32 • 5형식(지각동사+목적어+현재분사) 2	• It ~ for ... to부정사 10 • 계속적 용법의 관계대명사 34	• 5형식(사역동사+목적어+동사원형) 2 • 동명사의 관용 표현 18	• 최상급 43, 44 • 접속사 since 39 • 관계대명사 what 32
• 현재완료진행 6 • 명사를 수식하는 분사 19	• 분사구문 21, 22 • 접속사 if, whether 38	• It ~ for ... to부정사 10 • 명사를 수식하는 분사 19	• It ~ that 강조구문 53 • 5형식(동사+목적어+목적격보어) 1	• The+비교급, the+비교급 42 • to부정사의 의미상 주어 10	• 5형식(동사+목적어+to부정사) 1 • 명사를 수식하는 분사 19 • 관계대명사 whose 31
• It ~ that 강조구문 53 • 5형식(have+목적어+과거분사) 2	• The+비교급, the+비교급 42 • It ~ that 강조구문 53	• not only *A* but also *B* 37 • 관계부사 33	• 관계대명사 what 32 • 5형식(사역동사+목적어+동사원형) 2	• not only *A* but also *B* 37 • I wish 가정법 과거 47	• 목적격 관계대명사 31 • 조동사가 있는 수동태 25 • 가정법 과거 45
• to부정사의 의미상 주어 10 • 가정법 과거 45	• 접속사 although 39 • seem to 14	• 과거완료 5 • to부정사 부사적 용법 12	• 과거완료 5 • 분사구문 21, 22	• 과거완료 5 • 원급 비교 41	• 현재완료 3, 4 • enough+to부정사 13 • The+비교급, the+비교급 42
• 과거완료 5 • so that(목적) 39	• 관계대명사 what 32 • 현재완료진행 6	• 부정대명사 one • 분사구문 21, 22	• 의문사+to부정사 9 • The+비교급, the+비교급 42	• so ~ that 39 • 5형식(지각동사+목적어+목적격보어) 2	• 강조 53 • 접속사 while 39 • 과거완료 5
• 계속적 용법의 관계대명사 34 • to부정사 부사적 용법 12	• 원급 비교 41 • 과거완료 5	• It ~ that 강조구문 53 • 접속부사 however 40	• 화법 전환 51, 52 • 5형식(지각동사+목적어+현재분사) 2	• It ~ that 강조구문 53 • 분사구문 21, 22	• be worth -ing 18 • 접속사 whether 38 • to부정사 명사적 용법 9
• 간접의문문 how 38 • The+비교급, the+비교급 42	• 가정법 과거 45 • so that(목적) 39	• 가정법 과거 45 • 5형식(동사+목적어+형용사) 1	• 가정법 과거 45 • so ~ that 39	• enough+to부정사 13 • 도치(so+동사+주어) 54	• 계속적 용법의 관계대명사 34 • the+형용사 • 가목적어 it ~ to부정사 10
• 분사구문 21, 22 • be worth -ing 18	• not only *A* but also *B* 37 • 접속사 while 39	• too ~ to부정사 13 • 부정 구문		• 간접의문문 38 • It is time +가정법	• feel like -ing 18 • 도치 54 • 부정대명사
					• It ~ that 강조구문 53 • 5형식(have+목적어+과거분사) 2 • I wish 가정법 과거 47

바로 쓰는 문법 LEVEL 3 목차

바로 쓰는 문법 공부 계획표

실력을 키우는 계획표 세우기

1 Level 3는 총 54강입니다. 하루에 몇 강씩, 일주일에 몇 번 공부할지 생각해 보세요.
2 공부한 날을 쓰고, 내가 성취한 항목에 체크(✔)하세요.
3 체크(✔)하지 않은 항목은 복습할 때 꼭 확인해서 빈칸이 없도록 하세요.

단원	목차	공부한 날	복습한 날	나의 성취도 체크 ✔				
		월 / 일	월 / 일	개념이해	문제풀이	오답점검	누적복습	단원평가
UNIT 1 문장의 형식	01 5형식 1							
	02 5형식 2							
UNIT 2 시제	03 현재완료 1_완료, 경험							
	04 현재완료 2_계속, 결과							
	05 과거완료 / 미래완료							
	06 완료 진행							
UNIT 3 조동사	07 had better / would rather / used to / would							
	08 조동사 + have + p.p.							
UNIT 4 to부정사	09 명사적 용법							
	10 가주어, 의미상 주어, 가목적어, It takes ~ to							
	11 형용사적 용법							
	12 부사적 용법							
	13 too ~ to / enough to							
	14 seem to							
UNIT 5 동명사	15 동명사의 역할							
	16 동명사의 의미상 주어와 시제							
	17 동명사와 to부정사							
	18 관용적 표현							
UNIT 6 분사와 분사구문	19 현재분사와 과거분사							
	20 감정을 나타내는 분사							
	21 분사구문							
	22 분사구문의 시제와 태							
	23 독립분사구문							
	24 with + 명사(구) + 분사							

단원	목차	공부한 날	복습한 날	나의 성취도 체크 ✔				
		월 / 일	월 / 일	개념이해	문제풀이	오답점검	누적복습	단원평가
UNIT 7 수동태	25 수동태의 의미와 형태, 시제							
	26 4형식 문장의 수동태							
	27 5형식 문장의 수동태							
	28 동사구의 수동태							
	29 by 이외의 전치사를 쓰는 수동태							
	30 that절을 목적어로 하는 문장의 수동태							
UNIT 8 관계사	31 관계대명사_주격, 소유격, 목적격							
	32 관계대명사 what과 that							
	33 관계부사							
	34 관계대명사의 계속적 용법							
	35 복합 관계대명사							
	36 복합 관계부사							
UNIT 9 접속사	37 상관접속사							
	38 간접의문문							
	39 부사절을 이끄는 접속사							
	40 접속부사							
UNIT 10 비교 구문	41 원급 비교							
	42 여러 가지 비교급 표현							
	43 여러 가지 최상급 표현							
	44 원급과 비교급을 이용한 최상급 표현							
UNIT 11 가정법	45 가정법 과거와 과거완료							
	46 혼합 가정법							
	47 I wish 가정법 / as if 가정법							
	48 Without 가정법							
UNIT 12 일치, 화법, 특수 구문	49 수 일치							
	50 시제 일치							
	51 평서문의 화법 전환							
	52 의문문과 명령문의 화법 전환							
	53 강조							
	54 도치							

BACKGROUND KNOWLEDGE

01 문장의 기본 구성 요소

문장은 단어들이 일정한 순서로 모여 의미를 전달하는 것이다. 문장을 이루는 기본 구성 요소에는 뼈대가 되는 주어, 동사, 목적어, 보어와 살을 붙이는 수식어가 있다.

These books are interesting.
(These books: 주어 / are: 동사 / interesting: 보어)

My uncle teaches Korean in America.
(My uncle: 주어 / teaches: 동사 / Korean: 목적어 / in America: 수식어)

주어 ~은/는, ~이/가 — **동사** ~이다, ~하다 — **목적어** ~을/를, ~에게 / **보어** '~이다, ~가 되다' 앞에 오는 말

주어 Subject | 동사가 나타내는 동작이나 상태의 주체가 되는 말로, 주로 문장 맨 앞에 쓴다.

I am a middle school student. 나는 중학생이다.

My parents love me. 나의 부모님께서는 나를 사랑하신다.

동사 Verb | 주어의 상태나 주어가 하는 동작을 나타내는 말로, 주로 주어 뒤에 쓴다.

Julia and I are good friends. Julia와 나는 좋은 친구이다. 〈상태〉

I walk to school with my friend. 나는 친구와 학교에 걸어간다. 〈동작〉

목적어 Object	동사가 나타내는 행위의 대상이 되는 말로, 주로 동사 뒤에 쓴다.

My grandfather wears glasses. 나의 할아버지께서는 안경을 쓰신다.

Mark bought his sister a guitar. Mark는 그의 누나에게 기타를 사 주었다.
(his sister: 간접목적어, a guitar: 직접목적어)

보어 Complement	주어나 목적어를 보충해서 설명하는 말로, 주로 동사나 목적어 뒤에 쓴다.

He is my uncle. 그는 나의 삼촌이다. 〈주어 He를 보충 설명: 주격 보어〉

The sofa looks comfortable. 그 소파는 편하게 보인다. 〈주어 The sofa를 보충 설명: 주격 보어〉

Her voice makes me sleepy. 그녀의 목소리는 나를 졸리게 한다. 〈목적어 me를 보충 설명: 목적격 보어〉

수식어 Modifier	문장의 요소를 꾸며 그 의미를 더 자세하고 풍부하게 해 주는 말로 주어, 동사, 목적어, 보어를 수식한다.

The book on the desk is mine. 책상 위에 있는 책은 내 것이다. 〈주어 수식〉

They talked loudly. 그들은 큰 소리로 말했다. 〈동사 수식〉

바로 개념 확인 1 상자 안에 제시된 부분이 어떤 문장 구성 요소인지 쓰시오. Answers p. 1

01 | The girl | in the yellow dress | gave | me | this rose | .

The girl	in the yellow dress	gave	me	this rose

02 | We | found | the movie | exciting | .

We	found	the movie	exciting

02 8품사

단어를 성격이 비슷한 것끼리 분류한 것으로, 영어에는 8품사가 있다.

Ah, that looks wonderful.
감탄사 대명사 동사 형용사

The small and lovely parrot in the cage is very noisy.
관사 형용사 접속사 형용사 명사 전치사 관사 명사 동사 부사 형용사

동사 Verb

사람이나 사물, 동물 등의 상태(~이다) 또는 동작(~하다)을 나타내는 말

walk

be동사	'~이다, ~에 있다'의 의미로 주어의 신분이나 상태를 나타내는 동사 현재형: am, are, is 과거형: was, were
조동사 (助도울 조動詞)	be동사나 일반동사 앞에서 의미를 더하는 동사 can(~할 수 있다), may(~일지도 모른다), will(~할 것이다), must(~해야 한다) 등
일반동사	be동사와 조동사를 제외한 나머지 동사 walk(걷다), speak(말하다), write(쓰다) 등

명사 Noun

사람, 사물, 개념 등의 이름을 나타내는 말로 문장에서 주어, 목적어, 보어로 쓰임

dog

셀 수 있는 명사	★보통명사: 일정한 모양이 있어서 하나만 있어도 무엇인지 쉽게 알 수 있는 것 dog, bus, book, ring 등 ★집합명사: 여럿이 모여야 무엇인지 알 수 있는 것 family, class, team 등
셀 수 없는 명사	★고유명사: 세상에 딱 하나뿐인 것(첫 글자는 항상 대문자) Korea, the Eiffel Tower, 사람 이름 등 ★물질명사: 일정한 형태가 없는 air, water, sugar 등 ★추상명사: 눈으로 볼 수 없는 love, peace, beauty 등
명사 짝꿍 [관사 Article]	셀 수 있는 명사 앞에 쓰는 a, an 서로 알고 있는 것을 가리킬 때 쓰는 the

대명사 Pronoun

명사의 반복을 피하기 위해 명사 대신 쓰는 말로 명사처럼 주어, 목적어, 보어로 쓰임

지시 대명사

가까이 있는 것을 가리킬 때: this / these
멀리 있는 것을 가리킬 때: that / those

인칭대명사

사람이나 사물을 대신해서 가리키는 말
Julia is my best friend. She is nice.
Look at the dog. It is cute.

부정(不定정할 정) 대명사

불특정한 사람·사물이나 일정하지 않은 수량을 나타내는 말
one, other, some, any 등

형용사 Adjective

사람·사물의 상태나 모양, 성질, 수량 등을 설명하는 말로 명사를 꾸밈

성질, 상태, 종류 등을 나타내는 형용사

She is happy. (주어의 상태를 설명)
Mia is a kind girl. (명사의 성질을 설명)

수량 형용사

I have many friends. (많은 친구)
└ 셀 수 있는 명사
We don't have much time. (많은 시간)
└ 셀 수 없는 명사

부사 Adverb

시간, 장소, 방법, 정도, 빈도 등을 나타내는 말로 동사, 형용사, 다른 부사, 또는 문장 전체를 꾸밈

often

It is very expensive. (매우 비싼: 형용사 expensive 꾸밈)

They live happily. (행복하게 산다: 동사 live 꾸밈)

You got up too late. (너무 늦게: 부사 late 꾸밈)

Fortunately, I passed the test. (다행스럽게도: 문장 전체 꾸밈)

전치사 Preposition

명사나 대명사 앞에 쓰여 시간, 장소, 방향, 이유, 수단 등을 나타내는 말

- The store opens at 10 on Sundays. (시간)
- Mom is in the living room. (장소)
- We ran to the park. (방향)
- I go to school by bus. (수단)

접속사 Conjunction

'그러나', '그리고'처럼 두 말(단어와 단어, 구와 구, 문장과 문장)을 이어주는 말

등위접속사 and, but, or	문법적으로 대등한 것을 연결 *I'm Jenny* and *I'm from Canada.* Do you like *dogs* or *cats*?
종속접속사 that, when, before, because 등	대장 역할을 하는 문장에 속해 있는 문장을 연결 I think that you are right. He stays at home when it rains. (= When it rains, he stays at home.)

감탄사 Interjection

놀람, 기쁨, 슬픔 등의 감정을 나타내며 저절로 나오는 말

ah, oops, oh, ouch, hooray, hey, wow 등	Ouch! It hurts. (아픔) Hooray! We won the game. (기쁨) Wow! What a beautiful day! (놀람)

바로 개념 확인 2

상자 안에 주어진 단어의 품사가 무엇인지 쓰시오. Answers p. 1

[When] I [scored] a [brilliant] [goal], [they] [shouted] [with] [joy], "[Hooray]! We [finally] [won]!"

03 구와 절

'구(phrase)'는 두 개 이상의 단어가 모여 만들어진 말로, 「주어+동사」를 포함하지 않는다. '절(clause)'은 「주어+동사」를 포함한 여러 단어가 모여 만들어진 말이다. 둘 다 문장에서 명사, 형용사, 부사처럼 쓰인다.

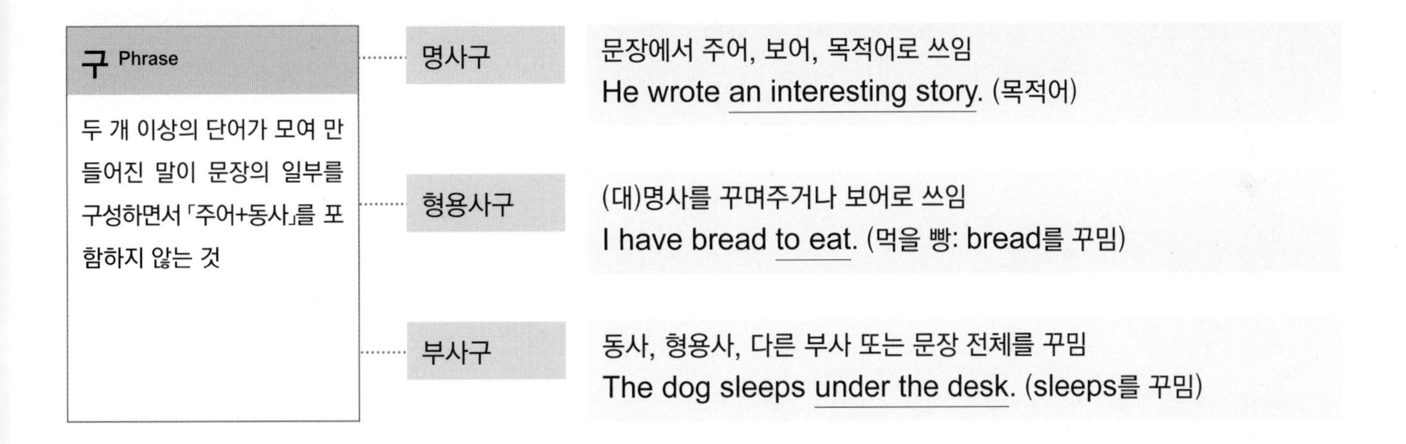

구 Phrase

두 개 이상의 단어가 모여 만들어진 말이 문장의 일부를 구성하면서 「주어+동사」를 포함하지 않는 것

- **명사구**: 문장에서 주어, 보어, 목적어로 쓰임
  He wrote an interesting story. (목적어)
- **형용사구**: (대)명사를 꾸며주거나 보어로 쓰임
  I have bread to eat. (먹을 빵: bread를 꾸밈)
- **부사구**: 동사, 형용사, 다른 부사 또는 문장 전체를 꾸밈
  The dog sleeps under the desk. (sleeps를 꾸밈)

절 Clause

두 개 이상의 단어가 모여서 문장의 일부를 구성하면서 「주어+동사」를 포함하는 것

- **등위절**: 등위접속사 and, but, or로 연결
  Whales live in the water, but they are not fish.
- **종속절**
  - 명사절
  - 형용사절
  - 부사절

  종속접속사 that, when, because, if 등으로 연결
  I think that he is smart. (명사절: 목적어로 쓰임)
  He likes a girl who has big eyes. (형용사절: a girl을 꾸밈)
  I will buy this cap because it looks nice. (부사절: 이유)

바로 개념 확인 3 상자 안에 제시된 부분이 구인지 절인지 쓰시오. Answers p. 1

01 Here is the best place [to see the sunset]. ______

02 Everyone in my class thinks [that Julia is a friendly girl]. ______

03 Do you have a friend [who is good at singing]? ______

04 12시제

시간 관계를 나타내는 문법 범주를 시제(tense)라고 하며, 영어의 시제에는 크게 과거, 현재, 미래가 있다. 그리고 이를 다시 진행형, 완료형과 결합시켜 12시제로 쓸 수 있다.

UNIT 01

문장의 형식

핵심 개념 바로 확인 I know! ☺ No idea! ☹

- 5형식은 「주어 + 동사 + 목적어 + 목적격 보어」로 이루어진 문장이다. ☺ ☹
- 목적격 보어는 목적어를 보충 설명해 주는 말이다. ☺ ☹

개념 01 5형식 1

월 일

The book made him a rich man.
목적어와 목적격 보어가 동격

The book made him rich.
목적격 보어가 목적어를 수식

I want you to call me later.
네가 전화하기를 원하다

My mom told me not to waste money.
내게 낭비하지 말라고 말했다

5형식 | 주어 + 동사 + 목적어 + 목적격 보어

- 명사, 형용사
  - ① 목적어와 목적격 보어가 [주어+서술어] 관계
  - ② name, call, choose, elect, think, keep, consider, find, make 등
- to부정사
  - ① 목적격 보어는 목적어가 하는 동작을 나타냄
  - ② want, wish, ask, tell, expect, require, order, advise, encourage, allow 등

바로 개념

1 5형식은 「주어 + 동사 + 목적어 + 목적격 보어」의 형태로 쓰며, 목적격 보어는 목적어의 성질이나 상태를 보충 설명한다.
2 목적격 보어가 명사나 형용사일 때 목적어와 목적격 보어는 의미상 주어와 서술어의 관계이며, 목적격 보어로 부사는 쓸 수 없다.
3 목적격 보어가 to부정사일 때 목적격 보어는 목적어가 하는 동작을 나타내며, 부정은 「not+to부정사」로 나타낸다.

고르며 개념 확인

Answers p. 1

01 My parents never allow me ○ keeping ○ to keep a pet.

02 The court ordered the man ○ to pay ○ pay a fine.

03 The customer's behavior made her ○ happily ○ happy .

04 I asked the taxi driver ○ turn ○ to turn down the radio.

05 You will find this book very ○ useful ○ use .

06 Emma thought herself ○ bravely ○ brave when she went skydiving.

07 The teacher wanted us ○ to not touch ○ not to touch anything in the science lab.

쓰며 개념 정리 (한 번씩만 쓸 것)

08 Their limitless love made him ______ .

09 Ms. Green advised us ______ for class.

10 Did you really expect me ______ ?

11 Everyone at school calls me ______ .

12 Dad always encourages me ______ .

- to believe you
- Brainy
- not to be late
- a better man
- to follow my dream

5형식 2

월 일

I saw a cat run after a mouse.
진행 중인 동작을 강조하려면 running

My brother let me use his computer.
목적어와 목적격 보어가 능동 관계

Sue had her hair dyed red.
목적어와 목적격 보어가 수동 관계

Dad got me to eat healthy food.
목적어와 목적격 보어가 능동 관계

Jake helped Mom (to) wash her car.

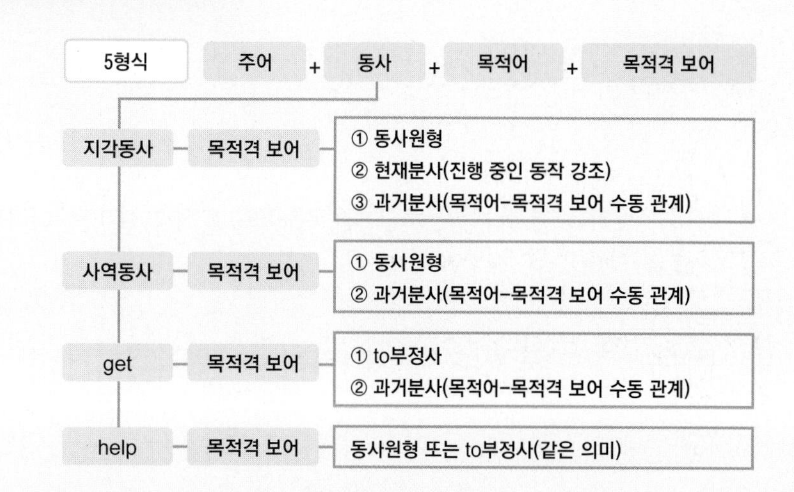

바로 개념

1 지각동사(see, watch, feel, smell, hear, listen to 등)는 목적격 보어로 동사원형과 분사를 쓴다.
2 사역동사(make, have, let 등)는 목적격 보어로 동사원형과 과거분사를 쓴다. 단, let은 과거분사를 쓸 수 없다.
3 get은 '~에게 …하도록 시키다'라는 사역의 의미일 때 목적격 보어로 to부정사와 과거분사를 쓴다.
4 help는 목적격 보어로 동사원형 또는 to부정사를 둘 다 쓸 수 있고, 이때 의미는 동일하다.

고르며 개념 확인

Answers p. 1

01 Technology helps us ○ live ○ living a better life.

02 The man made the bellboy ○ moved ○ move his luggage.

03 I sometimes feel someone ○ to look ○ look at me.

04 His parents wouldn't let him ○ sleep ○ sleeping at a friend's house.

05 She got me ○ to answer ○ answer the question.

06 My father had the broken door ○ repair ○ repaired .

07 We all heard you ○ sing ○ to sing a song.

쓰며 개념 정리

08 Music always makes me ________.

09 I saw a man ________.

10 He got the kids ________.

11 This app helps you ________.

12 She will have the room ________.

- to pick up the trash
- feel alive
- painted light blue
- begging for money
- to find your way

개념 01 5형식 1

1 5형식은 「주어 + 동사 + 목적어 + 목적격 보어」의 형태로 쓰며, 목적격 보어는 목적어의 성질이나 상태를 보충 설명한다.

2 목적격 보어가 명사나 형용사일 때 목적어와 목적격 보어는 의미상 주어와 서술어의 관계이며, 목적격 보어로 ________는 쓸 수 없다.

3 목적격 보어가 to부정사일 때 목적격 보어는 목적어가 하는 ________을 나타내며, 부정은 「________ + to부정사」로 나타낸다.

5형식 주어 + 동사 + 목적어 + 목적격 보어

________ – ① 목적어와 목적격 보어가 [주어+서술어] 관계
② name, call, choose, elect, think, keep, consider, find, make 등

________ – ① 목적격 보어는 목적어가 하는 동작을 나타냄
② want, wish, ask, tell, expect, require, order, advise, encourage, allow 등

개념 02 5형식 2

1 ________(see, watch, feel, smell, hear, listen to 등)는 목적격 보어로 동사원형과 분사를 쓴다.

2 사역동사(make, have, let 등)는 목적격 보어로 동사원형과 과거분사를 쓴다. 단, ________은 과거분사를 쓸 수 없다.

3 ________은 '~에게 …하도록 시키다'라는 사역의 의미일 때 목적격 보어로 to부정사와 과거분사를 쓴다.

4 ________는 목적격 보어로 동사원형 또는 to부정사를 둘 다 쓸 수 있고, 이때 의미는 동일하다.

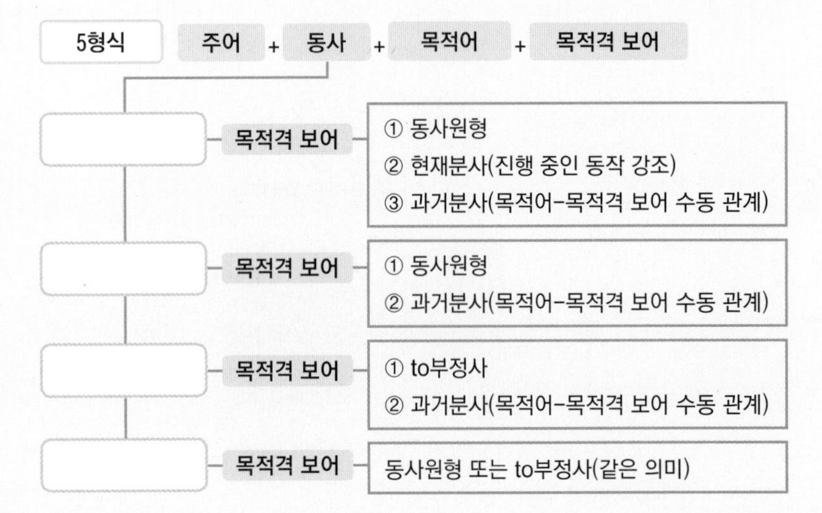

Answers p. 1

A 다음 주어진 단어를 빈칸에 알맞은 형태로 쓰시오.

01 sprain — I had my wrist ______ while playing tennis.

02 wait — She asked the passenger ______ for a second.

03 sleep — You shouldn't let your dog ______ in your bed.

04 play — I was listening to some teens ______ music on the street.

05 break — My father found his car ______ this morning.

06 quietly — Mom always keeps me ______ at a restaurant.

07 solve — There was no one who helped me ______ the problem.

08 raise — Ms. Evans got her students ______ their hands if they had a question.

B 우리말과 같도록 괄호 안의 표현을 이용하여 문장을 완성하시오.

01 그녀는 내가 피아노 치는 법을 배우게 했다. (make, me, learn)

→ She ______ how to play the piano.

02 그들은 화재 경보가 울리는 것을 듣지 못했다. (hear, the fire alarm, go)

→ They didn't ______ off.

03 인터넷은 네가 정보를 빨리 찾을 수 있게 도와준다. (help, you, get)

→ The Internet ______ information quickly.

04 너는 네 이름이 불리는 것을 듣지 못했니? (hear, your name, call)

→ Didn't you ______?

05 그의 부모님은 그가 의대에 가기를 바라셨다. (want, him, go)

→ His parents ______ to medical school.

06 아이를 차에 혼자 두지 마라. (leave, your child, alone)

→ Don't ______ in the car.

07 그녀는 기차가 역에서 떠나는 것을 보았다. (watch, the train, leave)

→ She ______ the station.

문장 바르게 고쳐 쓰기

001 I had my bed design by experts.

I had my bed designed by experts.

002 Living together in one building keeps them safely.

003 People often see animals to suffer from plastic waste.

004 We wanted the next generation be able to see these animals.

005 The manager let us painted anything we wanted.

006 Psychology can help you finding a solution to your problem.

007 Luigi watched the queen whispered in a servant's ear.

008 Volcanoes can make big islands to appear or destroy entire cities like Pompeii.

Answers p. 1

배열하여 문장 쓰고 해석하기

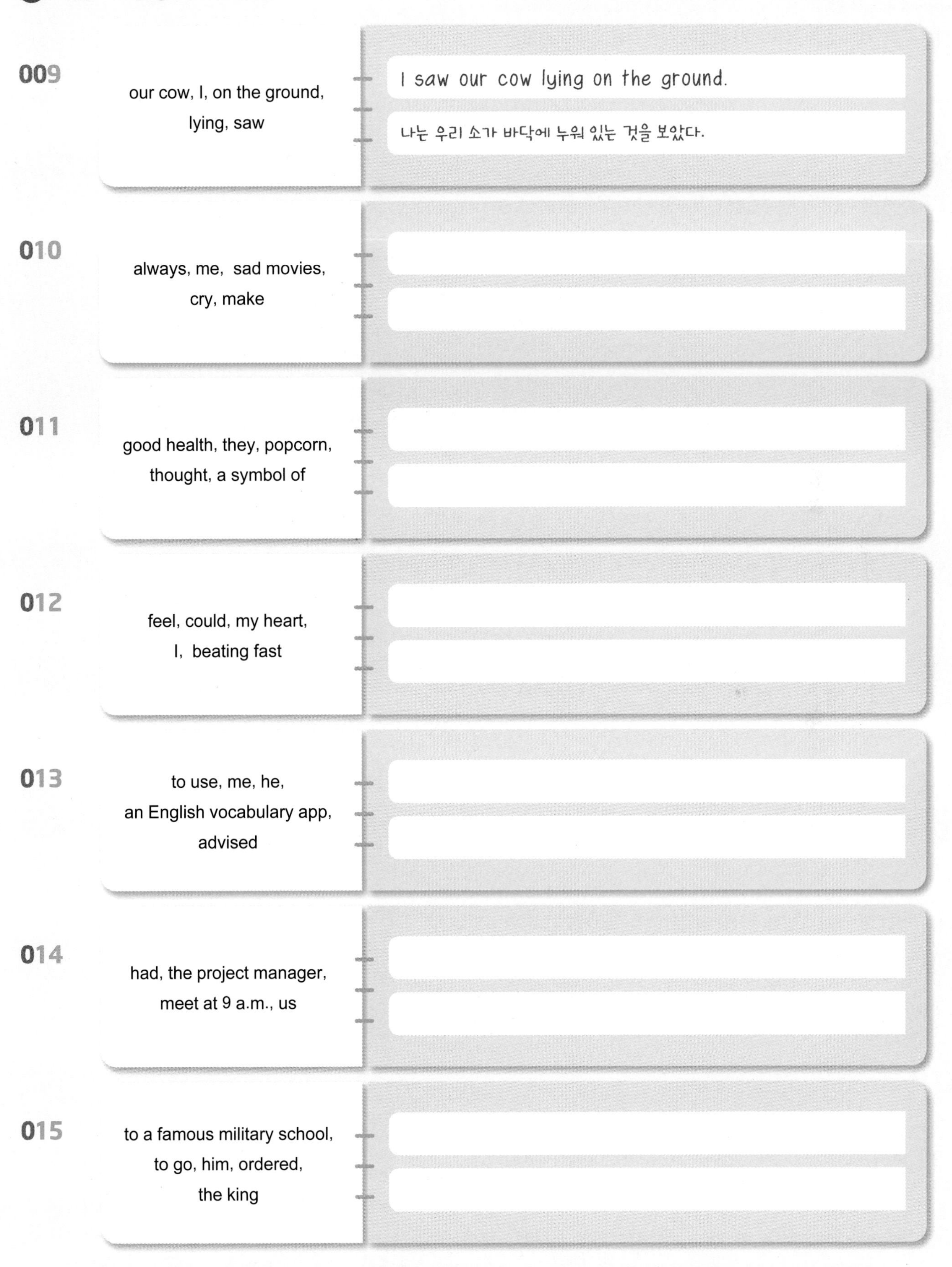

[Self-Editing Checklist] 대 • 소문자를 바르게 썼나요? Y N 철자와 문장 부호를 바르게 썼나요? Y N

REVIEW TEST UNIT 01 문장의 형식

대표유형 01 목적격 보어가 명사·형용사·to부정사인 5형식

01 〈보기〉의 밑줄 친 부분과 역할이 같은 것을 모두 고르면?

> 보기 Good eating habits will keep you healthy.

① People elected Mr. Jones mayor.
② Please get me the blanket on the sofa.
③ He called me a fool in front of my friends.
④ My friend made me a delicious dinner.
⑤ I found my cell phone in the drawer.

02 다음 중 〈보기〉의 문장과 형식이 같은 것은?

> 보기 I always think you a good person.

① He believes his girlfriend pretty.
② She showed me an interesting painting.
③ Brian made his little sister a paper doll.
④ Can you lend me a hand, please?
⑤ He bought me a dozen roses.

03 밑줄 친 동사의 올바른 형태가 나머지 넷과 다른 것은?

① Mom told my brother turn off the TV.
② Mr. Green advised Sam focus on study.
③ Jessica made me change my mind.
④ The coach wanted them play fair.
⑤ The guard didn't allow him get into the building.

[04-05] 다음 문장의 빈칸에 가장 알맞은 것을 고르시오.

04

> Mark considers William ________.

① strictly ② diligently ③ friendly
④ differently ⑤ clearly

05

> My brother asked me not ________ his cell phone.

① use ② used ③ be used
④ using ⑤ to use

06 다음 문장의 빈칸에 공통으로 알맞은 것은?

> • She ________ you to arrive on time.
> • Mr. Brown ________ us to finish writing the essay by tomorrow.

① has ② makes ③ expects
④ lets ⑤ finds

대표유형 02 사역동사가 있는 5형식

07 다음 문장의 빈칸에 들어갈 말로 어색한 것은?

> She ________ her children do the chores.

① let ② had ③ got
④ made ⑤ helped

08 다음 중 밑줄 친 부분의 쓰임이 어색한 것은?

① I found the dog wounded.
② You must get your hair cut.
③ Don't leave her waiting in the rain.
④ My sister had her bike steal yesterday.
⑤ The doctor made the patient stay in bed.

09 다음 우리말과 같도록 할 때 빈칸에 필요 없는 것은?

> 나는 오늘 치아를 뽑았다.
> → ____________________ today.

① had ② pulled ③ I ④ to ⑤ a tooth

10 다음 문장 중 어법상 어색한 것은?

① I had the car repaired.
② The teacher had me copy the file.
③ I'll let you know his phone number later.
④ Did you make your son cleaning the room?
⑤ The citizens helped the man get out of the car.

11 다음 우리말과 같도록 할 때 빈칸에 알맞은 것은?

> 엄마는 내가 채소를 좀 더 먹게 했다.
> → Mom made me ________ more vegetables.

① eat ② ate ③ eating
④ eaten ⑤ to eat

12 다음 문장의 빈칸에 들어갈 말로 알맞은 것은?

Julia ________ her students play a lot.

① let ② asked ③ wanted
④ got ⑤ told

13 다음 문장의 빈칸에 공통으로 알맞은 것은?

• He ________ his house painted white.
• My boss ________ me to type the report.

① made ② got ③ had ④ saw ⑤ kept

14 두 문장의 의미가 같도록 빈칸에 알맞은 것끼리 짝지은 것은?

Telephones allow people ________ easily over long distances.
= Telephones let people ________ easily over long distances.

① communicate — communicate
② communicate — to communicate
③ to communicate — to communicate
④ to communicate — communicate
⑤ to communicate — communicating

대표유형 03 지각동사가 있는 5형식

15 다음 우리말을 영어로 바르게 나타낸 것을 2개 고르면?

그는 내가 시험에서 부정행위를 하는 것을 보았다.

① He saw me cheat on the exam.
② He saw me to cheat on the exam.
③ He saw me cheating on the exam.
④ He saw me cheated on the exam.
⑤ He saw me to cheating on the exam.

16 다음 괄호 안 단어의 형태로 알맞은 것은?

There was an earthquake right before, and I felt the building (shake).

① shook ② shaking ③ shakes
④ shaken ⑤ to shake

대표유형 04 통합형

17 각 문장의 빈칸에 들어갈 말을 순서대로 바르게 짝지은 것은?

• The clerk's attitude made me ________.
• The doctor advised me ________ enough water.
• I heard someone ________ for help.

① angrily — drink — scream
② angrily — to drink — screaming
③ angry — to drink — screamed
④ angry — to drink — screaming
⑤ angry — drink — scream

18 다음 문장 중 빈칸에 to를 쓸 수 있는 것은?

① I saw you ________ sit alone on the grass.
② He felt a hand ________ touch his shoulder.
③ She helped me ________ change the light bulbs.
④ Mike had his car ________ towed.
⑤ We heard the dog ________ bark at night.

19 다음 문장 중 어법상 알맞은 것끼리 묶은 것은?

ⓐ Drinking soda made him fat.
ⓑ The manager got me wipe the dirt.
ⓒ My parents want me to be a pilot.
ⓓ I saw a man carry to the hospital.
ⓔ Mr. Kim had us to take the stairs.

① ⓐ, ⓒ ② ⓑ, ⓔ ③ ⓐ, ⓑ
④ ⓒ, ⓓ ⑤ ⓓ, ⓔ

20 다음 중 밑줄 친 부분이 어법상 어색한 것은?

① I had the table covered with a tablecloth.
② Mark always keeps the door closing.
③ The jury found him guilty of murder.
④ The experience helped me move forward.
⑤ He felt something crawling on his neck.

01 다음 우리말을 주어진 〈조건〉에 맞게 영작하시오.

(1) 그는 그의 거북이를 Edison이라고 이름 지었다.

[조건] **1.** name, turtle을 이용할 것
2. 5단어의 완전한 문장으로 쓸 것

→ ____________________

(2) 나는 네가 택시에서 내리는 것을 보았다.

[조건] **1.** see, get out of를 이용할 것
2. 4단어를 추가하여 완전한 문장으로 쓸 것

→ ____________________

(3) 이 사진은 내가 그 여행을 기억하도록 도와준다.

[조건] **1.** picture, remember, trip을 이용할 것
2. 4단어를 추가하여 완전한 문장으로 쓸 것

→ ____________________

02 다음 대화를 읽고, 괄호 안의 단어를 이용하여 질문에 답하시오.

Daniel Emma, what's wrong?
Emma Brian and I were supposed to meet at 3 yesterday, but he showed up late as usual.
Daniel Oh, no! You felt annoyed, didn't you?
Emma Yeah, I did.

Q. What did Brian do to Emma? (make, feel)

A. He ____________________.

03 다음 글을 읽고, 어법상 어색한 문장을 2개 찾아 밑줄 치고 바르게 고치시오.

My family cleaned up the house last Saturday. Mom had Dad clean the windows. Dad made me to clean the bathroom. I got my brother clean his room.

(1) ____________________

(2) ____________________

[Self-Editing Checklist] ✔ 대 • 소문자를 바르게 썼나요? Y N ✔ 철자와 문장 부호를 바르게 썼나요? Y N

UNIT 02

시제

핵심 개념 바로 확인 I know! ☺ No idea! 😐

- 완료 시제는 어떤 일이 또 다른 시점이나 사건 이전에 일어난 것을 나타낸다.
- 완료 진행 시제는 어느 시점에 일어난 일이 또 다른 사건이 일어날 때까지 진행 중이라는 것을 나타낸다.

개념 03 현재완료 1_완료, 경험

I have just completed the science project.
〈지금 막 끝냈다: 현재의 불특정한 시점에 완료함〉

(과거 시제: I completed the science project yesterday.)
〈어제 끝냈다: 끝낸 시점이 '어제'로 명확함〉

He has never been to Dokdo before.
〈지금까지 독도에 가 본 적이 없다: 과거의 경험〉

(과거 시제: He went to Dokdo when he was 20.)
〈20살 때 독도에 갔다: 과거의 특정 사건〉

쓰임	의미	함께 자주 쓰이는 표현
완료	(과거에 시작한 일이 현재) 막 ~했다, 이미 ~했다	already, just, yet, still 등
경험	(과거부터 현재까지) ~한 적이 있다	ever, never, once, twice, ~ times, before, 최상급 등

바로 개념

1 현재완료는 「have [has]+과거분사」의 형태로, 과거에 일어난 일이 현재까지 영향을 줄 때 사용한다.
2 부정문은 「주어+have [has]+not+과거분사 ~.」이고, 의문문은 「(의문사+)Have [Has]+주어+과거분사 ~?」이다.
3 현재완료는 현재와 관련 있는 어떤 과거의 일을 나타내며, 과거 시제는 현재와 전혀 관련 없는 과거의 일을 나타낸다.
4 과거를 나타내는 부사(구)인 ago, last, yesterday, just now, then 등과 when은 현재완료와 함께 쓸 수 없다.

고르며 개념 확인

Answers p. 3

01 Have you already made your plans? ○ 완료 ○ 경험

02 I have never seen anything like this before. ○ 완료 ○ 경험

03 The man has not fixed the broken machine yet. ○ 완료 ○ 경험

04 Have you read any good books recently? ○ 완료 ○ 경험

05 Sally has just found some mistakes in her writing. ○ 완료 ○ 경험

★**06** This is the most beautiful song I have ever heard. ○ 완료 ○ 경험
★ 「최상급+현재완료」 지금까지 ~한 것 중 가장 …한

07 How many times have you flown in an airplane? ○ 완료 ○ 경험

현재완료 쓰며 개념 정리

08 그 편지는 아직 도착하지 않았다. (arrive) The letter still ______.

09 너는 롤러코스터를 타 본 적이 있니? (ever, ride) ______ a roller coaster?

10 그 경기는 벌써 시작했다. (already, start) The game ______.

11 그는 방금 치과에 다녀왔다. (just, be) ______ to the dentist.

12 나는 그것에 대해 들어 본 적이 없다. (hear) ______ about it before.

현재완료 2_계속, 결과

월 일

She has been a teacher for ten years.
〈10년전부터 지금까지 선생님이다〉

(과거 시제: She was a teacher for ten years, from 2008 to 2017.)
〈2008년부터 2017년까지 10년 동안 선생님이었다〉

I have lost my English textbook.
〈영어책을 잃어버렸고 지금도 찾지 못했다는 것 강조〉

(과거 시제: I lost my English textbook.)
〈단순히 영어책을 잃어버렸다는 행동 강조〉

쓰임	의미	함께 자주 쓰이는 표현
계속	(과거부터 현재까지) 계속 ~해 왔다	since(~부터), for(~ 동안), so far, how long 등
결과	(과거에) ~한 결과 (현재는) …이다	go, lose, grow, buy, leave 등

바로 개념

1 전치사 for 뒤에는 a week, two hours처럼 시간의 길이를 나타내는 표현을 쓴다.
2 전치사 since 뒤에는 yesterday, last week처럼 특정한 시점을 나타내는 표현을 쓴다. 접속사 since가 이끄는 부사절에는 과거 시제를 쓴다.
3 have gone to는 '~에 가 버렸다'는 결과를 나타내고, have been to는 '~에 가 본 적이 있다'는 경험을 나타낸다.
4 have got은 현재완료형이지만 구어체에서는 보통 have(소유하다)의 의미로 쓰인다.

고르며 개념 확인

Answers p. 3

01 She has left her scarf in the restaurant. ○ 계속 ○ 결과
02 Snowboarding has become popular these days. ○ 계속 ○ 결과
03 My sister has learned Chinese since she was 10. ○ 계속 ○ 결과
04 Liam has worked at the UN for 20 years. ○ 계속 ○ 결과
05 Bora has gone to Canada to study English. ○ 계속 ○ 결과
06 He has been good at math since elementary school. ○ 계속 ○ 결과
07 Have you bought a new cell phone? ○ 계속 ○ 결과

현재완료 쓰며 개념 정리

08 그들은 다섯 시간 동안 춤을 췄다. (dance) ________ for five hours.
09 나뭇가지가 길게 자랐다. (grow) The branch ________ long.
10 나는 그때 이후로 피아노를 치지 않았다. (play) ________ the piano since then.
11 너는 얼마나 오래 버스를 기다렸니? (wait) How long ________ for the bus?
12 이틀 내내 비가 왔다. (rain) ________ for two days.

개념 03 현재완료 1_완료, 경험

1 현재완료는 「[ ]+과거분사」의 형태로, 과거에 일어난 일이 현재까지 영향을 줄 때 사용한다.

2 부정문은 「주어+have [has]+[ ]+과거분사 ~.」이고, 의문문은 「(의문사+)Have [Has]+주어+과거분사 ~?」이다.

3 현재완료는 현재와 관련 있는 어떤 과거의 일을 나타내며, 과거 시제는 현재와 전혀 관련 없는 과거의 일을 나타낸다.

4 과거를 나타내는 부사(구)인 ago, last, yesterday, just now, then 등과 [ ]은 현재완료와 함께 쓸 수 없다.

쓰임	의미	함께 자주 쓰이는 표현
완료	(과거에 시작한 일이 현재) [ ]	already, just, yet, still 등
경험	(과거부터 현재까지) [ ]	ever, never, once, twice, ~ times, before, 최상급 등

개념 04 현재완료 2_계속, 결과

1 전치사 [ ] 뒤에는 a week, two hours처럼 시간의 길이를 나타내는 표현을 쓴다.

2 전치사 [ ] 뒤에는 yesterday, last week처럼 특정한 시점을 나타내는 표현을 쓴다. 접속사 since가 이끄는 부사절에는 과거 시제를 쓴다.

3 have [ ] to는 '~에 가 버렸다'는 결과를 나타내고, have [ ] to는 '~에 가 본 적이 있다'는 경험을 나타낸다.

4 have got은 현재완료형이지만 구어체에서는 보통 have(소유하다)의 의미로 쓰인다.

쓰임	의미	함께 자주 쓰이는 표현
계속	(과거부터 현재까지) [ ]	since(~부터), for(~ 동안), so far, how long 등
결과	(과거에) ~한 결과 (현재는) …이다	go, lose, grow, buy, leave 등

Answers p. 3

A 다음 문장의 밑줄 친 부분을 바르게 고치시오.

01 We have four tests so far this semester.

02 How long has she lives in this neighborhood?

03 Natalie has walked to school early this morning.

04 He is the best English teacher that I never met.

05 I read this book ten times since I first read it.

06 Have you think about living in a foreign country?

07 She has visited the zoo since it opens in 2016.

08 When has he returned the book to the library?

B 다음 우리말과 같도록 〈보기〉에서 알맞은 단어를 골라 형태를 바꿔 쓰시오.

보기 see feel sleep lose eat move

01 그녀는 텐트에서 자 본 적이 있다.

→ She ______ in a tent.

02 나는 지난 화요일부터 목에 통증이 있다.

→ I ______ pain in my neck since last Tuesday.

03 그녀는 어제 지하철에서 지갑을 잃어버렸다.

→ She ______ her wallet on the subway yesterday.

04 우리는 2년 동안 그를 본 적이 없다.

→ We ______ him for two years.

05 그들은 두 달 전에 서울로 이사했다.

→ They ______ to Seoul two months ago.

06 그는 어젯밤 이후로 먹은 것이 없다.

→ He ______ anything since last night.

배열하여 문장 쓰기

016 자연은 세계의 많은 건축가에게 영감을 주어 왔다. (many architects, around the world, has, nature, inspired)

Nature has inspired many architects around the world.

017 몇몇 사람들은 지구를 구할 수 있는 창의적인 방법을 찾았다.
(have, to save the earth, creative ways, found, some people)

018 나는 입후보하는 것에 대해 생각해 본 적이 없다. (never, about running, I, thought, have)

019 많은 해녀들은 가족의 생계비를 버는 가장이 되었다.
(have, the breadwinners, many haenyeo, for their families, become)

★ breadwinner는 '생계를 책임지는 사람, 가장'이라는 의미임

020 바람이 화재를 악화시켰다. (has, worse, the fires, the wind, made)

021 물고기가 새를 잡기 위해 물 밖으로 뛰어오르는 것을 본 적 있니?
(ever, to catch a bird, jump out of the water, have, seen, you, a fish)

022 나는 한국 주변의 바다에 살고 있는 다양한 물고기를 연구해 왔다.
(have, living in the seas, many kinds of fish, I, studied, near Korea)

023 그때 이후로, 많은 사람들이 그의 발명품을 다양한 방식으로 이용해 왔다.
(many people, his invention, have, in many different ways, used)

Since then,

Answers p. 3

표현 이용하여 현재완료 문장 쓰기

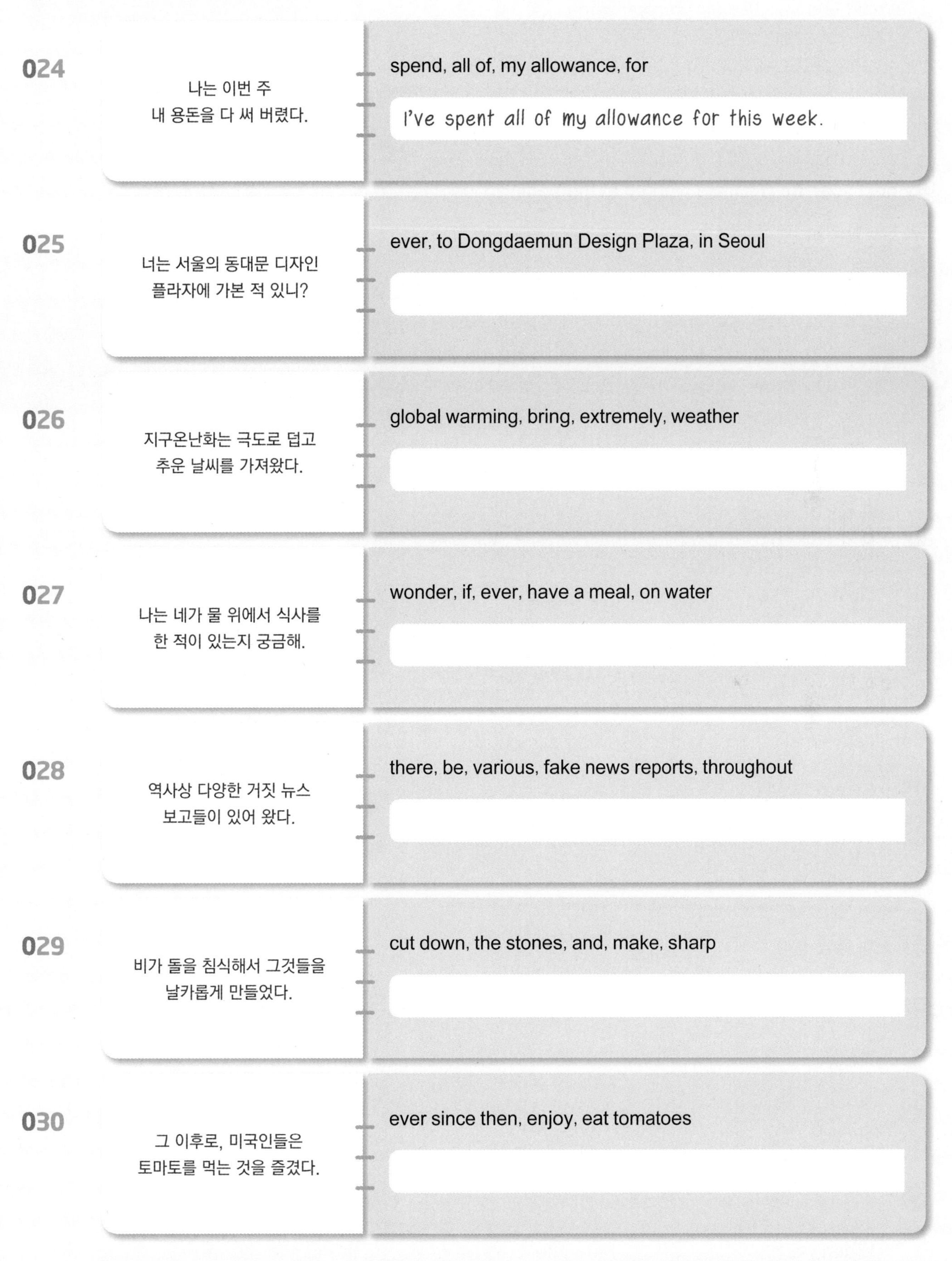

024 나는 이번 주 내 용돈을 다 써 버렸다.

spend, all of, my allowance, for

I've spent all of my allowance for this week.

025 너는 서울의 동대문 디자인 플라자에 가본 적 있니?

ever, to Dongdaemun Design Plaza, in Seoul

026 지구온난화는 극도로 덥고 추운 날씨를 가져왔다.

global warming, bring, extremely, weather

027 나는 네가 물 위에서 식사를 한 적이 있는지 궁금해.

wonder, if, ever, have a meal, on water

028 역사상 다양한 거짓 뉴스 보고들이 있어 왔다.

there, be, various, fake news reports, throughout

029 비가 돌을 침식해서 그것들을 날카롭게 만들었다.

cut down, the stones, and, make, sharp

030 그 이후로, 미국인들은 토마토를 먹는 것을 즐겼다.

ever since then, enjoy, eat tomatoes

[Self-Editing Checklist] 대 • 소문자를 바르게 썼나요? Y N 철자와 문장 부호를 바르게 썼나요? Y N

개념 05 과거완료 / 미래완료

월 일

Jina said she had been to Europe twice.
말하는 시점보다 더 이전 시점 〈경험〉

I had left before Emma got there.
Emma가 도착한 시점보다 더 이전 시점 〈결과〉

I will have finished this work by 3 o'clock.

By next year, he will have worked at the bank for ten years.

	과거완료	미래완료
긍정문	주어+had+과거분사 ~.	주어+will have+과거분사 ~.
부정문	주어+had not+과거분사 ~.	주어+will not have+과거분사 ~.
의문문	(의문사+) Had+주어+과거분사 ~?	(의문사+) Will+주어+have+과거분사 ~?

바로 개념

1 과거완료는 「had+과거분사」의 형태로, 과거 특정 시점보다 더 이전에 일어난 일이 특정 시점까지 영향을 줄 때 사용한다. 이때 먼저 일어난 일을 과거완료형으로 나타내며 이를 대과거라고 한다.

2 미래완료는 「will have+과거분사」의 형태로, 현재부터 미래의 또 다른 어느 시점까지 영향을 주는 일을 나타낸다. 함께 자주 쓰이는 표현은 until, 「by+미래년도」, 「by the time+미래 시점」 등이 있다.

고르며 개념 확인

Answers p. 3

01 I lost the bike that my uncle ○ bought ○ had bought for me.

02 Judy returned the book that she ○ has borrowed ○ had borrowed from me.

03 It's 4:30. He ○ had cooked ○ will have cooked dinner by 6 p.m.

04 I saved all the money that I ○ had earned ○ earned doing chores.

05 By next week, it ○ won't have stopped ○ had stopped raining.

06 The movie had already finished when I ○ arrived ○ arrive at the theater.

쓰며 개념 정리

07 그는 누군가 그의 사무실에 침입했던 것을 발견했다. (find, break)

He ______ that someone ______ into his office.

08 부모님이 도착하실 때쯤이면 우리는 집 청소를 다 해 놓았을 것이다. (clean)

By the time my parents arrive, we ______ the house.

09 우리가 Peter를 만났을 때, 그는 파리에서 20년째 살고 있었다. (meet, live)

When we ______ Peter, he ______ in Paris for 20 years.

개념 06 완료 진행

월 일

I had been waiting for Sam for two hours when he arrived.
Sam이 도착하기 전에 2시간 동안 그를 기다리고 있었다

I have been looking for my ring for a week.
일주일 전부터 지금까지도 찾고 있는

It has been ranining all day.

	과거완료 진행	현재완료 진행
긍정문	주어+had been+현재분사 ~.	주어+have [has] been+현재분사 ~.
부정문	주어+had not been+현재분사 ~.	주어+have [has] not been+현재분사 ~.
의문문	(의문사+)Had+주어+been+현재분사 ~?	(의문사+) Have [Has]+주어+been+현재분사 ~?

바로 개념

1 과거완료 진행형은 「had been+현재분사」의 형태로, 과거의 특정 시점보다 더 이전에 일어난 일이 특정 시점까지 계속 진행되었다는 것을 나타낼 때 쓴다.
2 현재완료 진행형은 「have [has] been+현재분사」의 형태로, 과거의 일이 현재까지 계속 진행되고 있다는 것을 강조할 때 쓴다. 함께 자주 쓰이는 표현은 for, since, all day [week] 등이 있다.
3 현재완료는 이전에 시작한 동작이 완료된 결과를 말하고, 현재완료 진행형은 현재까지도 계속되고 있는 것을 말한다.

고르며 개념 확인

Answers p. 3

01 Bill started to swim 15 years ago. He is still swimming.

→ Billl ○ has been ○ had been swimming for 15 years.

02 I got home. My son was watching TV.

→ My son ○ has been ○ had been watching TV when I got home.

03 Julia began to travel around the world three years ago. She is still traveling.

→ Julia ○ has been ○ had been traveling around the world for three years.

04 We started preparing for the party last Monday. We are still preparing for it.

→ We ○ have been ○ had been preparing for the party since last Monday.

쓰며 개념 정리

05 stand — She felt tired because she ______ ______ ______ all day.

06 think — He said that he ______ ______ ______ about making a film.

07 do — What ______ you ______ ______ for the last hour?

08 study — I ______ ______ ______ hard as final exams start tomorrow.

개념 05 과거완료 / 미래완료

1 과거완료는 「 +과거분사」의 형태로, 과거 특정 시점보다 더 이전에 일어난 일이 특정 시점까지 영향을 줄 때 사용한다. 이때 먼저 일어난 일을 과거완료형으로 나타내며 이를 대과거라고 한다.

2 미래완료는 「 +과거분사」의 형태로, 현재부터 미래의 또 다른 어느 시점까지 영향을 주는 일을 나타낸다. 함께 자주 쓰이는 표현은 until, 「by+미래년도」, 「by the time+미래 시점」 등이 있다.

	과거완료	미래완료
긍정문	주어 + + ~.	주어 + + ~.
부정문	주어 + + 과거분사 ~.	주어 + + 과거분사 ~.
의문문	(의문사+) + 주어 + 과거분사 ~?	(의문사+) Will + 주어 + have + 과거분사 ~?

개념 06 완료 진행

1 은 「had been+현재분사」의 형태로, 과거의 특정 시점보다 더 이전에 일어난 일이 특정 시점까지 계속 진행되었다는 것을 나타낼 때 쓴다.

2 은 「have [has] been+현재분사」의 형태로, 과거의 일이 현재까지 계속 진행되고 있다는 것을 강조할 때 쓴다. 함께 자주 쓰이는 표현은 for, since, all day [week] 등이 있다.

3 현재완료는 이전에 시작한 동작이 완료된 결과를 말하고, 현재완료 진행형은 현재까지도 계속되고 있는 것을 말한다.

	과거완료 진행	현재완료 진행
긍정문	주어 + + ~.	주어 + + ~.
부정문	주어 + + 현재분사 ~.	주어 + + 현재분사 ~.
의문문	(의문사+) Had + 주어 + been + 현재분사 ~?	(의문사+) Have [Has] + 주어 + been + 현재분사 ~?

Answers p. 4

A 우리말과 같도록 괄호 안에 주어진 표현을 이용하여 문장을 완성하시오.

01 나는 그가 회의에서 일찍 떠난 것을 알아채지 못했다. (notice, leave)

→ I ______ that he ______ the meeting early.

02 그녀는 버스가 오기 전에 30분 동안 기다리고 있었다. (wait, come)

→ She ______ for 30 minutes before the bus ______.

03 그들은 몇 시간 동안 축구를 하고 있어서 완전히 지쳤다. (be, play)

→ They ______ exhausted because they ______ soccer for hours.

04 우리는 전화 통화를 하기 전에 만난 적이 없었다. (meet, talk)

→ We ______ before we ______ on the phone.

05 나는 엄마가 오실 때쯤이면 숙제를 끝냈을 것이다. (finish, come)

→ I ______ my homework by the time Mom ______.

B 다음 두 문장을 한 문장으로 만들 때, 그 의미가 통하도록 문장을 완성하시오.

01
• He talked about the movie. • He saw the movie before.

→ He talked about the movie that ______.

02
• I started writing the essay this morning. • I still haven't finished it.

→ ______ since this morning.

03
• I arrived home. • My family already had dinner.

→ When I arrived home, ______.

04
• Mike got home. • His sister was trying to fix the computer for hours.

→ When Mike got home, ______ for hours.

05
• She moved to London. • She lived in Seoul before.

→ She ______ before she moved to London.

배열하여 문장 쓰기

031 has, it, been, heavily, for over three hours, snowing

It has been snowing heavily for over three hours.

032 for three years, in America, been, I, living, have

033 20, will, I, have, 100 books, am, I, read

By the time

034 no one else, before, discovered, been, places, had

He

035 had, an earthquake, I, gone, hit, to bed

After

036 he, he, that, surprised, hadn't, the door, was, locked

037 who, their tests, had, 19 other warriors, passed, were

There

038 I, been, in Spanish, writing, my shopping lists, have

Answers p. 4

표현 이용하여 문장 쓰기

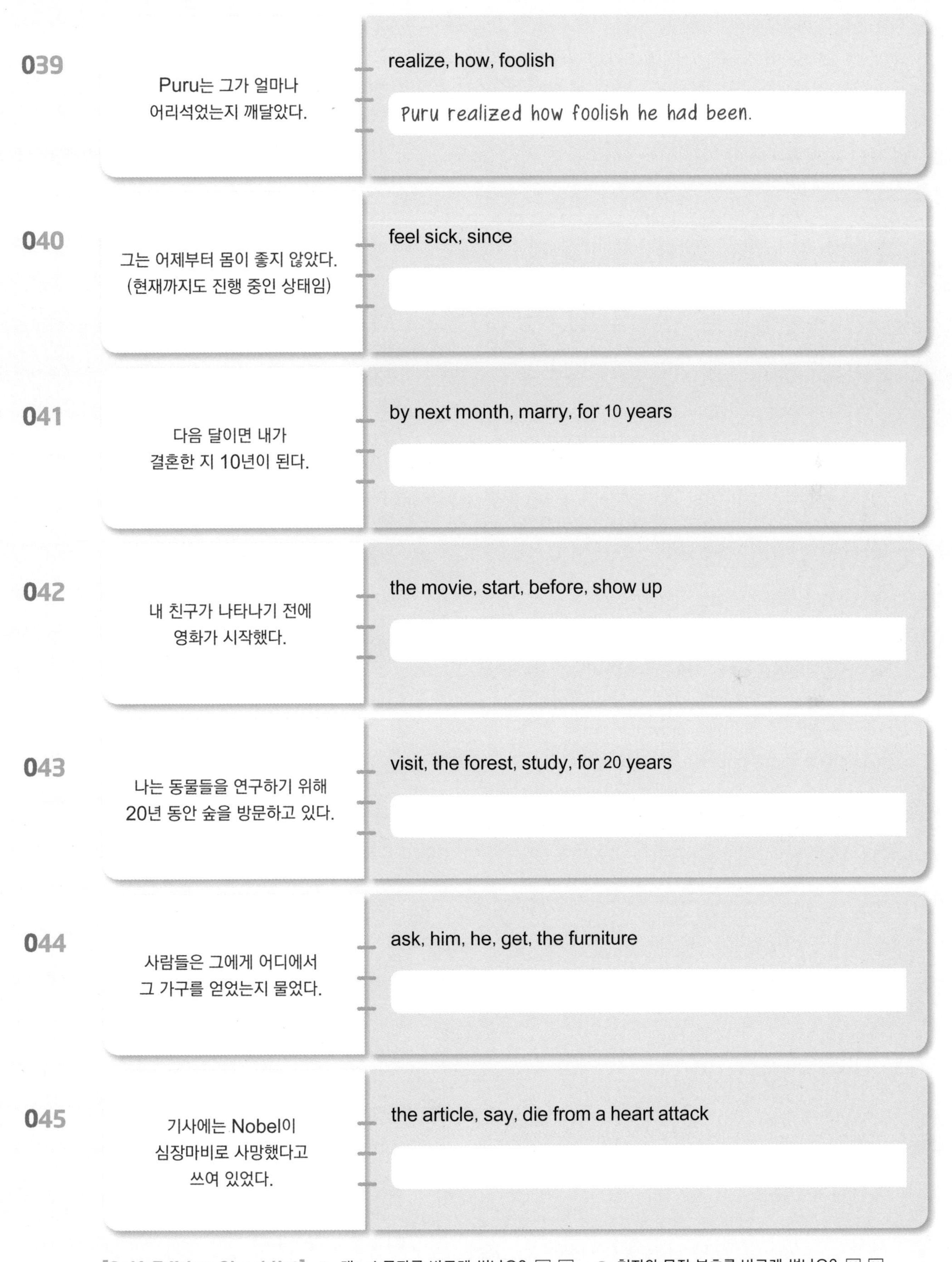

039 Puru는 그가 얼마나 어리석었는지 깨달았다.
realize, how, foolish
Puru realized how foolish he had been.

040 그는 어제부터 몸이 좋지 않았다. (현재까지도 진행 중인 상태임)
feel sick, since

041 다음 달이면 내가 결혼한 지 10년이 된다.
by next month, marry, for 10 years

042 내 친구가 나타나기 전에 영화가 시작했다.
the movie, start, before, show up

043 나는 동물들을 연구하기 위해 20년 동안 숲을 방문하고 있다.
visit, the forest, study, for 20 years

044 사람들은 그에게 어디에서 그 가구를 얻었는지 물었다.
ask, him, he, get, the furniture

045 기사에는 Nobel이 심장마비로 사망했다고 쓰여 있었다.
the article, say, die from a heart attack

[Self-Editing Checklist] ✔ 대 • 소문자를 바르게 썼나요? Y N ✔ 철자와 문장 부호를 바르게 썼나요? Y N

대표유형 01 현재완료

01 다음 문장 중 어법상 어색한 것은?

① We have been together since we are young.
② I haven't finished reading the magazine yet.
③ You have already missed the bus.
④ He has just decided to quit his job.
⑤ Kate has had this bag for 5 years.

02 다음 문장의 빈칸에 들어갈 말을 바르게 짝지은 것은?

• Lisa has been in this class ______ six months.
• A major earthquake has ______ occurred in Chile.

① since — yet ② for — just
③ since — just ④ for — yet
⑤ since — already

03 다음 중 밑줄 친 부분의 쓰임이 어색한 것은?

① My sister has lost weight in the past year.
② I have bought this backpack last month.
③ Winter is over and finally spring has come.
④ He has left his umbrella in the library.
⑤ The building has become a popular place to visit.

[04-05] 다음 대화의 빈칸에 알맞은 것을 고르시오.

04

A Have you climbed Mt. Halla?
B ______ I wish I could do it someday.

① Yes, I did. ② No, I didn't.
③ Yes, I have. ④ No, I haven't.
⑤ Of course, I did.

05

A ______ have you been in Korea?
B For five years.

① How ② When ③ How long
④ How often ⑤ How many times

06 다음 중 〈보기〉의 밑줄 친 부분과 쓰임이 같은 것은?

보기 I haven't made up my mind yet.

① Have you tried surfing?
② I have never won the lottery.
③ They have already taken the history class.
④ Liam has been sick since last week.
⑤ I have worked in this company for a year.

07 다음 우리말을 영어로 바르게 나타낸 것은?

나는 전에 무지개를 본 적이 없다.

① I have seen a rainbow before.
② I have never seen a rainbow before.
③ I have not saw a rainbow before.
④ I did not seen a rainbow before.
⑤ I did not see a rainbow before.

대표유형 02 과거완료 / 미래완료

08 다음 문장의 밑줄 친 동사의 형태로 알맞은 것은?

When the man was introduced to her, he remembered he meet her before.

① met ② meets ③ has met
④ had met ⑤ had meet

09 다음 문장의 빈칸에 들어갈 말로 알맞은 것은?

I couldn't get into the house because I ______ the lock password.

① forget ② forgot
③ had forgotten ④ have forgot
⑤ have forgotten

10 다음 문장의 빈칸에 had가 들어갈 수 없는 것은?

① She ______ never seen snow so far.
② I ______ never drunk coffee until I was 20.
③ My sister destroyed the kite I ______ made.
④ He told me he ______ not met Amy for years.
⑤ Kate ______ never played tennis until then.

Answers p. 4

11 다음 우리말과 같도록 빈칸에 알맞은 말끼리 짝지은 것은?

> 그는 내가 머리카락을 자른 것을 몰랐다.
> → He ________ that I ________ my hair cut.

① noticed — had
② noticed — had had
③ didn't noticed — had
④ didn't notice — had had
⑤ didn't noticed — have had

12 다음 글에서 어법상 어색한 부분을 바르게 고친 것은?

> I went to the beach last Sunday. As I arrived there, I saw a boy drowning in the water. Fortunately, the coast guard rescues the boy before he died.

① went → have been ② arrived → have arrive
③ saw → were seen ④ drowning → drowned
⑤ rescues → had rescued

13 다음 문장 중 어법상 어색한 것은?

① Will they have completed the construction by the end of this month?
② He had worked there before he left school.
③ In a few years they have discovered a cure for cancer.
④ The concert had already started when we arrived at the theater.
⑤ By next year, my family will have lived here for ten years.

대표유형 03 완료 진행

14 다음 문장 중 어법상 어색한 것은?

① Recently I have been feeling tired.
② He wasn't at home because he had gone shopping.
③ They have been building a hotel since last year.
④ Had you been exercising lately?
⑤ She has been reviewing her report all day.

[15-16] 다음 빈칸에 들어갈 수 있는 것을 모두 고르시오.

15

> Had you ________ long before the taxi arrived?

① waited ② wait
③ waiting ④ been waiting
⑤ been waited

16

> My mom has been cooking ____________.

① since 5 o'clock
② before breakfast
③ on weekends
④ for several hours
⑤ an hour ago

17 다음 두 문장을 한 문장으로 바르게 나타낸 것은?

> • She was playing the violin.
> • She is still playing it.

① She likes to play the violin.
② She is playing the violin now.
③ She sometimes plays the violin.
④ She has been playing the violin.
⑤ She had been playing the violin.

18 두 문장의 의미가 같을 때 빈칸에 들어갈 말로 알맞은 것은?

> Mia and I started arguing two hours ago, and we are still arguing at this moment.
> = Mia and I ____________ for two hours.

① had argued
② will have argued
③ has been arguing
④ had been arguing
⑤ have been arguing

01 다음 두 문장을 의미가 통하는 한 문장으로 바꿔 쓰시오.

(1) I started knitting a sweater for Mom a month ago. I'm still knitting it.

→ ________________________________ for a month.

(2) Julia found her credit card. She lost it in the subway.

→ Julia ________________ that ________________.

02 다음 우리말을 주어진 〈조건〉에 맞게 영작하시오.

(1) 내일 아침이면 길은 얼어 붙어 있을 것이다.

[조건] **1.** 미래완료로 쓸 것
2. The street, freeze, by를 이용할 것

→ ________________________________

(2) 우리는 두 시간을 헤맨 후에 그 호텔을 찾았다.

[조건] **1.** 과거완료 진행형으로 쓸 것
2. After, wander, find를 이용할 것

→ ________________________________

03 다음 달력과 제시된 정보를 보고, 빈칸에 알맞은 말을 써 넣어 문장을 완성하시오.

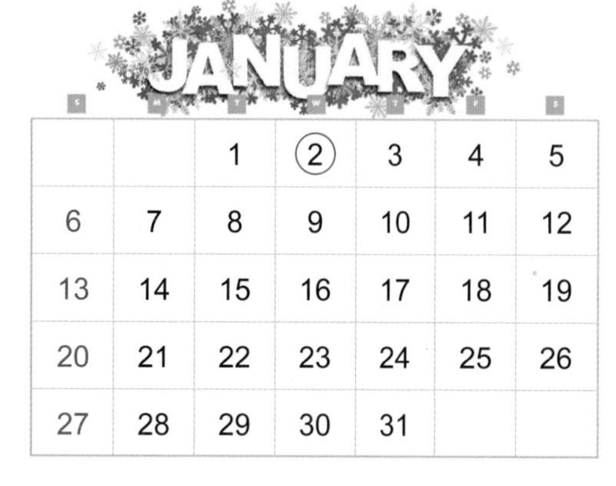

		1	(2)	3	4	5
6	7	8	9	10	11	12
13	14	15	16	17	18	19
20	21	22	23	24	25	26
27	28	29	30	31		

Olivia started learning Spanish on January 2, and today is January 16.

(1) Olivia ________________ for two weeks.

(2) By January 9, Olivia ________________ for one week.

(3) By January 23, Olivia ________________ for three weeks.

[Self-Editing Checklist] ✔ 대 · 소문자를 바르게 썼나요? Y N ✔ 철자와 문장 부호를 바르게 썼나요? Y N

UNIT 03

조동사

07 had better / would rather / used to / would

08 조동사 + have + p.p.

핵심 개념 바로 확인 I know! ☺ No idea! 😐

- 조동사는 동사의 기본 의미에 '충고, 선호, 과거의 습관이나 상태' 등의 의미를 더한다. ☺ 😐
- 「조동사 + have + p.p.」는 과거에 대한 추측, 후회나 유감 등을 나타낸다. ☺ 😐

개념 07 had better / would rather / used to / would

월 일

You had better cut down on snacks.
축약형 : You'd better

I would rather walk than take a bus.
축약형 : I'd rather

Victoria used to [would] go on a bike ride.
과거의 습관

There used to be a big tree in this garden.
과거의 상태를 나타내므로 would는 쓸 수 없음

조동사 구문	의미	
had better + 동사원형	충고 · 경고	~하는 게 좋겠다 부정: had better not
would rather + 동사원형 [A] (+ than + 동사원형 [B])	선호	(B하기 보다는 차라리) A하겠다 부정: would rather not
used to + 동사원형	현재는 지속되지 않는 과거의 습관·상태	~하곤 했다, ~이었다 부정: used not to / didn't use(d) to
would + 동사원형	과거의 습관	~하곤 했다

바로 개념

1 조동사 구문을 이용하여 충고, 선호, 과거의 습관·상태 등을 나타낼 수 있다.
2 used to와 would는 둘 다 과거의 습관을 나타낼 때 쓸 수 있지만 상태동사(be, have, like 등)와 함께 과거의 상태를 나타낼 때는 used to만 가능하고 would는 쓸 수 없다.

고르며 개념 확인

Answers p. 5

01 You'd better ○ keep ○ to keep in mind what I said.

02 I would rather stay home than ○ go ○ goes out.

03 ○ I'd not rather ○ I'd rather not attend her party.

04 She ○ used to ○ would like watching the sunset from the beach.

05 My dad used to ○ read ○ reading storybooks to me when I was a child.

★06 Ella soon got used to ○ wear ○ wearing contact lenses.

★「be [get] used to + 동명사」: ~하는 데 익숙하다[익숙해지다]

쓰며 개념 정리

07 너는 계획을 바꾸는 것이 좋겠다. (change) You ______ your plan.

08 그는 늦지 않는 것이 좋을 거야. (be) He ______ late.

09 나는 경기를 보느니 잠을 자겠다. (sleep) I ______ than watch the game.

10 나는 요리를 하느니 외식을 하겠다. (cook) I'd rather eat out ______ for myself.

11 나는 어릴 때 서울에 살았다. (현재는 아님) (live) I ______ in Seoul when I was young.

★12 그녀는 일요일마다 등산을 가곤 했다. (go, hike) She ______ on Sundays.

★「go + -ing」: ~하러 가다

조동사 + have + p.p.

월 일

I fell down the steps. I should have been more careful.
→ I'm sorry that I wasn't more careful.

Her eyes are red. She must have cried.
→ It's certain that she cried.

I can't find my bag. I may [might] have left it in the taxi.
→ It's possible that I left it in the taxi.

Brian can't have been sick. I saw him playing tennis.
→ It's certain that Brian wasn't sick.

형태	의미	해석
should have p.p.	과거의 일에 대한 후회나 유감	~했어야 했다
must have p.p.	과거의 일에 대한 강한 추측	~이었음에 틀림없다
may [might] have p.p.	과거의 일에 대한 약한 추측	~했을지도 모른다
cannot have p.p.	과거의 일에 대한 강한 의심	~이었을 리가 없다
could have p.p.	과거의 일에 대한 가능성	~할 수도 있었다

바로 개념

1 「조동사 + have + p.p.」는 과거에 대한 추측, 후회나 유감 등을 나타내는 표현이다.

2 「should have p.p.」: ~했어야 했다 (과거에 하지 못한 일에 대한 후회)
「shouldn't have p.p.」: ~하지 말았어야 했다 (과거에 했던 일에 대한 후회)

고르며 개념 확인

Answers p. 5

01 You should have ○ do ○ done your homework.

02 Wesley might have ○ wrote ○ written this letter.

03 I feel sick. I ○ shouldn't have eaten ○ should haven't eaten so much.

04 The ground is wet. It ○ must ○ can't have rained during the night.

05 I couldn't get a ticket for the concert. I ○ should ○ must have booked earlier.

06 Eva is a smart girl. She ○ can't ○ might have said such a stupid thing.

쓰며 개념 정리

07 그녀는 매우 바빴음에 틀림없다. (be) — She ______ really busy.

08 Ted는 더 열심히 공부했어야 했다. (study) — Ted ______ harder.

09 그 강아지는 길을 잃었던 것일지도 모른다. (lose) — The dog ______ its way.

10 그들은 그를 도울 수도 있었다. (help) — They ______ him.

11 그는 어젯밤에 잠을 잘 잤을 리가 없다. (sleep) — He ______ well last night.

12 나는 그녀에게 초대장을 보냈어야 했다. (send) — I ______ her an invitation card.

Answers p. 5

개념 07 had better / would rather / used to / would

1 조동사 구문을 이용하여 충고, 선호, 과거의 습관 · 상태 등을 나타낼 수 있다.

2 used to와 would는 둘 다 과거의 습관을 나타낼 때 쓸 수 있지만 상태동사(be, have, like 등)와 함께 과거의 상태를 나타낼 때는 ______ 만 가능하고 ______ 는 쓸 수 없다.

조동사 구문	의미		
______ + 동사원형	충고 · 경고	~하는 게 좋겠다	부정: ______
______ + 동사원형 [A] (+ than + 동사원형 [B])	선호	(B하기 보다는 차라리) A하겠다	부정: ______
______ + 동사원형	현재는 지속되지 않는 과거의 습관 · 상태	~하곤 했다, ~이었다	부정: ______ / ______
______ + 동사원형	과거의 습관	~하곤 했다	

cf. 「be [get] used to + 동명사」: ~하는 데 익숙하다 [익숙해지다]
「be used to + 동사원형」: ~하는 데 이용되다

개념 08 조동사 + have + p.p.

1 「조동사 + ______ + p.p.」는 과거에 대한 추측, 후회나 유감 등을 나타내는 표현이다.

2 「should have p.p.」: ~했어야 했다 (과거에 하지 못한 일에 대한 후회)
「______」: ~하지 말았어야 했다 (과거에 했던 일에 대한 후회)

should have p.p.	과거의 일에 대한 후회나 유감	~했어야 했다
	과거의 일에 대한 강한 추측	~이었음에 틀림없다
	과거의 일에 대한 약한 추측	~했을지도 모른다
	과거의 일에 대한 강한 의심	~이었을 리가 없다
	과거의 일에 대한 가능성	~할 수도 있었다

Answers p. 5

A 다음 문장에서 밑줄 친 부분을 어법에 맞게 고치시오.

01 You'd better making a reservation in advance.

02 You'd not better skip breakfast for your health.

03 I'd rather keep on moving to be sitting still.

04 The concert was really fantastic. You should have came.

05 Sam is used to taking a nap after lunch, but now he doesn't.

06 Mr. Watson got used to sleep on the sofa.

07 We would rather to lose a game than win the wrong way.

08 He used to not eat anything before an important test.

09 Melanie might has break up with her boyfriend.

10 I should have not forget to set my alarm clock.

B 〈보기〉와 같이 「조동사+have+p.p.」의 형태를 이용하여 주어진 문장을 바꿔 쓰시오.

보기 I'm sorry that I didn't call Joshua last night.
→ I should have called Joshua last night.

01 I regret that I wasn't more patient.

→ I ______.

02 It's certain that David didn't lie to me.

→ David ______.

03 I'm sorry that you didn't think twice.

→ You ______.

04 It's possible that you heard this song before.

→ You ______.

05 It's certain that they had a hard time making this film.

→ They ______.

06 I'm sorry that she drove so fast.

→ She ______.

비교하며 문장 쓰기

046	나는 제주도에 살았다.	I lived in Jejudo.
	나는 예전에 제주도에 살았다. (현재는 아님)	
047	우리 할머니는 요리사였다.	My grandmother was a cook.
	우리 할머니는 예전에 요리사였다. (현재는 아님)	
048	너는 더 조심해야 한다.	You should be more careful.
	너는 더 조심했어야 했다. (과거의 일에 대한 유감)	
049	나는 내 지출을 기록해야 한다.	I should keep track of my spending.
	나는 내 지출을 기록했어야 했다. (과거의 일에 대한 후회)	
050	너는 불필요한 것들을 사지 말아야 한다.	You shouldn't buy unnecessary things.
	너는 그것들을 사지 말았어야 했다. (과거의 일에 대한 유감)	
051	그는 감기에 걸렸다.	He caught a cold.
	그는 감기에 걸렸을지도 모른다. (과거의 일에 대한 약한 추측)	
052	그것은 그에게 힘든 일이었다.	It was tough for him.
	그것은 그에게 힘든 일이었음이 틀림없다. (과거의 일에 대한 강한 추측)	
053	그녀는 그 운동을 매우 좋아했다.	She loved the sport very much.
	그녀는 그 운동을 매우 좋아했음이 틀림없다. (과거의 일에 대한 강한 추측)	

Answers p. 5

표현 이용하여 문장 쓰기

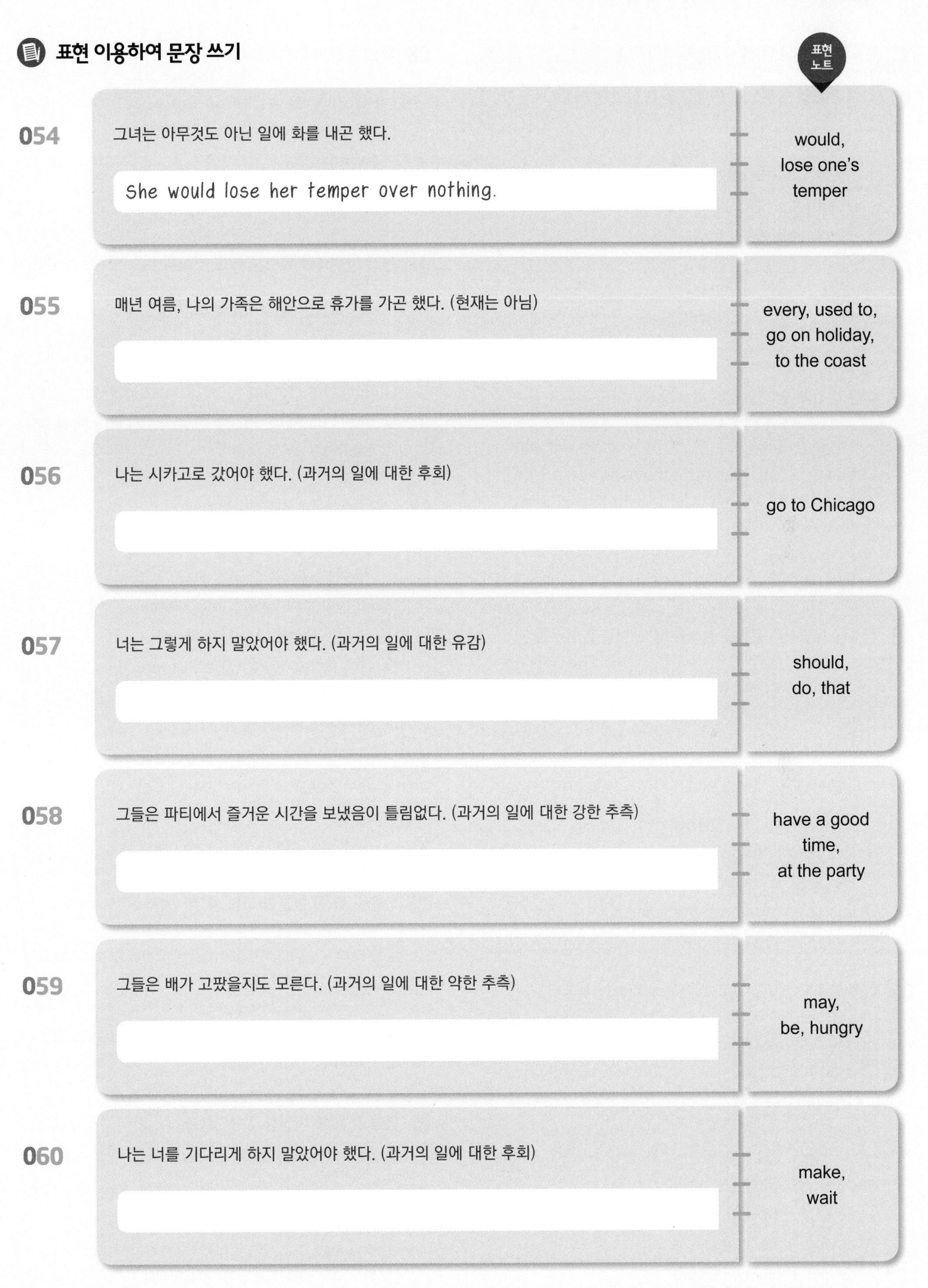

[Self-Editing Checklist] ✓ 대 • 소문자를 바르게 썼나요? Y N ✓ 철자와 문장 부호를 바르게 썼나요? Y N

대표유형 01 had better / would rather / used to / would

01 다음 빈칸에 공통으로 들어갈 말로 알맞은 것은?

• Minho ________ jog every morning last year, but he doesn't any more.
• Cathy ________ be active, but she seems to be very quiet now.

① may ② used to ③ should
④ will ⑤ would

02 다음 빈칸에 들어갈 말이 바르게 짝지어진 것은?

I would rather ________ a walk in the park than ________ fishing in the river.

① take – go ② takes – goes
③ to take – go ④ taking – going
⑤ taking – to go

03 다음을 배열하여 문장을 완성할 때 네 번째로 오는 것은?

had, eat, not, too, better, out, often, you

① had ② eat ③ not ④ too ⑤ better

04 다음 중 밑줄 친 부분의 의미가 나머지 넷과 다른 것은?

① They used to be models.
② We used to throw a big party.
③ He used to watch cartoons a lot.
④ It is used to remove the stains.
⑤ I used to have a dog when I was a kid.

05 다음 빈칸에 들어갈 말이 바르게 짝지어진 것은?

• I'm not used to ________ on the left.
• Salt is used to ________ snow on roadways.
• People used to ________ that the Earth was flat.

① drive – melting – believe
② driving – melting – believe
③ driving – melt – believe
④ drive – melt – believing
⑤ driving – melt – believing

06 다음 문장의 밑줄 친 부분 중 어법상 어색한 것은?

I would(①) rather lie(②) on the beach than(③) goes(④) swimming(⑤).

07 다음 우리말을 영어로 옮긴 문장의 빈칸에 알맞은 것은?

나는 어렸을 때 토마토를 먹지 않았다.
→ I ________ tomatoes when I was young.

① didn't use to eat ② used not eat
③ didn't used to eating ④ wasn't used eating
⑤ wasn't used to eat

08 다음 중 해석이 잘못된 것은?

① You'd better follow her advice.
→ 너는 그녀의 충고를 따르는 게 좋겠다.
② I'd rather have tea than coffee.
→ 나는 커피보다는 차를 마시겠다.
③ This is the dress I used to wear.
→ 이것은 내가 예전에 입곤 했던 드레스이다.
④ I'm used to living in a big city.
→ 나는 예전에 대도시에서 살았다.
⑤ Jim would hide in the closet when his mom came.
→ Jim은 엄마가 오시면 옷장에 숨곤 했다.

09 다음 밑줄 친 부분과 바꿔 쓸 수 있는 것은?

When my parents were away, my grandmother used to take care of me.

① would ② should ③ could
④ might ⑤ must

10 다음 문장 중 어법상 옳은 것은?

① Andy is used to be mean to me.
② You'd better to make a copy of your passport.
③ I'd rather stay home than visit a museum.
④ You had not better cheat on an exam.
⑤ There would be a bridge called the White Ford Bridge.

Answers p. 6

대표유형 02 조동사 + have + p.p.

11 다음 빈칸에 들어갈 말로 알맞은 것은?

> I missed the train. I ________ have come earlier.

① must ② should ③ can ④ may ⑤ might

12 다음 두 문장이 같은 의미가 되도록 할 때 빈칸에 들어갈 말로 알맞은 것은?

> I'm sorry that I wasn't honest with you.
> = I ________________ honest with you.

① should been ② must been have
③ might be ④ should have been
⑤ can't have been

13 다음 빈칸에 공통으로 들어갈 말로 알맞은 것은?

> • Excuse me, but ________ I have a glass of water?
> • Suji hasn't come yet. Perhaps she ________ have taken a wrong bus.

① may ② must ③ should
④ shall ⑤ will

14 다음 대화의 빈칸에 들어갈 말로 알맞은 것은?

> **A** I'm in big trouble. I used up all my allowance.
> **B** Oh, you ________ so much money on clothes.

① could have spent ② should have spent
③ can't have spent ④ must not have spent
⑤ shouldn't have spent

15 다음 문장의 의미와 가장 가까운 것은?

> I should have eaten less for lunch.

① I regret that I ate too much for lunch.
② I'm sorry that I ate too little for lunch.
③ It's possible that I ate little for lunch.
④ I'm sure that I ate too much for lunch.
⑤ I'm not sure whether I ate too much or not.

16 다음 두 문장이 같은 의미가 되도록 할 때 빈칸에 들어갈 말로 알맞은 것은?

> I'm certain that Claire saw the show already.
> = Claire ________ the show already.

① can't seen ② must have seen
③ could have seen ④ should have seen
⑤ might have seen

17 다음 빈칸에 들어갈 말로 알맞은 것은?

> Joey is an honest boy. He ________ your purse.

① should have stolen ② must have stolen
③ may have stolen ④ could have stolen
⑤ can't have stolen

18 다음 문장 중 어법상 옳은 것은?

① Mr. Warren cannot have be rich.
② You should have wore a warmer coat.
③ He might have met Julia somewhere before.
④ Sam may have feels disappointed at the result.
⑤ She must has misunderstood what I said.

19 다음 대화의 밑줄 친 부분 중 어법상 어색한 것은?

> **A** Have you ① heard ② that they won the game?
> **B** Yes, I ③ have. They must have ④ be proud of ⑤ themselves.

20 다음 대화에서 밑줄 친 부분의 쓰임이 어색한 것은?

① **A** Becky didn't show up yesterday.
  B She might have forgotten the appointment.
② **A** I couldn't finish the project.
  B You should have started it earlier.
③ **A** Julia's performance was amazing.
  B I agree. She must have practiced a lot.
④ **A** What he said really hurt me.
  B He shouldn't have said that.
⑤ **A** I just saw Ivan at the theater.
  B It must have been Ivan. He has gone to Paris.

01 다음 우리말에 맞게 빈칸에 알맞은 말을 쓰시오.

(1) 너는 그와 어울리지 않는 게 좋겠다.

→ You'd ____________ ____________ hang out with him.

(2) 나는 어렸을 때 이 강에서 수영을 하곤 했다.

→ I ____________ ____________ ____________ in this river when I was young.

(3) 나는 전화로 얘기하느니 차라리 문자 메시지를 보내겠다.

→ I would ____________ ____________ a text message ____________ ____________ on the phone.

02 (A)와 (B)에서 각각 알맞은 것을 골라 대화를 완성하시오. (단, 한 번씩만 사용할 것)

(A)	(B)
should	be
shouldn't	lie
must	leave
might	bring

(1) **A** Have you seen my science book?

B I'm not sure, but you ________________________ it in the library.

(2) **A** It looks like rain. I ________________________ an umbrella.

B Don't worry. You can share my umbrella.

(3) **A** Nobody in the class passed the test.

B Really? It ________________________ very difficult.

(4) **A** Is Jason still mad at me?

B Yes. You ________________________ to him. You hurt his feelings.

수행평가 유형 조건 제시형

03 다음 상황을 읽고 〈조건〉에 맞게 문장을 완성하시오.

Yesterday Mark had an important business meeting. But he was late for the meeting, and he lost a *contract. He regrets that he was late for the meeting. What would you say to him about yesterday's situation?

*contract 계약

[조건] 「조동사 + have + p.p.」의 형태를 이용하여 과거의 일에 대한 유감을 나타낼 것

→ You ____.

[Self-Editing Checklist] ✔ 대 • 소문자를 바르게 썼나요? Y N ✔ 철자와 문장 부호를 바르게 썼나요? Y N

UNIT 04

to부정사

핵심 개념 바로 확인 I know! ☺ No idea! ☹

- to부정사는 「to + 동사원형」의 형태이고 명사, 형용사, 부사의 역할을 한다. ☺ ☹
- 주어나 목적어 역할을 하는 to부정사가 길어질 경우, 각각 가주어 it과 가목적어 it을 쓴다. ☺ ☹

개념 09

명사적 용법

월 일

To eat blueberries is good for your eyes. 〈주어〉
= Eating / to부정사(구) 주어는 단수 취급

Her dream is to become a famous rapper. 〈보어〉
= becoming

They all agreed to go to the beach. 〈목적어〉

We don't know what to do.
= what we should do

Jiho decided not to join the rock band.

to부정사를 목적어로 쓰는 동사				
want	hope	wish	expect	plan
need	choose	decide	learn	agree
promise	refuse	manage	pretend	would like

의문사 + to부정사	
what + to부정사	무엇을 ~할지
when + to부정사	언제 ~할지
where + to부정사	어디로 ~할지
how + to부정사	어떻게 ~할지, ~하는 방법
which + to부정사	어느 것을 ~할지
who(m) + to부정사	누가 [누구를] ~할지

바로 개념

1 to부정사는 「to + 동사원형」의 형태로 명사처럼 문장의 주어, 보어, 목적어 역할을 할 수 있으며 '~하는 것, ~하기'라고 해석한다.
2 「의문사 + to부정사」는 명사처럼 쓰이며 「의문사 + 주어 + should + 동사원형」으로 바꿔 쓸 수 있다.
3 to부정사의 부정은 「not[never] + to부정사」의 형태이다.

고르며 개념 확인

Answers p. 7

01 ○ Do ○ To do your best is the easiest way to succeed.

02 Her goal is ○ to raise ○ to raising funds by next month.

03 I managed ○ to get ○ getting to the airport on time.

04 The important thing is ○ to listen ○ to listened to your friend in trouble.

05 Do you know ○ how ○ what to distinguish twins?

06 They chose ○ to not spread ○ not to spread the rumor.

쓰며 개념 정리

★07 플라스틱 병을 재활용하는 것은 중요하다. ____ plastic bottles ____ important. (recycle)
★ to부정사(구) 주어는 단수 취급

08 나의 꿈은 동물 보호소를 짓는 것이다. My dream is ____ an animal shelter. (build)

★09 너는 왜 마음을 바꾸기로 결심했니? Why have you ____ your mind? (decide, change)
★ 현재완료 의문문 형태에 주의

10 나는 그가 하는 말에 관심 있는 척했다. I ____ interested in what he said. (pretend, be)

11 너는 돈을 절약하는 법을 배워야 한다. You should learn ____ money. (save)

12 나는 Sam을 위해 무엇을 사야 할지 모르겠다. I have no idea ____ for Sam. (buy)

개념 10 가주어, 의미상 주어, 가목적어, It takes ~ to

월 일

It is important to protect our nature.
가주어 / 진주어

It is hard for him to make a speech in public.
가주어 / 의미상 주어 / 진주어

He found it hard to make new friends.
가목적어 / 목적격 보어 / 진목적어

It took me an hour to finish the homework.
= It took an hour for me to finish the homework.

가주어	「가주어 it ~ to부정사」	
의미상 주어	「for + 목적격」	일반적인 to부정사의 의미상 주어
	「of + 목적격」	사람의 성격을 나타내는 형용사가 보어로 쓰였을 때 *kind, rude, polite, generous, wise, foolish, careful 등
가목적어	「주어 + 동사 + 가목적어 it + 목적격 보어(형용사/명사) + 진목적어」 (← 5형식) * 가목적어를 주로 쓰는 동사: think, believe, find, make, consider 등	

바로 개념

1 to부정사가 주어로 쓰일 때 주로 가주어 it을 주어 자리에 쓰고 to부정사(구)는 뒤로 보낸다. 가주어 it은 해석하지 않는다.
2 to부정사의 행위의 주체가 문장의 주어와 다를 때 to부정사 앞에 「for / of + 목적격」을 써서 의미상 주어를 나타낸다.
3 to부정사가 목적어로 쓰일 때 가목적어 it을 목적어 자리에 쓰고 to부정사(구)는 뒤로 보낸다. 가목적어 it은 해석하지 않는다.
4 「It takes + 목적격 + 시간 + to부정사」는 '~가 …하는 데 시간이 걸리다'라는 의미이다.

고르며 개념 확인

Answers p. 7

01 ○ It ○ That is illegal to drive a car without a license.

*02 It took ○ her a week ○ a week her to recover from the flu.

03 It is stupid ○ of ○ for you to believe every word she said.

04 Is it necessary ○ of ○ for him to attend the meeting?

05 I make ○ it a rule ○ make a rule it to go swimming every morning.

06 Social media has ○ made possible ○ made it possible to share your ideas with others.

★「It takes + 목적격 + 시간 + to부정사」
→「It takes + 시간 + for + 목적격 + to부정사」

쓰며 개념 정리 배열하기

07 그가 임무를 완수하는 것은 불가능하다. (is, to complete, impossible, for, it, him)

________ his mission.

*08 나는 그를 설득하기가 어렵다고 느꼈다. (to persuade, it, found, difficult)

I ________ him. ★ 가목적어 위치 주의하기

09 내가 이 책을 읽는 데는 오랜 시간이 걸렸다. (me, it, to read, took, a long time)

________ this book.

Answers p. 7

개념 09 명사적 용법

1 to부정사는 「to + 동사원형」의 형태로 명사처럼 문장의 주어, 보어, 목적어 역할을 할 수 있으며 ‘[ ], [ ]’라고 해석한다.

2 「의문사 + to부정사」는 명사처럼 쓰이며 「의문사 + 주어 + [ ] + 동사원형」으로 바꿔 쓸 수 있다.

3 to부정사의 부정은 「[ ] [[ ]] + [ ]」의 형태이다.

to부정사를 목적어로 쓰는 동사				
want	hope	wish	expect	plan
need	choose	decide	learn	agree
promise	refuse	manage	pretend	would like

의문사 + to부정사	
what + to부정사	무엇을 ~할지
[ ] + to부정사	언제 ~할지
[ ] + to부정사	어디로 ~할지
[ ] + to부정사	어떻게 ~할지, ~하는 방법
[ ] + to부정사	어느 것을 ~할지
[ ] + to부정사	누가 [누구를] ~할지

개념 10 가주어, 의미상 주어, 가목적어, It takes ~ to

1 to부정사가 주어로 쓰일 때 주로 가주어 [ ]을 주어 자리에 쓰고 to부정사(구)는 뒤로 보낸다. 가주어 it은 해석하지 않는다.

2 to부정사의 행위의 주체가 문장의 주어와 다를 때 to부정사 앞에 「for / of + 목적격」을 써서 의미상 주어를 나타낸다.

3 to부정사가 목적어로 쓰일 때 가목적어 [ ]을 목적어 자리에 쓰고 to부정사(구)는 뒤로 보낸다. 가목적어 it은 해석하지 않는다.

4 「[ ] [ ] + 목적격 + 시간 + to부정사」는 ‘~가 …하는 데 시간이 걸리다’라는 의미이다.

가주어	「가주어 it ~ to부정사」	
의미상 주어	「[ ] + 목적격」	일반적인 to부정사의 의미상 주어
	「[ ] + 목적격」	사람의 성격을 나타내는 형용사가 보어로 쓰였을 때 *kind, rude, polite, generous, wise, foolish, careful 등
가목적어	「주어 + 동사 + [ ] + [ ](형용사/명사) + [ ]」(← 5형식) * 가목적어를 주로 쓰는 동사: think, believe, find, make, consider 등	

Answers p. 7

A 다음 문장에서 밑줄 친 부분을 어법에 맞게 고치시오.

01 Get enough sleep helps you learn better.

02 The biggest challenge is faces my fears.

03 We promise deliver within 48 hours.

04 Can you explain how set up this printer?

05 It is generous him to offer to pay for us.

06 It is natural of teens to want more privacy.

07 After the fight, Anne decided never meet him again.

08 It was polite you to apologize to the old lady.

09 It took three hours them to put out the fire.

10 Credit cards made possible to buy things without cash.

B 다음 문장을 가주어 it 또는 가목적어 it을 사용하여 바꿔 쓰시오.

01 To study abroad will be nice. (가주어)

→

02 He found that it was hard to refuse our invitation. (가목적어)

→ He ______.

03 It was impossible to sleep well because of the noise. (가목적어)

→ The noise made ______.

04 To find a way to control your feelings may be a good idea. (가주어)

→

05 To consume too much caffeine is not good for your health. (가주어)

→

06 We believe that it is necessary to teach about cultural differences. (가목적어)

→ We ______.

조건에 맞게 문장 바꿔 쓰기

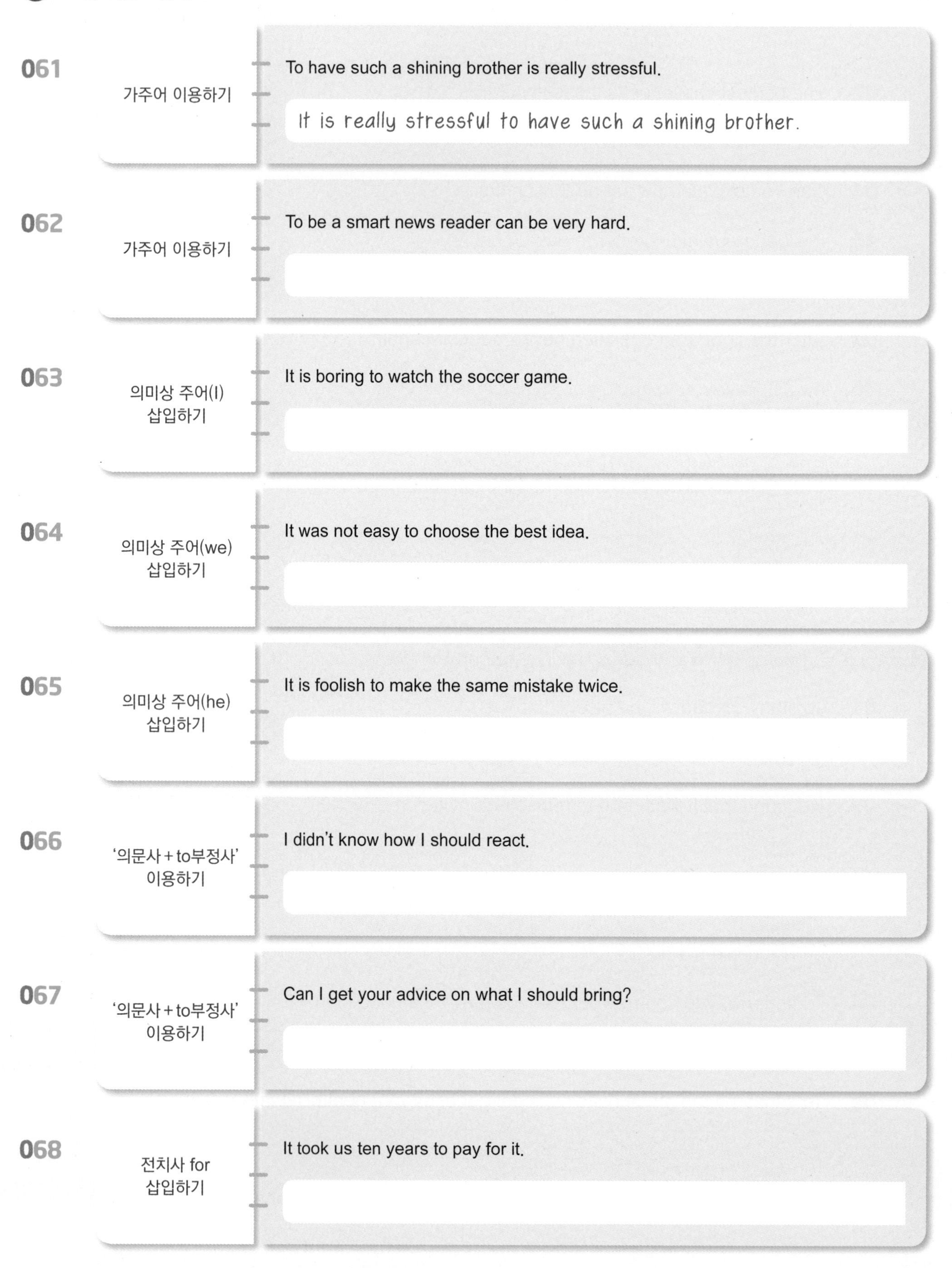

061 가주어 이용하기
To have such a shining brother is really stressful.
It is really stressful to have such a shining brother.

062 가주어 이용하기
To be a smart news reader can be very hard.

063 의미상 주어(I) 삽입하기
It is boring to watch the soccer game.

064 의미상 주어(we) 삽입하기
It was not easy to choose the best idea.

065 의미상 주어(he) 삽입하기
It is foolish to make the same mistake twice.

066 '의문사+to부정사' 이용하기
I didn't know how I should react.

067 '의문사+to부정사' 이용하기
Can I get your advice on what I should bring?

068 전치사 for 삽입하기
It took us ten years to pay for it.

Answers p. 7

배열하여 문장 쓰기

069 그 프로젝트는 우리 마을에 벽화를 그리는 것이었다.
(a wall painting, was, to do, in our neighborhood)

The project

070 부자는 돈을 불리는 방법을 안다.
(knows, a rich man, to make, grow, money, how)

071 내가 머리를 손질하는 데 시간이 좀 걸렸다.
(to do, me, it, my hair, some time, took)

072 당신은 스마트폰 사용에 대한 몇 가지 규칙을 정할 필요가 있다.
(for you, it, for using your smartphone, to set some rules, necessary, is)

073 아이슬란드는 많은 장소 섭외가들이 방문하기에 최적의 장소이다.
(to visit, for many location scouts, the best place, Iceland, is)

074 모두가 자원을 소중히 여기는 것이 중요하다.
(to value, for everyone, important, it, the resources, is)

075 나는 음악으로 사람들에게 영감을 주는 것이 가능하다는 것을 알았다.
(possible, it, people, to inspire, I, by music, found)

[Self-Editing Checklist] ✔ 대·소문자를 바르게 썼나요? Y N ✔ 철자와 문장 부호를 바르게 썼나요? Y N

개념 11 형용사적 용법

월 일

She wants some bread to eat.

I have something important to tell you.

The man asked for a fork to eat with.
← eat with a fork

His speech is to start soon. 〈예정〉

You are to report to Mr. Smith. 〈의무〉

No one was to be seen in the room. 〈가능〉

명사·대명사 수식 (~할, ~하는)	명사·대명사 + to부정사	
	-thing, -one, -body (+ 형용사) + to부정사	
	(대)명사 + to부정사 + 전치사	
be + to부정사	예정	~할 예정이다
	의무	~해야 한다
	가능	~할 수 있다
	운명	~할 운명이다
	의지	~할 작정이다

바로 개념

1 to부정사는 형용사처럼 명사 또는 대명사를 뒤에서 수식할 수 있고, 이때 to부정사는 '~할, ~하는'이라는 의미이다.
2 -thing, -one, -body로 끝나는 대명사가 쓰일 때 「-thing, -one, -body (+ 형용사) + to부정사」의 어순이다.
3 to부정사의 수식을 받는 명사가 전치사의 목적어일 때 to부정사 뒤에 전치사를 쓴다.
4 「be + to부정사」는 예정, 의무, 가능, 운명, 의지 등의 의미를 나타낸다.

고르며 개념 확인

Answers p. 7

01 Are you looking for ○ something different to do ○ different to do something ?

02 Is there ○ anybody to help ○ to help anybody me find my dog?

03 Stephen Hawking said, "Intelligence is the ability ○ to adapt ○ adapting to change."

04 Here are ○ some tips to relieve ○ to relieve some tips your stress.

05 Writing a diary is a good way ○ to improve ○ to improving your writing skills.

★**06** My family will rent an apartment ○ to live ○ to live in .

★ 「(대)명사 + to부정사 + 전치사」
- a house to live in
- a chair to sit on
- someone to talk to
- a toy to play with
- a pen to write with

쓰며 개념 정리 「be + to부정사」 쓰기

07 We are going to leave for Seoul at six.

= We [ ] for Seoul at six.

08 Not a sound could be heard.

= Not a sound [ ] heard.

09 If you intend to pass the exam this time, you should study hard.

= If you [ ] the exam this time, you should study hard.

부사적 용법

월 일

I went to the library to return books. 〈목적〉
= in order to return [so as to return]

We were happy to see Julia again. 〈감정의 원인〉

Steve must be adventurous to travel alone. 〈판단의 근거〉

He lived to see his son become a writer. 〈결과〉

These clothes are comfortable to wear. 〈형용사 수식〉

목적	~하기 위해서	= in order to [so as to]
감정의 원인	~해서, ~하니	감정을 나타내는 형용사를 뒤에서 수식 *glad, surprised, excited, shocked, disappointed 등
판단의 근거	~하다니	주로 함께 쓰는 표현: cannot, must 등
결과	…해서 (결국) ~하다	주로 함께 쓰는 표현: live, grow up, awake, wake up 등
형용사 수식	~하기에	to부정사가 형용사를 뒤에서 수식

바로 개념

1 to부정사는 부사처럼 동사, 형용사, 부사를 수식할 수 있다.
2 부사적 용법의 to부정사는 목적, 감정의 원인, 판단의 근거, 결과 등을 나타낸다.
3 「(in order / so as) not to + 동사원형」은 '~하지 않도록'이라는 의미이다.

고르며 개념 확인

Answers p. 7

01 Everyone was pleased to receive such a nice gift. ○ 감정의 원인 ○ 판단의 근거

02 He awoke to find himself lying on the sofa. ○ 목적 ○ 결과

03 Many people think that good friends are hard to find. ○ 감정의 원인 ○ 형용사 수식

04 David must be a fool to believe such a story. ○ 결과 ○ 판단의 근거

05 I turned down the volume to concentrate on studying. ○ 목적 ○ 결과

06 I learned that male house mice sing to attract females. ○ 목적 ○ 감정의 원인

쓰며 개념 정리

07 그 기사는 이해하기 어렵다. (understand) The article is difficult ______.

08 우리는 눈을 보고 신났다. (see) We were excited ______ the snow.

09 나는 Max를 태우기 위해 공항에 갔다. (pick) I went to the airport ______ up Max.

10 그녀는 자라서 배우가 되었다. (be) She grew up ______ an actress.

11 나는 아기를 깨우지 않도록 조용히 말했다. (wake) I spoke quietly ______ the baby.

12 그런 말을 하다니 그는 화가 난 것이 틀림없다.(say) He must be angry ______ such a word.

Answers p. 8

개념 11 형용사적 용법

1 to부정사는 형용사처럼 명사 또는 대명사를 뒤에서 수식하는 역할을 할 수 있고, 이때 to부정사는 '[ ], [ ]'이라는 의미이다.

2 -thing, -one, -body로 끝나는 대명사가 쓰일 때 「-thing, -one, -body (+ [ ])+ [ ]」의 어순이다.

3 to부정사의 수식을 받는 명사가 전치사의 목적어일 때 to부정사 뒤에 전치사를 쓴다.

4 「be + to부정사」는 예정, 의무, 가능, 운명, 의지 등의 의미를 나타낸다.

명사·대명사 수식 (~할, ~하는)	명사·대명사 + to부정사	
	-thing, -one, -body (+ 형용사) + to부정사	
	(대)명사 + to부정사 + 전치사	
be + to부정사	예정	~할 예정이다
	의무	
	가능	
	운명	
	의지	

개념 12 부사적 용법

1 to부정사는 부사처럼 동사, 형용사, 부사를 수식할 수 있다.

2 부사적 용법의 to부정사는 목적, 감정의 원인, 판단의 근거, 결과 등을 나타낸다.

3 「(in order / so as) [ ] + 동사원형」은 '~하지 않도록'이라는 의미이다.

목적	~하기 위해서	= [ ] [so as to]
감정의 원인		감정을 나타내는 형용사를 뒤에서 수식 *glad, surprised, excited, shocked, disappointed 등
판단의 근거		주로 함께 쓰는 표현: cannot, must 등
결과		주로 함께 쓰는 표현: live, grow up, awake, wake up 등
형용사 수식		to부정사가 형용사를 뒤에서 수식

A 다음 문장에서 어법상 어색한 부분에 밑줄을 긋고 바르게 고치시오.

01 Ryan is not a man tell a lie.

02 We're going to order spicy something eat.

★ 어순에 주의

03 Miranda was disappointed lost the game again.

04 Don't miss the opportunity join our team.

05 Your handwriting is to recognize impossible.

06 Doran lent me a pen to write.

★ write with a pen

07 You should do your best in order that achieve your goals.

B 다음 〈보기〉와 같이 두 문장이 같은 뜻이 되도록 to부정사를 이용하여 바꿔 쓰시오.

보기 My grandfather wore glasses because he wanted to read the letter.
→ My grandfather wore glasses to read the letter.

01 We dropped by the grocery store because we wanted to buy some flour.

→ We dropped by the grocery store ____________.

02 I had to take a taxi because I didn't want to miss my flight.

→ I had to take a taxi ____________.

★ to부정사의 부정: 「not [never] + to부정사」

03 Frank heard that his mom felt better, so he was glad.

→ Frank was glad ____________.

04 I woke up and found myself famous.

→ I woke up ____________.

05 Eva can answer the difficult questions, so she must be a genius.

→ Eva must be a genius ____________.

★ 6~8번은 「be + to부정사」 이용하기

06 The president is going to visit Switzerland next weekend.

→ The president ____________ next weekend.

07 You should not talk during the exam.

→ You ____________.

08 The princess was destined to get married to a poor man.

→ The princess ____________.

★ be destined to: ~할 운명이다

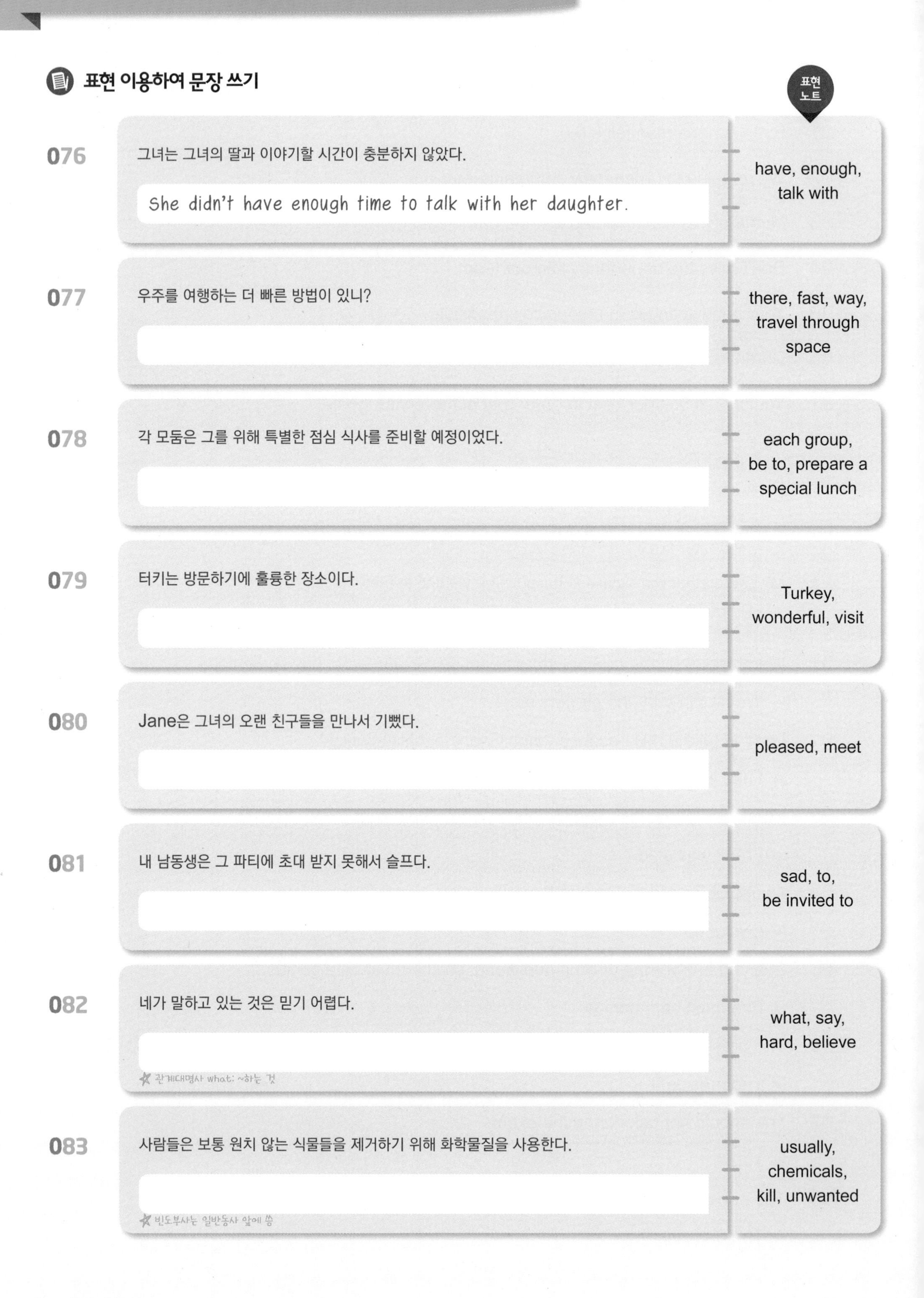

표현 이용하여 문장 쓰기

표현 노트

076 그녀는 그녀의 딸과 이야기할 시간이 충분하지 않았다.

She didn't have enough time to talk with her daughter.

have, enough, talk with

077 우주를 여행하는 더 빠른 방법이 있니?

there, fast, way, travel through space

078 각 모둠은 그를 위해 특별한 점심 식사를 준비할 예정이었다.

each group, be to, prepare a special lunch

079 터키는 방문하기에 훌륭한 장소이다.

Turkey, wonderful, visit

080 Jane은 그녀의 오랜 친구들을 만나서 기뻤다.

pleased, meet

081 내 남동생은 그 파티에 초대 받지 못해서 슬프다.

sad, to, be invited to

082 네가 말하고 있는 것은 믿기 어렵다.

★ 관계대명사 what: ~하는 것

what, say, hard, believe

083 사람들은 보통 원치 않는 식물들을 제거하기 위해 화학물질을 사용한다.

★ 빈도부사는 일반동사 앞에 씀

usually, chemicals, kill, unwanted

Answers p. 8

배열하여 문장 쓰기

084 이것은 내게 내 삶에 대해 생각해 볼 기회를 주었다.
(gave, a chance, my life, to think about, this, me)

085 나는 그녀가 자신의 일을 즐기고 있다는 것을 알고 놀랐다.
(to find, she, I, her job, was enjoying, surprised, that, was)

086 고대 중국에서, 사람들은 다음 해를 점치기 위해 옥수수를 펑 소리를 내며 튀겼다.
(people, for the coming year, popped, to tell fortunes, corn)

In ancient China,

087 더 많은 것들이 해저에 존재하는데, 그것들은 정확한 위치를 파악하기가 어렵다.
(hard, many more, underwater, and, are, are, to locate, they)

088 새로운 언어를 배우는 가장 좋은 방법은 그것을 매일 연습하는 것이다.
(to learn a new language, to practice it, is, the best way, every day)

089 그 항아리는 매우 귀중하니 그것을 깨지 않도록 조심해.
(very, is, precious, be, so, not, it, careful, the pot, to break)

090 대부분의 사람은 책을 읽기 위한 전통적인 종이책으로만 생각한다.
(think of, as, to read, traditional paper books, most people, books)

★ think of *A* as *B*: A를 B로 생각하다

[Self-Editing Checklist] ✔ 대 • 소문자를 바르게 썼나요? Y N ✔ 철자와 문장 부호를 바르게 썼나요? Y N

개념 13 too ~ to / enough to

월 일

The jeans are too tight for me to wear.
의미상 주어

→ The jeans are so tight that I can't wear them.
that절의 목적어가 필요

too + 형용사/부사 (+for+목적격) + to부정사
의미상 주어

→ so + 형용사/부사 + that + 주어 + can't + 동사원형

Mary was clever enough to solve the problem.

→ Mary was so clever that she could solve the problem.
시제 일치

형용사/부사 + enough (+for+목적격) + to부정사
의미상 주어

→ so + 형용사/부사 + that + 주어 + can + 동사원형

바로 개념

1 「too ~ to」는 '…하기에 너무 ~한/하게'라는 부정의 의미를 나타낸다.
2 「enough to」는 '…할 만큼 충분히 ~한/하게'라는 긍정의 의미를 나타낸다.
3 「too ~ to」와 「enough to」를 「so ... that ~」을 이용하여 바꿔 쓸 때 주어와 시제 일치, that절에 동사의 목적어가 필요한 경우 등에 유의한다.

고르며 개념 확인

Answers p. 8

01 Emma was ○ too ○ enough nervous to sleep.

02 Their parents think they are ○ too young to ○ so young that get married.

03 It was too hot ○ for ○ of us to leave the house.

04 The ice is so thin that it ○ can ○ can't bear his weight.

★05 This guitar is ○ small enough ○ enough small to fit in a backpack. ★ enough의 위치에 주의

06 Matt ran so fast that he ○ could ○ couldn't keep up with Jim.

쓰며 개념 정리

★07 I was too scared to shout out for help.

★ 과거 시제임에 유의

➔ I was ________ for help. (so ~ that ~ can)

★08 This table is so heavy that he can't move it.

★ 의미상 주어 나타내기

➔ This table is ________. (too ~ to)

09 She was so brave that she could run after the thief.

➔ She was ________. (enough to)

개념 14 seem to

단순부정사	「to + 동사원형」	to부정사의 시제가 본동사의 시제와 일치하거나 미래일 때	Anna seems to be sick. → It seems that Anna is sick. Anna seemed to be sick. → It seemed that Anna was sick.
완료부정사	「to + have + p.p.」	to부정사의 시제가 본동사보다 앞선 시제일 때	Anna seems to have been sick. → It seems that Anna was sick. Anna seemed to have been sick. → It seemed that Anna had been sick.

바로 개념

1 「seem to + 동사원형」은 '~인 것 같다'라는 의미이다.
2 「주어 + seem(s) to + 동사원형」은 「It seems that + 주어 + 동사 ~」로 바꿔 쓸 수 있다.
3 to부정사의 행위가 본동사의 시제보다 이전에 일어났을 때는 「주어 + seem(s) to + have + p.p.」로 나타낸다.

고르며 개념 확인

Answers p. 8

01 It seemed that the shepherd was a liar.

→ The shepherd seemed ○ to be ○ to have been a liar.

02 It seems that Lisa cried last night.

→ Lisa seems ○ to cry ○ to have cried last night.

03 Freddie seems to have loved her so much.

→ It seems that Freddie ○ loves ○ loved her so much.

04 The police seemed to have found some evidence.

→ It seemed that the police ○ have found ○ had found some evidence.

쓰며 개념 정리

05 It seemed that the teacher was angry. → The teacher seemed ______.

06 They seemed to be surprised. → It seemed that they ______.

07 It seems that Rachel lost her keys. → Rachel seems ______ her keys.

Answers p. 8

개념 13 too ~ to / enough to

1 「too ~ to」는 '　　　　　'라는 부정의 의미를 나타낸다.

2 「enough to」는 '　　　　　'라는 긍정의 의미를 나타낸다.

3 「too ~ to」와 「enough to」를 「so ... that ~」을 이용하여 바꿔 쓸 때 주어와 시제 일치, that절에 동사의 목적어가 필요한 경우 등에 유의한다.

개념 14 seem to

1 「seem to + 동사원형」은 '　　　　　'라는 의미이다.

2 「주어 + seem(s) to + 동사원형」은 「　　　　　+ 주어 + 동사 ~」로 바꿔 쓸 수 있다.

3 to부정사의 행위가 본동사의 시제보다 이전에 일어났을 때는 「주어 + seem(s) to + 　　　+ 　　　」로 나타낸다.

단순부정사	「to + 동사원형」	to부정사의 시제가 본동사의 시제와 일치하거나 미래일 때
완료부정사	「　　　　」	to부정사의 시제가 본동사보다 앞선 시제일 때

Answers p. 9

A 다음 〈보기〉와 같이 두 문장이 같은 뜻이 되도록 괄호 안의 표현을 이용하여 바꿔 쓰시오.

보기 I am too tired to go hiking. (so ~ that ~ can)
→ I am so tired that I can't go hiking.

01 The curry was so spicy that he couldn't eat it. (too ~ to)
★ 의미상 주어 쓰기
→

02 The boy is too poor to pay a bill. (so ~ that ~ can)
→

03 The problem was too difficult for me to answer. (so ~ that ~ can)
★ that절의 목적어 쓰기
→

04 I was lucky enough to get the ticket. (so ~ that ~ can)
→

05 He spoke so clearly that I could understand him. (enough)
★ 의미상 주어 쓰기
→

B 두 문장이 같은 뜻이 되도록 주어진 말로 시작하는 문장을 완성하시오.

01 It seemed that you were hungry.
→ You ______.

02 It seems that no one noticed it.
→ No one ______.

03 It doesn't seem that he misses us.
→ He ______.

04 It seems that they forgot my name.
→ They ______.

05 It seemed that Alice had been ill.
→ Alice ______.

조건에 맞게 문장 바꿔 쓰기

091 too ~ to 이용하기
Most people are so busy at school that they can't spend much time outdoors.
Most people are too busy at school to spend much time outdoors.

092 too ~ to 이용하기
She was so afraid that she couldn't go.

093 too ~ to 이용하기
People thought that art was so difficult that they couldn't understand it.

094 enough to 이용하기
Eric is so smart that he can solve difficult math problems.

095 It seems that ~ 이용하기
She seems to help to keep both their mind and body healthy.

096 seem to 이용하기
It seems that there are many natural disasters in Korea these days.

097 seem to 이용하기
It seemed that Mike thought it was nothing serious.

098 It seemed that ~ 이용하기
Nobody seemed to want his bike.

Answers p. 9

배열하여 문장 쓰기

099 그녀는 운 좋게도 디자이너 팀과 일할 수 있었다.
(was, enough, she, to work, fortunate, with a team of designers)

100 그것들 중 대부분은 사용하기에 너무 크거나 너무 어려웠다.
(most of, were, too big, them, or, to use, too difficult)

101 이 연구 과제는 노벨상을 받을 정도로 훌륭할까?
(to win, this research project, a Nobel Prize, enough, is, good)

102 그는 너무 욕심이 많아서 백성들과 나누지 않는다.
(with the people, to share, greedy, is, he, too)

103 개미는 항상 바쁘고 전혀 휴식을 취하지 않는 것처럼 보인다.
(to be, all the time, rest, never, and, ants, seem, busy)

104 당신은 메달을 따기에 너무도 크게 뒤떨어져 있었다는 것을 알고 있었다.
(that, you, you, too, to win, behind, a medal, far, were, knew)

105 그들은 그들의 캠핑이 안전하도록 하기 위해 무엇을 해야 하는지 알고 있는 것 같다.
(what, to make, they, safe, their camping trip, seem, to do, to know)

[Self-Editing Checklist] 대 • 소문자를 바르게 썼나요? Y N 철자와 문장 부호를 바르게 썼나요? Y N

대표유형 01 to부정사의 용법

01 다음 중 밑줄 친 부분의 쓰임이 〈보기〉와 같은 것은?

> 보기 We went outside to see the scenery.

① Edmund was the first man to climb Mt. Everest.
② They refused to donate the money to a charity.
③ It is relaxing to listen to classical music.
④ The boy yelled to draw someone's attention.
⑤ Our responsibility is to keep the Earth clean.

02 다음 밑줄 친 부분의 쓰임이 나머지 넷과 다른 것은?

① He was planning to do some volunteer work.
② I was excited to see the magic show.
③ They were sorry to miss the chance.
④ She was relieved to be able to get home.
⑤ We were all shocked to hear his suggestion.

03 다음 중 밑줄 친 부분의 쓰임이 〈보기〉와 같은 것은?

> 보기 There are many rules to follow.

① I did my best to win the race.
② He must be a fool to make such a mistake.
③ Bulgarians shake their head to show agreement.
④ They agreed to cooperate with each other.
⑤ Everyone has a right to express their opinions.

04 다음 중 밑줄 친 부분의 쓰임이 나머지 넷과 다른 것은?

① Sam and I are to meet at seven.
② The meeting is to be held on Monday.
③ Jeremy is to appear in court tomorrow.
④ If you are to be rich, you should be diligent.
⑤ The airplane is to land at the airport at noon.

05 다음 빈칸에 들어갈 수 없는 것은?

> Lisa ________ to meet her old friend.

① hoped ② decided ③ enjoyed
④ managed ⑤ expected

06 다음 중 어법상 옳은 문장끼리 묶인 것은?

> ⓐ Alice is looking for a roommate to live.
> ⓑ There's interesting nothing to read here.
> ⓒ Her son grew up to be a famous pianist.
> ⓓ You need to decide what to do first.
> ⓔ We were upset to hear about the accident.

① ⓐ, ⓑ ② ⓑ, ⓒ ③ ⓑ, ⓒ, ⓓ
④ ⓐ, ⓒ, ⓔ ⑤ ⓒ, ⓓ, ⓔ

07 다음 빈칸에 들어갈 수 없는 것을 모두 고르면?

> I went early so that I could get a good seat.
> = I went early ________ get a good seat.

① to ② for ③ in order to
④ in order that ⑤ so as to

08 다음 밑줄 친 말과 바꿔 쓸 수 있는 것은?

> We are to leave for Canada tonight.

① are going to ② seem to
③ had better ④ are able to
⑤ would like to

09 다음 빈칸에 들어갈 말로 알맞은 것은?

> I go to work by bike ________ the air.

① not pollute ② not to pollute
③ to pollute not ④ to not polluting
⑤ not being polluted

10 다음 두 문장이 같은 의미가 아닌 것은?

① I don't know where to go.
→ I don't know where I should go.
② If you are to succeed, work harder.
→ If you intend to succeed, work harder.
③ I woke up to find myself in the dark.
→ I woke up in order to find myself in the dark.
④ She was surprised because she saw him again.
→ She was surprised to see him again.
⑤ They were never to meet again.
→ They were destined never to meet again.

Answers p. 9

대표유형 02 가주어, 의미상 주어, 가목적어, It takes ~ to

11 다음 빈칸에 들어갈 말이 나머지 넷과 다른 것은?

① It was silly ______ him to say so.
② It is thoughtful ______ you to help her.
③ It is necessary ______ him to take this medicine.
④ It was foolish ______ you to lend him money.
⑤ It was careless ______ her to break the glass.

12 다음 문장의 밑줄 친 부분과 쓰임이 같은 것은?

> It is important to treat people with respect.

① It's 120 km from here to Busan.
② It was a lovely starry night with a full moon.
③ I suppose it easy to pass the exam.
④ I think it is quite boring to work alone.
⑤ You should explain it to her clearly.

13 다음 빈칸에 들어갈 수 없는 것은?

> It was ________ of you to behave like that.

① common ② rude ③ clever
④ wise ⑤ generous

14 다음 빈칸에 들어갈 말이 나머지 넷과 다른 것은?

① He makes ________ a rule to write a diary.
② We all consider ________ wrong to tell a lie.
③ This app will make ________ easier for you to find a place.
④ I think ________ using SNS is an effective way to make friends.
⑤ She found ________ interesting to learn about how people lived long ago.

15 다음 우리말과 같도록 주어진 표현을 배열할 때 네 번째로 오는 것은?

> 폭우 때문에 그들은 소풍을 갈 수 없었다.
> (to have, impossible, them, for, it, the heavy rain, a picnic, made)

① to have ② impossible ③ them
④ for ⑤ it

16 다음 문장 중 어법상 어색한 것은?

① It was amazing to see the pyramids of Egypt.
② It is natural for her to get upset about it.
③ It was selfish of them to expect you to do everything.
④ It took me half an hour to get to the fishing spot.
⑤ I found strange to drive on the left in Britain.

17 다음 빈칸에 한 번도 들어가지 않는 것은?

> He had a hard time admitting his failure.
> = ________ was hard ________ ________ ________ ________ his failure.

① to ② it ③ of ④ admit ⑤ him

대표유형 03 too ~ to, enough to, seem to

18 다음 문장과 의미가 가장 유사한 것은?

> Mars is so cold that humans can't survive.

① Mars is cold enough for humans to survive.
② Mars is cold enough for humans not to survive.
③ Mars is too cold for humans not to survive.
④ Mars is too cold of humans to survive.
⑤ Mars is too cold for humans to survive.

19 다음 우리말과 같도록 빈칸에 들어갈 말로 알맞은 것은?

> 그는 스스로 결정을 내릴 만큼 충분히 나이가 들었다.
> → He is ______________ his own decision.

① old enough to make ② old to make enough
③ to make old enough ④ enough old make to
⑤ enough old to make

20 다음 두 문장이 같은 뜻이 되도록 할 때 빈칸에 들어갈 말로 알맞은 것은?

> It seems that Robin met her before.
> = Robin ______________ her before.

① seems to meet ② seemed to meet
③ seems to have met ④ seems to had met
⑤ seemed to have met

01 주어진 표현을 이용하여 다음 그림의 상황을 나타내는 문장을 완성하시오.

(1)

(2)

(1) The pants are ______________________________. (too, wear, short, John)

(2) Helen is ______________________________. (tall, reach, enough, the top shelf)

02 다음 문장을 괄호 안의 지시대로 바꿔 쓰시오.

(1) It seems that they are annoyed.

→ ______________________________ (They를 주어로)

(2) No one seemed to care about the dog.

→ ______________________________ (It을 주어로)

(3) It seems that Kate misunderstood my intention.

→ ______________________________ (Kate를 주어로)

03 다음 〈조건〉에 맞게 두 문장을 한 문장으로 바꿀 때 빈칸에 알맞은 말을 쓰시오.

[조건] to부정사를 이용할 것

(1) He lost his passport. He was careless.

→ It was careless ______________________________.

(2) The little girl needs a friend. She wants to talk to a friend.

→ The little girl needs ______________________________.

(3) I was disappointed. Because I found out that the game was canceled.

→ I was disappointed ______________________________.

[Self-Editing Checklist] ✔ 대·소문자를 바르게 썼나요? Y N ✔ 철자와 문장 부호를 바르게 썼나요? Y N

UNIT 05

동명사

핵심 개념 바로 확인 I know! ☺ No idea! ☹

- 동명사는 「동사원형+-ing」의 형태로 명사 역할을 한다. ☺ ☹
- 동명사의 의미상의 주어를 나타내야 할 때 동명사 앞에 소유격 또는 목적격을 쓴다. ☺ ☹

개념 15

동명사의 역할

월 일

Using plastic bags is illegal in Kenya. 〈주어〉
= To use
동명사(구) 주어는 단수 취급

Her dream is climbing Mt. Everest. 〈보어〉
= to climb

I enjoy making miniature cars. 〈동사의 목적어〉

We were tired of waiting in line. 〈전치사의 목적어〉

They considered not sending their son to camp.
동명사의 부정

동명사를 목적어로 쓰는 동사			
enjoy	finish	keep	stop
quit	mind	avoid	admit
deny	recommend	practice	imagine
consider	dislike	give up	put off

cf. stop + to부정사: ~하기 위해 멈추다 〈to부정사의 부사적 용법〉

바로 개념

1 동명사는 「동사원형 + -ing」의 형태로, 문장 내에서 명사 역할(주어, 보어, 목적어)을 하며 '~하는 것, ~하기'라는 의미이다.
2 동명사의 부정은 「not [never] + 동명사」의 형태이다.
3 현재분사는 '~하는, ~하고 있는'의 의미로 진행형을 만들거나 명사 앞에서 명사를 수식한다.

고르며 개념 확인

Answers p. 10

01 ○ Learn ○ Learning never exhausts the mind.

02 My father's job was ○ protects ○ protecting wild animals.

03 You can't post pictures without ○ to ask ○ asking permission.

04 Serena seemed to avoid ○ to make ○ making eye contact with him.

05 Love means ○ never having ○ having never to say you're sorry.

06 The truck driver felt hungry and stopped ○ to eat ○ eating at a restaurant.

쓰며 개념 정리

07 약속을 깨는 것은 나쁘다. (break) ______ a promise is wrong.

08 내가 가장 좋아하는 활동은 자전거 타기이다. (cycle) My favorite activity is ______.

09 그녀는 그 책을 베낀 것을 인정했다. (copy) She admitted ______ the book.

10 그는 법률 공부를 포기했다. (study) He has given up ______ law.

11 Mandy는 직장을 구하는 데 성공했다. (find) Mandy succeeded in ______ a job.

12 제시간에 오지 못해 미안합니다. (come) I'm sorry for ______ on time.

개념 16 동명사의 의미상 주어와 시제

월 일

Parking is not allowed here.

I'm sure of winning the competition.
→ 내가 대회에서 이길 것을 확신하다

I'm sure of his winning the competition.
= him → 그가 대회에서 이길 것을 확신하다

There's little chance of that happening.

I am sorry for having lost your cap.
→ 모자를 잃어버린 일이 문장의 시제(am)보다 앞서 일어난 일임

동명사의 의미상 주어를 생략하는 경우	① 주어가 일반인일 때 ② 문장의 주어·목적어와 일치할 때
동명사의 의미상 주어	소유격 [목적격] + 동명사 *의미상 주어가 all, both, this [these], that [those], 또는 무생물일 때는 목적격을 씀
단순동명사(동사원형 + -ing)	본동사의 시제와 같거나 미래일 때
완료동명사(having + p.p.)	본동사의 시제보다 이전일 때

바로 개념

1 동명사의 의미상 주어가 일반인이거나, 문장의 주어·목적어와 일치할 때는 이를 생략할 수 있다.
2 동명사의 행위를 하는 주체가 문장의 주어와 다를 때 동명사 앞에 소유격을 써서 의미상 주어를 나타낸다. 구어체에서는 주로 목적격의 형태로 쓰기도 한다.
3 동명사가 문장의 시제보다 앞서 일어난 일을 나타낼 때는 「having + p.p.」로 쓴다.

고르며 개념 확인

Answers p. 10

01 I don't like ○ he ○ his being rude to me.

02 Do you mind ○ I turning ○ my turning off the TV?

03 I think Sue is the best runner in our class. I'm sure of ○ winning ○ her winning the race.

04 The boy denied ○ taken ○ having taken my money yesterday.

05 Please forgive me for ○ not having answered ○ having not answered your letter.

쓰며 개념 정리 배열하기

06 나는 이번에 그가 성공하지 못할 것을 확신한다.

I'm sure of ______ this time. (not, his, succeeding)

07 너의 부모님께서는 네가 늦게까지 밖에 있는 것을 언짢아하시니?

Do your parents ______ out so late? (mind, staying, you)

08 그녀는 아무 말도 하지 않았던 것에 대해 사과했다.

She apologized ______ anything. (not, said, for, having)

개념 15 동명사의 역할

1 동명사는 「[ ] + [ ]」의 형태로, 문장 내에서 명사 역할(주어, 보어, 목적어)을 하며 '~하는 것, ~하기'라는 의미이다.

2 동명사의 부정은 「[ ] [[ ]] + [ ]」의 형태이다.

3 현재분사는 '[ ], [ ]'의 의미로 진행형을 만들거나 명사 앞에서 명사를 수식한다.

동명사를 목적어로 쓰는 동사			
enjoy	finish	keep	stop
quit	mind	avoid	admit
deny	recommend	practice	imagine
consider	dislike	give up	put off

cf. stop + to부정사: '[ ]'라는 의미임 〈to부정사의 부사적 용법〉

개념 16 동명사의 의미상 주어와 시제

1 동명사의 의미상 주어가 일반인이거나, 문장의 주어·목적어와 일치할 때는 이를 생략할 수 있다.

2 동명사의 행위를 하는 주체가 문장의 주어와 다를 때 동명사 앞에 [ ]을 써서 의미상 주어를 나타낸다. 구어체에서는 주로 [ ]의 형태로 쓰기도 한다.

3 동명사가 문장의 시제보다 앞서 일어난 일을 나타낼 때는 「having + p.p.」로 쓴다.

동명사의 의미상 주어	소유격 [목적격] + 동명사 *의미상 주어가 all, both, this [these], that [those], 또는 무생물일 때는 목적격을 씀
단순동명사(동사원형 + -ing)	본동사의 시제와 같거나 미래일 때
완료동명사([ ] + [ ])	본동사의 시제보다 이전일 때

Answers p. 10

A 다음 문장에서 밑줄 친 부분을 어법에 맞게 고치시오.

01 Touch someone's head is rude in Thailand.

02 They have just finished to decorate her room.

03 Making mistakes are a lot better than not doing anything.
동명사(구) 주어는 단수 취급

04 I'm sure of she not leaving the town.

05 I apologize for have lose your cell phone.

06 One of her hobbies are plays badminton.
「one of + 복수명사」는 단수 취급

07 You can turn on the alarm system by press this button.

08 The baby is sleeping, so stop yell.

09 He was arrested for have steal a car last month.

10 Using not a cell phone for a day might be difficult.

B 다음 두 문장이 같은 뜻이 되도록 빈칸에 알맞은 말을 쓰시오.

01 Do you mind if I practice the piano here?
→ Do you mind ________ ________ the piano here?

02 I don't mind that my brother wears my clothes.
→ I don't mind ________ ________ ________ my clothes.

03 I couldn't imagine that she lied to me.
→ I couldn't imagine ________ ________ to me.

04 I am sure that Kate will be the class president.
→ I am sure of ________ ________ the class president.

05 I hate that he talks with his mouth full.
→ I hate ________ ________ with his mouth full.

06 I'm proud that you have a talent for art.
→ I'm proud of ________ ________ a talent for art.

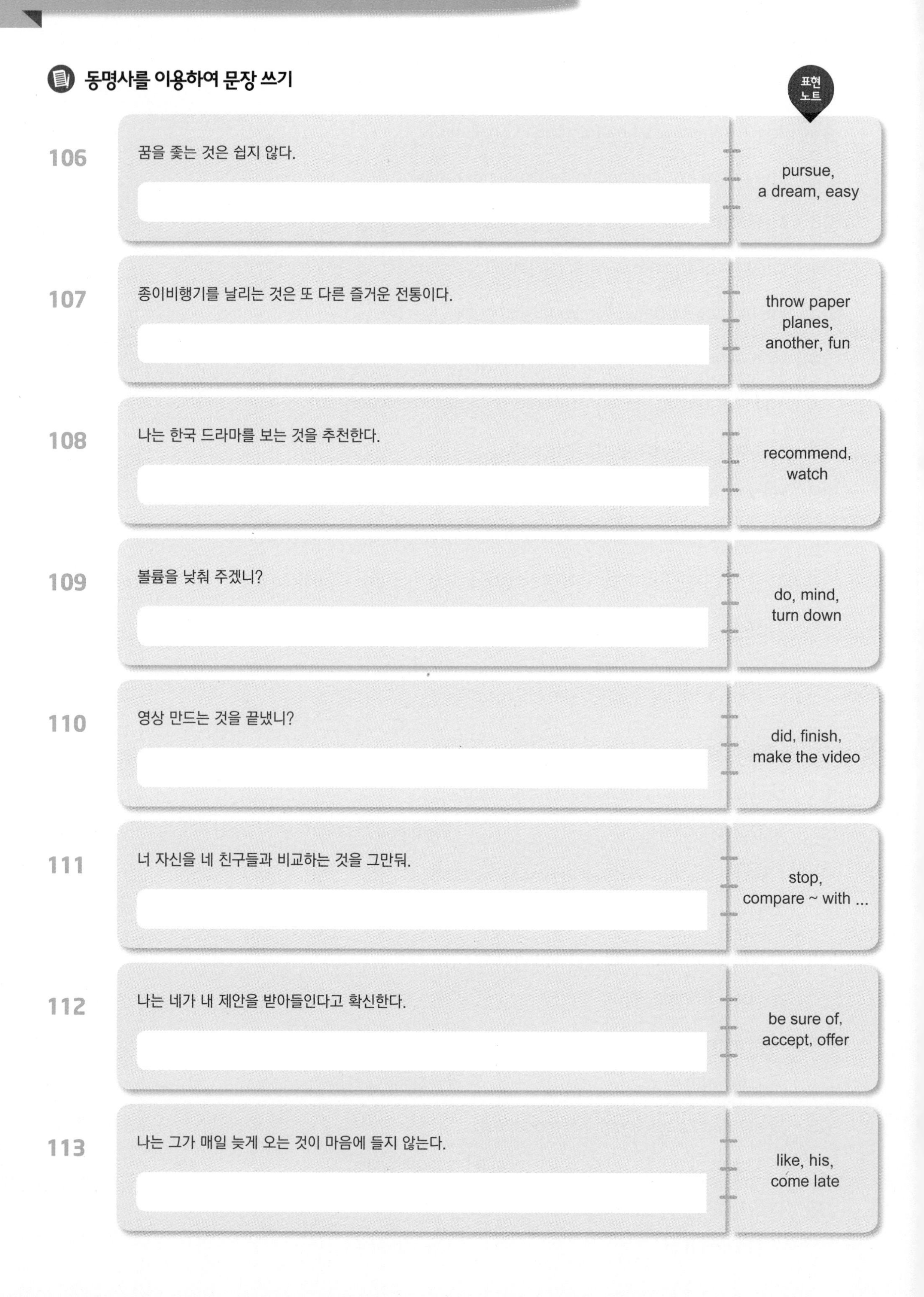

동명사를 이용하여 문장 쓰기

표현 노트

106 꿈을 좇는 것은 쉽지 않다.

pursue, a dream, easy

107 종이비행기를 날리는 것은 또 다른 즐거운 전통이다.

throw paper planes, another, fun

108 나는 한국 드라마를 보는 것을 추천한다.

recommend, watch

109 볼륨을 낮춰 주겠니?

do, mind, turn down

110 영상 만드는 것을 끝냈니?

did, finish, make the video

111 너 자신을 네 친구들과 비교하는 것을 그만둬.

stop, compare ~ with ...

112 나는 네가 내 제안을 받아들인다고 확신한다.

be sure of, accept, offer

113 나는 그가 매일 늦게 오는 것이 마음에 들지 않는다.

like, his, come late

Answers p. 11

배열하여 문장 쓰기

114 내 일은 영화를 촬영할 완벽한 장소를 찾는 것이다.
(finding, to shoot movies, is, perfect places)

My job

115 토마토를 먹는 것은 심장 질환에 걸릴 위험을 낮춰줄 수 있다.
(tomatoes, lower, of heart disease, eating, can, your risk)

116 때로 우리는 의도치 않게 사람들의 감정을 다치게 한다.
(we, people's feelings, intending to, hurt, without)

Sometimes

117 시장을 방문하는 것은 한 나라의 문화를 배우는 좋은 방법이다.
(about the culture of a country, to learn, a good way, is, visiting markets)

118 나는 네가 그의 집에서 저녁을 맛있게 먹길 바라.
(enjoy, dinner, at his house, you, having)

I hope

119 나의 아내는 내가 우리 집 창고를 어지럽히는 것에 싫증이 났다.
(my, our garage, messing up, my wife, got tired of)

120 나는 포기하지 않는 것이 왜 그토록 중요한지 알겠어.
(why, is, I, not, important, understand, so, giving up)

[Self-Editing Checklist] ✔ 대 • 소문자를 바르게 썼나요? Y N ✔ 철자와 문장 부호를 바르게 썼나요? Y N

월 일

개념 17 동명사와 to부정사

People kept donating for the boy's treatment.

We decided to donate our money to him.

I remember sending an email to David.
→ 과거에 보냈던 것을 기억하다

I have to remember to send an email to David.
→ 앞으로 보낼 것을 기억하다

★ 동명사와 to부정사를 모두 목적어로 쓸 수 있지만 의미가 달라지는 동사

forget	+동명사	(과거에) ~했던 것을 잊다
	+to부정사	(앞으로) ~할 것을 잊다
remember	+동명사	(과거에) ~했던 것을 기억하다
	+to부정사	(앞으로) ~할 것을 기억하다
regret	+동명사	(과거에) ~했던 것을 후회하다
	+to부정사	(현재 · 미래에) ~하게 되어 유감이다
try	+동명사	시험 삼아 (한번) ~해 보다
	+to부정사	~하려고 노력하다

바로 개념

1 동명사를 목적어로 쓰는 동사(74쪽)와 to부정사를 목적어로 쓰는 동사(52쪽)를 잘 구분해야 한다.
2 의미의 차이 없이 동명사와 to부정사를 모두 목적어로 쓰는 동사는 start, begin, like, love, hate, prefer, continue 등이 있다. 의미가 달라지는 동사는 forget, remember, regret, try 등이 있다.

고르며 개념 확인

Answers p. 11

01 I don't want ○ spoiling ○ to spoil your holiday.

02 Do you mind ○ typing ○ to type this article for me?

★03 My computer needs ○ repairing ○ to repair .
★「need + 동명사」: ~되어야 할 필요가 있다(수동의 의미)
cf.「need + to부정사」: ~할 필요가 있다

04 Surprisingly, everyone refused ○ signing ○ to sign the agreement.

05 I regret ○ telling ○ to tell him my secret. I shouldn't have done that.

06 We regret ○ telling ○ to tell you that your flight is delayed.

쓰며 개념 정리

07 나는 가만히 앉아 있는 것을 싫어한다. (sit) I hate ______ still.

08 비가 오후 내내 계속 내렸다. (fall) The rain continued ______ all afternoon.

09 많은 의사들은 환자들에게 걷기를 추천한다. (walk) Many doctors recommend ______ to patients.

10 난 Jim을 디즈니랜드에 데려가기로 약속했다. (take) I promised ______ Jim to Disneyland.

11 도착하면 그녀에게 다시 (한번) 전화해 볼게. (call) I'll try ______ her when I arrive.

12 그는 방 안에 열쇠를 두고 온 것을 잊었다. (leave) He forgot ______ the key in the room.

개념 18 관용적 표현

월 일

go -ing	~하러 가다	be busy -ing	~하느라 바쁘다
on [upon] -ing (= as soon as + 주어 + 동사)	~하자마자	be used to -ing	~하는 데 익숙하다
keep (on) -ing	계속 ~하다	How [What] about -ing?	~하는 게 어때?
be worth -ing	~할 만한 가치가 있다	look forward to -ing	~하기를 고대하다
feel like -ing (= would like to + 동사원형)	~하고 싶다	make a point of -ing (= make it a rule to + 동사원형)	~하는 것을 규칙으로 하다
far from -ing	전혀 ~이 아닌	on the point of -ing (= be about to + 동사원형)	막 ~하려고 하는
spend + 시간/돈 + -ing	~하느라 시간/돈을 쓰다	It is no use -ing	~해도 소용없다
not [never] ... without -ing	…하면 꼭 ~하다	keep [prevent] ... from -ing	…가 ~하지 못하게 막다
cannot help -ing (= cannot help but + 동사원형)	~하지 않을 수 없다	have trouble [difficulty] (in) -ing	~하는 데 어려움이 있다

고르며 개념 확인

Answers p. 11

01 The children are busy ○ packing ○ to pack for the trip.

02 The heavy rain kept us from ○ go ○ going on a picnic.

03 Alex has difficulty ○ fall ○ falling asleep.

★**04** The boy is used to ○ get ○ getting up early.

★ cf. 「be used to + 동사원형」: ~하는 데 이용되다

05 We're really looking forward ○ exploring ○ to exploring the Amazon.

06 It's worth ○ challenge ○ challenging the record even if we may fail.

쓰며 개념 정리 동명사의 관용적 표현 이용하기

07 나는 오늘 아무것도 먹고 싶지 않다. (eat) I don't ______ anything today.

08 런던에 도착하자마자 나는 Tim에게 전화했다. (arrive) ______ in London, I called Tim.

09 나는 그의 농담에 웃지 않을 수 없었다. (laugh) I ______ at his joke.

10 그와 언쟁해봤자 소용없다. (argue) It is ______ with him.

11 그들은 만나기만 하면 싸운다. (meet, quarrel) They never ______.

12 우리는 TV를 보며 3시간을 보냈다. (spend, watch) We ______ TV.

Answers p. 11

개념 17 동명사와 to부정사

동명사를 목적어로 쓰는 동사	enjoy, finish, keep, stop, quit, mind, avoid, admit, deny, recommend, practice, imagine, consider, dislike, give up, put off 등
to부정사를 목적어로 쓰는 동사	want, hope, wish, expect, plan, need, choose, decide, learn, agree, promise, refuse, manage, pretend, would like 등
의미의 차이 없이 동명사와 to부정사를 모두 목적어로 쓰는 동사	start, begin, like, love, hate, prefer, continue 등
동명사와 to부정사를 모두 목적어로 쓸 수 있지만 의미가 달라지는 동사	forget, remember, regret, try 등

forget	+ 동명사	(과거에) ~했던 것을 잊다
	+ to부정사	(앞으로) ~할 것을 잊다
remember	+ 동명사	
	+ to부정사	
regret	+ 동명사	
	+ to부정사	
try	+ 동명사	
	+ to부정사	

개념 18 관용적 표현

go -ing	~하러 가다		~하느라 바쁘다
on [upon] -ing (= as soon as + 주어 + 동사)			~하는 데 익숙하다
keep (on) -ing		How [What] about -ing?	
	~할 만한 가치가 있다		~하기를 고대하다
	~하고 싶다	make a point of -ing (= make it a rule to + 동사원형)	
	전혀 ~이 아닌	on the point of -ing (= be about to + 동사원형)	막 ~하려고 하는
spend + 시간/돈 + -ing			~해도 소용없다
not [never] ... without -ing		keep [prevent] ... from -ing	
cannot help -ing (= cannot help but + 동사원형)		have trouble [difficulty] (in) -ing	

Answers p. 11

A 다음 문장에서 밑줄 친 부분을 어법에 맞게 고치시오.

01 My friends and I will go ski this winter.

02 The old house needed to paint.

03 Why does everyone in the room keep stare at me?

04 Grace forgot take this medicine, so she got worse.

05 I remember see many stars in the sky when I was young.

06 Remember wear your helmet when you ride a bike.

07 I regret inform you that your request will not be accepted.

08 Lisa has always regretted give up her piano lessons.

09 We're looking forward spend time with you.

★ look forward to의 to는 전치사임

10 Do you think this musical is worth watch twice?

B 주어진 표현을 이용하여 우리말에 맞게 문장을 완성하시오.

01 나는 너와 함께 중국을 방문했던 것을 결코 잊지 못할 것이다.

→ I will never ______ with you. (visit)

02 그는 우산을 가져오는 것을 잊어서 비를 맞았다.

→ He ______ an umbrella with him, so he got wet. (bring)

03 그 사고에 대해 그를 탓해봤자 소용없다.

→ It is ______ him for the accident. (use, blame)

04 Mia는 아침 식사를 거르는 데 익숙하다.

→ Mia is ______ breakfast. (skip)

05 나는 매일 아침 규칙적으로 조깅을 한다.

→ I make ______ every morning. (point, jog)

06 너는 새 친구를 사귀는 데 어려움이 있니?

→ Do you have ______ new friends? (trouble)

07 부상 때문에 그는 내일 경기를 뛰지 못할지도 모른다.

→ His injury may prevent ______ in tomorrow's game. (play)

표현 이용하여 문장 쓰기

표현 노트

121 그 밴드는 축하 음악을 연주하기 시작했다.

start, play, celebration music

122 나는 돈을 절약하는 데 어려움이 있다.

have difficulty, save money

123 나는 내 가방에서 그것을 꺼냈던 것을 기억한다.

remember, take, out of

124 긴 바지 한 벌을 가져올 것을 기억해라.

remember, bring, long pants

125 (시험 삼아) 당근을 많이 먹어 봐.

try, eat, lots of

126 우리의 나쁜 습관들을 고치려고 노력하자.

let's, try, change, bad habits

127 나는 너와 함께 콘서트에서 연주하기를 고대하고 있어.

looking forward to, play in a concert

128 나는 종종 내 용돈을 모두 간식을 사는 데 써버렸다.

often, spend, all my pocket money, buy snacks

Answers p. 12

배열하여 문장 쓰기

129 팝 아트는 주목할 만한 가치가 있다.
(worth, pop art, paying attention to, is)

130 그는 자신이 원했던 모든 일들을 하지 못한 것을 후회했다.
(all the things, wanted to, doing, regretted, not, he, he)

131 눈물을 참으려고 노력해도 소용없었다.
(no use, to hold back, it, trying, the tears, was)

132 이것은 열이 교실로 들어오는 것을 막아줄 것이다.
(into the classroom, this, from, heat, will, getting, prevent)

133 우리 할머니는 남은 인생을 자신의 결정을 후회하면서 보내셨다.
(the rest of her life, spent, my grandmother, her decision, has, regretting)

134 나는 내가 얼마나 불행한지를 생각하지 않을 수 없었다.
(help, how, couldn't, unlucky, I, I, was, thinking)

135 바라건대, 건축가들은 새로운 친환경적인 아이디어를 계속해서 생각해낼 것이다.
(new eco-friendly ideas, will, coming up with, architects, keep)

Hopefully,

[Self-Editing Checklist] 대 • 소문자를 바르게 썼나요? Y N 철자와 문장 부호를 바르게 썼나요? Y N

대표유형 01 동명사의 역할

01 다음 빈칸에 들어갈 말로 알맞은 것은?

> ________ your "needs" and "wants" will help you spend money more wisely.

① Separate ② Separates
③ Separating ④ To separating
⑤ Having separated

02 다음 중 밑줄 친 부분의 쓰임이 나머지 넷과 다른 것은?

① I'm not very good at running.
② Do you know the girl talking to Jim?
③ His favorite hobby is baking cookies.
④ Persuading someone is not an easy job.
⑤ Amy enjoys doing outdoor activities.

03 다음 중 밑줄 친 부분의 쓰임이 나머지 넷과 다른 것은?

① Learning about other cultures is important.
② The key to happiness is making others happy.
③ The audience suddenly began shouting.
④ You can improve your English by reading more.
⑤ The problem is getting worse over time.

04 다음 밑줄 친 부분 중 어법상 어색한 것은?

> Watching(①) horror movies are(②) one of(③) my favorite things(④) to do(⑤).

05 다음 문장 중 어법상 어색한 것은?

① To be a volunteer is fun and helpful.
② I kept working instead of taking a nap.
③ The hardest part of my job is training dogs.
④ Many people die from drink dirty water.
⑤ Not getting enough sleep makes you feel tired.

06 다음 우리말에 맞게 not이 들어가기에 알맞은 곳은?

> 그는 숙제를 하지 않은 것에 대해 항상 변명한다.
> → He always (①) gives (②) excuses (③) for (④) doing (⑤) his homework.

대표유형 02 동명사의 의미상 주어, 시제

07 다음 대화의 빈칸에 들어갈 말로 알맞은 것은?

> **A** Do you mind ________ this window?
> **B** Not at all. Go ahead.

① my opening ② my to open
③ me for opening ④ me to open
⑤ my to opening

08 다음 두 문장의 의미가 같도록 할 때 빈칸에 들어갈 말로 알맞은 것은?

> He broke the glass yesterday, but he denies it.
> = He denies ________ the glass yesterday.

① breaking not ② having been broke
③ having broken ④ to have breaking
⑤ to have being broken

09 다음 중 어법상 옳은 것끼리 묶은 것은?

> ⓐ I appreciate your calling me back.
> ⓑ I don't like she driving too fast.
> ⓒ Everyone liked the idea of his to stay here.
> ⓓ I'm sorry for not having wrote sooner.
> ⓔ Ted admitted having made a mistake.

① ⓐ, ⓑ ② ⓐ, ⓔ ③ ⓑ, ⓒ, ⓓ
④ ⓑ, ⓓ, ⓔ ⑤ ⓒ, ⓓ, ⓔ

10 동명사를 이용하여 전환한 문장 중 잘못된 것은?

① I am proud that I was a pilot.
→ I am proud of being a pilot.
② He is sure that his son will pass the test.
→ He is sure of his son's passing the test.
③ The kid was ashamed that he couldn't write.
→ The kid was ashamed of not being able to write.
④ I can understand that she is upset.
→ I can understand her being upset.
⑤ She hates that someone calls her full name.
→ She hates someone calling her full name.

Answers p. 12

대표유형 03 동명사와 to부정사

11 다음 빈칸에 들어갈 수 없는 것을 모두 고르면?

> Jessica ________ learning Chinese.

① quit ② enjoys ③ decided ④ hates ⑤ refused

12 다음 빈칸에 들어갈 수 있는 것을 모두 고르면?

> My cell phone needs ________.

① to charge ② charging
③ to charging ④ being charge
⑤ to be charged

13 다음 중 밑줄 친 부분이 어법상 어색한 것은?

① The scientist continued to do research.
② We've been considering moving back to Busan.
③ They put off voting on the proposal until July.
④ Ken hid under the seat to avoid to pay the fare.
⑤ Have you ever pretended to be someone else?

14 다음 빈칸에 들어갈 말이 바르게 짝지어진 것은?

> • I remember ______ the car, but after that I don't know what happened.
> • Don't forget ______ your passport with you.

① hitting — to bring ② hitting — bringing
③ to hit — to bring ④ to hit — bringing
⑤ to hitting — to bring

15 다음 빈칸에 공통으로 들어갈 말로 알맞은 것은?

> • Her dream is ______ a flight attendant.
> • Mom said, "Stop ______ rude to your dad."

① to be ② being ③ to being
④ have being ⑤ to have been

16 다음 문장 중 어법상 옳은 것은?

① I can never imagine to live without you.
② Jean has just finished to read the detective story.
③ They have agreed taking part in the survey.
④ I expect completing the project by next week.
⑤ We should never give up chasing our dreams.

17 다음 두 문장의 의미가 같도록 할 때 빈칸에 들어갈 말로 알맞은 것은?

> I didn't make a copy of the letter, and I regret it.
> = I regret ____________ a copy of the letter.

① not to make ② not having to make
③ not having made ④ not being made
⑤ not to be made

대표유형 04 동명사의 관용적 표현

18 다음 빈칸에 들어갈 수 없는 것은?

> I'm really looking forward ____________.

① to visit my cousin
② to his play this year
③ to the New Year's Eve party
④ to receiving your letter
⑤ to watching the football game

19 다음 문장 중 어법상 어색한 것은?

① The park is worth visiting at least once.
② It was no use to complain about the weather.
③ We were busy preparing for the exam.
④ This tool is used to pull out the nails.
⑤ They spent a lot of money advertising the campaign.

20 다음 두 문장의 의미가 서로 다른 것은?

① On seeing the police, he ran away.
= As soon as he saw the police, he ran away.
② I have difficulty in remembering names.
= It is difficult for me to remember names.
③ He never leaves home without locking the door.
= He never locks the door when he leaves home.
④ I feel like going out for dinner.
= I would like to go out for dinner.
⑤ I can't help accepting his offer.
= I can't help but accept his offer.

01 다음 두 문장이 같은 뜻이 되도록 빈칸에 알맞은 말을 쓰시오.

(1) I'm sure that he will come here on time.

= I'm sure of __________ __________ here on time.

(2) She could not go out because of the storm.

= The storm prevented __________ __________ __________ __________.

(3) I apologize that I hurt your feelings.

= I apologize for __________ __________ your feelings.

02 다음 대화의 밑줄 친 부분에서 의미가 어색한 부분을 알맞게 고쳐 문장을 다시 쓰시오.

(1)
A How was your trip to Paris?
B It was amazing, and I especially liked the Eiffel Tower. I'll never forget to see it.

➔ ______________________________

(2)
A Would you please get me a fork? I'm not used to use chopsticks.
B Oh, of course. Here you are.

➔ ______________________________

수행평가 유형 글 완성하기

03 다음은 수민이의 장래희망을 나타낸 글이다. 〈보기〉에서 알맞은 말을 골라 쓰시오. (단, 한 번씩만 사용하되 알맞은 형태로 바꿀 것)

보기	
watch his movies	make short movies
be a movie director	study movie-making in college
see him in person	

I want ______________________ when I grow up. I'm interested in science-fiction movies, and I enjoy ______________________ in my free time. My role model is Steven Spielberg, a famous movie director. I spend a lot of my time ______________________. I look forward ______________________ someday. I'm now considering ______________________. I hope that my dream will come true.

[Self-Editing Checklist] ✔ 대·소문자를 바르게 썼나요? Y N ✔ 철자와 문장 부호를 바르게 썼나요? Y N

UNIT 06

분사와 분사구문

핵심 개념 바로 확인 I know! ☺ No idea! 😐

- 분사는 동사원형에 -ing나 -ed를 붙여 형용사처럼 쓰는 것이다. ☺ 😐
- 분사구문은 분사가 이끄는 부사구로 문장 전체를 수식한다. ☺ 😐
- 독립분사구문은 분사구문과 주절의 주어가 다르다. ☺ 😐

개념 19 현재분사와 과거분사

월 일

		현재분사 (진행/능동의 의미)	과거분사 (수동/완료의 의미)
형태		동사원형+-ing	동사원형+-ed 또는 불규칙 과거분사형
쓰임	명사 수식	I am afraid of a barking dog. (분사와 명사가 능동 관계)	I like the play written by Shakespeare. (분사와 명사가 수동 관계)
	보어 역할	The dog sat barking up the tree. (주격 보어) I saw a dog barking fiercely. (목적격 보어)	Shakespeare remained written in history. (주격 보어) I found a letter written in code. (목적격 보어)
	동사적 성격	The dog is barking fiercely. (진행형)	He has written his first play. (완료형) The play was written by Shakespeare. (수동태)

바로 개념

1 분사는 동사의 형태를 바꿔 형용사처럼 쓰는 것으로, 명사를 수식하는 한정적 용법과 보어로 쓰이는 서술적 용법이 있다.
2 분사가 단독으로 명사를 수식할 때는 분사를 명사 앞에 쓰고, 목적어나 수식어구가 붙어 있는 경우 명사 뒤에 쓴다.
3 분사는 「be동사+현재분사」의 진행형과 「have+과거분사」의 완료형, 그리고 「be동사+과거분사」의 수동태를 만든다.
4 「현재분사+명사」에서 현재분사는 명사의 동작이나 상태를 나타내고, 「동명사+명사」에서 동명사는 명사의 용도를 나타낸다.

고르며 개념 확인

Answers p. 13

01 ○ Fallen ○ Falling leaves covered the entire road.

02 Pour ○ boiling ○ boiled water over the tea bags and add honey.

03 He got his coat ○ dry-cleaning ○ dry-cleaned today.

04 Do you know the lady ○ waving ○ waved her hand?

05 He was ○ rescued ○ rescuing by a miracle.

06 She was 7th on the ○ waited ○ waiting list in the hospital.

07 Mr. Brown is ○ worn ○ wearing a light blue suit.

쓰며 개념 정리

08 나는 안경이 깨진 것을 발견했다. (break) → I found my glasses ______.

09 그는 수돗물이 없는 집에서 산다. (run) → He lives in a house without ______ water.

10 1900년대에 지어진 건물이 있다. (build) → There is a building ______ in the 1900s.

11 벌떼들이 윙윙거리는 소리를 내고 있다. (buzz) → A group of bees are making a ______ sound.

개념 20 감정을 나타내는 분사

월 일

You might be frustrated if you find out the truth.

Your explanation about the process is confusing to the audience.

Chris was annoyed by the noise from next door late at night.

She put me in an embarrassing situation.

현재분사 (주어가 감정의 원인)	과거분사 (주어가 감정을 느낌)
boring 지루한	bored 지루해하는
frustrating 좌절감을 주는	frustrated 좌절감을 느끼는
annoying 짜증스러운	annoyed 짜증이 난
surprising 놀라운	surprised 놀란
depressing 우울하게 만드는	depressed 우울한
embarrassing 당황하게 하는	embarrassed 당황한
confusing 혼란스러운	confused 혼란스러워 하는
disappointing 실망스러운	disappointed 실망한
frightening 무서운	frightened 겁먹은
satisfying 만족을 주는	satisfied 만족하는

바로 개념

1 감정을 나타내는 분사는 현재분사나 과거분사가 형용사처럼 쓰이는 것이다.
2 현재분사는 주어가 감정의 원인이 되는 것으로 주로 사물이 주어이거나 사물을 수식할 때 쓴다.
3 과거분사는 주어가 감정을 느끼는 것으로 주로 사람이 주어이거나 사람을 수식할 때 쓰이지만, 항상 그런 것은 아니다.
(e.g.) He is bored.(그는 지루하다.) He is boring. (그는 지루한 사람이다.)

고르며 개념 확인

Answers p. 13

01 It is ○ annoyed ○ annoying that some people blame alcohol for their actions.

02 The accountant looked ○ boring ○ bored with his job.

03 The news of the actor's death was ○ shocked ○ shocking .

04 My sister was ○ disappointed ○ disappointing because the shoes were sold out.

05 I was ○ embarrassed ○ embarrassing by my friend's snoring on the bus.

06 The story from a lady who took care of orphans was ○ touched ○ touching .

07 The timing of the announcement was ○ surprising ○ surprised .

쓰며 개념 정리

08 그 사용 설명서는 너무 헷갈린다. (confuse) → The manual is very ______.

09 나는 엄마의 깜짝 선물에 즐거웠다. (amuse) → I was ______ by Mom's surprise gift.

10 그것은 나에게 무서운 경험이었다. (frighten) → It was a ______ experience for me.

11 그는 마라톤을 끝낸 후 탈진했다. (exhaust) → He was ______ after finishing a marathon.

12 부모님은 내 점수에 충격 받았다. (shock) → My parents were ______ at my grades.

개념 19 현재분사와 과거분사

1 분사는 동사의 형태를 바꿔 (　　　) 처럼 쓰는 것으로, 명사를 수식하는 한정적 용법과 보어로 쓰이는 서술적 용법이 있다.

2 분사가 단독으로 명사를 수식할 때는 분사를 명사 앞에 쓰고, 목적어나 수식어구가 붙어 있는 경우 명사 뒤에 쓴다.

3 분사는 「be동사+ (　　　) 」의 진행형과 「have+과거분사」의 완료형, 그리고 「be동사+ (　　　) 」의 수동태를 만든다.

4 「현재분사+명사」에서 현재분사는 명사의 (　　　) 이나 상태를 나타내고, 「동명사+명사」에서 동명사는 명사의 (　　　) 를 나타낸다.

		현재분사 (진행/능동의 의미)	과거분사 (수동/완료의 의미)
형태		동사원형+-ing	동사원형+-ed 또는 불규칙 과거분사형
쓰임	명사 수식	I am afraid of a barking dog. (분사와 명사가 (　　　) 관계)	I like the play written by Shakespeare. (분사와 명사가 (　　　) 관계)
	보어 역할	The dog sat barking up the tree. (주격 보어) I saw a dog barking fiercely. (목적격 보어)	Shakespeare remained written in history. (주격 보어) I found a letter written in code. (목적격 보어)
	동사적 성격	The dog is barking fiercely. (진행형)	He has written his first play. (완료형) The play was written by Shakespeare. (수동태)

개념 20 감정을 나타내는 분사

1 감정을 나타내는 분사는 현재분사나 과거분사가 형용사처럼 쓰이는 것이다.

2 현재분사는 주어가 감정의 (　　　) 이 되는 것으로 주로 사물이 주어이거나 사물을 수식할 때 쓴다.

3 과거분사는 주어가 감정을 느끼는 것으로 주로 사람이 주어이거나 사람을 수식할 때 쓰이지만, 항상 그런 것은 아니다.

(e.g.) He is bored.(그는 지루하다.)　He is boring. (그는 지루한 사람이다.)

현재분사 (주어가 감정의 원인)		과거분사 (주어가 감정을 느낌)	
boring 지루한	embarrassing 당황하게 하는	bored 지루해하는	embarrassed 당황한
frustrating 좌절감을 주는	confusing 혼란스러운	frustrated 좌절감을 느끼는	confused 혼란스러워 하는
annoying 짜증스러운	disappointing 실망스러운	annoyed 짜증이 난	disappointed 실망한
surprising 놀라운	frightening 무서운	surprised 놀란	frightened 겁먹은
depressing 우울하게 만드는	satisfying 만족을 주는	depressed 우울한	satisfied 만족하는

Answers p. 13

A 다음 문장의 밑줄 친 부분의 알맞은 형태를 쓰시오.

01 The math problems looked challenge to me.

02 I heard a bunch of blue birds fly up into the sky.

03 He had his wisdom tooth pull out at the dentist's.

04 He really wanted to have his car repair as soon as possible.

05 I was greatly encourage by my homeroom teacher.

06 We took the injury people to the nearest hospital.

07 People frighten by the earthquake left the town.

08 She ordered pizza top with pepperoni.

B 다음 빈칸에 들어갈 말을 〈보기〉에서 찾아 알맞은 형태로 쓰시오.

보기 depress thrill confuse satisfy excite

01 (1) The temporary road signs were ______, so we got lost.

(2) We were ______ by the temporary road signs, so we got lost.

02 (1) The girls were not ______ with their test results.

(2) The test results were not ______ to the girls.

03 (1) I was ______ because my son failed the test.

(2) The news that my son failed the test was ______ to me.

04 (1) The child looked ______ when he found the hidden present.

(2) Finding the hidden present was ______ to the child.

05 (1) Watching a car racing game is ______.

(2) People are ______ about watching a car racing game.

배열하여 문장 쓰기

136 모로코 전통 의상을 입고 있는 사람들을 봐. (wearing, look at, traditional Moroccan clothes, the people)

137 매일 발행되는 '가짜' 뉴스들이 많다. (are, published, many "fake" news articles, there, every day)

138 나는 정글에서 사는 것이 정말 흥미진진할 것이라고 생각한다. (would, really, living, exciting, in a jungle, be)

I think

139 그는 옆에 앉아 있는 전혀 모르는 사람에게 그의 문제에 관해 얘기했다.
(a complete stranger, about his problem, told, sitting, he, beside him)

140 당신은 환상적인 경관에 놀랄 것이다. (by, will, you, the fantastic views, amazed, be)

141 시금치는 놀라운 용도로 사용될 수 있다. (can, spinach, in a surprising way, used, be)

142 다양한 음식을 포함하는 식사는 우리의 몸을 건강하게 유지시켜 준다.
(a variety of foods, containing, keeps, a diet, healthy, our bodies)

143 개미는 서로 소통하기 위해 '페로몬'이라고 불리는 화학물질을 분비한다.
(a chemical, a pheromone, with one another, produce, called, to communicate)

Ants

Answers p. 13

표현 이용하여 문장 쓰기

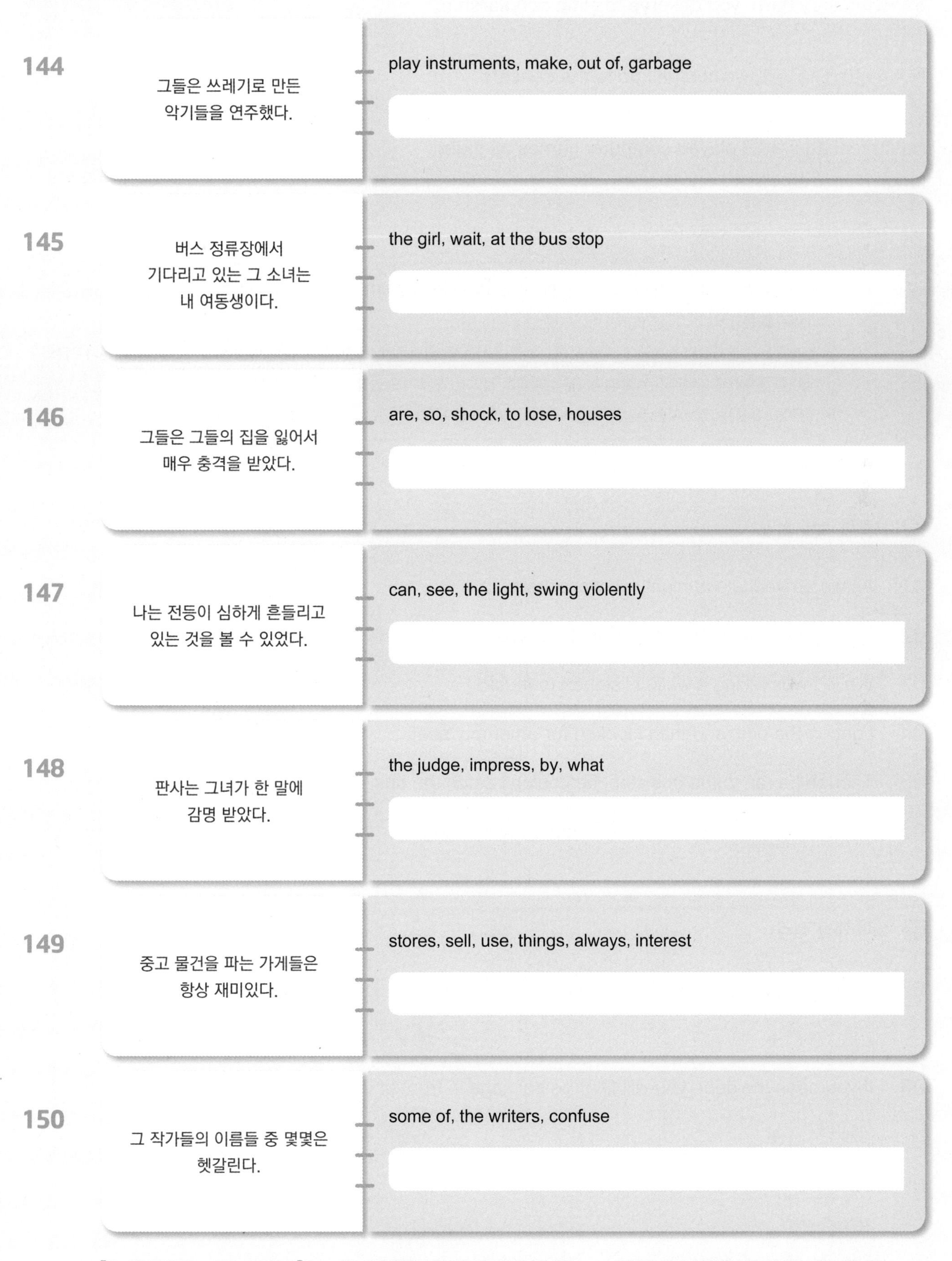

144 그들은 쓰레기로 만든 악기들을 연주했다.
play instruments, make, out of, garbage

145 버스 정류장에서 기다리고 있는 그 소녀는 내 여동생이다.
the girl, wait, at the bus stop

146 그들은 그들의 집을 잃어서 매우 충격을 받았다.
are, so, shock, to lose, houses

147 나는 전등이 심하게 흔들리고 있는 것을 볼 수 있었다.
can, see, the light, swing violently

148 판사는 그녀가 한 말에 감명 받았다.
the judge, impress, by, what

149 중고 물건을 파는 가게들은 항상 재미있다.
stores, sell, use, things, always, interest

150 그 작가들의 이름들 중 몇몇은 헷갈린다.
some of, the writers, confuse

[Self-Editing Checklist] 대·소문자를 바르게 썼나요? Y N 철자와 문장 부호를 바르게 썼나요? Y N

개념 21 분사구문

Studying very hard, **you deserve to get a scholarship.**

Not getting tickets, **we couldn't go to the concert.**

Never feeling tired, **I played computer games all night long.**

분사구문 만드는 법

As I entered the room, I switched the light on.

~~As~~ I entered the room, ~	① 접속사 생략
~~I~~ entered the room, ~	② 부사절의 주어 생략 (주절의 주어와 같을 때)
Entering the room, ~	③ 동사를 현재분사로 바꾸기 (주절의 시제와 같을 때)

바로 개념

1 분사구문은 부사절에서 접속사와 주어를 없애고 동사를 현재분사로 바꿔 부사구로 만든 것이다. 부정은 분사 앞에 not 또는 never를 쓴다.

2 분사구문은 부사절의 접속사에 따라 시간, 이유, 동시동작, 연속동작, 조건, 양보 등의 다양한 의미를 가지며, 분사구문의 의미를 명확하게 나타내기 위해 접속사를 생략하지 않고 남겨 두기도 한다.

3 조건을 나타내는 경우에는 주절에 보통 will, can, may 등이 있다.

고르며 개념 확인

Answers p. 14

01 As we arrived late at night, we were tired. ○ We arriving ○ Arriving

02 If you go to the library, you will find the book. ○ Going ○ If go

03 While I was taking a walk, I listened to music. ○ Taking ○ Be taking

04 I got on the bus, and then I looked for an empty seat. ○ looking for ○ looked for

05 Though he ran to the bus stop, he couldn't catch the bus. ○ Though ran ○ Running

06 When I cleaned out the drawer, I found my lost ring. ○ Cleaning ○ Cleaned

쓰며 개념 정리

07 While he was watching TV, he folded the laundry.

분사구문 → ______ 우리말 뜻 → ______

08 If you open the door, you will find the package in front of the door.

분사구문 → ______ 우리말 뜻 → ______

09 Because I didn't know what to do, I asked him for help.

분사구문 → ______ 우리말 뜻 → ______

개념 22

분사구문의 시제와 태

월 일

Having lost my passport, **I had to go to the embassy.**
(→ Because I had lost my passport)

Not having prepared for the exam, **she doesn't expect good scores.**
(→ As she didn't prepare for the exam)

(Being) Badly injured, **I couldn't walk.**
(→ Because I was badly injured)

(Having been) Born in England, **he is Korean.**
(→ Though he was born in England)

Having lived here all his life, **he knows a lot about the town.**
(→ As he has lived here all his life)

	단순 분사구문	완료 분사구문
능동	현재분사 ~	having+과거분사
수동	being+과거분사	having been+과거분사

바로 개념

1 완료형의 분사구문은 「having+과거분사」의 형태로 부사절의 시제가 주절보다 한 시제 앞선 시제일 때 쓴다. 부정은 「not [never]+having+과거분사」의 형태로 쓴다.
2 수동태의 분사구문에서는 보통 Being 또는 Having been을 생략하고 과거분사로 시작한다.
3 현재완료가 쓰인 부사절도 완료 분사구문으로 바꿔 쓸 수 있다.

고르며 개념 확인

Answers p. 14

01 Though we ate a box of pizza, we are still hungry.
○ Being eaten ○ Having eaten

02 As he was persuaded by his friends, Brutus decided to kill Caesar.
○ Persuading ○ Persuaded

03 Because she visited Paris in 2017, she is familiar with that area.
○ Having visited ○ Visiting

04 Since he was disappointed at the result, Andy couldn't do anything for days.
○ Disappointing ○ Disappointed

05 As I didn't take this class last year, I have to take it this year.
○ Not having taken ○ Not taking

쓰며 개념 정리

06 2002년에 지어진 이후로, 그것은 한국에서 가장 긴 다리이다. (build)
➜ ________ in 2002, it has been the longest bridge in Korea since then.

07 나는 그 영화를 여러 번 봐서 모든 대사를 다 기억한다. (watch)
➜ ________ the movie several times, I remember every single line.

개념 21 분사구문

1 분사구문은 부사절에서 접속사와 주어를 없애고 동사를 현재분사로 바꿔 부사구로 만든 것이다.

부정은 [   ] 앞에 not 또는 never를 쓴다.

2 분사구문은 부사절의 접속사에 따라 시간, 이유, 동시동작, 연속동작, 조건, 양보 등의 다양한 의미를 가지며, 분사구문의 의미를 명확하게 나타내기 위해 접속사를 생략하지 않고 남겨 두기도 한다.

3 조건을 나타내는 경우에는 주절에 보통 [   ], can, may 등이 있다.

분사구문 만드는 법

As I entered the room, I switched the light on.

~~As~~ **I entered the room**, I switched the light on. ① [   ] 생략

~~I~~ **entered the room**, I switched the light on. ② 부사절의 [   ] 생략 (주절의 주어와 같을 때)

Entering the room, I switched the light on. ③ 동사를 [   ]로 바꾸기 (주절의 시제와 같을 때)

개념 22 분사구문의 시제와 태

1 완료형의 분사구문은 「[   ] + 과거분사」의 형태로 부사절의 시제가 [   ]보다 한 시제 앞선 시제일 때 쓴다. 부정은 「not [never] + having + 과거분사」의 형태로 쓴다.

2 수동태의 분사구문에서는 보통 Being 또는 Having been을 생략하고 [   ]로 시작한다.

3 현재완료가 쓰인 부사절도 완료 분사구문으로 바꿔 쓸 수 있다.

	단순 분사구문	완료 분사구문
능동	현재분사 ~	having + 과거분사
수동	being + [ ]	having been + [ ]

Answers p. 14

A 다음 〈보기〉에서 알맞은 접속사를 찾아 분사구문을 부사절로 바꿔 쓰시오. (단, 한 번씩만 쓸 것)

보기 because if when though before

01 Forgiven by his sister, he still feels sorry for her.

→ ____________, he still feels sorry for her.

02 Joining our photography club, you can learn how to take good pictures.

→ ____________, you can learn how to take good pictures.

03 Having stayed up all night, I am really sleepy right now.

→ ____________, I am really sleepy right now.

04 Concentrating on mobile games, I couldn't hear anything.

→ ____________, I couldn't hear anything.

05 Going to bed, she finished reading the book.

→ ____________, she finished reading the book.

B 다음 문장의 빈칸에 알맞은 부사절을 〈보기〉에서 찾아 분사구문으로 바꿔 쓰시오.

보기
- After he tried *kimchi*
- Because I didn't make a reservation
- Since he has lived in Spain for 10 years
- Though I was embarrassed by my mistakes

01 ____________, he really loves it.

02 ____________, I tried to manage the situation.

03 ____________, he knows many great places to visit.

04 ____________, I have to be put on the waiting list.

문장 바르게 고쳐 쓰기

151 Used various methods, experts analyze big data.

152 Look for fantastic scenery, millions of tourists visit Mt. Halla.

153 Inspiring by the video, Whitacre decided to make a virtual choir.

154 Been very powerful and dangerous, volcanoes do harm to people in many ways.

155 I did my math homework, listen to classical music.

156 He was excited, think about the bike he planned to buy.

157 Knowing not the news was false, many people panicked.

158 When compare to other bicycles, his price was too high.

Answers p. 14

표현 이용하여 분사구문이 있는 문장 쓰기

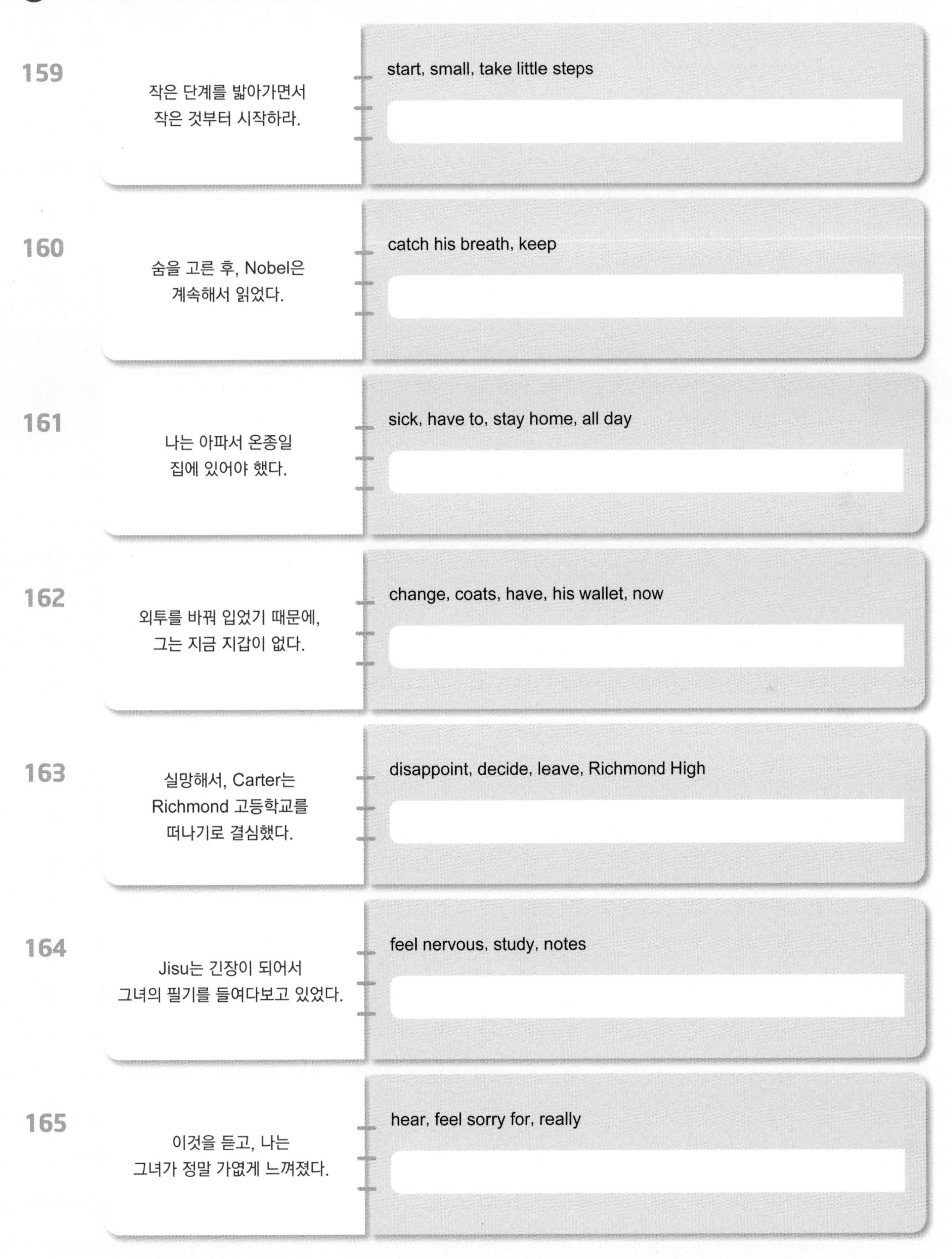

159 작은 단계를 밟아가면서 작은 것부터 시작하라.
start, small, take little steps

160 숨을 고른 후, Nobel은 계속해서 읽었다.
catch his breath, keep

161 나는 아파서 온종일 집에 있어야 했다.
sick, have to, stay home, all day

162 외투를 바꿔 입었기 때문에, 그는 지금 지갑이 없다.
change, coats, have, his wallet, now

163 실망해서, Carter는 Richmond 고등학교를 떠나기로 결심했다.
disappoint, decide, leave, Richmond High

164 Jisu는 긴장이 되어서 그녀의 필기를 들여다보고 있었다.
feel nervous, study, notes

165 이것을 듣고, 나는 그녀가 정말 가엾게 느껴졌다.
hear, feel sorry for, really

[Self-Editing Checklist] ✔ 대 • 소문자를 바르게 썼나요? Y N ✔ 철자와 문장 부호를 바르게 썼나요? Y N

월 일

개념 23 독립분사구문

It being fine, we go inline skating in the park.
(→ When it is fine, we go inline skating in the park.)

The tour guide walking so fast, I could not follow him.
(→ Since the tour guide walked so fast, I could not follow him.)

Judging from her look, she is in a bad mood.

Speaking of artists, I think Picasso is one of the greatest painters.

독립 분사구문	부사절 주어 ≠ 주절 주어	부사절의 주어를 생략하지 않고 분사 앞에 씀
비인칭 독립 분사구문	부사절 주어(일반인) ≠ 주절 주어	부사절의 주어 생략
	• frankly speaking (솔직히 말하면) • strictly speaking (엄밀히 말하면) • roughly speaking (대강 말하자면) • generally speaking (일반적으로 말하면) • speaking of (~ 이야기가 나와서 말인데) • judging from (~로 판단하건대) • considering ~ (~을 고려하면)	

바로 개념

1 독립분사구문은 부사절과 주절의 주어가 서로 다를 때, 부사절의 주어를 생략하지 않고 분사 앞에 남겨 둔 것이다.
2 비인칭 독립분사구문은 부사절의 주어가 we, you, people처럼 막연한 일반인일 때 주절의 주어와 다르더라도 생략하고 관용어처럼 쓰는 것이다.

고르며 개념 확인

Answers p. 14

01 ○ Beginning ○ The rain beginning to fall, I took a taxi.

02 ○ Generally speaking ○ Considering , dogs are faithful animals.

03 It ○ been ○ being a holiday today, the bank is closed.

04 ○ Judging from ○ Frankly speaking her accent, she must be Australian.

05 His car ○ being broken ○ be broken , he has to rent a car.

06 ○ Strictly speaking ○ Speaking of our teacher, she is very generous.

쓰며 개념 정리

07 너무 더워서, 나는 잠을 잘 수 없었다. ______ too hot, I couldn't sleep.

08 엄밀히 말해서, 그것은 공포 영화가 아니다. ______, it is not a horror movie.

09 그가 말한 것으로 판단하건대, 그는 무죄이다. ______ what he said, he is not guilty.

10 취미 얘기가 나와서 말인데, 너는 아직 기타를 치니? ______ hobbies, do you still play the guitar?

11 시험이 쉬워서, 그들은 좋은 점수를 받았다. The exam ______, they got good grades.

개념 24 with+명사(구)+분사

I can't work with you standing there.
네가 거기 서 있는 채로 (능동 관계)

Lisa took a walk with her dog following her.
그녀를 따라가는 개와 함께 (능동 관계)

I listened to music with the door closed.
문을 닫은 채로 (수동 관계)

Mr. Kim was sitting with his legs crossed.
다리를 꼰 채 (수동 관계)

with + 명사(구) + 현재분사	~가 …하고 있는 채로
with + 명사(구) + 과거분사	~가 …하여진 채로

바로 개념

1 「with+명사(구)+분사」는 '~한 채로, ~하면서'라는 의미로 동시에 일어나는 두 가지 상황을 나타낼 때 쓴다.
2 「with+명사(구)+현재분사」는 '~가 …하고 있는 채로'의 의미로 명사(구)와 분사가 능동의 관계이다.
3 「with+명사(구)+과거분사」는 '~가 …하여진 채로'의 의미로 명사(구)와 분사가 수동의 관계이다.
4 분사 대신 형용사나 부사(구)를 쓸 수도 있다.

고르며 개념 확인

Answers p. 15

01 Mark is standing with his arms ○ folded ○ folding .

02 She went to bed with the light ○ turned on ○ turning on .

03 The students listened to their teacher with their eyes ○ shining ○ shined .

04 You can't return the shirt with the tag ○ removing ○ removed .

05 Don't brush your teeth with the water ○ running ○ run .

06 The soccer player came to the hospital with his leg ○ breaking ○ broken .

쓰며 개념 정리

07 그는 커튼을 닫은 채로 TV를 봤다. (closed, with, the curtains)

➔ He watched TV ______ ______ ______.

08 그녀는 음식을 먹으며 말했다. (her mouth, full, with)

➔ She spoke ______ ______ ______.

09 나는 다리를 떨며 조용히 앉아 있었다. (shaking, with, my legs)

➔ I sat quietly ______ ______ ______.

개념 23 독립분사구문

1 독립분사구문은 부사절과 주절의 주어가 서로 다를 때, 부사절의 주어를 생략하지 않고 [ ] 앞에 남겨 둔 것이다.

2 비인칭 독립분사구문은 부사절의 주어가 we, you, people처럼 막연한 [ ] 일 때 주절의 주어와 다르더라도 생략하고 관용어처럼 쓰는 것이다.

독립분사구문	부사절 주어 ≠ 주절 주어	부사절의 주어를 생략하지 않고 분사 앞에 씀
비인칭 독립분사구문	부사절 주어(일반인) ≠ 주절 주어	부사절의 주어 생략
	• [ ] speaking (솔직히 말하면) • strictly speaking (엄밀히 말하면) • roughly speaking (대강 말하자면) • generally speaking (일반적으로 말하면) • speaking of (~ 이야기가 나와서 말인데) • [ ] from (~로 판단하건대) • considering ~ (~을 고려하면)	

개념 24 with + 명사(구) + 분사

1 「with+명사(구)+분사」는 '~한 채로, ~하면서'라는 의미로 [ ] 에 일어나는 두 가지 상황을 나타낼 때 쓴다.

2 「with+명사(구)+현재분사」는 '~가 …하고 있는 채로'의 의미로 명사(구)와 분사가 [ ] 의 관계이다.

3 「with+명사(구)+과거분사」는 '~가 …하여진 채로'의 의미로 명사(구)와 분사가 [ ] 의 관계이다.

4 분사 대신 [ ] 나 부사(구)를 쓸 수도 있다.

with+명사(구)+ [ ]	~가 …하고 있는 채로	Mom fell asleep [ ] the washing machine running. 엄마는 세탁기를 돌린 채로 잠이 들었다.
with+명사(구)+ [ ]	~가 …하여진 채로	I took a rest with my eyes [ ]. 나는 눈을 감고 휴식을 취했다.

Answers p. 15

A 다음 우리말과 같도록 괄호 안의 표현을 이용하여 문장을 완성하시오.

01 나는 내 휴대전화를 꺼둔 채로 공부를 했다. (turn)

→ I studied with my cell phone ______ off.

02 그의 신발이 없어졌기 때문에 그는 온 집안을 살폈다. (be, miss)

→ His shoes ______ ______, he looked all around the house.

03 그 책이 다 팔렸기 때문에, 나는 일주일을 더 기다려야 했다. (be, sell)

→ The book ______ ______ out, I had to wait one more week.

04 많은 사람들이 깃발을 흔들며 행진하고 있었다. (flags, wave)

→ A lot of people were marching with ______ ______.

05 그는 운동화 끈이 풀린 채로 계속 걸었다. (untie)

→ He kept walking with his sneakers ______.

B 다음 우리말과 같도록 빈칸에 알맞은 말을 〈보기〉에서 골라 쓰시오. (단, 한 번씩만 쓸 것)

보기		
judging from	considering	frankly speaking
strictly speaking	speaking of	generally speaking

01 솔직히 말해서, 그 모자는 너에게 잘 안 어울린다.

→ ______, the hat doesn't suit you well.

02 그녀의 외모로 판단하건데, 그녀는 30대처럼 보인다.

→ ______ her appearance, she looks around thirty.

03 일반적으로 말해서, 중국어는 배우기 쉽지 않다.

→ ______, Chinese is not easy to learn.

04 네 계획을 고려하면, 너는 그것을 가능한 한 빨리 끝내야 한다.

→ ______ your plan, you must finish it as soon as possible.

05 물리학 수업 이야기가 나왔으니 말인데, 나는 오늘 그 수업에 결석했다.

→ ______ the physics class, I skipped it today.

배열하여 문장 완성하기

166 그 당시의 제한된 기술을 고려하면, 그것은 불가능해 보였다.
(in those days, the limited technology, it, impossible, seemed, considering)

Considering the limited technology in those days, it seemed impossible.

167 나는 표지에 글씨가 적힌 작은 공책을 하나 발견했다. (some words, on the cover, with, written)

I found a small notebook

168 날씨가 좋아서, 우리는 해변에 갔다. (went, the weather, we, fine, being, to the beach)

169 Jenny는 손가락으로 별들을 하나하나 가리키며 세었다.
(counted, with, the stars, pointing at, her finger, each of them)

Jenny

170 엄밀히 말하면, 너는 그 사고에 대한 책임이 있다. (responsible, speaking, are, strictly, you, for the accident)

171 White 씨는 시계에 2분이 남은 채로 타임아웃을 요청했다. (left, with, on the clock, two minutes, time out, called)

Mr. White

172 추워서, 그는 따뜻한 재킷을 입었다. (cold, put on, it, he, being, a warm jacket)

173 우주의 웜홀은 두 개의 입과 그 둘을 연결하는 목구멍을 지니고 있을지도 모른다.
(a throat, the two, connecting, with)

Wormholes in space may contain two mouths,

Answers p. 15

표현 이용하여 문장 쓰기

174 솔직히 말하면, 나는 그 농담이 재미가 없었다.
frank, could, find, the joke, interest

175 다리를 뻗은 채 앉아라.
sit, with, your legs, extend

176 아이스크림에 대해 말하자면, 그것은 중국에서 발명되었다.
speak of, invent, in China

177 나는 심장이 매우 빠르게 뛰는 채로 그 책을 읽기 시작했다.
start, reading, with, my heart, beat, very fast

178 일반적으로 말해서, 기차는 버스보다 더 빠르다.
general, trains, than, buses

179 John의 개는 John이 그것의 뒤를 쫓고 있는 채로 달리고 있다.
run, with, chase after, it

180 그 종이를 들고 점들이 맞춰지도록 그것을 접어라.
take, the paper, fold, with, the dots, match up

[Self-Editing Checklist] 대 • 소문자를 바르게 썼나요? Y N 철자와 문장 부호를 바르게 썼나요? Y N

대표유형 01 현재분사와 과거분사

01 다음 중 밑줄 친 부분이 어법상 어색한 것은?

① I found my cell phone broken.
② Paul's invitation to dinner was surprising.
③ This is the museum building in 1920.
④ A girl sitting next to me kept coughing.
⑤ Look at the mountain covered with snow.

02 다음 중 밑줄 친 분사의 형태가 어색한 것은?

① I bought pants made in Pakistan.
② The boy raised his hands is Sam.
③ You must not keep him waiting so long.
④ Hold the baby sleeping in the cradle tight.
⑤ English has an alphabet consisting of 26 letters.

03 다음 문장 중 어법상 알맞은 것은?

① My job makes me depress.
② He sat surrounding by many fans.
③ The ideas presenting in that book are good.
④ I found her standing on the subway platform.
⑤ She is not satisfying with the result.

04 다음 중 composed가 들어갈 위치로 가장 알맞은 것은?

I always (①) listen to (②) the ninth Symphony (③) by Beethoven (④) when I (⑤) feel down.

05 다음 〈보기〉의 밑줄 친 부분과 쓰임이 같은 것을 모두 고르면?

보기 The actress set up a charity to help those living on the street.

① My job is protecting wild animals.
② We saw some shooting stars last night.
③ Racing cars can go as fast as 400 km per hour.
④ He thought it was an amazing movie.
⑤ There are two bedrooms and one living room in the house.

대표유형 02 분사구문

06 다음 빈칸에 들어갈 말끼리 바르게 짝지은 것은?

• ________ at the family album, I thought of my grandparents.
• ________ the flu, he took a week off work.

① Look — Having
② Looked — Had
③ Looking — Had
④ Looking — Having
⑤ Looking — Being had

07 다음 〈보기〉의 밑줄 친 부분과 쓰임이 같은 것은?

보기 Losing a lot of weight, he had to buy new clothes.

① Using the kitchen, you have to put things back.
② Living near his house, I've never seen him.
③ Knowing little of the city, we joined the city tour.
④ Coming home, I found the lock broken.
⑤ Buying this shirt today, you will get a 10 percent discount.

[08-09] 두 문장의 뜻이 같도록 빈칸에 알맞은 것을 고르시오.

08

Because the book is written with easy words, it is good for beginners.
➔ ________ with easy words, the book is good for beginners.

① Writing
② Being writing
③ Written
④ Having written
⑤ Having been writing

09

As I haven't read your report, I can't comment on it.
➔ ________ the book, I can't comment on it.

① Not reading
② Reading not
③ Not being read
④ Having read not
⑤ Not having read

Answers p. 15

10 다음 밑줄 친 부분 중 생략할 수 없는 것은?

① Being interrupted by the phone call, he became upset.
② Having been disappointed at his lies, I don't want to see him again.
③ Having been broken by the car accident, the fence should be repaired.
④ Having finished his assignment, he played with his friends.
⑤ Being written by a famous writer, the book sold a million copies.

11 다음 밑줄 친 분사구문을 부사절로 바르게 바꾼 것은?

① Being young, the rapper is a millionaire.
➔ As the rapper is young
② Practicing every day, you can master playing the guitar.
➔ Though you practice every day
③ Having slept well, she is not tired today.
➔ If she had slept well
④ Not knowing how to play this game, he read the instructions first.
➔ If he didn't know how to play this game
⑤ Seen from far away, the rock looks like a horse.
➔ When the rock is seen from far away

12 다음 문장 중 어법상 어색한 것은?

① Walking down the street, I met my teacher.
② There being no bus, I had to walk there.
③ Not saving enough money, she couldn't buy a new backpack.
④ Being born in Paris, she is able to speak French.
⑤ Turning to the left, you'll find the bookstore.

13 다음 밑줄 친 부분을 영작할 때 필요 없는 것은?

그 소설에 감명 받아서 나는 그것을 여러 번 읽었다.
➔ ______________, I read it several times.

① the ② by ③ I ④ moved ⑤ novel

대표유형 03 독립분사구문

14 다음 우리말과 같도록 빈칸에 알맞은 것은?

솔직히 말해서, 그 연극은 지루했다.
➔ ______________, the play was boring.

① Judging from ② Frankly speaking
③ Roughly speaking ④ Strictly speaking
⑤ Generally speaking

15 다음 문장의 빈칸에 들어갈 말로 알맞은 것은?

________ so windy, we couldn't go sailing.

① To be ② Being ③ It being
④ It been ⑤ Be

대표유형 04 with+명사(구)+분사

16 다음 문장의 빈칸에 들어갈 말로 알맞은 것은?

The event took place in the auditorium with all the students ________ on the chairs.

① seat ② being seat ③ seats
④ seated ⑤ seating

17 다음 문장 중 어법상 어색한 것은?

① You should not talk with your mouth full.
② Look at the board with your book closed.
③ A boy stood by me with his body shivering.
④ A big dog ran up to me with its tail wagged.
⑤ The player lay on the ground with his leg injured.

18 다음 문장의 빈칸에 들어갈 수 없는 것은?

Julia was sleeping ______________.

① with her hat on
② with the door closed
③ with her cat by her side
④ with her legs crossing
⑤ with her arms stretched

01 다음 그림의 상황을 나타내는 문장에서 어색한 부분을 바르게 고쳐 문장을 다시 쓰시오.

(1)

There is a lot of people waited outside the restaurant.

➜ ____

(2)

She is played the violin with her eyes close.

➜ ____

02 다음 주어진 문장을 분사구문을 포함한 문장으로 바꿔 쓰시오.

(1) Because she was not invited to the party, she did not come.

➜ ____

(2) As the concert was over, people went home.

➜ ____

03 다음 우리말을 〈조건〉에 맞게 영작하시오.

(1) 우리 웹 사이트에 방문하면, 록 페스티벌에 관한 정보를 얻을 수 있다.

[조건] **1.** 분사구문을 사용할 것 **2.** visit, can, get을 사용할 것

➜ ____ about the rock festival.

(2) 나는 할머니 댁 근처에 살지 않아서, 할머니를 자주 만날 수 없다.

[조건] **1.** 분사구문을 사용할 것 **2.** live, near, can't를 사용할 것

➜ ____ her often.

[Self-Editing Checklist] ✔ 대·소문자를 바르게 썼나요? Y N ✔ 철자와 문장 부호를 바르게 썼나요? Y N

UNIT 07

수동태

핵심 개념 바로 확인 I know! ☺ No idea! ☹

- 수동태는 행위의 대상을 주어로 하는 동사의 형태이다. ☺ ☹
- 수동태의 시제, 수 일치 등은 be동사로 나타낸다. ☺ ☹

개념 25 수동태의 의미와 형태, 시제

월 일

The plate **was broken** by my sister.

This movie **will be reviewed** by a famous director.

My dog **is being treated** by the vet.

Ten different factories **have been visited** by the engineers.

The packages **should be delivered** by Mr. Parker.

시제	수동태 형태
현재	am/is/are + 과거분사
과거	was/were + 과거분사
미래	will be + 과거분사 be동사 + going to be + 과거분사
진행	be동사 + being + 과거분사
완료	have/has/had/will have + been + 과거분사
조동사가 있을 때	조동사 + be + 과거분사

바로 개념

1 수동태는 행위의 대상을 주어로 하는 동사의 형태로, 「be동사 + 과거분사」로 쓴다. 행위의 주체는 「by + 행위자」로 나타낸다.
2 수동태의 시제는 be동사의 형태 변화로 나타낸다.
3 조동사가 있을 때 수동태는 be동사를 원형으로 쓴다.

고르며 개념 확인

Answers p. 16

01 Your drink will ○ refill ○ be refilled by the waiters.

02 The flowers in the park ○ water ○ are watered every morning.

03 The museum ○ has be visited ○ has been visited by millions of people.

04 The injured man should ○ be sent ○ was sent to the hospital right away.

05 All the lights ○ are turned ○ were turned off when I came into the house.

쓰며 개념 정리

06 The police must catch the thief.
→ The thief ________ by the police.

07 Mark has bought some of the author's books.
→ Some of the author's books ________ by Mark.

08 Ms. Smith was driving the car on the highway.
→ The car ________ by Ms. Smith on the highway.

09 He will have completed the housework by 11.
→ The housework ________ by him by 11.

개념 26 4형식 문장의 수동태

월 일

Mr. Owens was offered the seat by me.
4형식 문장의 간접목적어가 주어가 된 수동태 문장

The seat was offered to Mr. Owens by me.
4형식 문장의 직접목적어가 주어가 된 수동태 문장

The children are taught math by my father.

A favor was done for George by the nurse.

Questions will be asked of him by the audience.

4형식 문장의 형태
주어 + 동사 + 간접목적어(A) + 직접목적어(B)
간접목적어가 주어가 될 때
주어(A) + be동사 + 과거분사 + B + by + 행위자
직접목적어가 주어가 될 때
주어(B) + be동사 + 과거분사 + 전치사 + A + by + 행위자

직접목적어를 주어로 쓸 때 사용하는 전치사	
to를 쓰는 동사	give, teach, bring, send, show, tell, lend, sell, read, write, offer 등
for를 쓰는 동사	buy, choose, find, get, make, cook, do 등
of를 쓰는 동사	ask, request, inquire 등

바로 개념

1 4형식 문장의 수동태는 간접목적어나 직접목적어를 주어로 하는 두 종류의 문장으로 쓸 수 있다.
2 4형식으로 쓰인 동사가 buy, make, cook, sell, read, write, choose 등이면 직접목적어만 주어로 쓸 수 있다.
3 4형식 문장의 직접목적어를 주어로 하는 수동태 문장을 쓸 때 간접목적어였던 명사 앞에 전치사를 쓴다.

고르며 개념 확인

Answers p. 16

01 Some chairs were brought ○ to ○ of the people on the ground.

02 Delicious stew was cooked ○ to ○ for the guests.

03 I was shown ○ to ○ 없음 some old photos by my mother.

04 The small office was lent ○ to ○ for Noah by Mr. Lawrence.

05 A difficult question will be asked ○ to ○ of the doctor by a reporter.

쓰며 개념 정리

06 They offered me a cup of tea. ➔ I ______ by them.

07 Mr. Lee told her an interesting story.
➔ An interesting story ______ by Mr. Lee.

08 I sent my brother the concert tickets.
➔ My brother ______ by me.

09 Randy is going to make me a wooden shelf.
➔ A wooden shelf ______ by Randy.

Answers p. 16

개념 25 수동태의 의미와 형태, 시제

1 수동태는 행위의 대상을 주어로 하는 동사의 형태로, 「be동사 + 과거분사」로 쓴다. 행위의 주체는 「by + 행위자」로 나타낸다.

2 수동태의 시제는 be동사의 형태 변화로 나타낸다.

3 조동사가 있을 때 수동태는 be동사를 원형으로 쓴다.

시제	수동태 형태
현재	______ + ______
과거	______ + ______
미래	will be + 과거분사 / be동사 + going to be + 과거분사
진행	be동사 + ______ + ______
완료	have/has/had/will have + been + 과거분사
조동사가 있을 때	______ + ______ + ______

개념 26 4형식 문장의 수동태

1 4형식 문장의 수동태는 간접목적어를 주어로 쓸 수도 있고, 직접목적어를 주어로 쓸 수도 있다. 단, 동사가 buy, make, cook, sell, read, write, choose 등이면 ______ 만 주어로 쓸 수 있다.

2 4형식 문장의 직접목적어를 주어로 하는 수동태 문장을 쓸 때, 간접목적어였던 명사 앞에 동사에 따라 전치사 ______, ______, ______ 를 쓴다.

4형식 문장의 형태	주어 + 동사 + 간접목적어(A) + 직접목적어(B)	
______ 가 주어가 될 때	주어(A)(간접목적어) + be동사 + 과거분사 + B(직접목적어) + by + 행위자(주어)	
______ 가 주어가 될 때	주어(B)(직접목적어) + be동사 + 과거분사 + 전치사 + A(간접목적어) + by + 행위자(주어)	
	전치사 to를 쓰는 동사	give, teach, bring, send, show, tell, lend, sell, read, write, offer 등
	전치사 for를 쓰는 동사	buy, choose, find, get, make, cook, do 등
	전치사 of를 쓰는 동사	ask, request, inquire 등

Answers p. 17

A 다음 중 알맞은 것을 골라 문장을 완성하시오.

01 The car ○ be ○ will be repaired tomorrow morning.

02 The horses ○ are ○ were fed by the farmer just now.

03 The pool ○ uses ○ is used for a variety of activities.

04 Since he was eight, he ○ was ○ has been taught English.

05 The trash should ○ be ○ been dumped out soon.

06 They are going ○ to be ○ to being blamed by most people.

07 Something beautiful ○ is being ○ is been painted on the canvas now.

08 The film must ○ be ○ is edited by a professional editor.

09 The ducklings were ○ be ○ being guided on the road by their mother.

B 주어진 문장을 수동태 문장으로 바꿔 쓰시오.

01 I'll give him some flowers.

→ He ______ by me.

02 Clara read me a sad story.

→ A sad story ______ by Clara.

03 I cooked my family a nice brunch last Sunday.

→ A nice brunch ______ by me last Sunday.

04 Mark was telling us the news.

→ We ______ by Mark.

05 The chef showed her the new kitchen.

→ She ______ by the chef.

06 The boy wrote Mr. Hamilton an apology letter.

→ An apology letter ______ by the boy.

07 Did he ask you the question?

→ Was the question ______ by him?

문장 쓰기

표현 노트

	문장	표현 노트
181	그의 시는 모든 세대의 사랑을 받는다. His poems are loved by people of all ages.	poems, love, of all ages
182	그는 야생 동물들에 의해 공격당했다.	attack, wild animals
183	고대 이집트 때의 꿀은 오늘날 먹을 수 있다.	from ancient Egypt, can, eat
184	인공위성은 점점 더 많은 분야에서 이용되고 있다. ★ 현재진행 수동태로 쓸 것	satellites, use, in more and more fields
185	나는 네가 당선될 것이라고 확신한다.	have no doubt, that, will, elect
186	그녀의 대부분의 돈은 새로운 물건들을 사는 데 쓰인다.	most of, spend on, buy the new items
187	이 놀라운 형태는 빗방울에 의해 만들어졌다. ★ 현재완료 수동태로 쓸 것	amazing, shape, create, rainfall
188	화산은 연구되어야 하고, 이해되어야 한다.	volcanoes, should, study, understand

Answers p. 17

배열하여 문장 쓰기

189 많은 유명한 영화들이 뉴질랜드에서 만들어져 왔다.
(been, have, many famous movies, made, in New Zealand)

Many famous movies have been made in New Zealand.

190 3D 프린터는 우주 비행사들을 위한 음식을 출력하는 데 쓰일 것이다.
(will, used, food for astronauts, the 3D printer, be, to print out)

191 농작물에 해로운 화학 약품의 사용은 중단되어야 한다.
(on crops, be, the use of, must, stopped, harmful chemicals)

192 수리는 이번 주가 끝날 때까지 완료될 것이다.
(the repairs, of this week, completed, have, will, by, been, the end)

193 거기에는 그녀가 시카고에서 열리는 리그의 본 심사에 초청되었다고 적혀 있었다.
(had, she, invited, in Chicago, to the league's main tryouts, been)

It read that

194 불평하기 전에, 여러분이 선물을 받았다는 것을 명심하세요.
(that, been, given, you, a gift, have, remember)

Before you complain,

195 그것들 중 하나는 인도의 16살 소녀에게 주어졌다.
(to, one of them, in India, was, a 16-year-old girl, given)

[Self-Editing Checklist] ✔ 대 • 소문자를 바르게 썼나요? Y N ✔ 철자와 문장 부호를 바르게 썼나요? Y N

개념 27 5형식 문장의 수동태

월 일

Her parents believed her honest.
(honest: 목적격 보어)

→ She was believed honest by her parents.
(honest: 5형식에서 목적격 보어였던 말)

David was heard to cry out something.
(to cry: 5형식에서 목적격 보어였던 동사원형을 to부정사로 씀)

I was seen taking pictures in the library by the guard.
(taking: 5형식에서 목적격 보어였던 현재분사를 그대로 씀)

The dog was made to bring the ball by Jackson.
(to bring: 5형식에서 목적격 보어였던 동사원형을 to부정사로 씀)

5형식 문장(주어+동사+목적어+목적격 보어)의 수동태	
대부분의 동사	주어(목적어) + be동사 + 과거분사 + 보어(목적격 보어) + by + 행위자(주어)
지각동사 · 사역동사	• 목적격 보어인 동사원형을 to부정사로: 주어(목적어) + be동사 + 과거분사 + to부정사(목적격 보어) + by + 행위자(주어) • 목적격 보어가 현재분사면 그대로 쓴다. • 사역동사 let과 have는 수동태로 쓰지 않는다.

바로 개념

1 5형식 문장을 수동태 문장으로 바꿀 때 목적어를 수동태 문장의 주어로 쓰고 목적격 보어는 동사 바로 뒤에 쓴다.
2 5형식 문장의 동사가 지각동사나 사역동사일 때 목적격 보어인 동사원형은 수동태 문장에서 to부정사로 고쳐 쓴다.
3 5형식 문장의 동사가 지각동사일 때 목적격 보어가 현재분사면 그대로 동사 뒤에 쓴다.

고르며 개념 확인

Answers p. 17

01 I was called ○ Danny ○ by Danny by my family.

02 Eric was heard ○ talk ○ to talk on the phone by Sarah.

03 They were made ○ stay ○ to stay out of the hall during the show.

04 The girls were seen ○ played ○ playing baseball on the playground.

05 The kids were made ○ keep ○ to keep quiet by their teacher.

쓰며 개념 정리

06 한 손님이 불평하는 소리가 들렸다. (complain)
A customer was heard ______.

07 그녀는 강아지 때문에 행복하다. (happy)
She is made ______ by her puppy.

08 나는 집으로 돌아가게 되었다. (go)
I was made ______ back home.

09 그가 그 가게에 걸어 들어가는 것이 여러 사람에 의해 목격되었다. (walk)
He was seen ______ into the store by several people.

10 그 인형은 내 여동생에 의해 Mary라고 이름 붙여졌다. (Mary)
The doll was named ______ by my sister.

개념 28 동사구의 수동태

월 일

The clown is laughed at by kids.
laugh at: ~을 비웃다

The word was looked up in the dictionary by Ann.
look up: (사전에서) 찾다

The matter will be dealt with at the meeting.
deal with: ~을 다루다

The baby should be taken care of by him.
take care of: ~을 돌보다

She is spoken well of by her friends.
speak well of: ~을 좋게 말하다

동사구의 수동태

주어 + 동사 + 전치사/부사 + 목적어
⇩
주어 + be동사 + 과거분사 + 전치사/부사 + by + 행위자

1 '동사 + 전치사/부사'가 하나의 동사 역할을 할 때, 수동태는 '동사 + 전치사/부사'를 한 덩어리로 보아 「be동사 + 과거분사 + 전치사/부사」로 쓴다.

고르며 개념 확인

Answers p. 17

01 These tables have to be cleaned ○ by us up ○ up by us .

02 Their field trip was put ○ by off ○ off by the principal.

03 The bus will be caught up ○ with by ○ by with his car.

04 All the lights in the house were turned ○ on at a time ○ at a time on .

05 The festival is being looked ○ forward to by ○ by forward to all the students.

쓰며 개념 정리

06 The children made fun of Lily.
→ Lily [   ] by the children.

07 Anyone can make use of this fitness center.
→ This fitness center [   ] by anyone.

08 Jonathan looks up to the composer.
→ The composer [   ] by Jonathan.

09 I should look after my little sisters during the day.
→ My little sisters [   ] by me during the day.

Answers p. 17

개념 27 5형식 문장의 수동태

1 5형식 문장을 수동태 문장으로 바꿀 때 목적어를 수동태 문장의 주어로 쓰고 목적격 보어는 동사 바로 뒤에 쓴다.

2 5형식 문장의 동사가 지각동사나 사역동사일 때 목적격 보어인 동사원형은 수동태 문장에서 (   ) 로 고쳐 쓴다. 지각동사의 목적격 보어가 현재분사면 그대로 동사 뒤에 쓴다.

3 사역동사 (   ) 과 (   ) 는 수동태로 쓰지 않으므로 주의한다.

5형식 문장 (주어 + 동사 + 목적어 + 목적격 보어) 의 수동태	
대부분의 동사	주어(목적어) + be동사 + 과거분사 + 보어(목적격 보어) + by + 행위자(주어)
지각동사	목적격 보어가 동사원형일 때 → ( ) 주어(목적어) + be동사 + 과거분사 + ( )(목적격 보어) + by + 행위자(주어) 목적격 보어가 현재분사일 때 → ( ) 주어(목적어) + be동사 + 과거분사 + ( )(목적격 보어) + by + 행위자(주어)
사역동사	목적격 보어 (동사원형) → ( ) 주어(목적어) + be동사 + 과거분사 + ( )(목적격 보어) + by + 행위자

개념 28 동사구의 수동태

1 '동사+전치사/부사'가 하나의 동사 역할을 할 때, 수동태는 '동사 + 전치사/부사'를 한 덩어리로 취급하여 만든다. 따라서 전치사 또는 부사를 'be동사 + (   )' 바로 뒤에 쓴다.

능동태	주어 + 동사 + 전치사/부사 + 목적어
수동태	주어 + be동사 + 과거분사 + 전치사/부사 + by + 행위자

Answers p. 17

A 다음 문장에서 어법상 틀린 부분을 고르시오.

01 The boy ①was called ②of Oliver ③by his uncle.

02 The choir ①will be seeing ②to sing on the stage by ③lots of people.

03 ①Over 1,000 soda cans were ②giving away ③to the people by the volunteers.

04 They ①were heard ②to played ③the instruments in the music room.

05 Yunsu ①was seen ②be entering that house ③alone.

06 The building ①was believed ②to safe ③from earthquakes.

07 We ①were making ②to watch ③the boring movie by the teacher.

08 The event ①was put ②off the company ③because of bad weather.

B 주어진 문장을 수동태 문장으로 바꿔 쓰시오.

01 She made up the story about the monster.

→ The story about the monster was [   ].

02 Tom should take care of the three kittens.

→ The three kittens should be [   ].

03 My parents made me help my sister.

→ I was [   ].

04 The zookeeper named the monkey Jack.

→ The monkey was [   ].

05 Ms. Skinner saw Chad standing on the street.

→ Chad was [   ].

06 Baseball fans are looking forward to the next season.

→ The next season is being [   ].

배열하여 문장 쓰기

196
뉴질랜드인들은 때때로 키위라고 불린다.
(are, Kiwis, New Zealanders, sometimes, called)

New Zealanders are sometimes called Kiwis.

197
민경이는 그녀의 반 남학생에게 데이트 신청을 받았다.
(by, out, in her class, was, a boy, asked)

Minkyeong

198
갑자기, 익숙한 노래가 독일 군인들의 참호로부터 들려왔다.
(was, coming, a familiar song, from the German trenches, heard)

Suddenly,

199
그 개는 아이들에 의해 Kong이라고 이름이 지어졌다.
(the dog, named, the children, Kong, by, was)

200
시금치는 지구상에서 가장 건강한 식품 10개 중 하나로 여겨진다.
(is, one of, considered, on the planet, the ten healthiest foods, spinach)

201
이 동물들은 그녀에 의해 돌보아졌니?
(these animals, taken, by, of, have, been, her, care)

202
그것들은 우리에게 어느 전등을 켜야 하는지 말해준다.
(turned, they, us, which light, be, on, should, tell)

203
Boggis 씨가 돌아왔을 때, 탁자의 다리는 잘려 있었다.
(cut, been, off, of the table, had, the legs)

When Mr. Boggis came back,

Answers p. 17

문장 쓰기

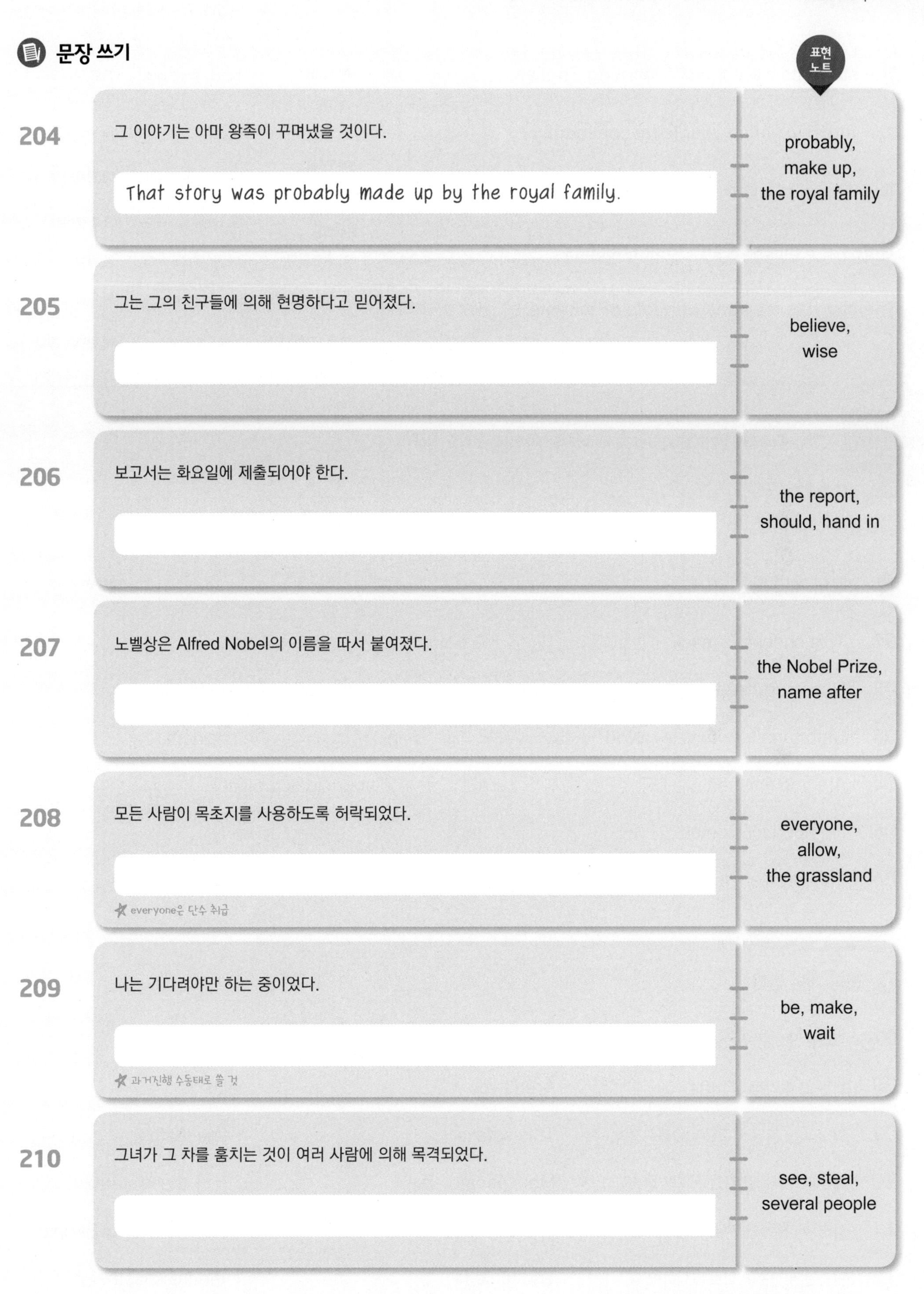

표현 노트

204 그 이야기는 아마 왕족이 꾸며냈을 것이다.

That story was probably made up by the royal family.

probably, make up, the royal family

205 그는 그의 친구들에 의해 현명하다고 믿어졌다.

believe, wise

206 보고서는 화요일에 제출되어야 한다.

the report, should, hand in

207 노벨상은 Alfred Nobel의 이름을 따서 붙여졌다.

the Nobel Prize, name after

208 모든 사람이 목초지를 사용하도록 허락되었다.

everyone은 단수 취급

everyone, allow, the grassland

209 나는 기다려야만 하는 중이었다.

과거진행 수동태로 쓸 것

be, make, wait

210 그녀가 그 차를 훔치는 것이 여러 사람에 의해 목격되었다.

see, steal, several people

[Self-Editing Checklist] 대・소문자를 바르게 썼나요? Y N 철자와 문장 부호를 바르게 썼나요? Y N

월 일

개념 29 by 이외의 전치사를 쓰는 수동태

The students were tired of learning English.

Are you involved in your local community?

The island is covered with pine trees.

They were pleased with their success.

The city was crowded with lots of tourists.

be surprised at	~에 놀라다	be covered with	~으로 덮여 있다
be interested in	~에 관심이 있다	be filled with	~으로 가득 차다
be tired of	~에 싫증나다	be pleased with	~에 기뻐하다
be worried about	~에 관해 걱정하다	be satisfied with	~에 만족하다
be concerned about	~에 관해 염려하다	be crowded with	~으로 붐비다
be involved in	~에 관련되다	be finished with	~을 끝내다
be made of + 성질이 변하지 않는 재료	~으로 만들어지다	be accustomed to	~에 익숙하다
be made from + 성질이 변하는 재료	~으로 만들어지다	be related to	~에 관련이 있다

바로 개념

1 수동태의 행위자를 나타낼 때 by 이외의 전치사를 쓰기도 한다.

고르며 개념 확인

Answers p. 18

01 This cheese is made ○ by ○ from goat milk.

02 I was surprised ○ at ○ by the horror movie poster.

03 Unfortunately, he is involved ○ by ○ in the accident.

04 Are you finished ○ by ○ with your class project?

05 I'm not accustomed ○ by ○ to getting up early.

06 This problem is related ○ by ○ to the air pollution.

쓰며 개념 정리

07 그녀는 영화를 찍는 데 관심이 있다. She is ______ ______ making films.

08 너는 그를 걱정하지 않니? Aren't you ______ ______ him?

09 이 소파는 좋은 가죽으로 만들어졌다. This sofa is ______ ______ fine leather.

10 대부분의 사람들은 그 식당에 만족한다. Most people are ______ ______ the restaurant.

11 강당은 많은 사람으로 붐볐다. The auditorium was ______ ______ a lot of people.

12 탁자는 두꺼운 식탁보로 덮여 있다. The table is ______ ______ the thick cloth.

개념 30

that절을 목적어로 하는 문장의 수동태

월 일

People believe that she is a millionaire.

→ It is believed that she is a millionaire.

→ She is believed to be a millionaire.

They expected (that) the strike would end soon.

→ It was expected that the strike would end soon.

→ The strike was expected to end soon.

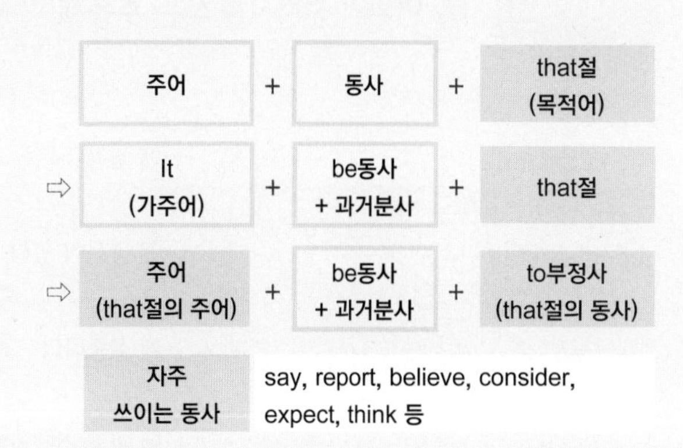

바로 개념

1 that절을 목적어로 하는 문장의 수동태는 가주어 it을 사용하여 만들 수 있다.

2 that절을 목적어로 하는 문장의 수동태는 that절의 주어를 문장의 주어로 하여 만들 수도 있다.

3 주로 전달, 사고와 관련된 동사가 많이 쓰인다.

고르며 개념 확인

Answers p. 18

01 Jack is said ○ that ○ to get a role in the play.

02 It is considered ○ that ○ to that Sydney is the best vacation spot.

03 Second-hand smoking is reported ○ that ○ to harm your health.

04 It is thought ○ that ○ to be smartphones have a bad influence on children.

쓰며 개념 정리

05 People say that the man is genius.

→ It __________ the man is a genius.

06 They expect that he will come back next week.

→ He __________ back next week.

07 They believed that Ms. Marple was popular among kids.

→ It __________ Ms. Marple was popular among kids.

08 We consider that the new rules will decrease the school violence.

→ The new rules __________ decrease the school violence.

Answers p. 18

개념 29 by 이외의 전치사를 쓰는 수동태

be surprised ( )	~에 놀라다	be covered ( )	~으로 덮여 있다
be interested ( )	~에 관심이 있다	be filled ( )	~으로 가득 차다
be tired ( )	~에 싫증나다	be pleased ( )	~에 기뻐하다
be worried ( )	~에 관해 걱정하다	be satisfied ( )	~에 만족하다
be concerned ( )	~에 관해 염려하다	be crowded ( )	~으로 붐비다
be involved ( )	~에 관련되다	be finished ( )	~을 끝내다
be made ( ) + 성질이 변하지 않는 재료	~으로 만들어지다	be accustomed ( )	~에 익숙하다
be made ( ) + 성질이 변하는 재료	~으로 만들어지다	be related ( )	~에 관련이 있다

개념 30 that절을 목적어로 하는 문장의 수동태

1 that절을 목적어로 하는 문장의 수동태는 가주어 ( )을 사용하거나, that절의 ( )를 수동태 문장의 주어로 하여 쓸 수 있다.

2 주로 say, report, believe, consider, expect, think 등 전달, 사고와 관련된 동사가 쓰인다.

목적어가 that절인 문장	주어 + 동사 + that절(목적어)
가주어 it을 수동태 문장의 주어로 쓸 때	It(가주어) + be동사 + 과거분사 + that절(진주어)
that절의 주어를 수동태 문장의 주어로 쓸 때	주어(that절의 주어) + be동사 + 과거분사 + ( )(that절의 동사) ~

Answers p. 18

A 다음 우리말에 맞게 주어진 동사를 활용하여 빈칸에 알맞은 말을 쓰시오.

01 이 귀걸이는 은으로 만들어진다. (make)

→ These earrings ______ ______ ______ silver.

02 나는 혼자 식사하는 것에 익숙하지 않다. (accustom)

→ I ______ ______ ______ ______ eating alone.

03 그 여자는 그 사건에 관련되어 있니? (involve)

→ ______ the woman ______ ______ that case?

04 우리 할머니는 어떤 것에도 놀라지 않으신다. (surprise)

→ My grandmother ______ ______ ______ ______ anything.

05 Andy는 그들이 그에게 해 주는 모든 것에 기뻐했다. (please)

→ Andy ______ ______ ______ everything they did for him.

06 그 박물관은 항상 외국인 여행객들로 붐빈다. (crowd)

→ The museum ______ always ______ ______ foreign tourists.

B 두 문장의 뜻이 같도록 빈칸에 알맞은 말을 쓰시오.

01 People think that Venice is a beautiful city.

→ ______ is ______ ______ Venice is a beautiful city.

02 It is expected that he will win a medal at the Olympics.

→ He is ______ ______ ______ a medal at the Olympics.

03 It is said that the song is the best song of this year.

→ The song is ______ ______ ______ the best song of this year.

04 She is believed to have saved several people.

→ It is ______ ______ ______ ______ saved several people.

05 It was reported that Mr. Roland had been hit by a car.

→ ______ was ______ to ______ ______ hit by a car.

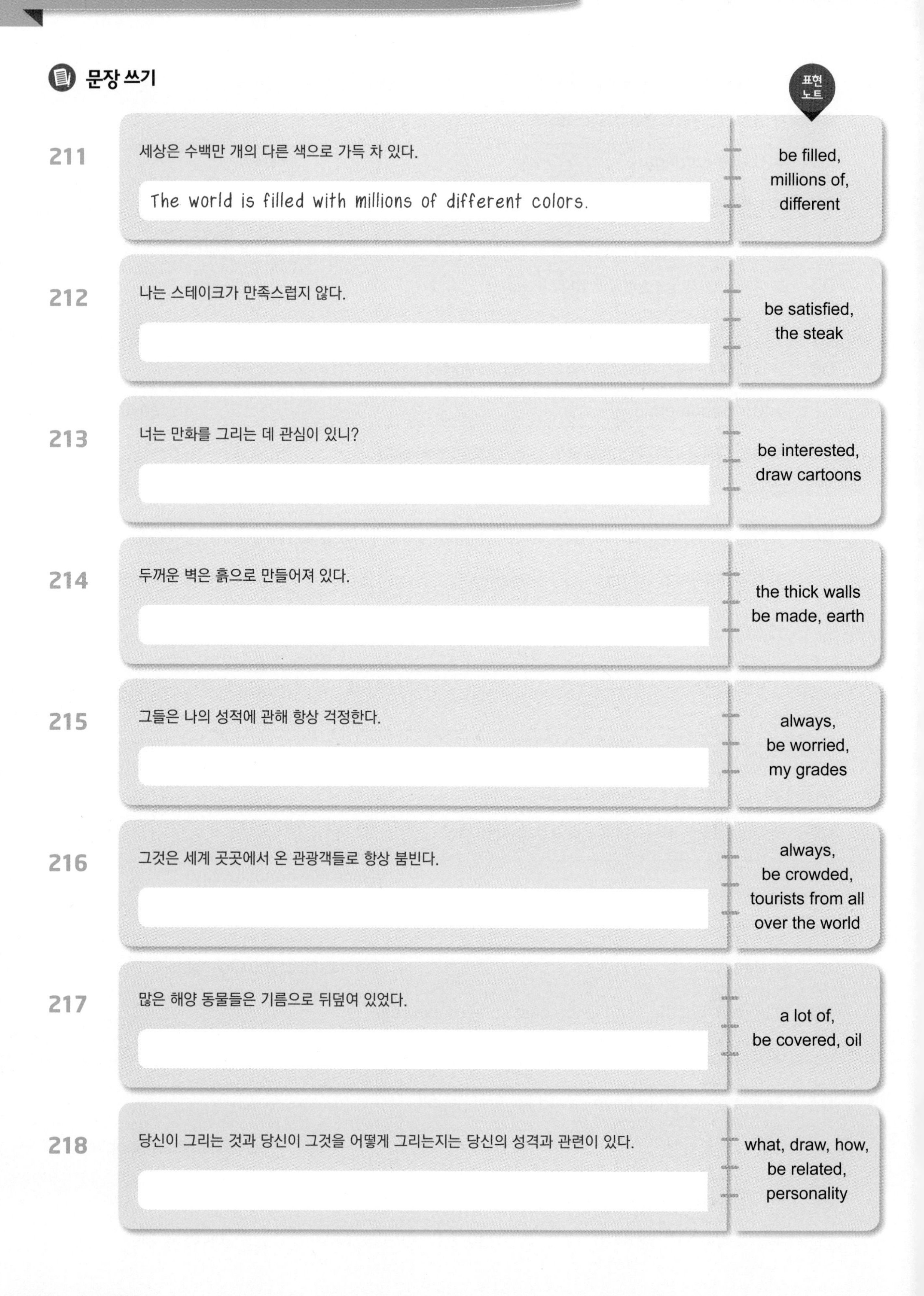

문장 쓰기

표현 노트

211 세상은 수백만 개의 다른 색으로 가득 차 있다.

The world is filled with millions of different colors.

be filled, millions of, different

212 나는 스테이크가 만족스럽지 않다.

be satisfied, the steak

213 너는 만화를 그리는 데 관심이 있니?

be interested, draw cartoons

214 두꺼운 벽은 흙으로 만들어져 있다.

the thick walls be made, earth

215 그들은 나의 성적에 관해 항상 걱정한다.

always, be worried, my grades

216 그것은 세계 곳곳에서 온 관광객들로 항상 붐빈다.

always, be crowded, tourists from all over the world

217 많은 해양 동물들은 기름으로 뒤덮여 있었다.

a lot of, be covered, oil

218 당신이 그리는 것과 당신이 그것을 어떻게 그리는지는 당신의 성격과 관련이 있다.

what, draw, how, be related, personality

Answers p. 18

that절을 목적어로 하는 문장의 수동태 쓰기

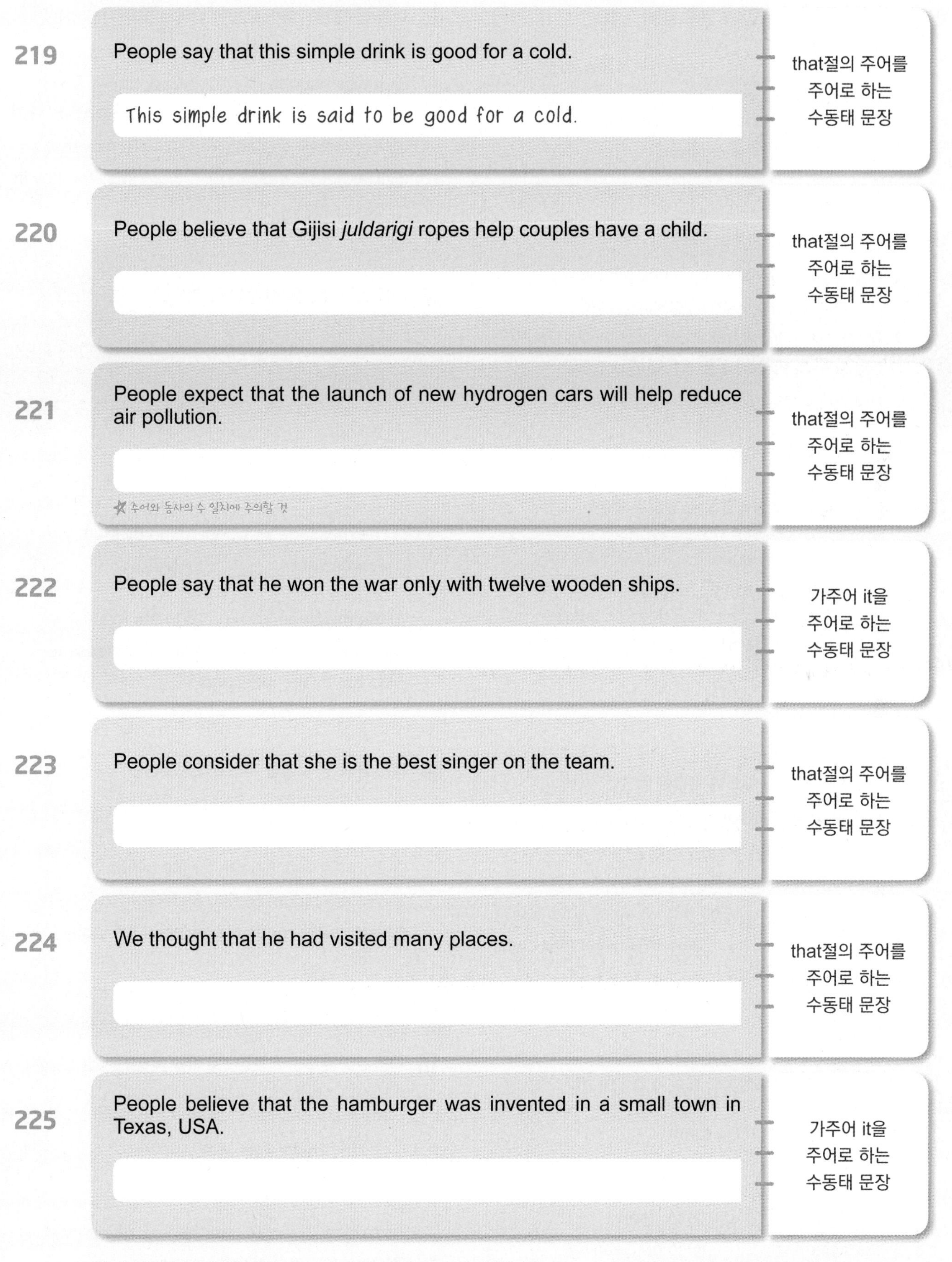

219 People say that this simple drink is good for a cold.

This simple drink is said to be good for a cold.

that절의 주어를 주어로 하는 수동태 문장

220 People believe that Gijisi *juldarigi* ropes help couples have a child.

that절의 주어를 주어로 하는 수동태 문장

221 People expect that the launch of new hydrogen cars will help reduce air pollution.

★ 주어와 동사의 수 일치에 주의할 것

that절의 주어를 주어로 하는 수동태 문장

222 People say that he won the war only with twelve wooden ships.

가주어 it을 주어로 하는 수동태 문장

223 People consider that she is the best singer on the team.

that절의 주어를 주어로 하는 수동태 문장

224 We thought that he had visited many places.

that절의 주어를 주어로 하는 수동태 문장

225 People believe that the hamburger was invented in a small town in Texas, USA.

가주어 it을 주어로 하는 수동태 문장

[Self-Editing Checklist] ✔ 대 • 소문자를 바르게 썼나요? Y N ✔ 철자와 문장 부호를 바르게 썼나요? Y N

대표유형 01 수동태의 시제와 형태

01 다음 문장의 빈칸에 들어갈 말로 알맞은 것은?

The trees will ________ down in a few days.

① be cut ② have cut ③ were cut
④ been cut ⑤ be cutting

02 다음 문장 중 어법상 어색한 것은?

① This theater is visited by many people.
② The pigs should been treated by a vet.
③ We're going to be taught physics by Dr. Green.
④ The speakers will be fixed by tomorrow.
⑤ The church is being built by a famous architect.

03 다음 대화의 빈칸에 들어갈 말로 알맞은 것은?

A Who made Hangeul?
B It ________ made by King Sejong in 1443.

① is ② was ③ were
④ has been ⑤ will be

04 다음 문장 중 밑줄 친 부분이 어법상 어색한 것은?

① This keyboard is being used by me.
② The decision has been made yesterday.
③ My work will have been completed by 3 p.m.
④ The old things must be thrown away right now.
⑤ The animals will be moved to another zoo next week.

05 다음 문장을 수동태 문장으로 바꿀 때 빈칸에 알맞은 말은?

You have to clean the room.
➔ The room has ________ by you.

① be clean ② to clean
③ been cleaned ④ to be cleaning
⑤ to be cleaned

대표유형 02 4형식과 5형식의 수동태

06 다음 중 빈칸에 들어갈 말이 나머지 넷과 다른 것은?

① The book was given ________ me by him.
② It was bought ________ Gary by Mr. Ahn.
③ The news was told ________ us by Alvin.
④ A letter will be sent ________ Tom by me.
⑤ The house was sold ________ Ms. Todd by its owner today.

07 다음 문장의 밑줄 친 부분 중 어법상 어색한 것은?

I ① was ② made ③ washing ④ the dishes ⑤ by my sister.

08 다음 두 문장의 뜻이 통하도록 할 때 빈칸에 알맞은 말은?

The message was sent to me by Matt.
= I was sent ________ by Matt.

① the message ② to the message
③ by the message ④ for the message
⑤ to me by the message

09 다음 문장 중 어법상 자연스러운 것은?

① Drinks were offered of the guests.
② I was seen walk into the house by him.
③ This hat was bought for my father.
④ We are taught by Ms. Anderson science.
⑤ They were made to staying in the lobby.

대표유형 03 동사구의 수동태

10 다음 문장을 수동태 문장으로 바꿀 때 빈칸에 알맞은 말은?

My mom has taken care of the matter.
➔ The matter has been taken ________ my mom.

① care of ② care by ③ care by of
④ care of by ⑤ by of care

Answers p. 18

11 다음 어구를 알맞게 배열하여 문장을 쓸 때, 네 번째로 오는 것은?

> out, was, filled, the student, the form, by

① out ② was ③ filled
④ the student ⑤ by

12 주어진 우리말과 같도록 할 때 빈칸에 들어갈 말로 알맞은 것은?

> 강아지는 그 꼬마에게 종종 놀림을 당한다.
> ➔ The puppy is often ________ the kid.

① make fun of ② making fun by
③ made fun by ④ made by fun of
⑤ made fun of by

대표유형 04 by 이외의 전치사를 쓰는 수동태

13 두 문장의 빈칸에 알맞은 말이 순서대로 짝지어진 것은?

> • Don't be concerned ________ my health.
> • My parents seem to be worried ________ my school grades.

① about – in ② at – about
③ with – by ④ by – with
⑤ about – about

14 다음 우리말을 바르게 영작한 것은?

> 그는 도시 생활에 익숙하지 않다.

① He is not accustomed by city life.
② He is not accustomed to city life.
③ He is not accustomed to by city life.
④ He is accustomed with not to city life.
⑤ He is accustomed with not by city life.

15 각 문장의 괄호 안에서 알맞은 것을 골라 순서대로 짝지은 것은?

> • Are you finished (to / with) your English homework?
> • I am not interested (by / in) working for a bank.
> • This wine is made (from / of) berries.

① to – by – of ② to – in – from
③ with – by – of ④ with – in – from
⑤ with – by – from

대표유형 05 that절을 목적어로 하는 문장의 수동태

16 다음 두 문장의 뜻이 통하도록 할 때 빈칸에 알맞은 말은?

> It is expected that his suggestion will help solve the traffic problem.
> = His suggestion is expected ________ solve the traffic problem.

① help ② helping ③ to help
④ will help ⑤ that helps

17 다음 문장의 빈칸에 들어갈 말로 알맞은 것은?

> It is believed ________ drinking enough water is good for your health.

① if ② that ③ to
④ of ⑤ so

18 다음 문장의 밑줄 친 부분의 형태로 알맞은 것은?

> The old man is thought <u>be</u> very kind to his neighbors.

① be ② is ③ being
④ to be ⑤ been

01 어법상 어색한 부분을 찾아 바르게 고쳐 문장을 다시 쓰시오.

(1) The plant has been using in medical treatment by many doctors.

→ ______________________________

(2) His old desk was always covered at dust.

→ ______________________________

02 다음 문장을 주어진 말을 주어로 하는 두 개의 수동태 문장으로 바꿔 쓰시오.

(1) My grandfather sent me a nice present.

→ I ______________________________.

→ A nice present ______________________________.

(2) CNN reported that the fire was four times the size of Manhattan.

→ It ______________________________.

→ The fire ______________________________.

수행평가 유형 대화 완성하기

03 다음은 학생들이 현재 하고 있는 일과 하지 않는 일을 나타낸 표이다. 표를 보고 질문에 완전한 문장으로 답하여 대화를 완성하시오.

이름	하고 있는 일	하지 않는 일
Tom	clean the living room	make cookies
Susie	make cookies	clean the living room
Kyle	clean the living room	make cookies

A Is the living room being cleaned by Susie?

B No, (1) ______________________________.

A What is being made by Susie?

B (2) ______________________________

A Are the cookies being made by Tom and Kyle?

B No, the cookies are not being made by them.

A What is being cleaned by them?

B (3) ______________________________

[Self-Editing Checklist] ✔ 대 • 소문자를 바르게 썼나요? Y N ✔ 철자와 문장 부호를 바르게 썼나요? Y N

UNIT 08

관계사

31 관계대명사_주격, 소유격, 목적격

32 관계대명사 what과 that

33 관계부사

34 관계대명사의 계속적 용법

35 복합 관계대명사

36 복합 관계부사

핵심 개념 바로 확인 I know! ☺ No idea! 😐

- 관계대명사와 관계부사는 선행사를 꾸미는 절을 이끈다. ☺ 😐
- 관계대명사는 〈접속사 + 대명사〉의 역할을 하고 관계부사는 〈접속사 + 부사〉의 역할을 한다. ☺ 😐

개념 31 관계대명사_주격, 소유격, 목적격

I have a friend who loves to travel.
(a friend: 선행사 / who: 주격 관계대명사 = that)

I know a girl whose sister is a famous singer.
(a girl: 선행사 / whose: 소유격 관계대명사)

She ate a sandwich which her son made.
(a sandwich: 선행사 / which: 목적격 관계대명사 = that)

Tim is a true friend on whom I can rely.
(= whom I can rely on)

선행사	주격	소유격	목적격
사람	who	whose	who(m)
사물, 동물	which	whose / of which	which
사람, 사물, 동물	that	–	that

관계대명사의 생략

① 「주격 관계대명사 + be동사 + 분사(형용사)」 구문에서 「주격 관계대명사 + be동사」는 생략 가능
② 목적격 관계대명사는 생략 가능

바로 개념

1 주격 관계대명사는 관계사절 안에서 주어 역할을 한다. 바로 뒤에는 동사가 오며 동사의 수는 선행사에 일치시킨다.
2 소유격 관계대명사는 관계사절 안에서 소유격 역할을 한다. 소유격 관계대명사 뒤에는 명사가 온다.
3 목적격 관계대명사는 관계사절 안에서 목적어 역할을 한다. 목적격 관계대명사 뒤에는 「주어 + 동사」를 쓴다.
4 선행사가 전치사의 목적어일 때 「전치사 + 관계대명사」의 형태로 쓰거나 전치사를 관계사절 끝에 쓴다.

고르며 개념 확인

Answers p. 19

01 Seals are animals ○ who ○ which live both on land and in water.

02 Megan ran into the couple ○ that ○ which lives next door.

03 The boy ○ whom ○ whose I met at the store was my classmate.

04 Heaven helps those ○ who ○ which help themselves.

05 A shoplifter is someone ○ that steal ○ who steals things from shops.

★**06** This is the house in ○ which ○ that my parents live.

★ 관계대명사 that을 쓸 수 없는 경우
• 앞에 전치사가 있을 때 쓸 수 없음
• 소유격 관계대명사 대신 쓸 수 없음

쓰며 개념 정리

07 The reporter interviewed the swimmer. She won the gold medal.

→ The reporter interviewed the swimmer ______________.

08 The paintings were beautiful. + He showed them to me.

→ The paintings ______________ were beautiful.

★**09** Do you know the girl? + Leo is talking with the girl.

→ Do you know the girl ______________?

★ 전치사의 위치에 주의

개념 32

관계대명사 what과 that

월 일

What I can't stand is his rude attitude. 〈주어 역할〉

This is not what I wanted to have for lunch. 〈보어 역할〉

I can't understand what she explains. 〈목적어 역할〉

You can choose anything that you like.
(anything: 선행사)

All that glitters is not gold.
(All: 선행사)

관계대명사 what	관계대명사 that
명사절을 이끎	형용사절을 이끎
선행사 없음	선행사 있음
관계대명사 what + 불완전한 문장	관계대명사 that + 불완전한 문장

바로 개념

1 관계대명사 what은 명사처럼 쓰여 주어, 보어, 목적어 역할을 하며 '~하는 것'이라는 의미이다.
2 관계대명사 what은 선행사를 포함하므로 앞에 선행사가 없고, the thing(s) which [that]와 바꿔 쓸 수 있다.
3 관계대명사 that은 주격·목적격 관계대명사 who(m), which 대신 쓸 수 있으며 that 앞에는 선행사가 있다.
4 선행사에「사람+사물」,「사람+동물」, all, the only, -thing, -body, -one, 최상급, 서수가 있으면 주로 관계대명사 that을 쓴다.

고르며 개념 확인

Answers p. 19

★ 부분 부정: not + always: 항상 ~인 것은 아니다

*01 ○ What ○ That you see is not always true.

02 It is the most boring movie ○ who ○ that I've ever seen.

03 The future depends on ○ which ○ what we do in the present.

04 Is this really ○ that ○ what you have been looking for?

05 Could you please repeat ○ which ○ what you've just said?

06 Every word ○ that ○ what she said was true.

쓰며 개념 정리 관계대명사 what 또는 that 쓰기

07 난 그런 뜻이 아니었다. That's not ______ I meant.

08 내게 가장 인상적이었던 것은 그녀의 용기였다. ______ impressed me most was her courage.

09 그는 그가 저지른 일에 대해 벌을 받을 것이다. He'll be punished for ______ he has done.

10 이것은 내가 어제 잃어버렸던 책이다. This is the book ______ I lost yesterday.

11 너는 내가 방금 들은 것을 못 믿을 거야. You wouldn't believe ______ I just heard.

12 사랑은 우리를 구원할 유일한 것이다. Love is the only thing ______ will save us.

Answers p. 20

개념 31 관계대명사_주격, 소유격, 목적격

1 주격 관계대명사는 관계사절 안에서 주어 역할을 한다. 바로 뒤에는 [ ] 가 오며 동사의 수는 선행사에 일치시킨다.

2 소유격 관계대명사는 관계사절 안에서 소유격 역할을 한다. 소유격 관계대명사 뒤에는 [ ] 가 온다.

3 목적격 관계대명사는 관계사절 안에서 목적어 역할을 한다. 목적격 관계대명사 뒤에는 「주어 + 동사」를 쓴다.

4 선행사가 전치사의 목적어일 때 「전치사 + 관계대명사」의 형태로 쓰거나 전치사를 관계사절 끝에 쓴다.

선행사	주격	소유격	목적격
사람			
사물, 동물			
사람, 사물, 동물		-	

관계대명사의 생략	① 「주격 관계대명사 + be동사 + 분사(형용사)」 구문에서 「주격 관계대명사 + be동사」는 생략 가능 ② 목적격 관계대명사는 생략 가능
관계대명사 that을 쓸 수 없는 경우	① 앞에 전치사가 있을 때 쓸 수 없음 ② 소유격 관계대명사 대신 쓸 수 없음

개념 32 관계대명사 what과 that

1 관계대명사 what은 명사처럼 쓰여 [ ], [ ], [ ] 역할을 하며 '[ ]' 이라는 의미이다.

2 관계대명사 what은 선행사를 포함하므로 앞에 선행사가 없고, the thing(s) which [that]와 바꿔 쓸 수 있다.

3 관계대명사 that은 주격·목적격 관계대명사 [ ], [ ] 대신 쓸 수 있으며 that 앞에는 선행사가 있다.

4 선행사에 「사람+사물」, 「사람+동물」, all, the only, -thing, -body, -one, 최상급, 서수가 있으면 주로 관계대명사 that을 쓴다.

관계대명사 what	관계대명사 that
[ ] 절을 이끎	[ ] 절을 이끎
선행사 [ ]	선행사 [ ]
관계대명사 what + [ ] 문장	관계대명사 that + [ ] 문장

Answers p. 20

A 다음 문장에서 밑줄 친 부분을 어법에 맞게 고치시오.

01 Rachel has a daughter which resembles her very much.

02 I like the red dress who Bella is wearing.

03 There is one thing what upsets me.

04 The girl is sitting next to Jake is my best friend Jina.

★ 「주격 관계대명사 + be동사」는 함께 생략할 수 있음

05 This is the hospital which my son was born.

06 They're helping the children who suffers from a disease.

07 The bike of which I bought last weekend is expensive.

08 Daniel is the singer whom everyone loves him.

09 The student that computer was stolen called the police.

10 Which makes the desert beautiful is that somewhere it hides a well.

B 다음 〈보기〉와 같이 두 문장을 who, which, whom, whose를 이용하여 한 문장으로 쓰시오.

보기 This is a bridge. + It was built about 50 years ago.
➔ This is a bridge which was built about 50 years ago.

01 The police arrested the thief. The thief broke into her store yesterday.

➔

02 He is my new neighbor. + I talked about him.

★ 전치사를 생략하지 않도록 주의

➔

03 I met a woman. Her hobby is rock-climbing.

➔

04 This is one of the films. I'd like to watch it.

➔

05 Most people didn't show up. Kate invited them to her house.

➔

관계대명사 who, whom, which, whose를 이용하여 한 문장으로 쓰기

226 The farmer visited a close friend. + He had four children.

The farmer visited a close friend who had four children.

227 Thulin wanted a sturdy, yet light bag. + It would last for ages.

228 It was written by a woman. + Her husband was far away.

229 He is one of the three gods. + They created humans.

230 This is the woman. + I worked with her.

231 They decided to adopt the dog. + They saw it at the animal shelter.

232 Birbal came back with two pots. + Their necks were really narrow.

233 Ants live in colonies. + They have lots of residents living together.

Answers p. 20

배열하여 문장 쓰기

234 나는 나와 이름이 같은 한 소녀를 만났다.
(the same, is, name, a girl, whose, met, as mine, I)

235 기사를 주의 깊게 읽었던 사람들은 크게 웃었다.
(read, those, laughed out, loud, carefully, who, the article)

★ those: ~한 사람들

236 나는 아이슬란드에서 찍은 사진들로 사진 경연대회에 참가했다.
(in Iceland, took, I, I, a photo contest, entered, with the pictures)

★ 목적격 관계대명사가 생략된 형태

237 여러분은 계란처럼 생긴 건물을 상상할 수 있나요?
(you, can, imagine, that, an egg, looks like, a building)

238 내가 고등학교를 시작했을 때 썼던 이 시가 당신의 마음에 들기를 바랍니다.
(which, this poem, wrote, I, I, high school, started, when)

I hope you like

239 화산이 하는 일이 인류에게 항상 나쁜 것만은 아니다.
(do, is, always, for humans, what, not, volcanoes, bad)

★ not always는 부분 부정으로 '항상 ~인 것은 아닌'이라는 의미임

240 작가가 말하는 것을 뒷받침하는 증거가 있는가?
(there, is, that, any evidence, what, supports, says, the writer)

[Self-Editing Checklist] 대 • 소문자를 바르게 썼나요? Y N 철자와 문장 부호를 바르게 썼나요? Y N

개념 33 관계부사

월 일

Friday is the day when I am busiest.
= on which

This is the place where I was born.
= in which

Do you know the reason why he left here?
= for which

I want to know how you solved the problem.
= the way (in which)

	선행사	관계부사	전치사 + 관계대명사
시간	the day, the time, the week 등	when	in / at / on+which
장소	the place, the town, the city 등	where	in / at / on+which
이유	the reason	why	for which
방법	(the way)	how	in which

바로 개념

1 관계부사는 시간, 장소, 이유, 방법을 나타내는 선행사를 수식하는 절을 이끌며 접속사와 부사의 역할을 한다.
2 관계부사는 「전치사 + 관계대명사」와 바꿔 쓸 수 있다.
3 관계부사 how와 선행사 the way는 함께 쓰일 수 없으므로 둘 중 하나는 생략해야 한다.
4 관계부사의 선행사가 the day, the place, the reason 등과 같이 일반적일 때 관계부사와 선행사 중 하나를 생략할 수 있다.

고르며 개념 확인

Answers p. 20

01 2002 was the year ○ when ○ where Korea hosted the World Cup.

02 We need to book a hotel ○ where ○ which we can rest for a while.

03 Fred is selfish. That's ○ why ○ how I hate him.

04 Could you explain ○ the way ○ the way how this washing machine works?

★05 This is the place ○ where ○ which Ted and I used to hide in.
★ 끝에 전치사가 있음에 주의

06 There's a reason for ○ why ○ which Cindy didn't attend the meeting.

쓰며 개념 정리 알맞은 관계부사 쓰기

07 나는 너를 만났던 날을 기억한다. I remember the day ______ I met you.

08 그는 병원이 없는 마을에 살고 있다. He lives in a village ______ there are no hospitals.

09 이런 일이 일어나는 이유를 알겠니? Can you guess the reason ______ this happens?

10 난 그녀가 사람들을 대하는 방식이 마음에 안 든다. I don't like ______ she treats people.

11 1월은 눈이 많이 오는 달이다. January is the month ______ we have a lot of snow.

12 이곳은 내가 자주 점심을 먹는 구내식당이다. This is the cafeteria ______ I often have lunch.

개념 34 관계대명사의 계속적 용법

제한적 용법	계속적 용법
선행사를 직접 수식함	선행사에 대한 보충 설명을 함
관계사 앞에 콤마(,)가 없음	관계사 앞에 콤마(,)가 있음
'~한, ~하는'으로 해석함	관계사 앞의 절부터 해석하고 and, but 등의 접속사를 넣어 관계사 뒤의 절을 해석함
He has two sons who are teachers. 그에게는 교사인 아들이 두 명 있다. (→ 아들이 둘 이상일 수 있음)	He has two sons, who(= and they) are teachers. 그에게는 아들이 둘 있고, 그들은 교사이다. (→ 아들이 둘 뿐임)

바로 개념

1 관계대명사의 계속적 용법은 선행사에 대한 부가적인 정보를 제공할 때 쓰인다.
2 관계대명사가 계속적 용법으로 쓰일 때 관계사 앞에 콤마(,)를 쓰며, 명사뿐만 아니라 구나 절도 선행사가 될 수 있다.
3 계속적 용법으로 쓰인 관계대명사는 생략할 수 없고, 관계대명사 that과 what은 계속적 용법으로 쓰일 수 없다.

고르며 개념 확인

Answers p. 20

01 Brian has a dog, ○ which ○ that can swim very well.

02 We want to hire Ms. Anderson, ○ who ○ which can speak three languages.

03 Kelly does a lot of walking, ○ who ○ which keeps her healthy.

04 I have a collection of dolls, ○ which ○ what I used to play with.

★**05** The hotel is run by three sisters, ○ all of whom ○ all of which are friendly.

★ 계속적 용법에서 콤마(,) 다음에 「부정대명사 + of + 관계대명사」의 형태로 쓰임

쓰며 개념 정리

06 Grace was named after her grandmother, and she died a year ago.
= Grace was named after her grandmother, ______ ______ a year ago.

★**07** The old man, though he is poor, is happy.
= The old man, ______ ______ poor, is happy. ★ 관계사절이 삽입된 경우에는 절 앞뒤로 콤마를 씀

08 A lot of people visit Iceland, and it is famous for its natural beauty.
= A lot of people visit Iceland, ______ ______ famous for its natural beauty.

09 Max was late for school, and it made his teacher angry.
= Max was late for school, ______ ______ his teacher angry.

Answers p. 20

개념 33 관계부사

1 관계부사는 시간, 장소, 이유, 방법을 나타내는 선행사를 수식하는 절을 이끌며 접속사와 부사의 역할을 한다.

2 관계부사는 「[   ] + [   ]」와 바꿔 쓸 수 있다.

3 관계부사 [   ]와 the way는 함께 쓰일 수 없으므로 둘 중 하나는 생략해야 한다.

	선행사	관계부사	전치사 + 관계대명사
시간	the day, the time, the week 등		
장소	the place, the town, the city 등		
이유	the reason		
방법	(the way)		

개념 34 관계대명사의 계속적 용법

1 관계대명사의 계속적 용법은 선행사에 대한 부가적인 정보를 제공할 때 쓰인다.

2 관계대명사가 계속적 용법으로 쓰일 때 관계사 앞에 [   ]를 쓰며, 명사뿐만 아니라 구나 절도 선행사가 될 수 있다.

3 계속적 용법으로 쓰인 관계대명사는 생략할 수 없고, 관계대명사 [   ]과 [   ]은 계속적 용법으로 쓰일 수 없다.

제한적 용법	계속적 용법
선행사를 직접 수식함	선행사에 대한 보충 설명을 함
관계사 앞에 콤마(,)가 없음	관계사 앞에 콤마(,)가 있음
'~한, ~하는'으로 해석함	관계사 앞의 절부터 해석하고 and, but 등의 접속사를 넣어 관계사 뒤의 절을 해석함
He has two sons who are teachers. 그에게는 교사인 아들이 두 명 있다. (→ 아들이 둘 이상일 수 있음)	He has two sons, who(= [ ]) are teachers. 그에게는 아들이 둘 있고, 그들은 교사이다. (→ 아들이 둘 뿐임)

A 다음 문장들이 같은 뜻이 되도록 빈칸에 알맞은 말을 쓰시오.

01 I still remember the day. Jiwon left Seoul on the day.

= I still remember the day [ ] Jiwon left Seoul.

= I still remember the day [ ] [ ] Jiwon left Seoul.

02 This is the town. I spent my childhood in the town.

= This is the town [ ] I spent my childhood.

= This is the town [ ] [ ] I spent my childhood.

03 She told us the way. She raised money in the way.

= She told us [ ] she raised money.

= She told us the way [ ] [ ] she raised money.

04 We learned about the reasons. Birds migrate for the reasons.

= We learned about the reasons [ ] birds migrate.

= We learned about the reasons [ ] [ ] birds migrate.

B 다음 문장을 관계대명사의 계속적 용법을 이용하여 바꿔 쓰시오.

01 I have two close friends, and they are very different from each other.

➔ [ ]

02 My teacher recommended this novel, and it changed my life.

➔ [ ]

03 My favorite artist is Gustav Klimt, and his work is full of patterns and colors.

➔ [ ]

04 I met Sophia, and I hadn't seen her for ages.

➔ [ ]

05 The man said he didn't know Anne, but it was a lie.

➔ [ ]

관계부사 이용하여 한 문장으로 쓰기

241 This is the day. + My parents got married on the day.

This is the day when my parents got married.

242 Turkey is a country. + East meets West in the country.

243 That's the reason. + He hasn't finished the painting yet for the reason.

244 Calli should pick a time. + Her mom is ready to listen at the time.

245 This letter shows the way. + People got over these difficulties in the way.

246 That is the place. + My dog hides his food in the place.

247 Sunmin's sister disliked the way. + Sunmin had treated her in the way.

248 Cancun is a city. + 4.8 million tourists travel there every year.

Answers p. 21

계속적 용법을 이용하여 문장 바꿔 쓰기

249 I share a room with my sister, and she is two years older than me.

I share a room with my sister, who is two years older than me.

250 People use ROFL quite often, and it means "Rolling On the Floor Laughing."

251 The book is about King Sejong, and he invented Hangeul.

252 Most buildings need air conditioning, and it uses a lot of energy.

253 Walnuts also have wrinkles, and the brain has them too.

254 All the rules were explained by an old man in a suit, and he sounded very serious and unkind.

255 Uncle Ben went on a trip to Africa, and it was his lifelong dream.

[Self-Editing Checklist] 대 • 소문자를 바르게 썼나요? Y N 철자와 문장 부호를 바르게 썼나요? Y N

개념 35 복합 관계대명사

월 일

Whoever comes first will have this ticket.
명사절 (= Anyone who)

Whoever comes first, I'll give this ticket to the person.
양보의 부사절 (= No matter who)

I believe whatever she says.
명사절(= anything that)

Whatever she says, I'm not going to believe her.
양보의 부사절 (= No matter what)

복합 관계대명사	명사절	양보의 부사절
whoever	anyone who ~하는 누구든지	no matter who 누가 ~하더라도
whomever	anyone whom ~하는 누구든지	no matter whom 누구를 ~하더라도
whichever	anything which ~하는 어느 것이든지	no matter which 어느 것이[을] ~하더라도
whatever	anything that ~하는 무엇이든지	no matter what 무엇이[을] ~하더라도

바로 개념

1 복합 관계대명사는 「관계대명사 + -ever」의 형태로 자체에 선행사를 포함하고 있다.
2 복합 관계대명사는 문장 내에서 주어 또는 목적어 역할을 하는 명사절이나 양보의 부사절을 이끈다.
3 복합 관계대명사가 주어일 때는 단수 동사를 쓴다.

고르며 개념 확인

Answers p. 21

01 I hate anyone ○ who ○ whoever lies to me.

02 You can eat ○ which ○ whichever you want.

03 Give it to ○ who ○ whoever needs it.

04 ○ No matter who ○ Anyone who calls me, tell them I'm not home.

05 The shirt comes in three sizes. Choose ○ which ○ whichever you prefer.

06 ○ Whomever ○ Whatever he wears, he looks perfect to his fans.

쓰며 개념 정리

07 무엇을 하든 최선을 다하려고 노력해라. ______ you do, try to do your best.

08 누가 문을 두드리더라도 문을 열지 마. ______ knocks on the door, don't open it.

09 네가 내게 원하는 것은 무엇이든 할 것이다. I'll do ______ you want me to do.

10 누굴 만나도 그는 그들과 사이좋게 잘 지낸다. ______ he meets, he gets along well with them.

★11 어느 길을 택하든, 시간이 오래 걸릴 것이다. It will take long, ______ route you take.
★ whichever/whatever는 명사 앞에서 명사를 꾸밀 수 있음.

12 춤에 관심 있는 사람은 누구든 우리와 함께할 수 있다. ______ is interested in dancing can join us.

개념 36 복합 관계부사

I feel gloomy whenever it rains.
시간의 부사절 (= at any time when)

Wherever he went, he was welcomed.
양보의 부사절 (= No matter where)

However rich people are, they want more.
양보의 부사절 (= No matter how)

복합 관계부사	시간, 장소의 부사절	양보의 부사절
whenever	at any time when ~할 때마다	no matter when 언제 ~하더라도
wherever	at any place where ~한 곳 어디에나	no matter where 어디에서 ~하더라도
however	–	no matter how 아무리 ~하더라도

바로 개념

1 복합 관계부사는 「관계부사+-ever」의 형태로 자체에 선행사를 포함하고 있다.
2 복합 관계부사는 시간, 장소의 부사절이나 양보의 부사절을 이끈다.
3 however는 양보의 부사절만 이끌며 어순은 대개 「however+형용사/부사+주어+동사 ~」이다.

고르며 개념 확인

Answers p. 21

01 ○ Whomever ○ Whenever he talks to Julia, his face turns red.

02 No matter ○ when ○ where I call, night or day, Aaron is never home.

03 ○ Wherever ○ However careful I try to be, I always end up making mistakes.

04 You can get off ○ wherever ○ however you need to.

05 ○ However you tired ○ However tired you may be, you must finish the report.

06 ○ Where ○ Wherever you choose to live, there'll always be disadvantages.

쓰며 개념 정리 배열하기

07 그 개는 그녀가 어디를 가든 따라다닌다.

The dog follows her __________. (goes, she, wherever)

08 당신이 원할 때면 언제든지 나를 찾아와도 좋다.

You can visit me __________. (like, whenever, you)

09 문제가 아무리 어렵더라도 그녀는 그것을 풀 것이다.

__________, she'll solve it. (the problem, be, however, may, hard)

Answers p. 21

개념 35 복합 관계대명사

1 복합 관계대명사는 「 ______ + ______ 」의 형태로 자체에 선행사를 포함하고 있다.

2 복합 관계대명사는 문장 내에서 주어 또는 목적어 역할을 하는 ______ 이나 양보의 부사절을 이끈다.

3 복합 관계대명사가 주어일 때는 단수 동사를 쓴다.

복합 관계대명사	명사절	양보의 부사절
whoever	anyone who ~하는 누구든지	______ 누가 ~하더라도
______	______ ~하는 누구든지	no matter whom 누구를 ~하더라도
______	anything which ~하는 어느 것이든지	no matter which 어느 것이[을] ~하더라도
______	______ ~하는 무엇이든지	______ 무엇이[을] ~하더라도

개념 36 복합 관계부사

1 복합 관계부사는 「 ______ + ______ 」의 형태로 자체에 선행사를 포함하고 있다.

2 복합 관계부사는 시간, 장소의 부사절이나 ______ 의 부사절을 이끈다.

3 however는 양보의 부사절만 이끌며 어순은 대개 「 ______ + ______ + 주어 + 동사 ~」이다.

복합 관계부사	시간, 장소의 부사절	양보의 부사절
whenever	at any time when ~할 때마다	no matter when 언제 ~하더라도
______	______ ~한 곳 어디에나	______ 어디에서 ~하더라도
______	–	______ 아무리 ~하더라도

Answers p. 22

A 주어진 표현과 복합 관계사를 이용하여 우리말과 같도록 문장을 완성하시오.

01 법을 어기는 사람은 누구든 벌을 받을 것이다. (breaks the law)

→ [   ] will be punished.

02 네가 뭐라고 하든, 난 그녀와 친구가 되고 싶지 않다. (say)

→ [   ], I don't want to be friends with her.

03 나는 피곤함을 느낄 때면 초콜릿을 약간 먹는다. (feel tired)

→ I eat some chocolate [   ].

04 날씨가 아무리 춥더라도 그는 항상 수영하러 간다. (cold, it)

→ [   ], he always goes swimming.

B 주어진 문장과 같은 뜻이 되도록 빈칸에 알맞은 말을 쓰시오.

01 You can take anything that you like.

= You can take _______ _______ _______.

02 Anyone who gets home first should open all the windows.

= _______ _______ _______ _______ should open all the windows.

03 No matter how hard I tried, I couldn't catch up with him.

= _______ _______ _______ _______, I couldn't catch up with him.

04 Whatever happens, don't give up the game.

= _______ _______ _______ _______, don't give up the game.

05 The gifts will go to whoever passes the finish line.

= The gifts will go to _______ _______ _______ the finish line.

06 My brother always blames me at any time when anything goes wrong.

= My brother always blames me _______ _______ _______ _______.

07 No matter where she is, she thinks of her daughter.

= _______ _______ _______, she thinks of her daughter.

08 No matter how loudly he might shout, no one could hear him.

= _______ _______ _______ _______ _______, no one could hear him.

복합 관계사를 이용하여 문장 바꿔 쓰기

256 At any time when I lose my temper, she tries to support me.

Whenever I lose my temper, she tries to support me.

257 No matter what you do, you leave behind a digital footprint.

258 At any time when I do my best, they tell me I don't try hard enough.

259 We all know that people are the same no matter where we go.

260 Anyone who has a healthy mind is capable of reading other people's minds.

261 Please take anything that you want from the fridge.

262 At any time when he invented something, he experimented many times.

263 No matter how difficult it is, I don't care.

Answers p. 22

배열하여 문장 쓰기

264 야구 방망이는 칠 때마다 반응하여 진동한다.
(struck, a bat, is, whenever)

_______________, it vibrates in response.

265 당신이 누구이든, 그리고 무엇을 하든 당신을 소중히 여겨라.
(and, whatever, are, you, you, whoever, do)

Value yourself, _______________

266 우리는 당신을 돕기 위해 필요한 일은 무엇이든 할 것이다.
(we, to help, necessary, whatever, do, is, will, you)

____

267 파티에 오는 누구나 환영받을 것이다.
(comes, will, welcome, whoever, to the party, be)

____

268 그 개는 혼자 남겨질 때마다 매우 혼란스러워하고 우울해졌다.
(she, alone, left, whenever, was)

The dog became very upset and depressed _______________

269 미래에 내가 어떤 직업을 갖더라도, 나는 주변의 장애물을 극복하기 위해 노력할 것이다.
(I, in the future, job, have, whatever)

_______________, I'll try to overcome the obstacles around me.

270 상황이 아무리 심각해도, 희망이 없는 것은 아니다.
(serious, is, the situation, however)

_______________, it is not hopeless.

[Self-Editing Checklist] 대 • 소문자를 바르게 썼나요? Y N 철자와 문장 부호를 바르게 썼나요? Y N

대표유형 01 관계대명사

01 다음 빈칸에 들어갈 말이 바르게 짝지어진 것은?

• Ms. Parker is a poet ________ I have known since last year.
• The word "bully" is a word ________ meaning has changed over time.

① whose – which ② whom – that ③ whom – whose ④ that – who ⑤ that – whom

02 다음 중 밑줄 친 부분을 that과 바꿔 쓸 수 있는 것은?

① Look at the man whose hair is blond.
② I can't understand what you've just said.
③ This is the house in which Beth was born.
④ David failed the test again, which surprised us.
⑤ Sue is wearing a sweater which her mom made.

03 다음 빈칸에 들어갈 말로 가장 알맞은 것은?

He gave me the thing. I wanted to have it.
→ He gave me ________ I wanted to have.

① who ② whose ③ what ④ which ⑤ that

04 다음 우리말에 맞게 괄호 안의 단어를 배열할 때 ★에 들어갈 말로 알맞은 것은?

안내견은 앞을 볼 수 없는 사람을 돕는 개다.
→ A guide dog is a dog ________ ________ ________ ★ ________ ________.
(who, people, helps, cannot, which, see)

① who ② people ③ helps ④ cannot ⑤ which

05 다음 중 빈칸에 들어갈 말이 나머지 넷과 다른 것은?

① This is not ________ I ordered.
② He said something ________ hurt my feelings.
③ ________ we saw there amazed us.
④ Josh didn't believe ________ I told him.
⑤ ________ scared me most was the silence.

06 다음 빈칸에 들어갈 말이 바르게 짝지어진 것은?

• She tried to swim across the river, ________ was impossible.
• The victims, ________ were injured in the accident, were taken to the hospital.

① that – who ② what – which ③ which – that ④ who – what ⑤ which – who

07 다음 빈칸에 들어갈 말로 알맞은 것은?

Sally is the girl ________ Jack is waiting.

① for that ② for whom ③ whom to ④ whom ⑤ to whose

대표유형 02 관계대명사의 쓰임 구별

08 다음 중 밑줄 친 부분의 쓰임이 나머지 넷과 다른 것은?

① Tom liked the girl that he met at the party.
② Have you found the cell phone that you lost?
③ She's the actress that the director wanted to cast.
④ We watched the musical that our teacher recommended.
⑤ He blamed me for the accident that happened yesterday.

09 다음 중 밑줄 친 부분의 쓰임이 나머지 넷과 다른 것은?

① This is the tallest tree that I've ever seen.
② A friend is someone that you believe in.
③ The song that he wrote for me was amazing.
④ I told the police that I had seen him before.
⑤ I want to visit the island that has beautiful beaches.

10 다음 중 밑줄 친 부분의 쓰임이 나머지 넷과 다른 것은?

① Is that what your daughter painted?
② You can't always get what you want.
③ I don't know what her address is.
④ What he likes best is reading.
⑤ You must do what I told you to do.

Answers p. 22

대표유형 03 관계대명사의 생략

11 다음 빈칸에 생략된 말로 알맞은 것은?

This is a picture ________ painted by Lisa.

① which ② which was ③ whose was
④ that are ⑤ who is

12 다음 밑줄 친 부분 중 생략할 수 없는 것을 모두 고르면?

① I just said anything that came into my head.
② He is the president whom everyone respects.
③ The fish which we had for dinner was delicious.
④ This house has a bedroom, which faces south.
⑤ She is reading a novel which was written by Hemingway.

13 다음 중 생략된 말이 잘못된 것은?

① That is the woman (whom) I told you about.
② The car (which) she rented broke down.
③ There lived a powerful god (that) named Zeus.
④ Look at the stars (which are) shining brightly.
⑤ I like the songs (that were) composed by the Beatles.

14 다음 문장에서 관계대명사 that이 생략된 곳은?

I'm asking (①) everyone (②) I know to donate to (③) my campaign (④) instead of giving me presents (⑤) for my birthday.

대표유형 04 관계부사

15 다음 빈칸에 들어갈 말로 알맞은 것은?

The Sahara Desert is a place ________ only 250 mm of rain falls in a year.

① which ② where ③ whose ④ when ⑤ how

16 다음 중 빈칸에 들어갈 말이 나머지 넷과 다른 것은?

① Now is the time ________ we must work hard.
② That was the moment ________ I felt thrilled.
③ Sunday is the day ________ comes after Saturday.
④ That was the year ________ they got married.
⑤ July is the month ________ the vacation starts.

17 다음 문장 중 어법상 어색한 것은?

① I don't know why he gave up becoming a vet.
② This is the cafe where the party will be held.
③ Jun misses the country where he used to live.
④ That is the way how he overcame the challenge.
⑤ April Fool's Day is the day when we play jokes on people.

18 다음 빈칸에 들어갈 말로 알맞은 것은?

I don't know the reason why he disappeared.
= I don't know the reason ________ he disappeared.

① for which ② in where ③ of whom
④ for what ⑤ on which

대표유형 05 복합 관계사

19 다음 괄호 안의 단어를 바르게 배열한 것은?

(may, life, difficult, seem, however), there is always something you can do.

① Difficult however life may seem
② Life may seem however difficult
③ However life may seem difficult
④ However difficult life may seem
⑤ Difficult may seem however life

20 다음 밑줄 친 부분 중 쓰임이 어색한 것은?

① Sit wherever you like.
② I eat some hot soup whenever I get a cold.
③ However late you are, be sure to call me.
④ Whatever I suggest, he always disagrees.
⑤ Anyone whoever makes a mess must clean it up.

01 (A)와 (B)에서 각각 알맞은 것을 골라 문장을 완성하시오. (단, 한 번씩만 사용할 것)

(A) who
which
that
what

(B) was a shame
I did yesterday
has many fans worldwide
she could do to win first prize

(1) I apologize for ________________.

(2) Selena did all ________________.

(3) Their friendship didn't last long, ________________.

(4) Yuna Kim is a famous figure skater ________________.

02 다음 중 어법상 어색한 문장을 두 개 찾아 기호를 쓴 뒤 옳은 문장으로 다시 쓰시오.

ⓐ Cecile told me how she prepared for the audition.
ⓑ He explained everything what he had experienced.
ⓒ However busy she is, she goes jogging every morning.
ⓓ Venice is a city where is located on the seacoast in the north of Italy.

________ → ________________

________ → ________________

03 친구를 소개하는 메모를 보고, 관계대명사 또는 관계부사를 이용하여 문장을 알맞게 완성하시오.

My friend ...
• Name: Monica
• Nickname: Supergirl
• Born: August 5
• good at singing K-pop songs

(1) Monica is my best friend ________________ Supergirl.

(2) August is the month ________________.

(3) I like Monica, ________________.

[Self-Editing Checklist] ✔ 대 · 소문자를 바르게 썼나요? Y N ✔ 철자와 문장 부호를 바르게 썼나요? Y N

UNIT 09

접속사

핵심 개념 바로 확인

I know! ☺ No idea! 😐

- 의문문이 종속절처럼 다른 문장의 일부로 쓰인 것을 간접 의문문이라고 한다. ☺ 😐
- 접속부사는 연결의 의미를 갖는 부사로, 문장 전체를 꾸민다. ☺ 😐

개념 37 상관접속사

월 일

Both Tom and Judy are absent from school.

I want not only some bread but also some butter.

I think you as well as Billy are responsible fot it.

Not Danny but the others have to quit the job.

You should neither raise your voice too loud nor remain silent.

both *A* and *B*	A와 B 둘 다
not only *A* but also *B*	A뿐만 아니라 B도
A as well as *B*	B뿐만 아니라 A도
not *A* but *B*	A가 아니라 B
either *A* or *B*	A 또는 B 둘 중 하나
neither *A* nor *B*	A도 B도 아닌

바로 개념

1 상관접속사는 두 개 이상의 단어가 짝을 이루는 접속사로, 문법적으로 동등한 요소를 연결한다.

2 상관접속사가 연결하는 말이 주어일 때 동사의 수는 B에 맞춘다. 단, 「both *A* and *B*」가 주어로 올 때에는 복수로 쓰고, 「*A* as well as *B*」일 때는 A에 맞춘다.

고르며 개념 확인

Answers p. 23

01 It will not only rain but also ○ snow ○ snowing today.

02 The exam results were neither good ○ or ○ nor bad.

03 I am going to vote for either Megan or ○ Max ○ for Max .

04 The blue coat as well as the red shoes ○ is ○ are quite new.

쓰며 개념 정리

05 William뿐만 아니라 Dana도 나를 보고 놀랐다.

→ Dana ______ ______ ______ William was surprised to see me.

06 남동생이나 내가 공항에 너를 마중 나갈 것이다.

→ ______ my brother ______ I am going to pick you up at the airport.

07 바람뿐만 아니라 비 때문에 나는 외출하지 못했다.

→ Not ______ the wind but ______ the rain kept me from going out.

08 그 소년이 아니라 그의 부모가 이 상황에 책임이 있다.

→ ______ the boy ______ his parents are responsible for this situation.

간접의문문

월 일

She might know where Beth went yesterday.
← Where did Beth go yesterday?

What do you think I brought to them?
← What did I bring to them?

I wonder if he can return by six.
← Can he return by six?

I don't know whether she heard that news.
← Did she hear that news?

cf. Do you know that Jose planned to go abroad?
~라는 것

의문사가 있는 의문문	기본: 의문사 + 주어 + 동사 (└ 접속사 역할) 주절의 동사가 think, believe, guess 등일 때: 의문사 + do you think [believe, guess, ...] + 주어 + 동사 ...?
의문사가 없는 의문문	if + 주어 + 동사 / whether + 주어 + 동사

바로 개념

1 의문문이 다른 문장의 일부(주어, 보어, 목적어)가 되는 것을 간접의문문이라고 한다.
2 의문사가 있는 의문문은 간접의문문이 될 때 「의문사 + 주어 + 동사 ...」로 쓴다. 주절의 동사가 think, believe, guess, suppose, imagine 등일 때에는 의문사를 문장 맨 앞에 쓴다.
3 의문사가 없는 의문문은 접속사 if 또는 whether가 이끄는 절로 쓴다.

고르며 개념 확인

Answers p. 23

01 Can you tell me ○ that ○ what causes earthquakes?

02 Do you know ○ how long ○ how many the movie is?

03 It is certain ○ if ○ that the world is getting smaller.

04 I wonder ○ that ○ whether she is a great singer.

05 My little brother wonders ○ that ○ why we can't see air.

쓰며 개념 정리

06 나는 은행이 이 근처에 있는지 알고 싶다. (a bank, near, there, here, is, if)

→ I'd like to know ________________.

07 나는 내가 강아지들을 어떻게 돌봐야 하는지 모르겠다. (I, the puppies, how, take, of, should, care)

→ I don't know ________________.

08 너는 비행기가 언제 이륙할 거라고 추측하니? (you, do, the flight, guess, will, take off)

→ When ________________?

개념 37 상관접속사

1 상관접속사는 두 개 이상의 단어가 짝을 이루는 접속사이다.

2 상관접속사는 문법적으로 [ ] 요소를 연결한다.

3 상관접속사가 연결하는 말이 주어로 쓰일 때 동사의 수에 유의한다.

상관접속사	의미	주어로 쓰일 때 동사의 수
both *A* and *B*		복수 취급
not only *A* but also *B*	A뿐만 아니라 B도	
A as well as *B*		A에 맞춤
not *A* but *B*	A가 아니라 B	
either *A* or *B*		B에 맞춤
neither *A* nor *B*		

개념 38 간접의문문

1 간접의문문은 의문문이 다른 문장의 일부로 쓰인 것을 말하고, 주어, 목적어, 보어 역할을 한다.

2 의문사가 있는 의문문은 간접의문문이 될 때 「의문사+주어+동사 ...」 형태로 쓴다. 주절의 동사가 think, believe, guess, suppose, imagine 등일 때에는 [ ] 를 문장 맨 앞에 쓴다.

3 의문사가 없는 의문문은 접속사 [ ] 또는 [ ] 가 이끄는 절로 쓴다.

종류	형태
의문사가 있는 의문문	[ ] + [ ] + [ ] 주절의 동사가 think, believe, guess, suppose, imagine 등일 때: 의문사 + do you think [believe, guess, ...] + 주어 + 동사 ...?
의문사가 없는 의문문	[ ] + 주어 + 동사 / [ ] + 주어 + 동사

Answers p. 23

A 자연스러운 문장이 되도록 빈칸에 알맞은 말을 쓰시오.

01 The house was ______ cozy nor tidy.

02 I know you like ______ William but Taylor.

03 His birthday is not in January ______ in December.

04 Both singing ______ dancing are my favorite hobbies.

05 Neither Emma ______ her brother helped their parents.

06 You should either keep quiet ______ get out of here.

07 I am interested in playing basketball ______ well ______ writing stories.

08 Not only the curtains ______ ______ the windows need to be cleaned.

09 We can ______ fly there or take a train. Choose one.

10 Noah ______ ______ prepared lunch but also washed the dishes.

B 간접의문문 형식을 활용하여 두 문장을 한 문장으로 쓰시오.

01 I want to know. Can you bake a cake in an hour?

→ I want to know ______.

02 Do you guess? Where are they going?

→ Where ______?

03 They don't know. Will Julia like the new school?

→ They don't know ______.

04 Tell me. How many people are in the hall?

→ Tell me ______.

05 Do you think? When will Mr. Baron get back to his hometown?

→ When ______?

06 Do you recognize? Who is this woman in the photo?

→ Do you recognize ______?

비교하며 문장 쓰기

			표현 노트
271	그는 긴장됨과 흥분을 동시에 느꼈다.	He felt both nervous and excited.	both, happy, sad
	그는 기쁨과 슬픔을 동시에 느꼈다.	He felt both happy and sad.	
272	나는 랩탑이 아니라 전화기가 필요해.	I need not a laptop but a phone.	what, need, tools, cats
	그들이 필요한 것은 공구가 아니라 고양이다.		
273	그들은 과일도 채소도 팔지 않는다.	They sell neither fruit nor vegetables.	fish, meat
	그녀는 생선이나 고기를 살 것이다.		
274	너는 그것이 정확히 무슨 의미인지 모른다.	You don't know what that means exactly.	have no idea, do, it
	그는 자신이 왜 그렇게 했는지 알 수 없었다.		
275	나는 내가 이 문제를 어떻게 풀 수 있을지 궁금했다.	I wondered how I could solve this problem.	wonder, if, for those girls
	나는 내가 그 소녀들을 위해 무언가 할 수 있을지 궁금했다.		
276	그는 강하지도 체격이 좋지도 않았다.	He was neither strong nor athletic.	a politician, a soldier
	그는 정치인도 군인도 아니었다.		
277	너뿐만 아니라 그도 거기에 가고 싶어 한다.	Not only you but also he wants to go there.	be awarded, the Nobel Prize
	Marie Curie 뿐만 아니라 그녀의 딸도 노벨상을 탔다.		
278	너는 다빈치의 위대함이 어디서 왔는지 아니?	Do you know where da Vinci's greatness came from?	where, think
	너는 다빈치의 위대함이 어디서 왔다고 생각하니?		

Answers p. 24

배열하여 문장 쓰기

279
너는 우리에게 희망뿐만 아니라 용기도 주었다.
(as, you, us, well, hope, as, gave, courage)

You gave us courage as well as hope.

280
그녀는 일어서서 자리를 양보하거나 또는 불의에 맞설 수 있었다.
(stand up to, either, she, stand up, injustice, to give up her seat, could, or)

★ stand up to: ~에 맞서다

281
세상에 얼마나 많은 화산이 있는지 아무도 확실하게 알지 못한다.
(how many volcanoes, nobody, for sure, are, in the world, there, knows)

282
당신은 시장에서 꽃을 조금 살 수 있는지 궁금할 것이다.
(wonder, may, whether, you, just a few flowers, you, buy, can, at the market)

283
넌 내가 무엇을 해야 한다고 생각하니?
(I, you, what, do, do, should, think)

284
처음에, 나는 그가 사실을 말하고 있는지 확실히 알 수 없었다.
(sure, he, if, I, not, telling, was, was, the truth)

At first,

285
당신은 자신에 대해 확신을 느낄 뿐만 아니라 다른 사람들이 보기에도 자신감이 있어 보일 것이다.
(not only, will, to other people, feel sure, but also, you, about yourself, look confident)

[Self-Editing Checklist] ✔ 대 • 소문자를 바르게 썼나요? Y N ✔ 철자와 문장 부호를 바르게 썼나요? Y N

월 일

개념 39 부사절을 이끄는 접속사

시간	when	~할 때
	while	~하는 동안
	as	~하면서
	until	~할 때까지
	as soon as	~하자마자
	since	~ 이후로
이유	because	~ 때문에
	as	
	since	

조건	if	만일 ~라면
	unless	만일 ~ 아니라면 (= if ~ not)
	in case (that)	~할 경우에는 (= in case of + 명사)
양보	though, although, even though	비록 ~이지만, ~에도 불구하고 (= in spite of / despite + 명사)

결과	so	그래서
	so ~ that	매우 ~해서 …하다
	so ~ that ... can	매우 ~해서 …할 수 있다 (= ~ enough + to부정사)
	so ~ that ... can't	너무 ~해서 …할 수 없다 (= too ~ to부정사)
목적	so that ... *can, in order that ... *can	~하기 위해 (= in order + to부정사 / to부정사) *조동사 may, will 등도 쓰임

바로 개념

1 부사절은 시간, 이유, 조건, 양보, 결과, 목적 등의 의미를 나타내며 주절의 앞이나 뒤에 쓰일 수 있다. 주절의 앞에 올 때에는 콤마(,)로 연결한다.

2 시간이나 조건을 나타내는 부사절에서는 미래를 나타낼 때 현재 시제를 쓴다.

고르며 개념 확인

Answers p. 24

01 Keep quiet ○ though ○ until the movie ends. (영화가 끝날 때까지)

02 ○ As ○ If you have a headache, take this medicine. (두통이 있다면)

03 ○ Although ○ In case you find the man, report it to the police. (그 남자를 찾는 경우에)

04 ○ Since ○ When I was in Paris, I went to see the Eiffel Tower. (내가 파리에 있을 때)

05 ○ As soon as ○ While you arrive, give me a call. (네가 도착하자마자)

쓰며 개념 정리

06 I had to prepare dinner, but I went out.

= I went out [ ] I had to prepare dinner.

07 The cell phone was too expensive for me to buy it.

= The cell phone was [ ] expensive [ ] I couldn't buy it.

08 Unless he comes early, I won't meet him.

= [ ] he does [ ] come early, I won't meet him.

09 I came alone so that I could talk to you privately.

= I came alone [ ] [ ] [ ] talk to you privately.

개념 40

접속부사

I have an important test tomorrow. Therefore, I have to study tonight.

This hotel is beautiful. Furthermore, it has a great view.

I love horror movies. On the other hand, my sister loves action movies.

We must hurry. Otherwise, we'll miss the bus.

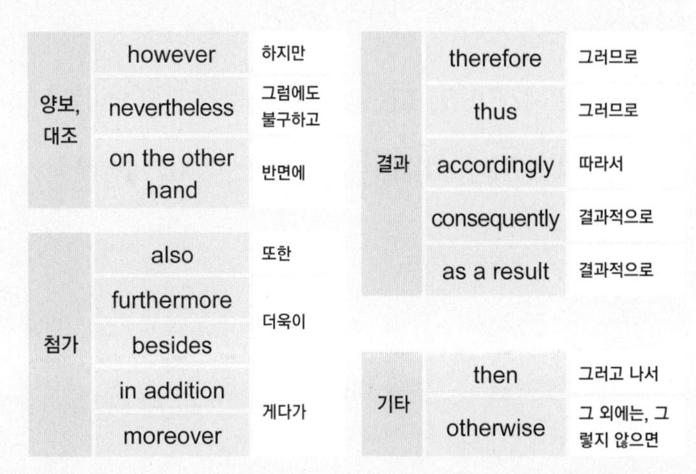

구분	접속부사	뜻
양보, 대조	however	하지만
	nevertheless	그럼에도 불구하고
	on the other hand	반면에
첨가	also	또한
	furthermore, besides	더욱이
	in addition, moreover	게다가

구분	접속부사	뜻
결과	therefore	그러므로
	thus	그러므로
	accordingly	따라서
	consequently	결과적으로
	as a result	결과적으로
기타	then	그러고 나서
	otherwise	그 외에는, 그렇지 않으면

바로 개념

1 접속부사는 문장을 꾸며 문장 사이를 자연스럽게 연결하는 부사로, 단어와 단어, 구와 구, 절과 절 등 문법적으로 대등한 요소를 연결하는 접속사와 역할을 구분해야 한다.

고르며 개념 확인

Answers p. 24

01 He was hungry. ○ Also ○ Thus , he looked for something to eat.

02 You should leave home now. ○ Otherwise ○ Then , you'll be late.

03 I tried to be polite. ○ Also ○ Nevertheless , I couldn't stand his rudeness.

04 I got enough allowance. ○ Accordingly ○ However , I didn't save any.

05 Our failure wasn't expected. ○ Accordingly ○ Besides , it was very disappointing.

06 I don't know her name. ○ Besides ○ On the other hand , I didn't ask her phone number.

07 Tom put on his jacket. ○ However ○ Then , he looked in the mirror.

08 He liked the novel. ○ Moreover ○ Otherwise , he memorized some parts of it.

09 Lisa insisted that she was correct. ○ However ○ Therefore , she was wrong.

10 Allan was short and thin. His brother, ○ on the other hand ○ in addition , was tall and big.

11 We have to reduce plastic waste. ○ Consequently ○ Otherwise , we will lose lots of wildlife.

12 Lily wrote the answer with incorrect grammar. ○ As a result ○ However , she got a bad grade.

개념 39 부사절을 이끄는 접속사

1 부사절은 시간, 이유, 조건, 양보, 결과, 목적 등의 의미를 나타내며 주절의 앞이나 뒤에 쓰일 수 있다.

2 시간이나 조건을 나타내는 부사절에서는 미래를 나타낼 때 [ ] 를 쓴다.

구분	접속사	의미
시간	when	
	while	
	as	~하면서
	until	
	as soon as	
	since	~ 이후로

구분	접속사	의미
결과	so	
	so ~ that	
	so ~ that ... can	매우 ~해서 …할 수 있다 (= ~ enough + to부정사)
	so ~ that ... can't	너무 ~해서 …할 수 없다 (= too ~ to부정사)

구분	접속사	의미
이유	because	
	as	
	since	

구분	접속사	의미
조건	if	
	unless	만일 ~ 아니라면 (= if ~ not)
	in case (that)	~할 경우에는 (= in case of + 명사)

구분	접속사	의미
목적	so that ... *can, in order that ... *can	~하기 위해 (= in order + to부정사 / to부정사) *조동사 may, will 등도 쓰임

구분	접속사	의미
양보	though, although, even though	비록 ~이지만, ~에도 불구하고 (= in spite of / despite + 명사)

개념 40 접속부사

구분	접속부사	의미
양보, 대조	however	하지만
	nevertheless	
	on the other hand	

구분	접속부사	의미
첨가	also	또한
	furthermore	
	besides	
	in addition	
	moreover	

구분	접속부사	의미
결과	therefore	그러므로
	thus	
	accordingly	
	consequently	결과적으로
	as a result	

구분	접속부사	의미
기타	then	
	otherwise	그 외에는, 그렇지 않으면

Answers p. 24

A 주어진 접속사를 이용하여 두 문장을 한 문장으로 바꿔 쓰시오.

01 I have learned English. I was 10. (since)

→ ____________________

02 The movie ended. They ran out of the theater. (as soon as)

→ ____________________

03 I was late for school. The bus had a flat tire. (because)

→ ____________________

04 It was very cold. I couldn't stay outside anymore. (so ~ that ... can't)

→ ____________________

05 You are lost. Install the map application on your phone. (in case)

→ ____________________

B 의미가 자연스럽도록 빈칸에 알맞은 접속사 또는 접속부사를 쓰시오.

01 I'd better write the words down. ______, I'll forget them.

02 ______ ______ he is my enemy, I will save him.

03 He was so sick ______ he ______ eat anything.

04 ______ it snows tomorrow, we'll have a snowball fight.

05 We should get up early ______ ______ we can catch the train.

06 I didn't prepare for the test. ______ ______ ______, I failed it.

07 Ann was too busy. ______, she decided to go to the gathering.

08 He moved to my town. ______ ______, his house is next to my place.

09 You must read the book ______ ______ to understand the movie.

10 I don't eat carrots. ______ ______ ______ ______, my sister likes them very much.

문장 쓰기

표현 노트

286 그 결과, 그의 대부분의 건축물들은 곡선의 돌을 사용한다.

As a result, most of his constructions use curved stones.

as a result, most of, constructions, curved

287 나는 파란 눈을 갖고 있다. 반면에 나의 형은 갈색 눈을 갖고 있다.

have, on the other hand

288 Boggis 씨는 너무 충격을 받아서 아무 말도 할 수 없었다.

so ~ that ..., shocked, anything

289 나는 베이징에 도착하자마자, 나의 민박 가족을 만났다.

as soon as, arrive, Beijing, host family

290 식사 중간에 목이 마르게 될 경우를 대비해서, 여러분은 물병을 가지고 다닐 수 있다.

, you can carry a water bottle with you.

in case, get thirsty, between meals

291 그녀는 스트레스를 너무 많이 받아서 그녀의 인생이 우울해 보일 때, 방을 청소한다.

, she cleans her room.

when, so ~ that ..., stressed, look, gloomy

292 비가 너무 심하게 오고 있다. 그러므로 우리는 집에 머물러야 한다.

too hard, therefore, stay at home

293 비록 우리는 작게 시작했지만, 큰 차이를 만들고 있다.

although, start small, make a big difference

Answers p. 25

의미 확장하여 문장 쓰기

294

꿈꾸는 것을 멈추지 마라. — Don't stop dreaming.

여러분의 꿈이 실현될 때까지 꿈꾸는 것을 멈추지 마라. — Don't stop dreaming until your dreams come true.

295

표제가 그의 눈길을 끌었다. — A headline caught his eye.

그가 그의 커피를 마시고 있는 동안, 한 표제가 그의 눈길을 끌었다.

296

부정적인 생각은 매우 해롭다. — Negative thoughts are very harmful.

부정적인 생각은 매우 해로워서 당신의 뇌를 손상시킬 수 있다.

damage: 손상시키다

297

우리는 정원을 손질해야 한다. — We have to tidy up the garden.

우리는 정원을 손질해야 한다. 게다가 파티도 준비해야 한다.

prepare for: ~을 준비하다

298

그들은 이 거짓 기사를 지어냈다. — They made up this fake article.

그들은 독자들의 주의를 끌기 위해 이 거짓 기사를 지어냈다.

draw one's attention: 주의를 끌다

299

독감 확산은 예방될 수 있다. — The spread of the flu can be predicted.

만약 이런 종류의 데이터가 현명하게 분석된다면, 독감 확산은 예방될 수 있다.

analyze: 분석하다, wisely: 현명하게

300

아이들은 극장에 들어갈 수 없다. — Children cannot enter the theater.

부모와 함께 하지 않는다면, 아이들은 극장에 들어갈 수 없다.

[Self-Editing Checklist] 대 • 소문자를 바르게 썼나요? Y N 철자와 문장 부호를 바르게 썼나요? Y N

대표유형 01 상관접속사의 형태와 쓰임

01 주어진 우리말과 같도록 할 때 빈칸에 알맞은 것은?

> 사과뿐만 아니라 바나나도 신선했다.
> ➔ Bananas ________ apples were fresh.

① either ② neither
③ both ④ as well as
⑤ not only

[02-03] 다음 문장 중 어법상 어색한 것을 고르시오.

02 ① Not only you but also I am tired.
② She has neither a pen nor a pencil.
③ Both Marvin and she likes the place.
④ Either Charles or Alvin will pick you up.
⑤ I will take not the book but the magazine.

03 ① I like both swimming and skating.
② He was not only kind but also helpful.
③ Roses as well as lilies are my favorite.
④ I wanted not desserts but take a walk.
⑤ You can have either cola or juice.

대표유형 02 간접의문문

04 다음 우리말을 바르게 영작한 것은?

> 은행에 어떻게 가는지 알려주실 수 있나요?

① How can I get to the bank do you know?
② How can you tell that I can get to the bank?
③ Can you tell me how I can get to the bank?
④ How can you tell me I can get to the bank?
⑤ Can you tell me how can I get to the bank?

05 다음 문장 중 어법상 자연스러운 것을 모두 고르면?
① I don't know if she goes to my school.
② Do you think that he is a great actor?
③ Do you guess what my nickname is?
④ He might know when was the boy found.
⑤ How do you think did John deceive us?

06 다음 문장 중 빈칸에 if가 들어가기에 어색한 것은?
① I'm not sure ________ he is at home.
② Do you think ________ I will win the game?
③ ________ it is not cold, we're going out.
④ I don't know ________ the cat is hungry.
⑤ Do you know ________ the store is open?

대표유형 03 시간, 이유, 조건, 양보의 부사절

07 다음 두 문장을 한 문장으로 쓸 때 빈칸에 알맞은 것은?

> The new girl was shy. She didn't know anyone in the class.
> ➔ The new girl was shy ________ she didn't know anyone in the class.

① as ② if ③ though
④ until ⑤ unless

[08-09] 다음 문장의 빈칸에 가장 알맞은 것을 고르시오.

08

> You should not say the answer ________ the teacher calls you.

① and ② that ③ because
④ unless ⑤ however

09

> I hope that he will take care of my dogs instead of me ________ I get back from holiday.

① so ② so that ③ while
④ until ⑤ as soon as

10 다음 문장의 밑줄 친 부분의 형태로 알맞은 것은?

> If it be sunny, they will look for shade.

① is ② are ③ to be
④ will be ⑤ has been

Answers p. 25

11 다음 문장 중 밑줄 친 부분의 쓰임이 어색한 것은?

① I got a cold, so I took two days off.
② Unless you want the recipe, I will tell you.
③ Since they were 12, they have been friends.
④ As soon as I saw Mr. Brown's car, I ran away.
⑤ Can you stir the sauce while I chop the carrots?

대표유형 04 so와 that을 사용한 구문

12 다음 문장과 의미가 가장 가까운 것은?

I was very happy, so I jumped for joy.

① I was too happy to jump for joy.
② I jumped for joy until I was happy.
③ I jumped for joy though I was happy.
④ I was happy so that I might jump for joy.
⑤ I was so happy that I jumped for joy.

13 다음 두 문장의 뜻이 통하도록 할 때, 빈칸에 들어갈 말로 알맞은 것을 모두 고르면?

They need to have a conversation so that they can understand each other.
= They need to have a conversation ________ each other.

① understanding ② to understand
③ so understand ④ in case understand
⑤ in order to understand

14 다음 문장의 빈칸에 들어갈 말로 어색한 것은?

The food was so ________ that they left most of it.

① salt ② terrible ③ cold
④ fatty ⑤ spicy

[15-16] 다음 빈칸에 알맞은 말을 쓰시오.

15

He is so weak that he can't run a marathon.
= He is ________ to run a marathon.

16

She was so smart that she could solve the problem.
= She was ________ to solve the problem.

대표유형 05 접속부사의 의미와 쓰임

17 다음 문장 중 밑줄 친 부분의 쓰임이 어색한 것은?

① First comes Monday, and then Tuesday.
② Anna felt sick. Besides, she felt dizzy.
③ I don't know him well. However, I like him.
④ Daniel was very tired. Nevertheless, he went on working.
⑤ I failed the test. Thus, I was not disappointed at all.

[18-19] 다음 문장의 뜻이 통하도록 할 때, 빈칸에 가장 알맞은 것을 고르시오.

18

I tried hard to finish the task though it seemed impossible.
= The task seemed impossible. ________, I tried hard to finish it.

① Then ② However ③ Thus
④ Accordingly ⑤ Furthermore

19

If you don't buy this book, you'll regret it later.
= Buy this book. ________, you'll regret it later.

① Also ② Therefore ③ Otherwise
④ Moreover ⑤ Nevertheless

20 다음 빈칸에 공통으로 알맞은 말은?

• Don't worry so much. It's not a big problem. ________, it's not your fault.
• I think you will be able to play the guitar well. ________, you will love it.

① Otherwise ② Therefore ③ That
④ Despite ⑤ Furthermore

01 다음 두 문장을 하나의 문장으로 바꿔 쓰시오. (단, 간접의문문 형식을 활용할 것)

(1) I'm not sure. Can we get there on time?

➔ ______________________________

(2) Where did he go during the vacation? Do you guess it?

➔ ______________________________

(3) Tell me. How many books can I check out at the library?

➔ ______________________________

02 주어진 문장을 조건에 맞게 비슷한 의미의 문장으로 다시 쓰시오.

[조건] **1.** so와 that을 사용할 것
2. 제시된 단어 수를 지킬 것

(1) I arrived at the restaurant too late to order dinner.

➔ ______________________________ (13단어)

(2) The man was strong enough to lift the heavy box.

➔ ______________________________ (12단어)

수행평가 유형 글 완성하기

03 다음 글을 읽고, 빈칸에 알맞은 접속사 또는 접속부사를 보기에서 찾아 글을 완성하시오.

Most people have different likes and dislikes. I also have things that I like to do and things that I don't like to do. For instance, I always enjoy watching TV and reading books. (1) ________, I like playing the drums and going to the movies. (2) ________, I don't like going swimming (3) ________ I'm afraid of water. (4) ________ I go to the pool, I sit on the poolside most of the time.

보기
- in fact
- as a result
- nevertheless
- on the other hand
- in addition
- because
- in case
- unless

[Self-Editing Checklist] ✔ 대 · 소문자를 바르게 썼나요? Y N ✔ 철자와 문장 부호를 바르게 썼나요? Y N

UNIT 10

비교 구문

핵심 개념 바로 확인

I know! ☺ No idea! ☹

- 비교급은 한 쪽이 다른 쪽보다 특정 상태나 성질의 정도가 더할 때 사용한다. ☺ ☹
- 최상급은 어떤 것의 특정 상태나 성질이 여럿 중 정도가 가장 높을 때 사용한다. ☺ ☹

개념 41 원급 비교

월 일

Your dog looks as energetic as you.

I think he is not as [so] talented as George.

You should run as fast as you can.

= You should run as fast as possible.

He tried to fix the machine as quickly as he could.

The book is three times as thick as the other.

원급 비교	*A* ~ as + 원급 + as + *B* A가 B만큼 ~하다
can을 활용한 원급 비교	as + 원급 + as + 주어 + can (= as + 원급 + as possible) …가 할 수 있는 한 ~한/하게
배수 표현을 사용한 비교	*A* ~ 배수 표현 + as + 원급 + as + *B* A는 B보다 …배만큼 ~하다 배수 표현: half, twice, three times, etc.

바로 개념

1 비교되는 두 대상의 성질 또는 수량이 같을 때 형용사와 부사의 원급을 이용하여 '…만큼 ~하다'라는 원급 비교의 의미를 나타낼 수 있다.

2 '몇 배'를 나타내는 배수 표현을 원급 비교 구문과 함께 써서 '…배만큼 ~하다'라는 의미를 나타낼 수 있다.

고르며 개념 확인

Answers p. 26

01 Matilda drove three times ○ as ○ than far as Bill.

02 Clean up your room as fast as you ○ are ○ can .

03 Today is not ○ so ○ than hot as yesterday.

04 The living room is ○ two ○ twice as large as the kitchen.

05 The actor is not as famous ○ as ○ than you think.

06 This bridge is as ○ long ○ longer as the Golden Gate Bridge.

쓰며 개념 정리

07 The wall is as solid as it looks. (it, as, as, looks, solid)

08 This car is ______. (car, her, so, not, expensive, as)

09 Your new app works ______. (as, half, fast, the old one, as)

10 Let's decorate this tree ______. (beautifully, as, we, can, as)

11 Could you move the tables ______? (you, quickly, can, as, as)

12 The light is ______. (three, the other one, times, bright, as, as)

개념 42 여러 가지 비교급 표현

월 일

Sarah is taller than her elder sister.

This pool looks much deeper than I expected.

Is this shirt slightly bigger than that white one?

His sight became clearer and clearer.

The bigger the sound wave is, the louder the sound is.

비교급 + than	…보다 더 ~한
much / a lot / far / even + 비교급	훨씬 더 ~한
a little / a bit / slightly + 비교급	약간 더 ~한
less + 원급 + than	…보다 덜 ~한
비교급 + and + 비교급	점점 더 ~한
the + 비교급 ~, the + 비교급 ...	더 ~할수록 더 …하다

바로 개념

1 비교급을 사용해 두 대상을 비교할 때 비교 대상 앞에 than을 쓴다.
2 비교급을 강조할 때 비교급 앞에 much, a lot, far, even 등을 쓴다.
3 비교급을 활용하여 다양한 비교 구문을 쓸 수 있다.

고르며 개념 확인

Answers p. 26

01 I have never felt ○ happier ○ so happy than now.

02 The English class became harder ○ and ○ or harder.

03 I think this color is ○ a few ○ a little darker than that.

04 Those tools were ○ little ○ less useful than I guessed.

05 The more attention you pay, ○ fewer ○ the fewer mistakes you will make.

쓰며 개념 정리

06 이 재킷은 내 것보다 훨씬 더 크다. (lot, mine, than, big, a)

→ This jacket is a lot bigger than mine.

07 요즘, 겨울 날씨는 점점 더 추워지고 있다. (cold, cold, and, getting)

→ Nowadays, the weather in winter is ______.

08 많이 잘수록 더 졸릴 것이다. (you, get, the, will, sleepy)

→ The more you sleep, ______.

09 태풍은 그들이 예측한 것보다도 훨씬 더 강했다. (strong, they, than, predicted, even)

→ The typhoon was ______.

Answers p. 26

개념 41 원급 비교

1 비교되는 두 대상의 성질 또는 수량이 같을 때 형용사와 부사의 ______ 을 이용하여 '…만큼 ~하다'라는 원급 비교의 의미를 나타낼 수 있다.

2 '몇 배'를 나타내는 배수 표현을 원급 비교 구문과 함께 써서 '…배만큼 ~하다'라는 의미를 나타낼 수 있다. 배수 표현은 half(절반), twice(두 번), ______ (세 번), ______ (네 번) 등으로 나타낸다.

원급 비교	*A* ~ as + 원급 + as + *B*
	의미:
can을 활용한 원급 비교	as + 원급 + as + 주어 + can (= as + 원급 + as possible)
	의미:
배수 표현을 사용한 비교	*A* ~ 배수 표현 + as + 원급 + as + *B*
	의미:

개념 42 여러 가지 비교급 표현

1 비교급을 사용해 두 대상을 비교할 때 비교 대상 앞에 ______ 을 쓴다.

2 비교급을 ______ 할 때 비교급 앞에 much, a lot, far, even 등을 쓴다.

3 비교급을 활용하여 다양한 비교 구문을 쓸 수 있다.

비교급 구문	의미
비교급 + than	…보다 더 ~한
much / a lot / far / even + 비교급	
a little / a bit / slightly + 비교급	
less + 원급 + than	
비교급 + and + 비교급	
the + 비교급 ~, the + 비교급 ...	

Answers p. 26

A 괄호 안의 단어를 알맞은 형태로 바꾸어 빈칸에 쓰시오. (바꿀 필요가 없으면 그대로 쓸 것)

01 This plum is as ______ as an apple. (big)

02 The mother's voice got ______ and louder. (loud)

03 I am half as ______ as my eldest brother. (old)

04 I like walking fast ______ than jogging. (much)

05 Do you know CO_2 is ______ than O_2? (heavy)

06 Please come back here as soon as you ______. (can)

07 The singer is less ______ than the actor. (popular)

08 The ______ your hair gets, the ______ it takes to dry. (long, long)

B 괄호 안의 단어를 활용하여 우리말과 같은 뜻의 문장을 완성하시오.

01 그는 너만큼 키가 크지 않니? (tall)

→ Isn't he ______ you?

02 그 초콜릿 아이스크림은 초콜릿보다 훨씬 더 달다. (sweet)

→ The chocolate ice cream is ______ chocolate.

03 이 학교는 우리 학교보다 약 세 배 크다. (big)

→ This school is about ______ my school.

04 나는 지난번보다 약간 더 좋은 점수를 받았다. (good)

→ I got ______ grades than the last time.

05 그녀는 할 수 있는 한 천천히 책을 읽었다. (slowly)

→ She read the book ______.

06 문제가 어려워질수록 많은 학생들이 풀기를 포기했다. (difficult, many)

→ ______ the problems got, ______ gave up solving them.

비교하며 문장 쓰기

			표현 노트
301	Jason은 Mike만큼 빨리 달릴 수 있다.	Jason can run as fast as Mike.	play the guitar, well
	Mina는 Joan만큼 기타를 잘 칠 수 있다.	Mina can play the guitar as well as Joan.	
302	나는 샌드위치가 김밥보다 훨씬 더 건강에 좋다고 생각한다.	I think sandwiches are much healthier than *gimbap*.	much, tasty, sandwiches
	치킨이 샌드위치보다 훨씬 더 맛있다.		
303	이것은 저것의 두 배만큼 크다.	This is twice as big as that.	times, long
	이것은 저것의 세 배만큼 길다.		
304	그 나무는 점점 더 키가 자랐다.	The tree grew taller and taller.	fight, hard
	그들은 점점 더 심하게 싸웠다.		
305	가능한 한 많은 단어를 찾아라.	Find as many words as you can.	try, get, much information
	가능한 한 많은 정보를 얻도록 노력해라.		
306	우리가 더 높이 오를수록, 더 멀리 본다.	The higher we go up, the farther we see.	hard, dig, fast, finish
	네가 더 열심히 팔수록, 너는 더 빨리 끝낼 것이다.		
307	이 방은 내가 예상했던 것만큼 넓지 않다.	This room is not so large as I expected.	restaurant, nice
	이 식당은 우리가 예상했던 것만큼 좋지 않다.		
308	그것은 현재 사용되고 있는 물질보다 더 싸다.	It is less expensive than the currently used materials.	comfortable, sofa
	이 의자는 저 소파보다 덜 편안하다.		

Answers p. 26

배열하여 문장 쓰기

309
우리가 더 많은 책을 공유할수록, 더 많이 배운다.
(we, more, the, learn, books, we, the, share, more)

The more books we share, the more we learn.

310
벽에 그리는 것은 종이에 그리는 것보다 훨씬 더 힘들었다.
(harder, drawing, was, on a wall, drawing, much, on paper, than)

311
내 오래된 자전거는 거의 새것만큼 좋다.
(good, a new one, almost, is, my old bike, as, as)

312
나는 가능한 한 빠르고 자연스럽게 슬리퍼를 내 뒤로 숨겼다.
(could, quickly, as, and, as, naturally, I)

I hid the slippers behind me

313
점점 더 많은 사람들이 재활용할 수 있는 가방을 사용하고 있다.
(are using, more, reusable bags, and, people, more)

314
우리는 우리 동네를 좀 더 밝고 행복하게 만들었다.
(our neighborhood, brighter, made, happier, we, and, a little)

315
당신의 사과가 더 진실할수록 그것은 더 잘 받아들여질 것이다.
(sincere, is, it, received, the, the, your apology, will be, better, more)

[Self-Editing Checklist] ✓ 대 • 소문자를 바르게 썼나요? Y N ✓ 철자와 문장 부호를 바르게 썼나요? Y N

개념 43 여러 가지 최상급 표현

월 일

I think it is the greatest painting in this museum.

Who do you think is the most powerful person of them?

Mr. Leigh is one of the most intelligent members in this group.

This is the most beautiful scene that I have ever seen.

the + 최상급 ~ + in + 장소/집단	…에서 가장 ~한
the + 최상급 ~ + of + 복수 명사	… 중에서 가장 ~한
one of the + 최상급 + 복수 명사	가장 ~한 … 중 하나
the + 최상급 + 명사 (+ that) + 주어 + have ever + 과거분사	지금까지 …한 것 중 가장 ~한

바로 개념

1 최상급 앞에는 대개 the를 쓴다.
2 최상급 표현 뒤에 비교 범위를 나타내는 부사구가 오는 경우가 많다.

고르며 개념 확인

Answers p. 27

01 Rudy is the wisest one ○ in ○ of his siblings.

02 The Nile is the ○ longer ○ longest river in the world.

03 It is ○ a funnier ○ the funniest movie that I've ever seen.

04 Yeosu is one ○ in ○ of the most beautiful cities in Korea.

05 Celine is known as ○ a smarter ○ the smartest student in her school.

06 Don't you think he is one of the greatest ○ artist ○ artists in the UK?

쓰며 개념 정리

07 그는 가족 중 가장 키가 작다. He is [ ] [ ] in his family.

08 Alice는 다섯 명 중 가장 어리다. Alice is [ ] [ ] [ ] the five.

09 Amelia는 나의 학교에서 가장 빠른 달리기 선수이다.

Amelia is [ ] [ ] runner [ ] my school.

10 Alfie는 우리가 만나 본 사람 중 가장 친절한 사람이야.

Alfie is [ ] [ ] person that we've [ ] [ ].

개념 44

원급과 비교급을 이용한 최상급 표현

월 일

This is the tallest building.

= This building is taller than any other building.

= This building is taller than all the other buildings.

= No building is taller than this building.

= No building is as tall as this building.

최상급의 의미를 갖는 여러 가지 표현

비교급 + than + any other + 단수 명사	다른 어떤 …보다 ~한
비교급 + than + all the other + 복수 명사	다른 모든 …보다 ~한
No (other) + 명사 ~ + 비교급 + than	어떤 -도 …보다 ~하지 않다
No (other) + 명사 ~ + as [so] + 원급 + as	어떤 -도 …만큼 ~하지 않다

바로 개념

1 원급 또는 비교급을 이용하여 최상급과 같은 의미를 나타낼 수 있다.
2 각 표현의 문장 구조에 유의한다.

고르며 개념 확인

Answers p. 27

01 No problem is more serious ○ as ○ than this.

02 ○ All ○ No flower's fragrance is as sweet as the rose's.

03 No poet is as famous ○ as ○ than Shakespeare.

04 Harper's idea was ○ as creative ○ more creative than any other's idea.

05 The goalkeeper played better than ○ all ○ any the other goalkeepers.

쓰며 개념 정리

06 This is the most exciting movie.

→ This movie is ______ any other movie.

→ This movie is ______ all the other movies.

→ ______ is more exciting than this movie.

→ No movie is as ______.

07 This is the smallest island in Korea.

→ This island is ______ any other island in Korea.

→ No island is smaller ______ in Korea.

개념 43 여러 가지 최상급 표현

1 최상급 앞에는 대개 [ ] 를 쓴다.

2 최상급 표현 뒤에 비교 범위를 나타내는 부사구가 오는 경우가 많다.

최상급 구문	의미
the + 최상급 ~ + in + 장소/집단	
the + 최상급 ~ + of + 복수 명사	
one of the + 최상급 + 복수 명사	
the + 최상급 + 명사 (+ that) + 주어 + have ever + 과거분사	

개념 44 원급과 비교급을 이용한 최상급 표현

원급 또는 비교급을 이용한 최상급 표현	의미
비교급 + than + [ ] + 단수 명사	다른 어떤 …보다 ~한
비교급 + than + all [ ] + 복수 명사	다른 모든 …보다 ~한
No (other) + 명사 ~ + 비교급 + than	어떤 –도 …보다 ~하지 않다
No (other) + 명사 ~ + [ ] + 원급 + as	어떤 –도 …만큼 ~하지 않다

Answers p. 27

A 우리말과 같은 뜻이 되도록 빈칸에 알맞은 말을 넣어 문장을 완성하시오.

01 그 건물은 이 근방에서 가장 오래되었다.

→ The building is ______ ______ ______ this neighborhood.

02 어떤 것도 우리의 건강보다 중요하지 않다.

→ Nothing is ______ ______ ______ our health.

03 Joan은 그들 중 가장 젊은 교사이다.

→ Joan is ______ ______ ______ ______ them.

04 그것은 내가 본 것 중 가장 훌륭한 그림이다.

→ It is the greatest painting that I ______ ______ ______.

05 그 산은 이 나라에서 가장 높은 산 중의 하나이다.

→ It is ______ ______ ______ ______ ______ in this country.

06 Jason은 그의 반의 어느 학생보다도 일찍 그곳에 도착했다.

→ Jason arrived there ______ ______ ______ ______ ______ ______ his class.

B 짝지어진 두 문장이 같은 의미가 되도록 빈칸에 알맞은 말을 쓰시오.

01 Mr. Hanks is the most talented actor.

= ______ than Mr. Hanks.

02 No other thing is more important for life than water.

= No other thing is ______ as water.

03 This is the fastest printer in our store.

= This printer is ______ all the other printers in our store.

04 I think my father is the most wonderful person in the world.

= I think my father is ______ any other person in the world.

문장 쓰기

표현 노트

		표현 노트
316	에베레스트산은 세상의 다른 어떤 산보다도 높다. Mt. Everest is higher than any other mountain in the world.	Mt. Everest, high, any other
317	사그라다 파밀리아 성당은 세상에서 가장 유명한 성당 중 하나이다. The Sagrada Familia is	famous, church
318	내 인생에서 가장 당혹스러운 날이 될 것이다.	will be, embarrassing, of
319	이것은 내가 지금까지 본 것 중 가장 놀라운 책이다.	amazing, that, ever, see
320	어떤 사람도 Joe만큼 기타를 빠르게 연주할 수 없다.	no one, can, play the guitar
321	나는 이 마을에서 가장 부유한 농부가 될 수 있다.	be, rich, farmer, village
322	팝콘은 전 세계적으로 가장 인기 있는 간식 중 하나이다.	popcorn, popular, snacks, around the world
323	그들은 다른 어떤 팀보다 훨씬 더 잘 공연했다.	perform, much, any other

Answers p. 27

배열하여 문장 쓰기

324 네덜란드는 세계에서 가장 큰 꽃 시장을 소유하고 있다.
(the, has, in the world, the Netherlands, flower market, largest)

The Netherlands has the largest flower market in the world.

325 이것은 내가 맛본 것 중 가장 훌륭한 소고기야!
(the best, I've, is, tasted, beef, this, ever)

326 너는 게임 디자이너에게 필요한 가장 중요한 기술이 무엇이라고 생각하니?
(do, think, most important, a game designer, what, you, needs, is, the, skill)

✯ 간접의문문 문장에서 주절의 동사가 think일 때 어순에 주의

327 레오나르도 다빈치는 역사상 가장 위대한 화가 중 한 명으로 알려져 있다.
(one, painters, known, of all time, the greatest, of, is, as)

Leonardo da Vinci

✯ be known as: ~로 알려져 있다

328 다른 어떤 것도 이 문제를 해결하는 것보다 긴급하지 않다.
(other thing, this problem, urgent, than, no, solving, more, is)

329 이것은 내가 먹어본 다른 어떤 잼보다 더 낫다.
(better, I've, had, is, than, ever, any other jam, this)

330 여왕의 생각에는 세상의 온갖 보석보다 새끼 고양이가 훨씬 더 가치 있었다.
(far, was, more than, in the world, worth, the kitten, all the jewels)

In the queen's mind,

✯ far는 비교급 more를 강조하는 표현

[Self-Editing Checklist] ✔ 대 • 소문자를 바르게 썼나요? Y N ✔ 철자와 문장 부호를 바르게 썼나요? Y N

대표유형 01 원급 비교 구문

01 다음 우리말을 바르게 영작한 것은?

Sam은 너만큼 재치가 있어.

① Sam is wittier than you.
② Sam is as witty as you.
③ You are wittier than Sam.
④ Sam is not as witty as you.
⑤ Either Sam or you are witty.

02 다음 문장의 빈칸에 들어갈 말로 가장 알맞은 것은?

The book is not ________ difficult as you might think.

① so ② than ③ more
④ most ⑤ like

03 다음 문장과 의미가 가장 가까운 것은?

My room is half as big as yours.

① My room is as small as yours.
② My room is bigger than yours.
③ Your room is smaller than mine.
④ Your room is twice as big as mine.
⑤ My room is twice as big as yours.

04 주어진 우리말과 같은 의미가 되도록 할 때 빈칸에 알맞은 것은?

그는 할 수 있는 한 빠르게 걸었다.
➔ He walked as fast as he ________.

① can ② could ③ walks
④ walked ⑤ will do

05 다음 문장의 빈칸에 들어갈 말로 어색한 것은?

The cat is ________ as old as my dog.

① not ② so ③ twice
④ half ⑤ three times

대표유형 02 비교급 구문

06 다음 두 문장의 의미가 같을 때, 밑줄 친 부분의 형태로 알맞은 것끼리 짝지어진 것은?

As you go farther, you can see more.
= Far you go, much you can see.

① Far – much ② Farer – more
③ Farther – more ④ Farthest – most
⑤ The farther – the more

07 다음 문장 중 밑줄 친 부분이 어법상 어색한 것은?

① I got up a lot earlier than my father.
② It looks a bit smaller than others.
③ This bag is less heavier than that one.
④ I have never felt sadder than now.
⑤ The river looks deeper than before.

08 다음 문장의 빈칸에 들어갈 말로 알맞은 것은?

Amy was short when she was young. Now, she is much ________ than before.

① tall ② taller ③ tallest
④ the tallest ⑤ more taller

09 다음 문장 중 어법상 어색한 것을 모두 고르면?

① His face turned pale and pale.
② You look more healthier than last year.
③ This pasta is less salty than your.
④ The school is bigger than I guessed.
⑤ I think this chair is nicer than that one.

10 주어진 우리말과 같은 의미가 되도록 할 때 빈칸에 들어갈 말이 순서대로 바르게 짝지어진 것은?

더 많이 배울수록 더 현명해질 것이다.
➔ ________ you learn, ________ you will become.

① Much – wise ② A lot – much wiser
③ More – wiser ④ The more – the wiser
⑤ The most – the wisest

11 다음 중 밑줄 친 부분의 쓰임이 <u>어색한</u> 것은?

① The sky is getting <u>darker and darker</u>.
② <u>The more you have</u>, the more you want.
③ I'm sure he will get <u>better and better</u>.
④ The sea looked <u>a lot farther suddenly</u>.
⑤ Yena is <u>even outgoing than</u> I am.

대표유형 03 최상급 구문

12 다음 문장 중 밑줄 친 부분이 어법상 자연스러운 것은?

① He is <u>fastest one</u> on his team.
② I love this song <u>the more in this album</u>.
③ I'm <u>one of the oldest members</u> in my club.
④ It was <u>the longest movie so that</u> I've ever seen.
⑤ The blue whale is <u>one of biggest animals</u>.

13 다음 짝지어진 문장 중 서로 의미가 <u>다른</u> 것은?

① Lily is taller than the other two.
= Lily is the tallest of the three.
② He ran the fastest of the students.
= He ran faster than the other students.
③ She studied harder than the others.
= She studied the hardest of them.
④ This is the oldest tree in the park.
= This is one of the oldest trees in the park.
⑤ This is the funniest webtoon I've ever read.
= I've never read a funnier webtoon than this.

14 주어진 우리말과 같은 의미가 되도록 할 때 빈칸에 알맞은 것은?

이 스마트폰 모델은 매장에서 가장 최신의 것이다.
➔ This smartphone model is ________ in the store.

① late ② later ③ the latest
④ latter ⑤ the last

대표유형 04 원급과 비교급을 이용한 최상급 표현

15 다음 문장 중 나머지 넷과 의미가 <u>다른</u> 것은?

① This is the biggest statue.
② No statue is as big as this statue.
③ No statue is bigger than this statue.
④ This statue is one of the biggest statues.
⑤ This statue is bigger than any other statue.

16 다음 문장과 바꿔 쓸 수 있는 것은?

No book is older than this book.

① This book is older than that book.
② Any other book is older than this book.
③ No book is as new as this book.
④ This book is older than any other book.
⑤ This book is as old as all the other books.

17 다음 두 문장의 의미가 통하도록 빈칸에 알맞은 말을 고르면?

No one was more careful than Ms. Murphy of the participants.
= No participant was ________ Ms. Murphy.

① the most careful of
② as careful as
③ not so careful as
④ much more careful as
⑤ the most careful in

18 다음 문장 중 어법상 <u>어색한</u> 것은?

① My sister is the busiest in my family.
② No one is as friendlier as Michael.
③ A lemon is one of the healthiest fruits.
④ No other movie is more exciting than this movie.
⑤ Seoul is more crowded than any other city in Korea.

01 괄호 안의 단어를 사용하여 주어진 문장과 비슷한 의미의 문장을 완성하시오.

(1) I think Ms. Brett is the best writer.

→ I think ______________________________. (no, than)

(2) Sometimes comfort is more important than price.

→ ______________________________ (less)

02 다음 표를 보고 물음에 완전한 문장으로 답하여 대화를 완성하시오.

이름	100m 달리기	키	나이
Christine	14초	157cm	15세
Anita	17초	173cm	16세
Lindsay	15초	165cm	14세

A Who is the fastest of all?
B (1) ______________________________
A Who is the tallest of all?
B (2) ______________________________
A Who is younger than Christine?
B (3) ______________________________

수행평가 유형 자기 소개하기

03 다음 〈보기〉와 같이 최상급 또는 비교급을 사용하여 자신을 설명하는 문장을 다섯 개 쓰시오.

보기
- I am taller than any other student in my class.
- I know the most songs in my family.

(1) ______________________________
(2) ______________________________
(3) ______________________________
(4) ______________________________
(5) ______________________________

[Self-Editing Checklist] ✔ 대 • 소문자를 바르게 썼나요? Y N ✔ 철자와 문장 부호를 바르게 썼나요? Y N

UNIT 11

가정법

핵심 개념 바로 확인 I know! ☺ No idea! 😐

- 가정법 과거는 현재 사실과 반대되는 가정을 할 때 쓴다. ☺ 😐
- 가정법 과거완료는 과거 사실과 반대되는 가정을 할 때 쓴다. ☺ 😐

개념 45 가정법 과거와 과거완료

I would buy that computer if it were cheaper.

If he didn't play mobile games much, he could read more books.

If Kate had been more careful, she would not have had the accident.

		if절	주절
가정법 과거	현재 사실의 반대	If + 주어 + were 또는 동사의 과거형 ~,	주어 + 조동사 과거형(would, could, might) + 동사원형 ~.
가정법 과거완료	과거 사실의 반대	If + 주어 + had + 과거분사 ~,	주어 + 조동사 과거형(would, could, might) + have + 과거분사 ~.

바로 개념

1 가정법 과거는 '(만약) ~한다면, …할 텐데[것이다]'라는 의미로 현재 사실과 반대되거나 실제로 일어날 가능성이 거의 없는 일을 가정할 때 쓴다. if절의 동사가 be동사인 경우 주어의 인칭과 수에 관계없이 were를 쓴다.

2 가정법 과거완료는 '(만약) ~했다면, …했을 텐데[것이다]'라는 의미로 과거 사실과 반대되는 일을 가정할 때 쓴다.

3 if절과 주절의 위치는 바꿀 수 있으며, 주절이 앞에 있을 때는 주절 뒤에 콤마(,)를 쓰지 않는다.

고르며 개념 확인

Answers p. 28

01 If she had more time, she ○ exercises ○ could exercise after work.

02 If I ○ moved ○ had moved to Canada, I would live in Vancouver.

03 I ○ would listen ○ would have listened to my parents if I had been wiser.

04 What ○ would ○ will you do if someone knew your secret?

05 Lisa would have gotten wet if she ○ hadn't worn ○ didn't wear a raincoat.

06 If they ○ have started ○ had started earlier, they could have finished the work on time.

쓰며 개념 정리

07 내가 천재라면, 나를 복제한 인간을 만들 텐데. (be, make)

→ If I ______ a genius, I ______ my clone.

08 내게 10억 달러가 있다면, 아프리카에 병원을 세울 수 있을 텐데. (have, build)

→ If I ______ a billion dollars, I ______ hospitals in Africa.

09 네가 일찍 일어났더라면, 너는 지각하지 않았을 텐데. (get, be)

→ If you ______ up early, you ______ late for school.

혼합 가정법

월 일

If I had learned foreign languages, I would have more job opportunities.
(과거에) 외국어를 배웠더라면 (현재) 직업을 가질 기회가 더 많을 텐데
(→ As I didn't learn foreign languages, I don't have more job opportunities.)

If he had not eaten the ice cream, he would not have a stomachache now.
(과거에) 아이스크림을 먹지 않았더라면 (현재) 배가 아프지 않을 텐데
(→ As he ate the ice cream, he has a stomachache now.)

		if절(가정법 과거완료)	주절(가정법 과거)
혼합 가정법	과거에 실현되지 못한 일이 현재까지 영향을 줄 때	If + 주어 + had + 과거분사 ~,	주어 + 조동사 과거형(would, could, might) + 동사원형 ~.

바로 개념

1 혼합 가정법은 if절에 가정법 과거완료를, 주절에 가정법 과거를 쓴 것으로 '(만약) ~했다면, …할 텐데'라는 의미이다. 과거에 실현되지 못한 일이 현재까지 영향을 줄 때 사용한다.
2 if절에는 주로 과거를 나타내는 부사(구)를 쓰고, 주절에는 현재를 나타내는 부사(구)를 쓴다.

고르며 개념 확인

Answers p. 28

01 If I had not eaten lunch, I ○ would be ○ am hungry now.

02 The street ○ isn't ○ wouldn't be messy today if it had not snowed yesterday.

03 If Brian ○ has checked ○ had checked the map yesterday, he would not be lost.

04 If I had not traveled for a year, I ○ wouldn't have ○ would have various experiences now.

05 If the patient ○ had followed ○ hadn't followed the doctor's advice, he would be healthy now.

쓰며 개념 정리

06 네가 창문을 닫았더라면, 지금 집이 따뜻할 텐데. (close, be)
→ If you ________ the window, the house ________ warm now.

07 Dave가 며칠 전에 다리를 다치지 않았더라면, 우리는 오늘 하이킹을 갈 수 있을 텐데. (break, go)
→ If Dave ________ his leg the other day, we ________ hiking today.

08 그녀가 어제 비를 맞으며 걷지 않았더라면, 그녀는 지금 감기에 걸려 있지 않을 텐데. (walk, have)
→ If she ________ in the rain, she ________ a cold now.

개념 45 가정법 과거와 과거완료

1 [ ] 는 '(만약) ~한다면, …할 텐데[것이다]'라는 의미로 현재 사실과 반대되거나 실제로 일어날 가능성이 거의 없는 일을 가정할 때 쓴다. if절의 동사가 be동사인 경우 주어의 인칭과 수에 관계없이 were를 쓴다.

2 [ ] 는 '(만약) ~했다면, …했을 텐데[것이다]'라는 의미로 과거 사실과 반대되는 일을 가정할 때 쓴다.

3 if절과 주절의 위치는 바꿀 수 있으며, 주절이 앞에 있을 때는 주절 뒤에 [ ] 를 쓰지 않는다.

		if절	주절
가정법 과거	현재 사실의 반대	If + 주어 + were 또는 동사의 과거형 ~,	주어 + 조동사 과거형(would, could, might) + [ ] ~.
가정법 과거완료	과거 사실의 반대	If + 주어 + [ ] + 과거분사 ~,	주어 + 조동사 과거형(would, could, might) + [ ] + 과거분사 ~.

개념 46 혼합 가정법

1 혼합 가정법은 if절에 가정법 [ ] 를, 주절에 가정법 [ ] 를 쓴 것으로 '(만약) ~했다면, …할 텐데'라는 의미이다. 과거에 실현되지 못한 일이 현재까지 영향을 줄 때 사용한다.

2 if절에는 주로 [ ] 를 나타내는 부사(구)를 쓰고, 주절에는 [ ] 를 나타내는 부사(구)를 쓴다.

		if절 (가정법 과거완료)	주절 (가정법 과거)
혼합 가정법	과거에 실현되지 못한 일이 현재까지 영향을 줄 때	If + 주어 + [ ] + 과거분사 ~,	주어 + 조동사 과거형(would, could, might) + 동사원형 ~.

Answers p. 29

A 다음 문장에서 밑줄 친 부분을 어법에 맞게 바르게 고치시오.

01 If Julia owned a car, she will drive to work.

02 I would have believed you now if you hadn't lied to me before.

03 We could save more money if we had eaten out less.

04 He could have been on time if he caught the bus.

05 If Sam didn't break my bike a week ago, I could ride it now.

06 I would have been happy if my parents allowed me to have a pet.

07 If the weather has been fine today, we could have played outside.

B 다음 문장을 가정법 문장으로 바꿔 쓰시오.

01 As Dad doesn't have time, he can't take me to the zoo.

→ If Dad ____ time, he ____ me to the zoo.

02 As I didn't nap after lunch, I'm tired now.

→ If I ____ after lunch, I ____ tired now.

03 As Emma made mistakes, she couldn't win the prize.

→ If Emma ____ mistakes, she ____ the prize.

04 As I left my wallet at home, I can't buy you dinner.

→ If I ____ my wallet at home, I ____ you dinner.

05 As my sister is afraid of driving, she can't get a driver's license.

→ If my sister ____ of driving, she ____ a driver's license.

06 He didn't see a dog crossing the street, so he hit the dog.

→ If he ____ a dog crossing the street, he ____ the dog.

조건에 맞게 문장 바꿔 쓰기

331 가정법 과거로
As he doesn't know my address, he won't send me a letter.

332 가정법 과거완료로
As the wind was so strong, we couldn't have tea outside.

333 가정법 과거로
The water inside doesn't quickly boil over as the lid has that hole.

334 혼합 가정법으로
As I didn't apologize to her, we are not friends now.

★ 혼합 가정법은 if절에 가정법 과거완료를 쓰고, 주절에 가정법 과거를 쓴다.

335 가정법 과거완료로
I didn't die because you saved my life.

336 가정법 과거로
As I don't have enough eggs, I can't bake bread for my family.

337 가정법 과거완료로
I received a passing grade because you helped me.

338 혼합 가정법으로
As I didn't have enough sleep last night, I am tired today.

Answers p. 29

표현 이용하여 문장 쓰기

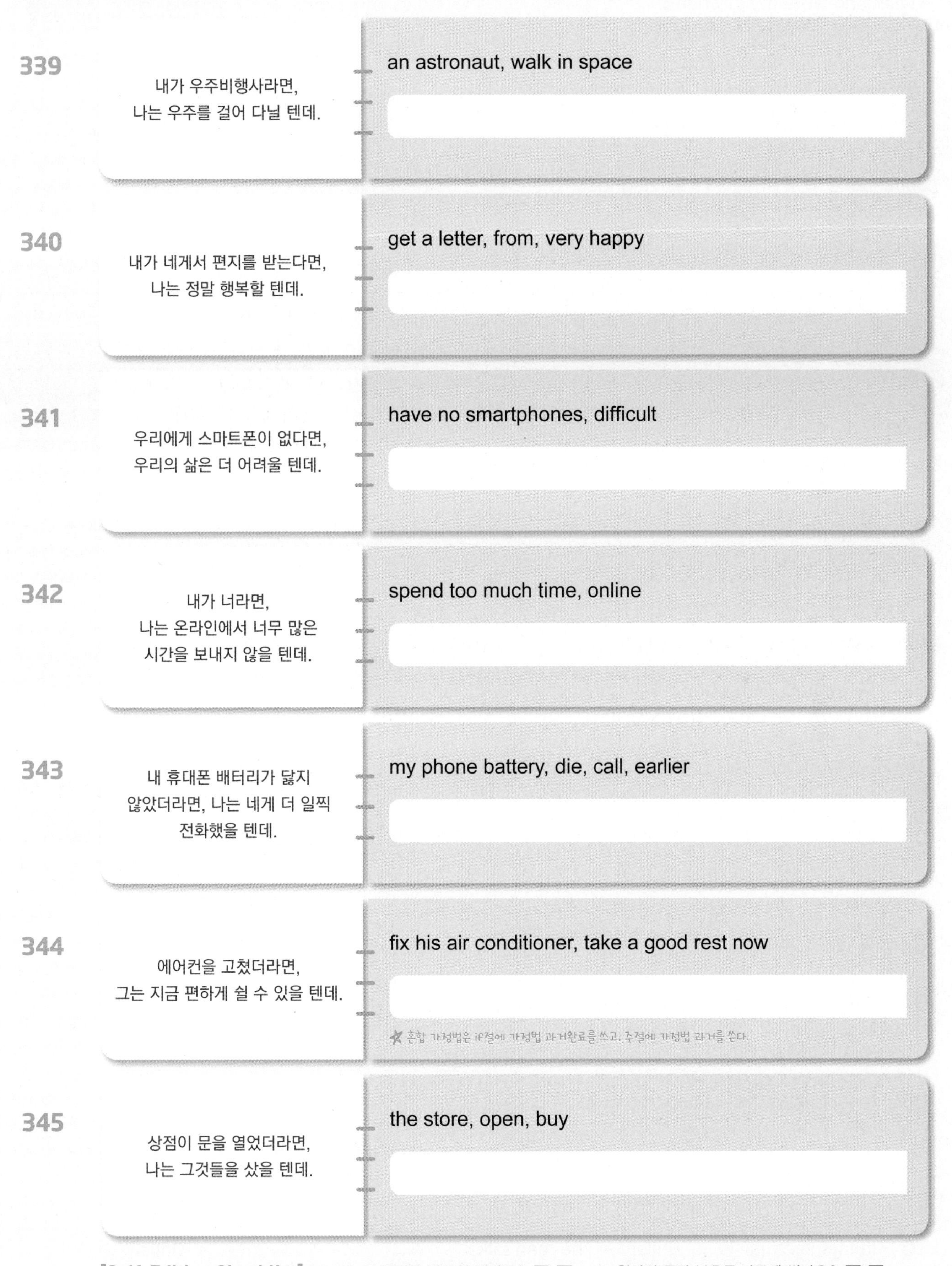

339 내가 우주비행사라면, 나는 우주를 걸어 다닐 텐데.
an astronaut, walk in space

340 내가 네게서 편지를 받는다면, 나는 정말 행복할 텐데.
get a letter, from, very happy

341 우리에게 스마트폰이 없다면, 우리의 삶은 더 어려울 텐데.
have no smartphones, difficult

342 내가 너라면, 나는 온라인에서 너무 많은 시간을 보내지 않을 텐데.
spend too much time, online

343 내 휴대폰 배터리가 닳지 않았더라면, 나는 네게 더 일찍 전화했을 텐데.
my phone battery, die, call, earlier

344 에어컨을 고쳤더라면, 그는 지금 편하게 쉴 수 있을 텐데.
fix his air conditioner, take a good rest now

★ 혼합 가정법은 if절에 가정법 과거완료를 쓰고, 주절에 가정법 과거를 쓴다.

345 상점이 문을 열었더라면, 나는 그것들을 샀을 텐데.
the store, open, buy

[Self-Editing Checklist] ✓ 대 • 소문자를 바르게 썼나요? Y N ✓ 철자와 문장 부호를 바르게 썼나요? Y N

개념 47 I wish 가정법 / as if 가정법

월 일

I wish she were my girlfriend.
(→ I'm sorry that she is not my girlfriend.)

I wish I had listened to your advice.
(→ I'm sorry that I did not listen to your advice.)

Dad treats me as if I were a genius.
(→ In fact, I am not a genius.)

Julia looks as if she had seen a ghost.
(→ In fact, she did not see a ghost.)

I wish 가정법	과거	I wish + 주어 + were 또는 동사의 과거형
	과거완료	I wish + 주어 + had + 과거분사
as if 가정법	과거	as if + 주어 + were 또는 동사의 과거형
	과거완료	as if + 주어 + had + 과거분사

바로 개념

1 I wish 가정법 과거는 '~라면 좋을 텐데'라는 뜻으로 현재 이루기 힘든 소망이나 현실에 대한 아쉬움을 나타낸다.
2 I wish 가정법 과거완료는 '~했더라면 좋을 텐데'라는 뜻으로 과거 이루지 못한 일에 대한 아쉬움을 나타낸다.
3 as if 가정법 과거는 '마치 ~인 것처럼'이라는 뜻으로 주절과 같은 시점의 사실과 반대되는 상황을 가정할 때 쓴다.
4 as if 가정법 과거완료는 '마치 ~이었던 것처럼'의 의미로 주절보다 앞선 시점의 사실과 반대되는 상황을 가정할 때 쓴다.

고르며 개념 확인

Answers p. 29

01 I wish I ○ am ○ were good at writing a song.

02 She talked as if she ○ had been ○ went to Europe several times.

03 I wish he ○ had not ○ has not spent all his money buying the car.

04 We all feel as if it ○ were ○ is summer again today.

05 I wish the man ○ had let ○ let the old lady have his seat yesterday.

06 Ed is not a grown-up, but he acts as if he ○ had been ○ were a grown-up.

쓰며 개념 정리

07 I'm sorry that I don't have a better memory.

➔ ______ a better memory.

08 In fact, Kate did not hear the news.

➔ Kate acts ______ the news for the first time.

09 I'm sorry that you didn't travel with me. ➔ ______ with me.

10 In fact, the man is not British. ➔ The man talks ______ British.

개념 48 Without 가정법

월 일

Without **you**, **I** could **not** live.

= But for **you**, **I** could **not** live.

= If it were not for **you**, **I** could **not** live.

Without 가정법	과거	Without + 명사(구), 주어 + 조동사 과거형 + 동사원형 ~.
	과거완료	Without + 명사(구), 주어 + 조동사 과거형 + have + 과거분사 ~.

Without **his dog, he** would have been **lonely.**

= But for **his dog, he** would have been **lonely.**

= If it had not been for **his dog, he** would have been **lonely.**

바로 개념

1 「Without + 명사(구), 가정법 과거」는 '~이 없다면, …할 것이다'라는 의미로 현재 있는 것이 없다고 가정할 때 쓴다. Without 대신 But for나 If it were not for로 바꿔 쓸 수도 있다.

2 「Without + 명사(구), 가정법 과거완료」는 '~이 없었다면, …했을 것이다'라는 의미로 과거에 있었던 것이 없었다고 가정할 때 쓴다. Without 대신 But for나 If it had not been for로 바꿔 쓸 수도 있다.

고르며 개념 확인

Answers p. 29

01 내 도움이 없다면, 너는 시험에 떨어질 것이다.

→ Without my help, you ○ would fail ○ would have failed the test.

02 친구들이 없었더라면, 내 인생은 힘들었을 것이다.

→ Without my friends, my life ○ would be ○ would have been difficult.

03 인터넷이 없다면, 우리는 정보를 빨리 얻기 어려울 것이다.

→ Without the Internet, we ○ can't get ○ couldn't get information quickly.

04 화재 알람이 없었더라면, 피해는 훨씬 더 컸을 것이다.

→ Without the smoke alarm, the damage ○ could have been ○ could be a lot worse.

쓰며 개념 정리

05 Without air, human beings could not survive.

→ If ______________, human beings could not survive.

06 But for the map, we could not find the museum.

→ If ______________, we could not find the museum.

07 Without my parents, I could not have gotten a good education.

→ If ______________, I could not have gotten a good education.

바로 개념 확인 노트

Answers p. 29

개념 47 I wish 가정법 / as if 가정법

1 I wish 가정법 과거는 ( ) 이루기 힘든 소망이나 현실에 대한 아쉬움을 나타낸다.

2 I wish 가정법 과거완료는 ( ) 이루지 못한 일에 대한 아쉬움을 나타낸다.

3 as if 가정법 과거는 주절과 같은 시점의 사실과 반대되는 상황을 가정할 때 쓴다.

4 as if 가정법 과거완료는 주절보다 앞선 시점의 사실과 반대되는 상황을 가정할 때 쓴다.

I wish 가정법	과거	( )	I wish + 주어 + were 또는 동사의 과거형
	과거완료	~했더라면 좋을 텐데	I wish + 주어 + ( ) + ( )
as if 가정법	과거	( )	as if + 주어 + were 또는 동사의 과거형
	과거완료	마치 ~이었던 것처럼	as if + 주어 + ( ) + ( )

개념 48 Without 가정법

1 「Without + 명사(구), 가정법 과거」는 현재 있는 것이 없다고 가정할 때 쓴다. Without 대신 ( )나 If it ( ) ( ) for로 바꿔 쓸 수도 있다.

2 「Without + 명사(구), 가정법 과거완료」는 과거에 있었던 것이 없었다고 가정할 때 쓴다. Without 대신 But for나 If it ( ) ( ) ( ) for로 바꿔 쓸 수도 있다.

Without 가정법	과거	~이 없다면, …할 것이다	Without + 명사(구), 주어 + 조동사 과거형 + ( ) ~.
	과거완료	~이 없었다면, …했을 것이다	Without + 명사(구), 주어 + 조동사 과거형 + ( ) + ( ) ~.

Answers p. 29

A 다음 문장에서 밑줄 친 부분을 어법에 맞게 고치시오.

01 I wish I am at the fireworks festival last month. ______

02 What's wrong? You look as if you have not slept well. ______

03 Without for his advice, I would have given up. ______

04 I wish I did not trust him at that time. ______

05 He feels as if something had been in his throat now. ______

06 If it were not smartphones, it would be very inconvenient. ______

07 I live in the country. I wish I had lived in the big city. ______

08 The lady doesn't know me. But she acts as if she knows me. ______

B 다음 문장과 같은 의미를 갖도록 가정법 문장을 완성하시오.

01 Without bees to spread seeds, many plants would die.

→ If ______ to spread seeds, many plants would die.

02 I'm sorry that there is homework today.

→ ______ no homework today.

03 If it had not been for him, the soccer team could not have won the championship.

→ ______, the soccer team could not have won the championship.

04 In fact, Dave doesn't get an A on the test.

→ Dave talks ______ an A on the test.

05 I'm sorry that I didn't buy the tickets online.

→ ______ the tickets online.

06 In fact, she took a shower this morning.

→ She looks ______ a shower this morning.

07 If it had not been for his sincere advice, I could not have entered university.

→ Without his sincere advice, ______ university.

가정법 문장 쓰고 해석하기

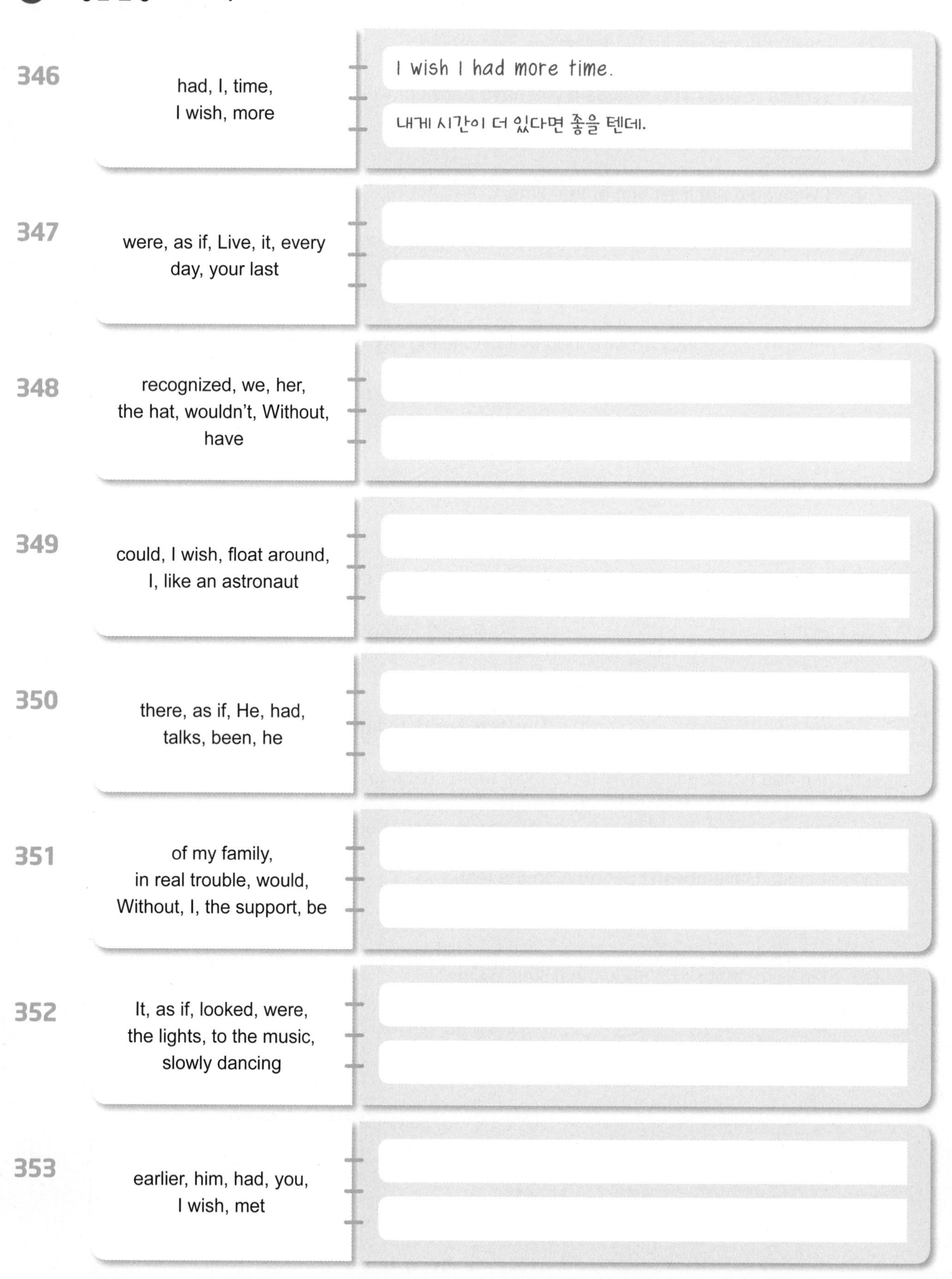

Answers p. 30

표현 이용하여 문장 쓰기

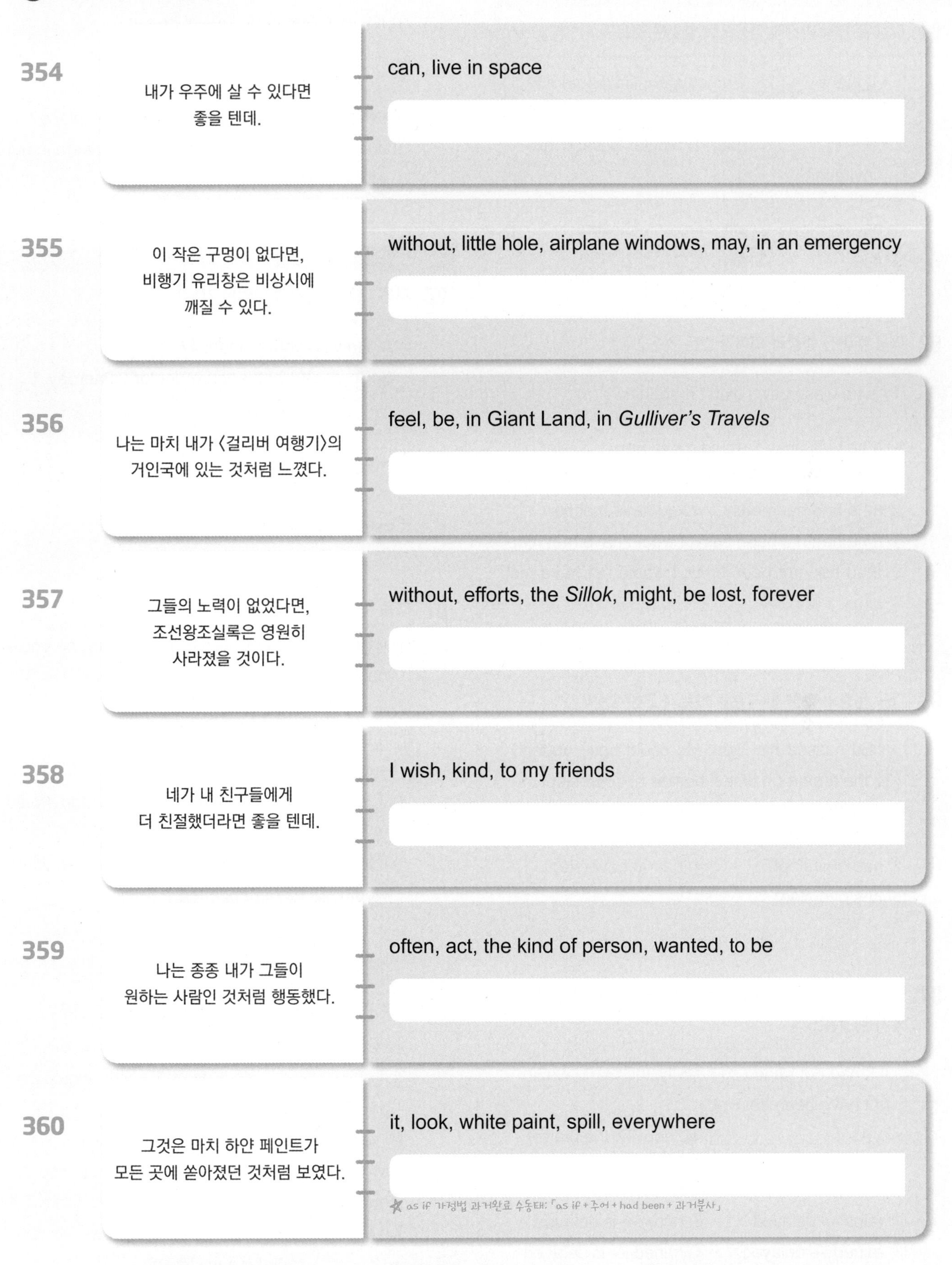

354 내가 우주에 살 수 있다면 좋을 텐데.

can, live in space

355 이 작은 구멍이 없다면, 비행기 유리창은 비상시에 깨질 수 있다.

without, little hole, airplane windows, may, in an emergency

356 나는 마치 내가 〈걸리버 여행기〉의 거인국에 있는 것처럼 느꼈다.

feel, be, in Giant Land, in *Gulliver's Travels*

357 그들의 노력이 없었다면, 조선왕조실록은 영원히 사라졌을 것이다.

without, efforts, the *Sillok*, might, be lost, forever

358 네가 내 친구들에게 더 친절했더라면 좋을 텐데.

I wish, kind, to my friends

359 나는 종종 내가 그들이 원하는 사람인 것처럼 행동했다.

often, act, the kind of person, wanted, to be

360 그것은 마치 하얀 페인트가 모든 곳에 쏟아졌던 것처럼 보였다.

it, look, white paint, spill, everywhere

★ as if 가정법 과거완료 수동태: 「as if + 주어 + had been + 과거분사」

[Self-Editing Checklist] ✔ 대 • 소문자를 바르게 썼나요? Y N ✔ 철자와 문장 부호를 바르게 썼나요? Y N

대표유형 01 가정법 과거와 과거완료

01 다음 문장의 빈칸에 공통으로 알맞은 것은?

> • If there ________ no oxygen, life would not exist.
> • If I ________ you, I would accept his invitation.

① be ② am ③ were
④ is ⑤ was

02 다음 주어진 문장과 의미가 같은 것은?

> As he was busy, I didn't meet him.

① If he was busy, I would meet him.
② If he were busy, I would meet him.
③ If he had been busy, I would have met him.
④ If he had not been busy, I would have met him.
⑤ If he had not been busy, I would not have met him.

03 다음 문장의 밑줄 친 부분을 바르게 고친 것은?

> Ed missed his flight. He could have gotten to the airport on time if he has not overslept.

① overslept ② didn't oversleep
③ had overslept ④ had not overslept
⑤ has overslept

04 다음 두 문장의 의미가 같을 때, 빈칸에 알맞은 말을 바르게 짝지은 것은?

> If it had not rained so heavily, the plane would not have been delayed.
> → As it ____________ so heavily, the plane ____________.

① rains — delayed ② rains — is delayed
③ rained — delayed ④ rained — is delayed
⑤ rained — was delayed

05 다음 중 밑줄 친 If [if]의 쓰임이 나머지 넷과 다른 것은?

① If it were not cold, I could go out.
② If I were you, I would refuse the offer.
③ If you do that again, I'll never talk to you.
④ What would you do if you were in my place?
⑤ Julia would answer the phone if she were in her office now.

대표유형 02 혼합 가정법

06 다음 대화의 빈칸에 알맞은 것은?

> **A** How do you feel today?
> **B** So-so. If I had seen a doctor yesterday, I ________ sick today.

① would not be ② am not
③ would have been ④ would be
⑤ would not have been

07 다음 문장 중 어법상 어색한 것은?

① If he had not hurt his leg at that time, he could be a soccer player now.
② If you wore this suit, you would look fantastic.
③ If I had not believed in myself, I could not have succeeded.
④ If it had not snowed last night, the road would not have been slippery now.
⑤ If the truck driver had slowed down, the accident would not have happened.

대표유형 03 I wish 가정법

08 다음 중 빈칸에 들어갈 말이 나머지 넷과 다른 것은?

① I wear glasses. I wish I ________ good eyesight.
② If she ________ no work to do, she would go and help her friend.
③ I wish it ________ not raining right now.
④ Mike is boring. I wish he ________ a sense of humor.
⑤ I would have given you the news if you ________ called me yesterday.

Answers p. 30

09 다음 우리말과 같도록 빈칸에 알맞은 것은?

> 내가 피아노 치는 법을 배웠다면 좋을 텐데.
> ➔ I wish I ________ how to play the piano.

① learned ② will learn ③ learn
④ had learned ⑤ would learn

10 다음 문장 중 의미가 나머지 넷과 다른 것은?

① I'm sorry that I didn't see the movie.
② I regret I didn't see the movie.
③ I wish I had seen the movie.
④ I shouldn't have seen the movie.
⑤ It's a pity that I didn't see the movie.

11 다음 두 문장의 뜻이 같을 때 빈칸에 알맞은 것은?

> I'm sorry that Nick doesn't help me.
> ➔ I wish Nick ________ me.

① helps ② didn't help ③ helped
④ has helped ⑤ had helped

12 다음 문장의 빈칸에 들어갈 말로 알맞은 것은?

> I was mean to Mom. I wish I ________ nice to her.

① was ② had been ③ would be
④ were ⑤ have been

대표유형 04 as if 가정법

13 다음 우리말을 영어로 바르게 나타낸 것은?

> 그는 마치 외계인을 만났던 것처럼 말한다.

① He talks as if he met an alien.
② He talked as if he met an alien.
③ He talks as if he has met an alien.
④ He talked as if he has met an alien.
⑤ He talks as if he had met an alien.

14 다음 문장이 의미하는 것으로 가장 알맞은 것은?

> Chris spends money as if he were rich.

① Chris wants to be rich.
② In fact, Chris is not rich.
③ In fact, Chris was not rich.
④ Chris said that he was rich.
⑤ Chris makes a lot of money.

15 다음 중 어법상 어색한 문장의 개수는?

> ⓐ I wish I could dance well.
> ⓑ She always acts as if she were an adult.
> ⓒ If we have been in a hurry, we could have taken the train.
> ⓓ He talked as if he hadn't done anything wrong.

① 1개 ② 2개 ③ 3개 ④ 4개 ⑤ 없음

16 다음 글의 흐름상 빈칸에 들어갈 알맞은 말을 쓰시오.

> Julia acts as if she had read the book. In fact, she ________ ________ it.

대표유형 05 Without 가정법

17 다음 문장의 빈칸에 들어갈 말로 알맞은 것은?

> ________ this translation app, I could not communicate with foreigners.

① But ② Not for ③ Because
④ Without ⑤ Thanks to

18 다음 밑줄 친 부분과 바꿔 쓸 수 있는 것을 모두 고르면?

> Without my grandpa, I would never have had the life I have.

① But my grandpa
② But for my grandpa
③ If it were for my grandpa
④ If it were not for my grandpa
⑤ If it had not been for my grandpa

01 다음 주어진 문장과 의미가 통하는 가정법 문장을 쓰시오.

(1) As I don't have enough strawberries, I can't make strawberry jam.

→ ______________________________

(2) Because we were wearing seatbelts, we were not seriously injured.

→ ______________________________

(3) I'm sorry that our classroom doesn't have an air conditioner.

→ ______________________________

02 다음 우리말을 〈조건〉에 맞게 영작하시오.

(1) 그는 마치 전부 이해했던 것처럼 고개를 끄덕였다.

[조건] **1.** 가정법 과거완료를 사용할 것
2. nod his head, understand, everything을 활용할 것

→ ______________________________

(2) 가족이 없다면 나는 아무것도 아닐 것이다.

[조건] **1.** 가정법 과거를 사용할 것
2. my family, nothing을 포함한 7단어로 쓸 것

→ ______________________________

03 다음 그림을 보고, 괄호 안의 표현을 이용하여 I wish 가정법 문장을 완성하시오.

→ ______________ last night instead of ______________.
(study, sleep)

[Self-Editing Checklist] ✔ 대·소문자를 바르게 썼나요? Y N ✔ 철자와 문장 부호를 바르게 썼나요? Y N

UNIT 12

일치, 화법, 특수 구문

핵심 개념 바로 확인 I know! ☺ No idea! 😐

- 문장에서 주어의 인칭이나 수에 따라 동사의 형태를 맞추는 것이 수의 일치이다. ☺ 😐
- 종속절의 시제를 주절의 시제에 맞추는 것이 시제의 일치이다. ☺ 😐

개념 49 수 일치

월 일

Every student has to arrive here in an hour.

Two hours is the usual time required.

One-third of the total time has passed.

One-third of the trees were already cut.

A number of people were standing on the ground.

주어의 종류	수
every / each + 명사	단수 취급
나라, 작품, 학문 이름	
시간, 거리, 금액, 무게	
the number of + 복수 명사	
분수, 부분 표현 + 단수 명사	
단일 개념의 「*A* and *B*」	
a number of + 복수 명사	복수 취급
the + 형용사 (복수의 의미)	
분수, 부분 표현 + 복수 명사	
both (*A* and *B*)	
항상 복수형인 명사 (e.g. socks)	

바로 개념

1 동사의 형태는 주어의 수와 인칭에 일치시킨다.
2 주어를 꾸미는 어구가 있을 때 주어가 무엇인지 잘 파악하여 동사의 수를 일치시킨다.

고르며 개념 확인

Answers p. 31

01 Those scissors ○ look ○ looks sharp and dangerous.

02 There ○ is ○ are a number of benches in this park.

03 Both of them ○ know ○ knows the fact that you did a great job.

04 One-fourth of the students ○ is ○ are from Japan.

05 These days the number of newborn babies ○ is ○ are decreasing.

06 Ten thousand dollars ○ is ○ are quite a lot of money for me.

쓰며 개념 정리

07 '로미오와 줄리엣'은 셰익스피어에 의해 쓰였다. *Romeo and Juliet* [ ] written by Shakespeare.

08 그 신발은 즉시 닦여야 한다. The shoes [ ] to be cleaned immediately.

09 각 소방관들이 불을 끄려고 노력하고 있다. Each firefighter [ ] trying to put out the fire.

10 눈의 2/3가 치워졌다. Two-thirds of the snow [ ] cleared.

11 물리는 내가 가장 좋아하는 과목이다. Physics [ ] my favorite subject.

12 대부분의 책이 불탔다. Most of the books [ ] burned.

개념 50 시제 일치

I know that she was in the hospital.
주절(현재) 종속절(과거)

I knew that she had been in the hospital.
주절(과거) 종속절(과거완료)

He said that one swallow doesn't make a summer.
주절(과거) 종속절(예외: 속담)

I learned that Edison invented the light bulb.
주절(과거) 종속절(예외: 역사적 사실)

I wished I were with you at that time.
주절(과거) 종속절(예외: 가정법)

시제 일치

주절의 시제	종속절의 시제
현재	시제 상관없음
과거	과거 / 과거완료

시제 일치의 예외

예외인 경우	종속절의 시제
불변의 진리, 속담, 현재의 사실, 습관 등	항상 현재
역사적 사실	항상 과거
가정법이 쓰인 종속절, 비교 구문 등	주절에 영향 받지 않음

바로 개념

1 영어 문장에서 종속절의 시제는 주절의 시제에 맞춘다.
2 주절의 시제가 현재일 때 종속절의 시제는 어느 것이나 쓸 수 있지만, 주절의 시제가 과거일 때에는 종속절의 시제를 과거 또는 과거완료로 쓴다. 단, 예외인 경우에는 주절의 시제와 상관없이 정해진 시제로 쓴다.

고르며 개념 확인

Answers p. 31

01 We knew that something ○ has happened ○ had happened .

02 She knew the fact that World War II ○ broke ○ had broken out in 1939.

03 We learned that the sun ○ sets ○ set in the west.

04 He looked healthier last year than he ○ does ○ did now.

쓰며 개념 정리

05 My aunt tells me that every cloud has a silver lining.
→ My aunt told me that ______.

06 I think that we did our best to win the game.
→ I thought that ______ to win the game.

07 Tom wonders if I can go with him to meet Mr. Morgan.
→ Tom wondered if ______ to meet Mr. Morgan.

★08 I want to ask him what he was looking for in the attic.
→ I wanted to ask him ______ in the attic.

★ 종속절의 일이 주절의 일보다 먼저 일어났다는 점에 유의한다.

Answers p. 31

개념 49 수 일치

1 동사의 형태는 주어의 [　　　　] 와 인칭에 일치시킨다.

주어의 종류	수	예
every / each + 명사	단수 취급	Every girl has ...
나라, 작품, 학문 이름		
시간, 거리, 금액, 무게		
the number of + 복수 명사		
분수, 부분 표현 + 단수 명사		Two-fifths of the cake was ...
단일 개념의 「*A* and *B*」		Curry and rice is ...
a number of + 복수 명사	복수 취급	
the + 형용사 (복수의 의미)		
분수, 부분 표현 + 복수 명사		
both (*A* and *B*)		
항상 복수형인 명사 (e.g. socks)		

* 알맞은 예를 생각하여 빈칸에 쓰세요.

개념 50 시제 일치

1 영어 문장에서 종속절의 시제는 [　　　　] 의 시제에 맞춘다. 그러나 항상 현재 시제 또는 과거 시제로 쓰이는 예외의 경우도 있다.

2 주절의 시제가 현재일 때 종속절의 시제는 어느 것이나 쓸 수 있지만, 주절의 시제가 과거일 때에는 종속절의 시제를 [　　　　] 또는 [　　　　] 로 쓴다.

시제 일치의 예외인 경우	종속절의 시제	예
불변의 진리, 속담, 현재의 사실, 습관 등	항상 현재	
역사적 사실	항상 과거	
가정법이 쓰인 종속절, 비교 구문 등	주절에 영향 받지 않음	

* 205쪽에서 각각의 경우에 해당하는 문장을 찾아 쓰세요.

Answers p. 31

A 밑줄 친 동사가 알맞으면 그대로 두고, 어색하면 고쳐 쓰시오.

01 Half of the students wants to join the club.

02 Did they know I will move to another city?

03 Every house has a small garden in that village.

04 My mother said that an early bird catches the worm.

05 I thought that I could do volunteer work in that area.

06 *A Tale of Two Cities* were first published in 1859.

07 A number of birds on the tree was twittering loudly.

08 Two-thirds of the salt was put into the boiling water.

09 Most of the mushrooms has to be used for making soup.

10 They found that Mr. Donovan has scratched my car that day.

B 괄호 안의 단어를 활용하여 우리말과 같은 뜻의 문장을 완성하시오.

01 매일은 모두에게 새로운 날이다. (each)

→ ______ ______ ______ a new day for everyone.

02 두 시간은 아이들이 조용히 있기에는 긴 시간이다. (hour)

→ ______ ______ ______ a long time for children to stay calm.

03 너는 내가 새 차를 샀다는 걸 그에게 말했니? (buy)

→ Did you tell him that ______ ______ ______ a new car?

04 우리는 세종대왕이 한글을 발명했다는 것을 배웠다. (invent)

→ We learned that King Sejong ______ Hangeul.

05 그녀는 늦게 잠자리에 들었다고 말했다. (go to bed)

→ She said that she ______ ______ ______ ______ late.

06 그 책들의 1/3은 한 작은 학교에 보내졌다. (send)

→ One-third of the books ______ ______ to a small school.

비교하며 문장 쓰기

			표현 노트
361	모든 언어가 처음엔 어렵다.	All languages are hard at first.	every
	모든 언어가 처음엔 어렵다.	Every language is hard at first.	
362	모든 그림들이 하루 만에 팔렸다.	All of the paintings were sold in a day.	most, the signs, on the stores
	가게의 간판들은 대부분 빨간색이었다.		
363	그는 그가 무엇을 잘못했는지 이제 깨닫는다.	He now realizes what he did wrong.	wrong
	그는 그가 무엇을 잘못했었는지 깨달았다. ★ 종속절을 과거완료 시제로 쓸 것		
364	미국은 북아메리카에 있다.	The United States is in North America.	The Netherlands, “low lands”
	네덜란드는 ‘저지대’를 의미한다.		
365	나는 그가 항상 늦게 일어난다는 것을 알고 있었어.	I knew that he always gets up late.	that day
	나는 그가 그날 늦게 일어났다는 것을 알고 있었어.		
366	사람들 중 절반이 애완동물을 소유하고 있다.	Half of the people have pets.	the money, steal
	돈의 절반이 도난당했다.		
367	학생들의 약 3분의 1은 안경을 쓴다.	About one-third of the students wear glasses.	the country, be covered with, forest
	그 나라의 3분의 2는 숲으로 뒤덮여 있다.		
368	각 팀에는 4명이 있다.	Each team has four people.	both, fight for the football
	양 팀은 미식축구 공을 차지하기 위해 싸우고 있었다.		

Answers p. 31

표현 이용하여 문장 쓰기

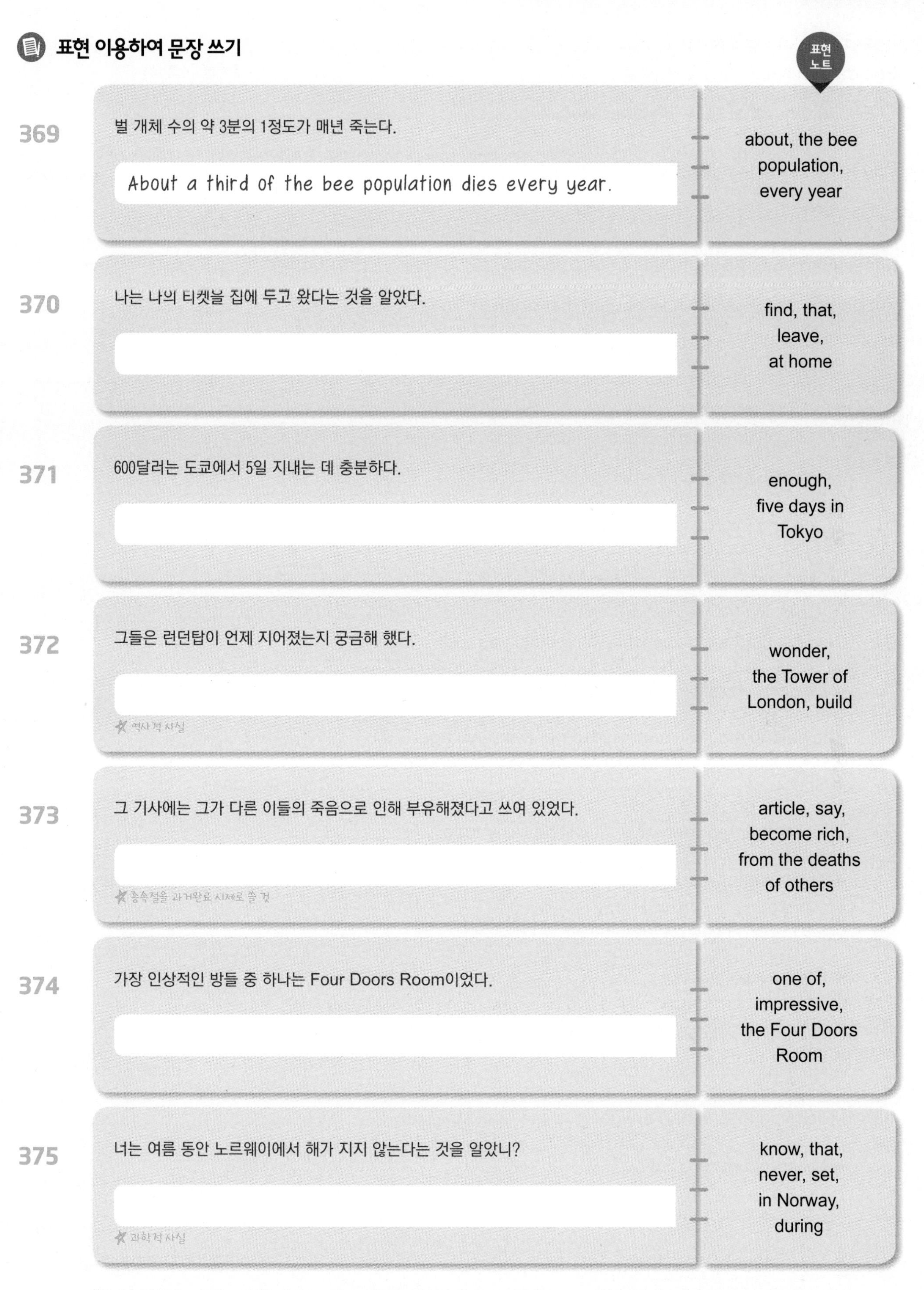

표현 노트

369 벌 개체 수의 약 3분의 1정도가 매년 죽는다.

About a third of the bee population dies every year.

about, the bee population, every year

370 나는 나의 티켓을 집에 두고 왔다는 것을 알았다.

find, that, leave, at home

371 600달러는 도쿄에서 5일 지내는 데 충분하다.

enough, five days in Tokyo

372 그들은 런던탑이 언제 지어졌는지 궁금해 했다.

★ 역사적 사실

wonder, the Tower of London, build

373 그 기사에는 그가 다른 이들의 죽음으로 인해 부유해졌다고 쓰여 있었다.

★ 종속절을 과거완료 시제로 쓸 것

article, say, become rich, from the deaths of others

374 가장 인상적인 방들 중 하나는 Four Doors Room이었다.

one of, impressive, the Four Doors Room

375 너는 여름 동안 노르웨이에서 해가 지지 않는다는 것을 알았니?

★ 과학적 사실

know, that, never, set, in Norway, during

[Self-Editing Checklist] ✓ 대·소문자를 바르게 썼나요? Y N ✓ 철자와 문장 부호를 바르게 썼나요? Y N

개념 51 평서문의 화법 전환

월 일

Eric said to her, "They like your idea."

→ Eric **told** her **that** they **liked** her idea.

Dad said, "Dinner will be ready soon."

→ Dad said **that** dinner **would** be ready soon.

Ella said to Joe, "I bought this book for you."

→ Ella **told** Joe **that** she **had bought that** book for **him**.

평서문의 화법 전환	
동사 전환	say는 그대로 / say to → tell
주절과 피전달문 연결	접속사 that으로 연결 (인용 부호, 콤마 등 생략)
피전달문 나머지 부분 일치시키기	• 주절의 동사가 과거일 때 시제 일치: 현재 → 과거 / 과거 → 과거완료 • 대명사와 부사(구): 내용과 주절의 시점에 맞춰 전환 this → that here → there now → then ago → before today → that day yesterday → the day before 등

바로 개념

1 다른 사람이 한 말을 그대로 전하는 것을 직접 화법이라고 한다. 직접 화법은 전달하는 사람의 입장에서 바꿔 말하는 간접 화법으로 전환하여 쓸 수 있다.

2 직접 화법을 간접 화법으로 전환할 때, 주어와 주절의 시점에 유의하여 시제와 대명사, 부사구 등을 전환한다.

쓰며 개념 정리

Answers p. 32

01 David said to me, "The white shirt suits you well."

➔ David [told] me that the white shirt [suited] [me] well.

02 She said to me, "My aunt visited me two days ago."

➔ She [ ] me that [ ] aunt had visited her two days [ ].

03 The weather reporter says, "It will be rainy today."

➔ The weather reporter says that [ ] [ ] [ ] rainy today.

04 Robby said, "I can't remember what she said."

➔ Robby said that he [ ] [ ] what she [ ] [ ].

05 Ms. Harrison said, "My family moved here three years ago."

➔ Ms. Harrison said that her family [ ] [ ] [ ] three years before.

06 Miller said to Karen, "I am going to the bookstore now."

➔ Miller told Karen that he [ ] [ ] to the bookstore [ ].

07 My mother said to me, "I will go on a trip tomorrow."

➔ My mother told me that [ ] [ ] [ ] on a trip the next day.

개념 52 의문문과 명령문의 화법 전환

월 일

He said, "Did you open the window?"

→ He asked if I had opened the window.

I said to him, "What will you have for lunch?"

→ I asked him what he would have for lunch.

Mr. Austin said to me, "Bring your umbrella."

→ Mr. Austin advised me to bring my umbrella.

	의문문의 화법 전환	명령문의 화법 전환
동사 전환	ask	• 지시: tell • 충고: advise • 부탁, 요청: ask • 명령: order
주절과 피전달문 연결	• 의문사 또는 if/whether로 연결 • 피전달문 어순: 의문사 / if [whether] + 주어 + 동사	• 긍정명령문: → to부정사 • 부정명령문: → not + to부정사
피전달문 나머지 부분 일치시키기	• 시제 일치 • 대명사와 부사(구) 일치시키기	

바로 개념

1 의문문의 직접 화법을 간접 화법으로 전환할 때, 피전달문을 연결하는 접속사로 의문사 또는 if [whether]를 사용한다.

2 명령문의 직접 화법을 간접 화법으로 전환할 때, 피전달문은 to부정사구로 바꾸어 쓴다.

고르며 개념 확인

Answers p. 32

01 She said to me, "Can I use the phone?"

→ She asked me ○ that ○ if she could use the phone.

02 The seller said to me, "Why did you buy the old car?"

→ The seller asked me why I ○ bought ○ had bought the old car.

03 She said to me, "Turn down the volume."

→ She told me ○ that ○ to turn down the volume.

04 I said to him, "How do you know her?"

→ I asked him ○ how ○ whether he ○ knows ○ knew her.

쓰며 개념 정리

05 그는 나에게 그를 기다리지 말라고 말했다. (to, him, not, wait, for)

→ He told me ______________________.

06 Lucy는 내게 Joe가 괜찮은지 물었다. (Joe, okay, if, was)

→ Lucy asked me ______________________.

07 그녀는 Brandon에게 그날 날씨가 어땠는지 물었다. (how, had, the weather, that day, been)

→ She asked Brandon ______________________.

개념 51 평서문의 화법 전환

1 다른 사람이 한 말을 그대로 전하는 것이 ______ 화법이고, 이것을 전달하는 사람의 입장에서 바꿔 말하는 ______ 화법으로 전환하여 쓸 수 있다.

2 직접 화법을 간접 화법으로 전환할 때, 주어와 주절의 시점에 유의하여 시제와 대명사, 부사구 등을 전환한다.

평서문의 화법 전환			
동사 전환	• say는 그대로 • say to → ______	주절과 피전달문 연결	접속사 ______으로 연결 (인용 부호, 콤마 등 생략)
피전달문 나머지 부분 일치시키기	• 주절의 동사가 과거일 때 시제 일치: 현재 → ______ / 과거 → ______ • 대명사와 부사(구): 내용과 주절의 시점에 맞춰 전환 this → ______ here → ______ now → ______ ago → ______ today → ______ yesterday → ______		

개념 52 의문문과 명령문의 화법 전환

	의문문의 화법 전환	명령문의 화법 전환
동사 전환	ask	• 지시: ______ • 충고: ______ • 부탁, 요청: ______ • 명령: ______
주절과 피전달문 연결	• 의문사 또는 ______로 연결 • 피전달문 어순: 의문사 / ______ + 주어 + 동사	• 긍정명령문: → to부정사 • 부정명령문: → ______ + to부정사
피전달문 나머지 부분 일치시키기	• 시제 일치 • 대명사와 부사(구) 일치시키기	

A 다음 문장을 간접 화법으로 전환하시오.

01 She said to me, "I haven't visited their office."

→ She told me that ________ their office.

02 Mr. White said, "She is going to meet me tomorrow."

→ Mr. White said that she was going to ________.

03 I said to him, "Whom did you recommend as a cook?"

→ I asked him ________ as a cook.

04 The baker said to the kids, "Taste these cookies."

→ The baker asked the kids ________.

05 Ms. Barry said to her students, "Don't make noise here."

→ Ms. Barry told her students ________.

06 Oscar's mother said to him, "Go to bed early."

→ Oscar's mother advised him ________.

07 A man said to me, "How can I get to Lincoln Park?"

→ A man asked me ________.

08 Gordon said to her, "What movie do you want to see today?"

→ Gordon asked her ________ that day.

09 The teacher said to me, "Why were you late for class?"

→ The teacher asked me ________ for class.

10 She said to him, "I didn't like your idea first."

→ She told him that ________ first.

11 I said to the girl, "Do you like playing basketball here?"

→ I asked the girl ________ there.

12 Annie says to me, "I will buy something nice for you on your birthday."

→ Annie says that ________ on my birthday.

화법 전환하기 1

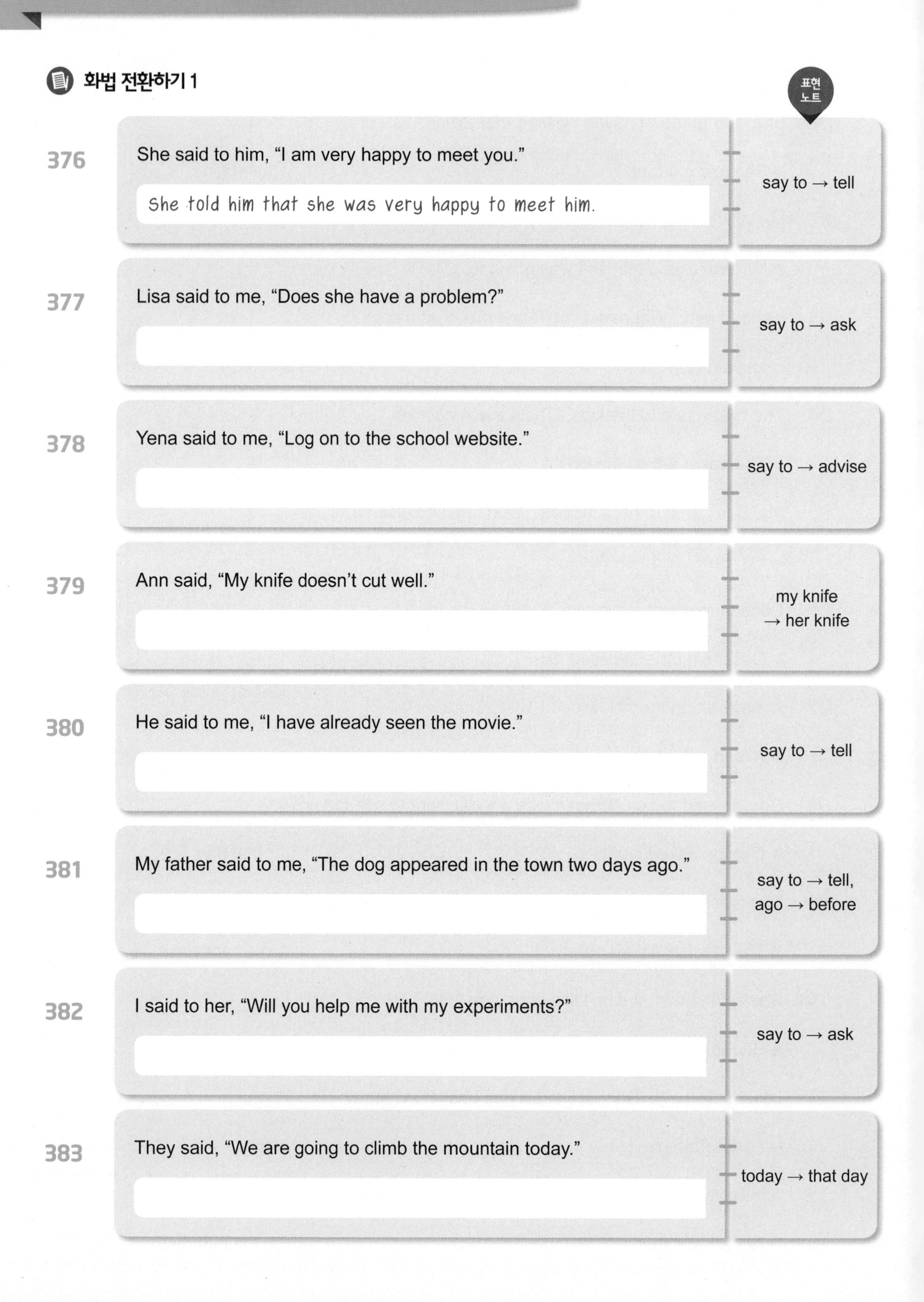

표현 노트

376 She said to him, "I am very happy to meet you."

She told him that she was very happy to meet him.

say to → tell

377 Lisa said to me, "Does she have a problem?"

say to → ask

378 Yena said to me, "Log on to the school website."

say to → advise

379 Ann said, "My knife doesn't cut well."

my knife → her knife

380 He said to me, "I have already seen the movie."

say to → tell

381 My father said to me, "The dog appeared in the town two days ago."

say to → tell, ago → before

382 I said to her, "Will you help me with my experiments?"

say to → ask

383 They said, "We are going to climb the mountain today."

today → that day

Answers p. 32

화법 전환하기 2

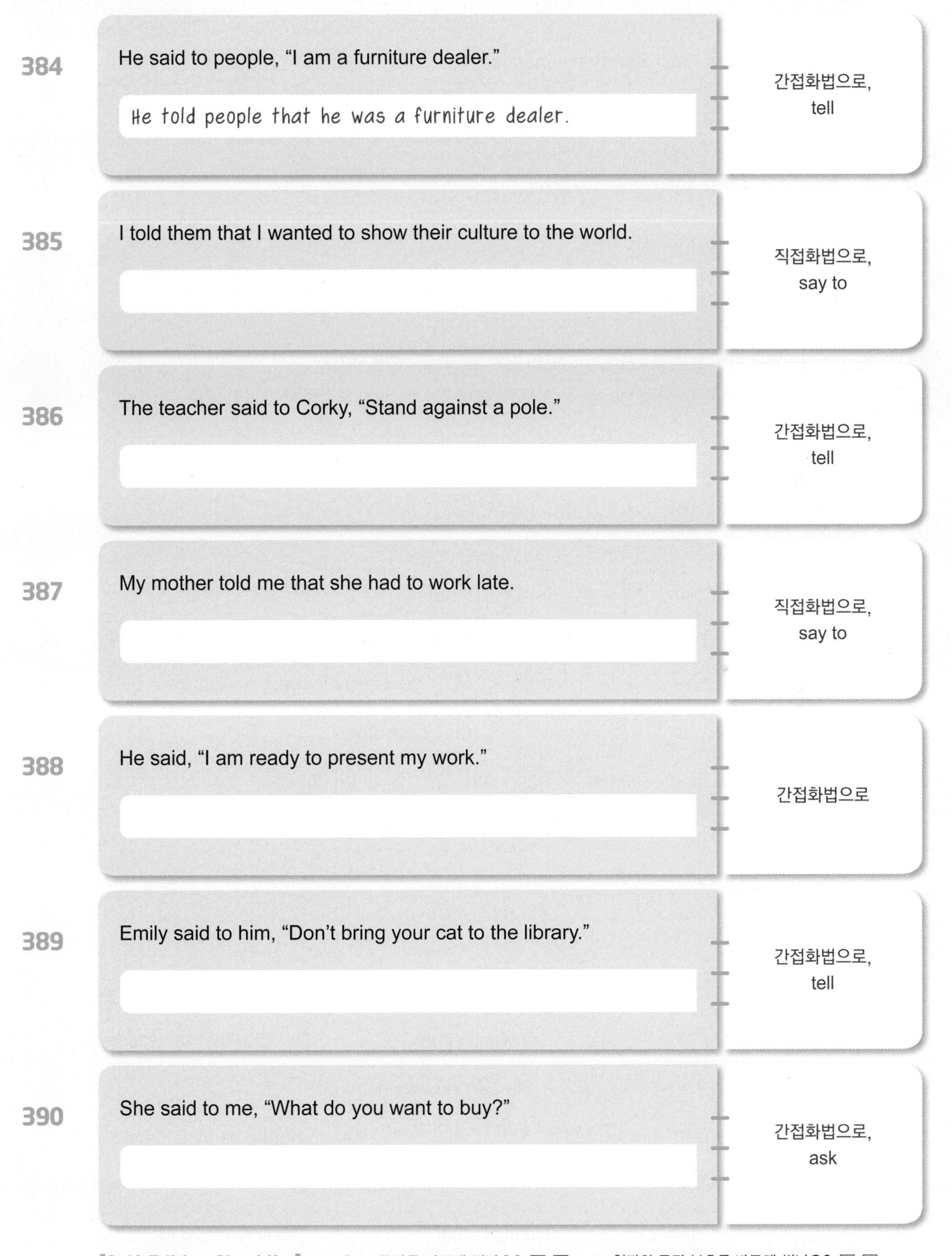

384 He said to people, "I am a furniture dealer."

He told people that he was a furniture dealer.

간접화법으로, tell

385 I told them that I wanted to show their culture to the world.

직접화법으로, say to

386 The teacher said to Corky, "Stand against a pole."

간접화법으로, tell

387 My mother told me that she had to work late.

직접화법으로, say to

388 He said, "I am ready to present my work."

간접화법으로

389 Emily said to him, "Don't bring your cat to the library."

간접화법으로, tell

390 She said to me, "What do you want to buy?"

간접화법으로, ask

[Self-Editing Checklist] ✔ 대 • 소문자를 바르게 썼나요? Y N ✔ 철자와 문장 부호를 바르게 썼나요? Y N

개념 53 강조

월 일

It is this old book that he has been looking for.
강조되는 말 (목적어)

It was in the park where I met Benny by chance.
강조되는 말 (부사구)

He did love the song, so he sang it every day.

This is the very painting she wants to buy.

I'm not sleepy at all.

「It ~ that」 강조 구문	It + be동사 + 강조할 말 + that ~ └ 주어, 목적어, 부사구 * 강조되는 말에 따라 that 대신 who, whom, when, where 등 사용 가능
동사 강조	do [does, did] + 동사원형
명사 강조	the very + 명사
부정어 강조	not ~ at all / not ~ in the least

바로 개념

1 「It ~ that」 강조 구문은 'It + be동사'와 that 사이에 강조하려는 어구를 넣는다.
2 동사는 조동사 do로, 명사는 the very로, 부정어는 at all과 in the least 등의 표현을 써서 강조한다.

고르며 개념 확인

Answers p. 32

01 It was two days ago ○ that ○ what the satellite stopped working.

02 It was Charles Darwin ○ when ○ who introduced the theory first.

03 Your parents ○ does ○ do feel sorry for you.

04 He did ○ believe ○ believed the ghost story.

05 I don't want to eat lunch with her ○ the least ○ in the least .

06 This is ○ so very ○ the very bicycle the famous athlete used.

쓰며 개념 정리

07 그녀를 가장 보고 싶어 하는 사람은 David이다. It is David ______ wants to see her most.

08 축제가 열린 것은 7월이었다. It was in July ______ the festival was held.

09 그는 전혀 피곤하지 않다고 말했다. He said he was not tired ______ ______.

10 나는 거기에서 누군가 노래하는 걸 분명히 들었다. I ______ hear someone singing there.

11 내가 배우고 있는 것은 한국어였다. It was the Korean language ______ I was learning.

12 이곳이 모차르트가 태어난 바로 그곳이다. This is the ______ place where Mozart was born.

개념 54 도치

월 일

Never did he think **he could find the treasure.**
일반동사일 때 do[does, did]를 이용해 도치

Hardly will you eat **anything after the surgery.**

Only then did we understand **the problem.**

On the platform stood a young boy.

Here comes the bus! / **Here he comes!**

A: I don't like sports. – B: Neither do I.

문장의 앞에 오는 어구	문장 구조
부정어	부정어 + 조동사 + 주어 + 동사 부정어 not, no, never, little, hardly, rarely, seldom, scarcely, ...
only를 포함한 부사구	부사구 + 조동사 + 주어 + 동사
장소·방향의 부사구	부사구 + 동사 + 주어 *주어가 대명사일 때: 부사구 + 주어 + 동사
there / here	There + be동사 + 주어 (…이 있다) Here + 동사 + 주어 * 주어가 대명사일 때: Here + 주어 + 동사
so / neither	So / Neither + (조)동사 + 주어 (…도 역시 그렇다)

1 주어와 동사의 위치가 바뀌는 것을 도치라고 한다.
2 주로 부정어나 부사구 등을 강조하기 위해 문장의 맨 앞에 쓸 때 도치가 일어난다.

고르며 개념 확인

Answers p. 33

01 Rarely ○ fought they ○ did they fight with other groups.

02 **A** I loved that show! – **B** ○ So I did. ○ So did I.

03 On their right side ○ the statue was ○ was the statue .

04 Scarcely ○ I could breathe ○ could I breathe because of the yellow dust.

쓰며 개념 정리 밑줄 친 부분 강조하여 문장 다시 쓰기

05 Some examples of his theory are <u>here</u>.

➔ ______________________

06 Mr. Hardy <u>seldom</u> takes off his hat in the office.

➔ ______________________ in the office.

07 The rain came <u>down</u> suddenly.

➔ ______________________ suddenly.

08 We have <u>never</u> met again since 2016.

➔ ______________________ since 2016.

Answers p. 33

개념 53 강조

「It ~ that」 강조 구문	( ) + be동사 + 강조할 말 + ( ) ~ └→ 주어, 목적어, 부사구 * 강조되는 말에 따라 ( ) 대신 who, whom, when, where 등 사용 가능
동사 강조	( ) + 동사원형
명사 강조	( ) + 명사
부정어 강조	not ~ ( ) / not ~ ( )

개념 54 도치

1 주어와 동사의 위치가 ( ) 것을 도치라고 한다.

2 주로 부정어나 부사구 등을 강조하기 위해 문장의 ( )에 쓸 때 도치가 일어난다.

문장의 앞에 오는 어구	문장 구조	예
부정어	부정어 + 조동사 + 주어 + 동사 부정어 not, no, never, little, hardly, rarely, seldom, scarcely, ...	
only를 포함한 부사구	부사구 + 조동사 + 주어 + 동사	
장소·방향의 부사구	부사구 + 동사 + 주어 * 주어가 대명사일 때: 부사구 + 주어 + 동사	
there / here	There + be동사 + 주어 (…이 있다) Here + 동사 + 주어 * 주어가 대명사일 때: Here + 주어 + 동사	
so / neither	So / Neither + (조)동사 + 주어 (…도 역시 그렇다)	

* 217쪽에서 각각의 경우에 해당하는 문장을 찾아 쓰세요.

Answers p. 33

A 다음 문장의 밑줄 친 부분을 강조하여 다시 쓰시오.

01 Dana called Maggie at noon.

→ It was ______.

02 They understood what you said.

→ They ______.

03 That was the part I wanted to tell.

→ That was ______.

04 He does not take care of the dogs.

→ He does not ______.

05 It was not a good result for me.

→ It was not ______.

06 Miguel noticed the error in the article.

→ It was ______.

07 My class is going to have a picnic at the park.

→ It is ______.

B 다음 문장의 밑줄 친 부분에서 어법상 틀린 부분을 고쳐 다시 쓰시오.

01 Never I have lied to my mom.

→ ______

02 **A** I liked the restaurant. **B** So I did.

→ ______

03 On the hill did the small school stand.

→ ______

04 Scarcely did they had breakfast.

→ ______

05 In front of the house a big apple tree was.

→ ______

비교하며 문장 쓰기

번호	우리말	영어	포인트
391	그는 문학을 가장 사랑했다.	He loved literature most.	「It ~ that」 강조 구문
	그가 가장 사랑한 것은 문학이었다.	It was literature that he loved most.	
392	Frodo에게 생명을 불어넣은 그 작가는 영국인이었다.	The writer who gave life to Frodo was British.	명사 강조, the very
	Frodo에게 생명을 불어넣은 바로 그 작가는 영국인이었다.		
393	이것은 무서워 보이지 않는다.	This one doesn't look scary.	부정어 강조, at all
	이것은 전혀 무서워 보이지 않는다.		
394	우리들은 가장 훌륭한 대장장이다.	We are the finest smiths.	「It ~ who」 강조 구문
	가장 훌륭한 대장장이는 우리들이다.		
395	난 네가 여기 올 것이라고 예상하지 못했어.	I never expected that you would come here.	부정어 강조, 도치
	난 네가 여기 올 것이라고 예상하지 못했어.		
396	중앙에 한 남자가 등장한다.	A man appears in the center.	장소의 부사구 강조, 도치
	중앙에 한 남자가 등장한다.		
397	시금치는 많은 영양분을 가지고 있다.	Spinach has a lot of nutrients.	동사 강조
	시금치는 정말 많은 영양분을 가지고 있다.		
398	1969년에 아폴로 11호가 달에 착륙했다.	Apollo 11 landed on the moon in 1969.	「It ~ that」 강조 구문
	아폴로 11호가 달에 착륙한 것은 1969년이었다.		

Answers p. 33

배열하여 문장 쓰기

399
튼튼한 뼈와 치아를 만드는 것은 칼슘이다.
(builds, and, calcium, it, teeth, is, that, strong bones)

It is calcium that builds strong bones and teeth.

400
당신을 기다리고 있는 멋진 동아리와 활동들이 많다.
(many, waiting for you, are, clubs and activities, there)

401
나는 Howard가 다른 사람들에게 나쁜 말을 하는 것을 거의 들어본 적이 없었다.
(hear, say, I, to others, bad words, hardly, Howard, did)

부정어를 강조하여 맨 앞에 쓸 것

402
호텔 바로 앞에 마켓 스퀘어가 있었다.
(the hotel, Market Square, in front of, was, right)

부사구를 강조하여 맨 앞에 쓸 것

403
내가 생일선물로 받고 싶은 것은 기타이다.
(to get, I, a guitar, it, for my birthday gift, is, want, that)

404
내가 사하라 사막에서 어린 왕자를 만난 것은 6년 전이었다.
(that, in the Sahara Desert, six years ago, it, I, was, the little prince, met)

405
저것이 그 기자가 전쟁 중에 찍은 바로 그 사진이다.
(that, the reporter, during, the very, is, photo, that, took, the war)

[Self-Editing Checklist] 대 • 소문자를 바르게 썼나요? Y N 철자와 문장 부호를 바르게 썼나요? Y N

대표유형 01 수의 일치

01 다음 문장 중 밑줄 친 부분이 어법상 어색한 것은?

① Politics is difficult for me to study.
② Sunglasses are needed to travel there.
③ Nothing was to be seen in the cave.
④ A number of students is waiting there.
⑤ The Netherlands is in Europe.

[02-03] 빈칸에 알맞은 말이 순서대로 짝지어진 것을 고르시오.

02

• Two-thirds of the peach which I was going to eat ________ rotten.
• Two-thirds of the children ________ running to the ballpark.

① is – is ② was – was ③ were – was
④ was – were ⑤ were – were

03

• Neither you nor he ________ to blame.
• This car together with those cars ________ to the company.

① is – belongs ② is – belong
③ are – belong ④ are – belongs
⑤ is – belonging

04 다음 문장 중 어법상 어색한 것은?

① Each girl has her own umbrella.
② All the money was spent by my sister.
③ Mathematics is an interesting subject.
④ Every member was eating snacks.
⑤ Half of the apples in the basket is red.

05 다음 문장의 밑줄 친 부분을 어법에 맞게 고친 것은?

Do you know whose socks this is?

① this are ② this was ③ is this
④ these is ⑤ these are

06 다음 문장 중 빈칸에 is가 들어갈 수 없는 것은?

① Ham and eggs ________ always delicious.
② Three miles ________ too long for the child.
③ The old ________ respected in our society.
④ The number of cars ________ increasing now.
⑤ *The Three Musketeers* ________ well-known to us.

대표유형 02 시제의 일치

07 다음 문장의 밑줄 친 부분 중 어법상 어색한 것은?

She didn't ①know that I ②tell a lie ③to her before. ④However, she didn't ⑤believe me.

08 다음 문장의 밑줄 친 동사를 과거형으로 바꾸어 다시 쓴 문장으로 알맞은 것은?

I think that he doesn't want it.

① I thought that he doesn't want it.
② I thought that he didn't want it.
③ I thought that he hasn't want it.
④ I thought that he hasn't wanted it.
⑤ I thought that he hadn't wanted it.

[09-10] 다음 중 어법상 어색한 것을 고르시오.

09
① I said that I get up at 7 every day.
② He told me that he would be back soon.
③ She said that an accident would happen.
④ Amy thought that the boy could survive.
⑤ We learned that Columbus had discovered America in 1492.

10
① I promise that I will never be late again.
② My mom knew that I hadn't had lunch.
③ Two thousand dollars is needed to help the children.
④ My neighbor said that she came back to the town the day before.
⑤ The students learned that the Earth goes around the Sun.

대표유형 03 화법의 전환

11 다음 문장을 간접 화법을 활용하여 바르게 전환한 것은?

> He said to me, "I need your help now."

① He told me that he needs my help now.
② He told me that he needed his help now.
③ He told me that he needs your help then.
④ He told me that he needed my help then.
⑤ He told me that he needed your help then.

12 주어진 문장을 다음과 같이 바꿔 쓸 때, 빈칸에 알맞은 말이 순서대로 바르게 짝지어진 것은?

> She said to me, "Can I use your pen?"
> ➔ She asked me if _____ could use _____ pen.

① she – her ② I – her ③ she – my
④ I – my ⑤ she – your

[13-14] 다음 문장 중 어법상 자연스러운 것을 고르시오.

13 ① Tom asked her where was she going.
② Ava told not me to open the window.
③ He told me that he will visit me soon.
④ She ordered us to leave there at once.
⑤ They asked if they can enter the house.

14 ① I told him that she will show me the way.
② John said me, "Shall I bring you water?"
③ She asked Liam where he had found the dog.
④ Jacob advised me that go to bed early.
⑤ I asked the baker if was the bread fresh.

15 다음 문장과 바꿔 쓸 수 있는 것은?

> She asked me what I had in the bag.

① She said me, "What do I have in the bag?"
② She asked me, "What you have in the bag?"
③ I said to her, "What do you have in the bag?"
④ She said to me, "What do you have in the bag?"
⑤ She said to me, "What you had in the bag?"

대표유형 04 강조와 도치

16 다음 중 밑줄 친 부분의 쓰임이 주어진 문장과 같은 것은?

> I did love the place.

① I did not go there.
② Do you know the truth?
③ They always do their best.
④ We do have our own plans.
⑤ Do your homework by yourself.

17 다음 대화에서 어법상 어색한 부분은?

> A ① Never ② I have seen ③ such a great film.
> B ④ Neither ⑤ have I.

18 다음 문장 중 어법상 어색한 것은?

① This car is even better than that one.
② There was a small bird on the roof.
③ She doesn't like junk food at all.
④ It was in this room that I saw the book.
⑤ Hardly realized I that the key was missing.

19 다음 두 문장의 빈칸에 공통으로 알맞은 것은?

> • The fact _______ she got married to the actor was surprising.
> • It was in this small town _______ the traveler stayed for several weeks.

① if ② that ③ so
④ where ⑤ whether

20 다음 문장 중 어법상 자연스러운 것은?

① Here they come.
② Here the bus comes.
③ Little I knew about him.
④ Down the hill did the truck run.
⑤ He didn't come, and neither she did.

01 조건에 맞게 대화를 완성하시오.

[조건] 1. 괄호 안의 말을 강조하여 완전한 문장으로 답할 것
2. 「It ~ that」 구문을 사용할 것

(1) **A** Where did he hear the news?

B ______________________________ (on the bus)

(2) **A** Who was being interviewed then?

B ______________________________ (Daniel)

02 다음을 간접 화법의 문장으로 고쳐 쓰시오.

(1) He said to Nancy, "Don't disturb me while I am studying."

→ He told ______________________________.

(2) Kate said to me, "How have you been?"

→ Kate asked ______________________________.

(3) I said to my sister, "Can I borrow your backpack tomorrow?"

→ I asked ______________________________.

수행평가 유형 글 완성형

03 글 (A)를 글 (B)로 고쳐 쓸 때 빈칸에 알맞은 말을 쓰시오.

(A)

I said to Judy, "Why didn't you tell me the news yesterday?" She said to me, "I didn't know it then." She had never lied to me by that time, so I believed her.

⇩

(B)

I asked Judy ______________________________ the day before. She told me that ______________________________. Never ______________________________ by that time, so I believed her.

[Self-Editing Checklist] ✔ 대 • 소문자를 바르게 썼나요? Y N ✔ 철자와 문장 부호를 바르게 썼나요? Y N

배움으로 행복한 내일을 꿈꾸는

천재교육 커뮤니티 안내

교재 안내부터 구매까지 한 번에!

천재교육 홈페이지

자사가 발행하는 참고서, 교과서에 대한 소개는 물론
도서 구매도 할 수 있습니다. 회원에게 지급되는 별을 모아
다양한 상품 응모에도 도전해 보세요!

다양한 교육 꿀팁에 깜짝 이벤트는 덤!

천재교육 인스타그램

천재교육의 새롭고 중요한 소식을 가장 먼저 접하고 싶다면?
천재교육 인스타그램 팔로우가 필수!
깜짝 이벤트도 수시로 진행되니 놓치지 마세요!

수업이 편리해지는

천재교육 ACA 사이트

오직 선생님만을 위한, 천재교육 모든 교재에 대한 정보가 담긴
아카 사이트에서는 다양한 수업자료 및 부가 자료는 물론
시험 출제에 필요한 문제도 다운로드하실 수 있습니다.

https://aca.chunjae.co.kr

천재교육을 사랑하는 샘들의 모임

천사샘

학원 강사, 공부방 선생님이시라면 누구나 가입할 수 있는 천사샘!
교재 개발 및 평가를 통해 교재 검토진으로 참여할 수 있는 기회는 물론
다양한 교사용 교재 증정 이벤트가 선생님을 기다립니다.

아이와 함께 성장하는 학부모들의 모임공간

튠맘 학습연구소

튠맘 학습연구소는 초·중등 학부모를 대상으로 다양한 이벤트와 함께
교재 리뷰 및 학습 정보를 제공하는 네이버 카페입니다.
초등학생, 중학생 자녀를 둔 학부모님이라면 튠맘 학습연구소로 오세요!

문장

바로 쓰는 문법

ANSWERS

CHUNJAE
EDUCATION, INC.

문장

바로 쓰는 문법

Background Knowledge

바로 개념 확인 1 p. 9

01

The girl	주어	in the yellow dress	수식어
gave	동사	me	목적어
this rose	목적어		

02

We	주어	found	동사
the movie	목적어	exciting	보어

바로 개념 확인 2 p. 12

When	접속사	scored	동사
brilliant	형용사	goal	명사
they	대명사	shouted	동사
with	전치사	joy	명사
Hooray	감탄사	finally	부사
won	동사		

바로 개념 확인 3 p. 13

01 구 02 절 03 절

UNIT 01 문장의 형식

개념 01 5형식 1 p. 16

01 to keep
02 to pay
03 happy
04 to turn
05 useful
06 brave
07 not to touch
08 a better man
09 not to be late
10 to believe you
11 Brainy
12 to follow my dream

개념 02 5형식 2 p. 17

01 live
02 move
03 look
04 sleep
05 to answer
06 repaired
07 sing
08 feel alive
09 begging for money
10 to pick up the trash
11 to find your way
12 painted light blue

바로 개념 확인 노트 개념 01–02 p. 18

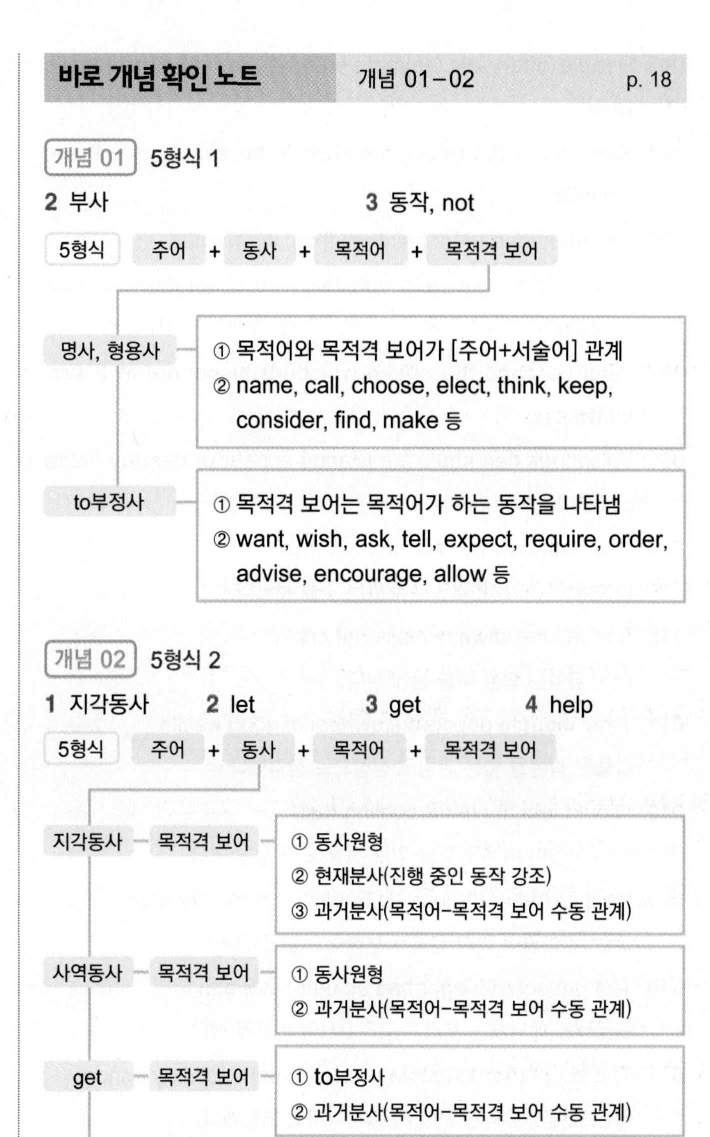

바로 기본 확인 노트 개념 01–02 p. 19

A
01 sprained
02 to wait
03 sleep
04 playing [play]
05 broken
06 quiet
07 (to) solve
08 to raise

B
01 made me learn
02 hear the fire alarm go [going]
03 helps you (to) get
04 hear your name called
05 wanted him to go
06 leave your child alone
07 watched the train leave [leaving]

교과서에서 뽑은 *405* 문장 마스터하기 pp. 20–21

001 I had my bed designed by experts.
002 Living together in one building keeps them safe.

003 People often see animals suffer[suffering] from plastic waste.

004 We wanted the next generation to be able to see these animals.

005 The manager let us paint anything we wanted.

006 Psychology can help you (to) find a solution to your problem.

007 Luigi watched the queen whisper[whispering] in a servant's ear.

008 Volcanoes can make big islands appear or destroy entire cities like Pompeii.

009 I saw our cow lying on the ground.
나는 우리 소가 바닥에 누워 있는 것을 보았다.

010 Sad movies always make me cry.
슬픈 영화는 항상 나를 울게 한다.

011 They thought popcorn a symbol of good health.
그들은 팝콘을 좋은 건강의 상징으로 생각했다.

012 I could feel my heart beating fast.
나는 심장이 빠르게 뛰고 있는 것을 느낄 수 있었다.

013 He advised me to use an English vocabulary app.
그는 내게 영어 어휘 앱을 사용하라고 충고했다.

014 The project manager had us meet at 9 a.m.
프로젝트 매니저는 우리가 오전 9시에 만나게 했다.

015 The king ordered him to go to a famous military school.
왕은 그에게 유명한 군사 학교에 가라고 명령했다.

REVIEW TEST pp. 22-24

01 ①, ③	02 ①	03 ③	04 ③	05 ⑤
06 ③	07 ③	08 ④	09 ④	10 ④
11 ①	12 ①	13 ②	14 ④	15 ①, ③
16 ②	17 ④	18 ③	19 ①	20 ②

서술형 • 수행평가형

01 (1) He named his turtle Edison.
(2) I saw you getting [get] out of the taxi [cab].
(3) This picture helps me remember the trip.

02 made her [Emma] feel annoyed

03 (1) Dad made me to clean the bathroom.
→ Dad made me clean the bathroom.
(2) I got my brother clean his room.
→ I got my brother to clean his room.

01 healthy, mayor, a fool은 5형식에 쓰인 목적격 보어이다. ②, ④ 4형식의 직접목적어 ⑤ 3형식 문장의 수식어구

02 <보기>와 ①은 「주어+동사+목적어+목적격 보어」의 5형식이고, 나머지는 모두 목적어가 두 개인 4형식이다.

03 ③의 made는 사역동사로 목적격 보어로 동사원형을 쓴다. 나머지는 모두 to부정사를 목적격 보어로 쓰는 동사이다.

04 5형식으로 빈칸에는 목적격 보어가 와야 하고 부사는 보어로 쓸 수 없다.

05 ask는 목적격 보어로 to부정사를 쓴다.

06 목적격 보어로 to부정사를 쓰는 동사는 expect이다.

07 get이 사역의 의미를 가질 때 목적격 보어로 to부정사를 쓴다.

08 목적어와 목적격 보어가 수동의 관계이므로 steal을 stolen으로 고친다.

09 목적어(a tooth)가 뽑히는 수동의 관계이므로 목적격 보어로 과거분사를 쓴다. I had a tooth pulled이다.

10 사역동사 make는 목적어와 목적격 보어가 능동의 관계일 때 목적격 보어로 동사원형을 쓴다. cleaning → clean

11 사역동사 make는 목적격 보어로 동사원형을 쓴다.

12 목적격 보어로 동사원형을 쓰는 동사는 let이다. 나머지는 모두 목적격 보어로 to부정사를 쓴다.

13 get이 사역의 의미를 가질 때 목적격 보어로 to부정사와 과거분사를 쓴다.

14 allow는 목적격 보어로 to부정사를 쓰고, let은 동사원형을 쓴다.

15 지각동사 see는 목적어와 목적격 보어가 능동의 관계일 때 목적격 보어로 동사원형과 현재분사 둘 다 쓸 수 있다.

16 지각동사 feel은 목적어와 목적격 보어가 능동의 관계일 때 목적격 보어로 동사원형 또는 현재분사를 쓸 수 있다.

17 첫 번째 빈칸: 부사는 목적격 보어로 쓸 수 없다.
두 번째 빈칸: advise는 to부정사를 목적격 보어로 쓴다.
세 번째 문장: 지각동사가 있고 목적어와 목적격 보어가 능동의 관계이므로 동사원형 또는 현재분사를 쓴다.

18 help는 목적격 보어로 동사원형과 to부정사 둘 다 쓸 수 있다.

19 ⓑ get이 사역의 의미일 때 to부정사를 목적격 보어로 쓴다. wipe → to wipe ⓓ 남자가 병원에 실려 가는 수동의 관계이므로 과거분사를 쓴다. carry → carried ⓔ 사역동사 have는 목적격 보어로 동사원형을 쓴다. to take → take

20 '문을 닫혀진 상태로 두다'라는 의미로 목적어와 목적격 보어가 수동의 관계이다. 과거분사 closed를 써야 한다.

서술형 • 수행평가형

01 (2) 지각동사는 목적격 보어로 동사원형 또는 현재분사를 쓴다.
(3) help는 목적격 보어로 동사원형과 to부정사를 쓸 수 있다. 4단어만 추가하면 되므로 동사원형으로 쓴다.

02 Brian은 늘 그렇듯이 약속에 늦어서 Emma를 짜증 나게 만들었다.

03 사역동사 make는 목적격 보어로 동사원형을 쓰고, get은 사역의 의미를 나타낼 때 목적격 보어로 to부정사를 쓴다.

UNIT 02 시제

개념 03 현재완료 1_완료, 경험 p. 26

01 완료 02 경험 03 완료 04 경험
05 완료 06 경험 07 경험
08 has not arrived
09 Have you ever ridden
10 has already started
11 He has just been
12 I have not [never] heard

개념 04 현재완료 2_계속, 결과 p. 27

01 결과 02 결과 03 계속 04 계속
05 결과 06 계속 07 결과
08 They have danced
09 has grown
10 I have not [never] played
11 have you waited
12 It has rained

바로 개념 확인 노트 개념 03-04 p. 28

개념 03 현재완료 1_완료, 경험

1 have [has] 2 not 4 when

쓰임	의미	함께 자주 쓰이는 표현
완료	(과거에 시작한 일이 현재) 막 ~했다, 이미 ~했다	already, just, yet, still 등
경험	(과거부터 현재까지) ~한 적이 있다	ever, never, once, twice, ~ times, before, 최상급 등

개념 04 현재완료 2_계속, 결과

1 for 2 since 3 gone, been

쓰임	의미	함께 자주 쓰이는 표현
계속	(과거부터 현재까지) 계속 ~해 왔다	since(~부터), for(~ 동안), so far, how long 등
결과	(과거에) ~한 결과 (현재는) …이다	go, lose, grow, buy, leave 등

바로 기본 확인 노트 개념 03-04 p. 29

A 01 have had 02 has she lived
03 walked 04 have ever met
05 have read 06 you thought
07 opened 08 did he return

B 01 has slept 02 have felt
03 lost 04 have not [never] seen
05 moved 06 has not [never] eaten

교과서에서 뽑은 *405* 문장 마스터하기 pp. 30-31

016 Nature has inspired many architects around the world.
017 Some people have found creative ways to save the earth.
018 I have never thought about running.
019 Many haenyeo have become the breadwinners for their families.
020 The wind has made the fires worse.
021 Have you ever seen a fish jump out of the water to catch a bird?
022 I have studied many kinds of fish living in the seas near Korea.
023 Since then, many people have used his invention in many different ways.
024 I've spent all of my allowance for this week.
025 Have you ever been to Dongdaemun Design Plaza in Seoul?
026 Global warming has brought extremely hot and cold weather.
027 I wonder if you have ever had a meal on water.
028 There have been various fake news reports throughout history.
029 Rain has cut down the stones and made them sharp.
030 Ever since then, Americans have enjoyed eating tomatoes.

개념 05 과거완료 / 미래완료 p. 32

01 had bought 02 had borrowed
03 will have cooked 04 had earned
05 won't have stopped 06 arrived
07 found, had broken 08 will have cleaned
09 met, had lived

개념 06 완료 진행 p. 33

01 has been 02 had been
03 has been 04 have been
05 had been standing 06 had been thinking
07 have, been doing 08 have been studying

바로 개념 확인 노트 개념 05-06 p. 34

개념 05 과거완료 / 미래완료

1 had 2 will have

	과거완료	미래완료
긍정문	주어+had+과거분사 ~.	주어+will have+과거분사 ~.
부정문	주어+had not+과거분사 ~.	주어+will not have+과거분사 ~.
의문문	(의문사+)Had+주어+과거분사 ~?	(의문사+)Will+주어+have+과거분사 ~?

개념 06 완료 진행

1 과거완료 진행형 2 현재완료 진행형

	과거완료 진행	현재완료 진행
긍정문	주어+had been+현재 분사 ~.	주어+have [has] been+현재분사 ~.
부정문	주어+had not been+현재분사 ~.	주어+have [has] not been+현재분사 ~.
의문문	(의문사+)Had+주어+been+현재분사 ~?	(의문사+)Have [Has]+주어+been+현재분사 ~?

바로 기본 확인 노트 개념 05-06 p. 35

A 01 did not [didn't] notice, had left
02 had been waiting, came
03 are, have been playing
04 had not [hadn't] met, talked
05 will have finished, comes

B 01 he had seen before
02 I have been writing the essay
03 my family had already had dinner
04 his sister had been trying to fix the computer
05 had lived in Seoul

교과서에서 뽑은 *405* 문장 마스터하기 pp. 36-37

031 It has been snowing heavily for over three hours.
032 I have been living in America for three years.
033 By the time I am 20, I will have read 100 books.
034 He discovered places no one else had been before.
035 After I had gone to bed, an earthquake hit.
036 He was surprised that he hadn't locked the door.
037 There were 19 other warriors who had passed their tests.
038 I have been writing my shopping lists in Spanish.
039 Puru realized how foolish he had been.
040 He has been feeling sick since yesterday.
041 By next month, I will have been married for 10 years.
042 The movie had started before my friend showed up. 또는 Before my friend showed up, the movie had started.
043 I've been visiting the forest to study animals for 20 years.
044 People asked him where he had got the furniture.
045 The article said (that) Nobel had died from a heart attack.

REVIEW TEST pp. 38-40

01 ①	02 ②	03 ②	04 ④	05 ③
06 ③	07 ②	08 ④	09 ③	10 ①
11 ④	12 ⑤	13 ③	14 ④	15 ①, ④
16 ①, ④	17 ④	18 ⑤		

서술형 • 수행평가형

01 (1) I have been knitting a sweater for Mom
(2) found her credit card, she had lost in the subway
02 (1) The street will have frozen by tomorrow morning.
(2) After we had been wandering for two hours, we found the hotel.
03 (1) has learned [has been learning] Spanish
(2) had learned [had been learning] Spanish
(3) will have learned Spanish

01 주절이 현재완료이면 부사절에는 과거 시제를 쓴다. are → were
02 첫 번째 문장: 시간의 길이를 나타내는 말이 있으므로 for를 쓴다. 두 번째 문장: 현재완료의 완료를 나타내는 문장으로 just가 적절하다.
03 last month는 과거를 나타내는 부사구로 현재완료와 함께 쓸 수 없다. have bought → bought
04 빈칸 뒤에 '언젠가 그것을 해 보고 싶다'는 I wish 가정법 과거 문장이 있으므로 한라산을 등반해 본 적이 없다는 부정의 응답이 와야 한다.
05 '5년 동안.'이라고 답한 것으로 보아 '얼마나 오래 한국에 있었니?'라는 질문이 와야 자연스럽다. How often과 How many times는 횟수를 묻는 표현이다.
06 <보기>와 ③은 완료를 나타낸다. ①, ② 경험 ④, ⑤ 계속
07 현재완료 부정문으로 주어가 I이므로 「have+not [never]+과거분사」로 쓴다.
08 전에 만났던 것을 기억했다는 의미로 과거완료를 쓴다.
09 잠금 비밀번호를 잊어버린 것은 주절의 과거 시제보다 더 이전에 일어난 일이므로 과거완료를 써야 한다.
10 so far(지금까지)는 과거부터 현재까지 영향을 주고 있는 것을 나타내는 표현으로 현재완료를 쓰고, 주어가 3인칭 단수이므로 has를 쓴다.
11 주절은 과거 시제 부정문이고, 머리카락을 자른 것은 그 전의 일이므로 과거완료를 쓴다.
12 물에 빠진 소년이 죽기 전에 구해졌으므로 과거완료로 쓴다.
해석 나는 지난 일요일에 해변에 갔다. 내가 거기 도착했을 때, 나는 물에 빠진 소년을 보았다. 다행스럽게도, 해양 경비원이 소년이 죽기 전에 구조했다.
13 in a few years(몇 년 안에)는 미래를 나타내는 말로 미래완료를 쓰는 것이 적절하다. have discovered → will have discovered
14 lately(최근에)는 현재까지 영향을 주는 말로 과거완료 진행형 대신 현재완료 진행형으로 쓰는 것이 더 자연스럽다. Had → Have
15 주어 앞에 Had가 있으므로 과거완료나 과거완료 진행형을 쓸 수 있다.

16 현재완료 진행형으로 since나 for를 이용한 표현이 적절하다.

17 바이올린을 연주하고 있었는데, 지금도 연주하고 있으므로 현재완료 진행형으로 나타낼 수 있다.

18 2시간 전부터 다투기 시작했는데 지금까지 다투고 있으므로 현재완료 진행형으로 나타낸다.

서술형 • 수행평가형

01 (1) 한 달 전부터 스웨터를 뜨기 시작해서 지금도 하고 있다는 것을 강조하고 있으므로 현재완료 진행형으로 쓴다.
(2) 찾은 시점은 과거이고, 잃어버린 시점은 과거완료이다.

02 (1) 미래완료는 「will have+과거분사」이다.
(2) 과거완료 진행형은 「had been+현재분사」이다.

03 (1) Olivia는 1월 2일에 스페인어를 배우기 시작했고, 오늘은 1월 16일이므로 그녀는 2주 동안 스페인어를 배웠다는 현재완료 또는 현재완료 진행형으로 쓸 수 있다.
(2) 1월 9일은 오늘보다 일주일 전이므로 과거완료 또는 과거완료 진행형으로 쓸 수 있다.
(3) 1월 23일은 오늘보다 일주일 뒤이므로 미래완료로 쓴다.

UNIT 03 조동사

개념 07 had better / would rather / used to / would p. 42

01 keep
02 go
03 I'd rather not
04 used to
05 read
06 wearing
07 had better change
08 had better not be
09 would rather sleep
10 than cook
11 used to live
12 used to [would] go hiking

개념 08 조동사 + have + p.p. p. 43

01 done
02 written
03 shouldn't have eaten
04 must
05 should
06 can't
07 must have been
08 should have studied
09 may [might] have lost
10 could have helped
11 can't have slept
12 should have sent

바로 개념 확인 노트 개념 07-08 p. 44

개념 07 had better / would rather / used to / would

2 used to, would

조동사 구문	의미		
had better + 동사원형	충고·경고	~하는 게 좋겠다	부정: had better not
would rather + 동사원형 [A] (+ than + 동사원형 [B])	선호	(B하기 보다는 차라리) A하겠다	부정: would rather not
used to + 동사원형	현재는 지속되지 않는 과거의 습관·상태	~하곤 했다, ~이었다	부정: used not to / didn't use(d) to
would + 동사원형	과거의 습관	~하곤 했다	

개념 08 조동사 + have + p.p.

1 have
2 shouldn't have p.p.

should have p.p.	과거의 일에 대한 후회나 유감	~했어야 했다
must have p.p.	과거의 일에 대한 강한 추측	~이었음에 틀림없다
may [might] have p.p.	과거의 일에 대한 약한 추측	~했을지도 모른다
cannot have p.p.	과거의 일에 대한 강한 의심	~이었을 리가 없다
could have p.p.	과거의 일에 대한 가능성	~할 수도 있었다

바로 기본 확인 노트 개념 07-08 p. 45

A
01 make
02 better not skip
03 than
04 come
05 used to [would] take
06 sleeping
07 lose
08 used not to [didn't use(d) to]
09 have broken
10 shouldn't have forgotten

B
01 should have been more patient
02 can't have lied to me
03 should have thought twice
04 may [might] have heard this song before
05 must have had a hard time making this film
06 shouldn't have driven so fast

교과서에서 뽑은 405 문장 마스터하기 pp. 46-47

046 I used to live in Jejudo.
047 My grandmother used to be a cook.
048 You should have been more careful.
049 I should have kept track of my spending.
050 You shouldn't have bought them.

051 He may[might] have caught a cold.

052 It must have been tough for him.

053 She must have loved the sport very much.

054 She would lose her temper over nothing.

055 Every summer, my family used to go on holiday to the coast.

056 I should have gone to Chicago.

057 You shouldn't have done that.

058 They must have had a good time at the party.

059 They may have been hungry.

060 I shouldn't have made you wait.

REVIEW TEST

pp. 48–50

01 ②	02 ①	03 ③	04 ④	05 ③
06 ④	07 ①	08 ④	09 ①	10 ③
11 ②	12 ④	13 ①	14 ⑤	15 ①
16 ②	17 ⑤	18 ③	19 ④	20 ⑤

서술형 • 수행평가형

01 (1) better not (2) used to swim
(3) rather send, than talk

02 (1) might have left (2) should have brought
(3) must have been (4) shouldn't have lied

03 shouldn't have been late for the meeting

01 used to는 현재는 지속되지 않는 과거의 습관이나 상태를 나타낼 때 사용한다. would는 과거의 습관은 나타낼 수 있지만 상태는 나타낼 수 없으므로 첫번째 빈칸에만 쓸 수 있다.

02 would rather *A* than *B*는 '*B*하기 보다는 차라리 *A*하겠다'라는 의미이고 이때 *A*와 *B*는 모두 동사원형으로 쓴다.

03 주어진 단어를 배열하면 You had better not eat out too often.(너는 너무 자주 외식하지 않는 것이 좋겠다.)이다.

04 ④의 used to는 be동사와 함께 쓰여 '~하기 위해 사용되다'라는 의미이다. 나머지는 모두 과거의 습관이나 상태를 나타내어 '~하곤 했다, ~이었다'라는 의미이다.

05 「be used to + 동명사」: ~하는 데 익숙하다, 「be used to + 동사원형」: ~하는 데 사용되다, 「used to + 동사원형」: ~하곤 했다, ~이었다

06 would rather *A* than *B*의 형태로 쓸 때 *A*와 *B*는 모두 동사원형을 써야 하므로 goes를 go로 고쳐야 한다.

07 used to의 부정은 used not to 또는 didn't use(d) to로 나타낸다.

08 ④ 「be used to + 동명사」는 '~하는 데 익숙하다'라는 의미이므로 '나는 대도시에 사는 것에 익숙하다'라고 해석해야 한다.

09 과거의 습관을 나타낼 때는 used to와 would를 모두 사용할 수 있다.

10 ① is used to → used to ② to make → make ④ had not better → had better not ⑤ would → used to

11 기차를 놓쳤다고 했으므로 좀 더 일찍 왔어야 했다고 후회하는 표현이 이어져야 자연스럽다. 「should have p.p.」: ~했어야 했다

12 과거에 하지 못한 일을 후회하는 표현인 should have been이 와야 한다.

13 첫 번째 빈칸에는 허가의 의미를 나타내는 may, 두 번째 빈칸에는 과거의 일에 대한 약한 추측을 나타내는 may가 와야 한다.

14 '옷 사는 데 돈을 그렇게 많이 쓰지 말았어야 했다'라는 응답이 되도록 shouldn't have spent가 와야 한다. 「shouldn't have p.p.」: ~하지 말았어야 했다

15 주어진 문장은 '난 점심을 더 적게 먹었어야 했다'라는 의미로, 점심을 많이 먹어서 후회한다는 내용과 의미가 통한다.

16 과거 사실에 대한 강한 추측은 「must have p.p.」로 나타낸다.

17 Joey가 정직한 소년이라고 했으므로 '너의 지갑을 훔쳤을 리가 없다'라는 내용이 이어져야 자연스럽다. 「can't have p.p.」: ~이었을 리가 없다

18 ① be → been ② wore → worn ④ feels → felt ⑤ has → have

19 과거 사실에 대한 강한 추측은 「must have p.p.」로 나타낸다.
④ be → been

20 ⑤ Ivan은 파리에 가고 여기 없다는 말이 이어지므로 '그건 Ivan이었을 리가 없다'라는 의미가 되도록 can't have been을 쓰는 것이 자연스럽다.

서술형 • 수행평가형

01 (1) 「had better not + 동사원형」: ~하지 않는 것이 좋겠다
(2) 「used to + 동사원형」: (예전에) ~하곤 했다
(3) would rather *A* than *B*: *B*하기 보다는 차라리 *A*하겠다

02 (1) 과학책을 봤는지 묻는 말에 확실하지는 않다고 답했으므로 과거 사실에 대한 약한 추측을 나타내는 표현을 이용해야 한다. 「might have p.p.」: ~했을지도 모른다
(2) 비가 올 것 같다는 말 다음에 '우산을 가져왔어야 했다'라고 후회하는 말이 이어져야 자연스럽다. 「should have p.p.」: ~했어야 했다
(3) 아무도 시험을 통과하지 못했다는 말에 과거 사실에 대한 강한 추측을 나타내는 표현을 이용하여 '시험이 어려웠음에 틀림없구나.'라고 응답해야 자연스럽다. 「must have p.p.」: ~이었음에 틀림없다
(4) Jason이 화가 나 있다고 했으므로 과거 사실에 대한 유감을 나타내는 표현을 이용하여 '너는 그에게 거짓말을 하지 말았어야 했다.'라고 해야 자연스럽다. 「shouldn't have p.p.」: ~하지 말았어야 했다

03 Mark는 모임에 늦어서 계약을 성사시키지 못했으므로 '모임에 늦지 말았어야 했다'라는 의미가 되도록 「shouldn't have p.p.」를 이용한다.

UNIT 04 to부정사

개념 09 명사적 용법 p. 52

01 To do
02 to raise
03 to get
04 to listen
05 how
06 not to spread
07 To recycle [Recycling], is
08 to build [building]
09 decided to change
10 pretended to be
11 how to save
12 what to buy

개념 10 가주어, 의미상 주어, 가목적어, It takes ~ to p. 53

01 It
02 her a week
03 of
04 for
05 it a rule
06 made it possible
07 It is impossible for him to complete
08 found it difficult to persuade
09 It took me a long time to read

바로 개념 확인 노트 개념 09–10 p. 54

개념 09 명사적 용법

1 ~하는 것, ~하기 2 should 3 not, never, to부정사

의문사 + to부정사	
what + to부정사	무엇을 ~할지
when + to부정사	언제 ~할지
where + to부정사	어디로 ~할지
how + to부정사	어떻게 ~할지, ~하는 방법
which + to부정사	어느 것을 ~할지
who(m) + to부정사	누가[누구를] ~할지

개념 10 가주어, 의미상 주어, 가목적어, It takes ~ to

1 it 3 it 4 It takes

가주어	「가주어 it ~ to부정사」	
의미상 주어	「for + 목적격」	일반적인 to부정사의 의미상 주어
	「of + 목적격」	사람의 성격을 나타내는 형용사가 보어로 쓰였을 때 * kind, rude, polite, generous, wise, foolish, careful 등
가목적어	「주어 + 동사 + 가목적어 it + 목적격 보어(형용사/명사) + 진목적어」(← 5형식) * 가목적어를 주로 쓰는 동사: think, believe, find, make, consider 등	

바로 기본 확인 노트 개념 09–10 p. 55

A
01 To get [Getting]
02 to face [facing]
03 to deliver
04 to set
05 of him
06 for
07 never to meet
08 of you
09 for them
10 made it possible

B
01 It will be nice to study abroad.
02 found it hard to refuse our invitation
03 it impossible to sleep well
04 It may be a good idea to find a way to control your feelings.
05 It is not good for your health to consume too much caffeine.
06 believe it necessary to teach about cultural differences

교과서에서 뽑은 405 문장 마스터하기 pp. 56–57

061 It is really stressful to have such a shining brother.
062 It can be very hard to be a smart news reader.
063 It is boring for me to watch the soccer game.
064 It was not easy for us to choose the best idea.
065 It is foolish of him to make the same mistake twice.
066 I didn't know how to react.
067 Can I get your advice on what to bring?
068 It took ten years for us to pay for it.
069 The project was to do a wall painting in our neighborhood.
070 A rich man knows how to make money grow.
071 It took me some time to do my hair.
072 It is necessary for you to set some rules for using your smartphone.
073 Iceland is the best place for many location scouts to visit.
074 It is important for everyone to value the resources.
075 I found it possible to inspire people by music.

개념 11 형용사적 용법 p. 58

01 something different to do
02 anybody to help
03 to adapt
04 some tips to relieve
05 to improve
06 to live in
07 are to leave
08 was to be
09 are to pass

개념 12 부사적 용법 p. 59

01 감정의 원인
02 결과
03 형용사 수식
04 판단의 근거
05 목적
06 목적
07 to understand
08 to see
09 to pick
10 to be
11 (in order/so as) not to wake
12 to say

바로 개념 확인 노트 개념 11–12 p. 60

개념 11 형용사적 용법

1 ~할, ~하는 2 형용사, to부정사

명사 · 대명사 수식 (~할, ~하는)	명사 · 대명사 + to부정사 -thing, -one, -body (+형용사) + to부정사 (대)명사 + to부정사 + 전치사	
be + to부정사	예정	~할 예정이다
	의무	~해야 한다
	가능	~할 수 있다
	운명	~할 운명이다
	의지	~할 작정이다

개념 12 부사적 용법

3 not to

목적	~하기 위해서	= in order to [so as to]
감정의 원인	~해서, ~하니	감정을 나타내는 형용사를 뒤에서 수식 *glad, surprised, excited, shocked, disappointed 등
판단의 근거	~하다니	주로 함께 쓰는 표현: cannot, must 등
결과	…해서 (결국) ~하다	주로 함께 쓰는 표현: live, grow up, awake, wake up 등
형용사 수식	~하기에	to부정사가 형용사를 뒤에서 수식

바로 기본 확인 노트 개념 11–12 p. 61

A
01 tell → to tell
02 spicy something eat → something spicy to eat
03 lost → to lose
04 join → to join
05 to recognize impossible → impossible to recognize
06 write → write with
07 that → to

B
01 to buy some flour
02 not to miss my flight
03 to hear that his mom felt better
04 to find myself famous
05 to answer the difficult questions
06 is to visit Switzerland
07 are not to talk during the exam
08 was to get married to a poor man

교과서에서 뽑은 405 문장 마스터하기 pp. 62–63

076 She didn't have enough time to talk with her daughter.
077 Is there a faster way to travel through space?
078 Each group was to prepare a special lunch for him.
079 Turkey is a wonderful place to visit.
080 Jane was pleased to meet her old friends.
081 My brother is sad not to be invited to the party.
082 What you're saying is hard to believe.
083 People usually use chemicals to kill unwanted plants.
084 This gave me a chance to think about my life.
085 I was surprised to find that she was enjoying her job.
086 In ancient China, people popped corn to tell fortunes for the coming year.
087 Many more are underwater, and they are hard to locate.
088 The best way to learn a new language is to practice it every day.
089 The pot is very precious, so be careful not to break it.
090 Most people think of books as traditional paper books to read.

개념 13 too ~ to / enough to p. 64

01 too 02 too young to 03 for
04 can't 05 small enough 06 could
07 so scared that I couldn't shout out
08 too heavy for him to move
09 brave enough to run after the thief

개념 14 seem to p. 65

01 to be 02 to have cried
03 loved 04 had found
05 to be angry 06 were surprised
07 to have lost

바로 개념 확인 노트 개념 13–14 p. 66

개념 13 too ~ to / enough to

1 …하기에 너무 ~한 / 하게
2 …할 만큼 충분히 ~한 / 하게

too + 형용사/부사 (+for+목적격) + to부정사
(for+목적격: 의미상 주어)
→ so + 형용사/부사 + that + 주어 + can't + 동사원형

형용사/부사 + enough (+for+목적격) + to부정사
(for+목적격: 의미상 주어)
→ so + 형용사/부사 + that + 주어 + can + 동사원형

개념 14 seem to

1 ~인 것 같다
2 It seems that
3 have, p.p.

단순부정사	「to + 동사원형」	to부정사의 시제가 본동사의 시제와 일치하거나 미래일 때
완료부정사	「to + have + p.p.」	to부정사의 시제가 본동사보다 앞선 시제일 때

바로 기본 확인 노트 개념 13-14 p. 67

A
01 The curry was too spicy for him to eat.
02 The boy is so poor that he can't pay a bill.
03 The problem was so difficult that I couldn't answer it.
04 I was so lucky that I could get the ticket.
05 He spoke clearly enough for me to understand.

B
01 seemed to be hungry
02 seems to have noticed it
03 doesn't seem to miss us
04 seem to have forgotten my name
05 seemed to have been ill

교과서에서 뽑은 405 문장 마스터하기 pp. 68-69

091 Most people are too busy at school to spend much time outdoors.
092 She was too afraid to go.
093 People thought that art was too difficult to understand.
094 Eric is smart enough to solve difficult math problems.
095 It seems that she helps to keep both their mind and body healthy.
096 There seem to be many natural disasters in Korea these days.
097 Mike seemed to think it was nothing serious.
098 It seemed that nobody wanted his bike.
099 She was fortunate enough to work with a team of designers.
100 Most of them were too big or too difficult to use.
101 Is this research project good enough to win a Nobel Prize?
102 He is too greedy to share with the people.
103 Ants seem to be busy all the time and never rest.
104 You knew that you were too far behind to win a medal.
105 They seem to know what to do to make their camping trip safe.

REVIEW TEST pp. 70-72

01 ④	02 ①	03 ⑤	04 ④	05 ③
06 ⑤	07 ②, ④	08 ①	09 ②	10 ③
11 ③	12 ④	13 ①	14 ④	15 ②
16 ⑤	17 ③	18 ⑤	19 ①	20 ③

서술형 • 수행평가형

01 (1) too short for John to wear
(2) tall enough to reach the top shelf
02 (1) They seem to be annoyed.
(2) It seemed that no one cared about the dog.
(3) Kate seems to have misunderstood my intention.
03 (1) of him to lose his passport
(2) a friend to talk to
(3) to find out that the game was canceled

01 보기와 ④는 목적을 나타내는 부사적 용법이다. ① 형용사적 용법 ② 명사적 용법(목적어 역할) ③ 명사적 용법(주어 역할) ⑤ 명사적 용법(보어 역할)
02 ①은 명사적 용법(목적어 역할)이고 나머지는 모두 감정의 원인을 나타내는 부사적 용법이다.
03 보기와 ⑤는 앞의 명사를 수식하는 형용사적 용법으로 쓰였다. ① 부사적 용법(목적) ② 부사적 용법(판단의 근거) ③ 부사적 용법(목적) ④ 명사적 용법(목적어 역할)
04 ④는 '~할 작정이다'라는 의미로 쓰였고 나머지는 모두 '~할 예정이다'라는 의미이다.
05 enjoy는 동명사를 목적어로 쓰는 동사이다.
06 ⓐ to live → to live with ⓑ interesting nothing to read → nothing interesting to read
07 목적의 의미를 나타내기 위해 (in order/so as) to를 쓸 수 있다. for 다음에는 명사(구) 또는 동명사(구)가 와야 하고 in order that 다음에는 절이 와야 한다.
08 「be + to부정사」가 예정의 의미로 쓰였으므로 be going to를 이용하여 바꿔 쓸 수 있다.
09 to부정사의 부정은 「not [never] + to부정사」로 나타낸다.
10 ③은 to부정사가 결과의 의미로 쓰여 '깨어보니 나는 어둠 속에 있었다'라고 해석한다. in order to는 '~하기 위해'라는 의미이다.
11 사람의 성격을 나타내는 형용사가 보어로 쓰였을 때는 의미상 주어를 「of + 목적격」으로 쓴다. necessary는 사람의 성격을 나타내지 않으므로 의미상 주어는 「for + 목적격」으로 쓴다.
12 주어진 문장과 ④는 가주어이다. ①, ② 비인칭 주어 ③ 가목적어 ⑤ 대명사
13 의미상 주어가 「of + 목적격」이므로 빈칸에는 사람의 성격을 나타내는 형용사가 와야 한다.
14 ④는 5형식이 아니며 두 개의 절을 잇는 접속사 that이 와야 한다. 나

머지는 모두 가목적어 it이 와야 한다.

15 바르게 배열하면 The heavy rain made it impossible for them to have a picnic.이다. 이때 it은 가목적어이다.

16 ⑤ 목적격 보어 앞에 가목적어 it을 써야 한다. → I found it strange to drive on the left in Britain.

17 주어진 문장은 It was hard for him to admit his failure.로 바꿔 쓸 수 있다.

18 「so + 형용사/부사 + that + 주어 + can't + 동사원형」은 「too + 형용사/부사 (+ for + 목적격) + to부정사」로 바꿔 쓸 수 있다.

19 「형용사/부사 + enough + to부정사」는 '…할 만큼 충분히 ~한/하게'라는 의미이다.

20 to부정사가 본동사보다 앞선 시제일 때 완료부정사 「to + have + p.p.」를 이용한다.

서술형 • 수행평가형

01 (1) 「too + 형용사/부사 (+ for + 목적격) + to부정사」는 '…하기에 너무 ~한/하게'라는 의미이다.
(2) 「형용사/부사 + enough + to부정사」는 '…할 만큼 충분히 ~한/하게'라는 의미이다.

02 (1) to부정사가 본동사의 시제와 일치하므로 단순부정사를 이용한다.
(2) 단순부정사이므로 It seemed that ~절로 바꿀 때 주절과 종속절의 시제를 일치시킨다.
(3) to부정사가 본동사보다 앞선 시제일 때 완료부정사 「to + have + p.p.」를 이용한다.

03 (1) 사람의 성격을 나타내는 형용사인 careless가 쓰였으므로 의미상 주어는 「of + 목적격」으로 쓴다.
(2) to부정사가 명사 뒤에서 명사를 수식하는 형용사적 용법으로 쓰인다. 수식을 받는 명사가 전치사의 목적어일 때 to부정사 뒤에 전치사를 써야 한다.
(3) to부정사가 감정을 나타내는 형용사를 뒤에서 수식하여 부사적 용법(감정의 원인)으로 쓰인다.

UNIT 05 동명사

개념 15 동명사의 역할 p. 74

01 Learning
02 protecting
03 asking
04 making
05 never having
06 to eat
07 Breaking [To break]
08 cycling [to cycle]
09 copying
10 studying
11 finding
12 not coming

개념 16 동명사의 의미상 주어와 시제 p. 75

01 his
02 my turning
03 her winning
04 having taken
05 not having answered
06 his not succeeding
07 mind you staying
08 for not having said

바로 개념 확인 노트 개념 15–16 p. 76

개념 15 동명사의 역할

1 동사원형, -ing 2 not, never, 동명사 3 ~하는, ~하고 있는

동명사를 목적어로 쓰는 동사			
enjoy	finish	keep	stop
quit	mind	avoid	admit
deny	recommend	practice	imagine
consider	dislike	give up	put off

cf. stop + to부정사: '~하기 위해 멈추다'라는 의미임 <to부정사의 부사적 용법>

개념 16 동명사의 의미상 주어와 시제

2 소유격, 목적격

동명사의 의미상 주어	소유격[목적격] + 동명사 *의미상 주어가 all, both, this [these], that [those], 또는 무생물일 때는 목적격을 씀
단순동명사(동사원형 + -ing)	본동사의 시제와 같거나 미래일 때
완료동명사(having + p.p.)	본동사의 시제보다 이전일 때

바로 기본 확인 노트 개념 15–16 p. 77

A 01 Touching [To touch] 02 decorating
03 is 04 her

05 having lost
06 is playing [to play]
07 pressing
08 yelling
09 having stolen
10 Not using

B 01 my [me] practicing
02 my brother('s) wearing
03 her lying
04 Kate('s) being
05 his [him] talking
06 your [you] having

07 feel like eating
08 On [Upon] arriving
09 couldn't help laughing
10 no use arguing
11 meet without quarreling
12 spent three hours watching

교과서에서 뽑은 405 문장 마스터하기 pp. 78–79

106 Pursuing a dream is not easy.
107 Throwing paper planes is another fun tradition.
108 I recommend watching Korean dramas.
109 Do you mind turning down the volume?
110 Did you finish making the video?
111 Stop comparing yourself with your friends.
112 I'm sure of your[you] accepting my offer.
113 I don't like his coming late every day.
114 My job is finding perfect places to shoot movies.
115 Eating tomatoes can lower your risk of heart disease.
116 Sometimes we hurt people's feelings without intending to.
117 Visiting markets is a good way to learn about the culture of a country.
118 I hope you enjoy having dinner at his house.
119 My wife got tired of my messing up our garage.
120 I understand why not giving up is so important.

개념 17 동명사와 to부정사 p. 80

01 to spoil
02 typing
03 repairing
04 to sign
05 telling
06 to tell
07 sitting [to sit]
08 falling [to fall]
09 walking
10 to take
11 calling
12 leaving

개념 18 관용적 표현 p. 81

01 packing
02 going
03 falling
04 getting
05 to exploring
06 challenging

바로 개념 확인 노트 개념 17–18 p. 82

개념 17 동명사와 to부정사

forget	+동명사	(과거에) ~했던 것을 잊다
	+to부정사	(앞으로) ~할 것을 잊다
remember	+동명사	(과거에) ~했던 것을 기억하다
	+to부정사	(앞으로) ~할 것을 기억하다
regret	+동명사	(과거에) ~했던 것을 후회하다
	+to부정사	(현재·미래에) ~하게 되어 유감이다
try	+동명사	시험 삼아 (한번) ~해 보다
	+to부정사	~하려고 노력하다

개념 18 관용적 표현

go -ing	~하러 가다	be busy -ing	~하느라 바쁘다
on [upon] -ing (= as soon as+주어+동사)	~하자마자	be used to -ing	~하는 데 익숙하다
keep (on) -ing	계속 ~하다	How [What] about -ing?	~하는 게 어때?
be worth -ing	~할 만한 가치가 있다	look forward to -ing	~하기를 고대하다
feel like -ing (= would like to+동사원형)	~하고 싶다	make a point of -ing (= make it a rule to+동사원형)	~하는 것을 규칙으로 하다
far from -ing	전혀 ~이 아닌	on the point of -ing (= be about to+동사원형)	막 ~하려고 하는
spend+시간/돈+-ing	~하느라 시간/돈을 쓰다	It is no use -ing	~해도 소용없다
not [never] ... without -ing	…하면 꼭 ~하다	keep [prevent] ... from -ing	…가 ~하지 못하게 막다
cannot help -ing (= cannot help but+동사원형)	~하지 않을 수 없다	have trouble [difficulty] (in) -ing	~하는 데 어려움이 있다

바로 기본 확인 노트 개념 17–18 p. 83

A 01 skiing
02 painting [to be painted]
03 staring
04 to take
05 seeing
06 to wear

07 to inform

08 giving

09 to spending

10 watching

B 01 forget visiting China

02 forgot to bring

03 no use blaming

04 used to skipping

05 a point of jogging

06 trouble (in) making

07 him from playing

교과서에서 뽑은 405 문장 마스터하기 pp. 84–85

121 The band started playing[to play] celebration music.

122 I have difficulty (in) saving money.

123 I remember taking it out of my bag.

124 Remember to bring a pair of long pants.

125 Try eating lots of carrots.

126 Let's try to change our bad habits.

127 I'm looking forward to playing in a concert with you.

128 I often spent all my pocket money buying snacks.

129 Pop art is worth paying attention to.

130 He regretted not doing all the things he wanted to.

131 It was no use trying to hold back the tears.

132 This will prevent heat from getting into the classroom.

133 My grandmother has spent the rest of her life regretting her decision.

134 I couldn't help thinking how unlucky I was.

135 Hopefully, architects will keep coming up with new eco-friendly ideas.

REVIEW TEST pp. 86–88

01 ③	02 ②	03 ⑤	04 ②	05 ④
06 ④	07 ①	08 ③	09 ②	10 ①
11 ③, ⑤	12 ②, ⑤	13 ④	14 ①	15 ②
16 ⑤	17 ③	18 ①	19 ②	20 ③

서술형 • 수행평가형

01 (1) his [him] coming (2) her from going out

(3) having hurt

02 (1) I'll never forget seeing it.

(2) I'm not used to using chopsticks.

03 to be a movie director, making short movies, watching his movies, to seeing him in person, studying movie-making in college

01 '필요한 것과 원하는 것을 구분하는 것'이라는 의미가 되도록 문장의 주어 역할을 하는 동명사 Separating 또는 To separate가 올 수 있다.

02 ②는 '이야기하고 있는'이라는 의미의 현재분사이고 나머지는 모두 동명사이다.

03 ⑤는 진행형 문장에 쓰인 현재분사이고 나머지는 모두 동명사이다.

04 ② are → is, 주어로 쓰인 동명사(구)는 단수 취급한다.

05 ④ drink → drinking, 전치사의 목적어로 동명사를 써야 한다.

06 동명사의 부정은 「not [never] + 동명사」의 형태이다.

07 동명사의 의미상의 주어는 동명사 앞에 소유격 또는 목적격을 써서 나타낸다.

08 동명사가 문장의 시제보다 앞선 일을 나타낼 때는 「having + p.p.」로 쓴다.

09 ⓑ she → her ⓒ to stay → staying

ⓓ having wrote → having written

10 ① → I am proud of having been a pilot. 동명사가 문장의 시제보다 앞선 일을 나타낼 때는 「having + p.p.」로 쓴다.

11 decide와 refuse는 to부정사를 목적어로 쓰는 동사이다.

12 「need + 동명사」: ~되어야 할 필요가 있다 (수동의 의미), 「need + to부정사」: ~할 필요가 있다

13 ④ to pay → paying, avoid는 동명사를 목적어로 취하는 동사이다.

14 「remember + 동명사」: (과거에) ~했던 것을 기억하다, 「forget + to부정사」: (앞으로) ~할 것을 잊다

15 첫 번째 빈칸에는 보어 역할을 하는 동명사 being 또는 to be가 들어갈 수 있다. 두 번째 빈칸에는 '~하는 것을 멈추다'라는 의미가 되도록 동명사 being이 들어가야 한다. (stop to: ~하기 위해 멈추다)

16 ① to live → living ② to read → reading ③ taking → to take ④ completing → to complete

17 동명사가 문장의 시제보다 앞선 일을 나타낼 때는 「having + p.p.」로 쓰고, 동명사의 부정은 동명사 앞에 not [never]을 써서 나타낸다.

18 look forward to 다음에는 명사(구) 또는 동명사(구)가 온다.

19 ② to complain → complaining, 「It is no use + 동명사」: ~해도 소용없다

20 「not [never] ... without -ing」는 '…하면 꼭 ~하다'라는 의미이므로 첫 번째 문장은 He locks the door whenever he leaves home.으로 바꿔 쓸 수 있다.

서술형 • 수행평가형

01 (1) 동명사의 의미상의 주어는 동명사 앞에 소유격 또는 목적격을 써서 나타내므로 his coming 또는 him coming을 써야 한다.

(2) 「keep [prevent] ... from -ing」는 '…가 ~하지 못하게 막다'라는

의미이다.

(3) 동명사가 문장의 시제보다 앞선 일을 나타낼 때는 「having + p.p.」로 쓴다.

02 (1) '그것을 봤던 것을 결코 잊지 못할 것이다'라는 의미가 되도록 고쳐야 한다. 「forget + 동명사」: (과거에) ~했던 것을 잊다

(2) '젓가락을 사용하는 것에 익숙하지 않다'라는 의미가 되도록 고쳐야 한다. 「be used to + 동명사」: ~하는 데 익숙하다, 「be used to+동사원형」: ~하는 데 이용되다

03 want는 to부정사를 목적어로 쓰는 동사이고 enjoy, consider는 동명사를 목적어로 쓴다. spend + 시간/돈 + -ing: ~하는 데 시간/돈을 쓰다, look forward to -ing: ~하기를 고대하다

UNIT 06 분사와 분사구문

개념 19 현재분사와 과거분사 p. 90

01 Fallen 02 boiling 03 dry-cleaned
04 waving 05 rescued 06 waiting
07 wearing 08 broken 09 running
10 built 11 buzzing

개념 20 감정을 나타내는 분사 p. 91

01 annoying 02 bored 03 shocking
04 disappointed 05 embarrassed 06 touching
07 surprising 08 confusing 09 amused
10 frightening 11 exhausted 12 shocked

바로 개념 확인 노트 개념 19–20 p. 92

개념 19 현재분사와 과거분사

1 형용사 3 현재분사, 과거분사 4 동작, 용도

		현재분사 (진행/능동의 의미)	과거분사 (수동/완료의 의미)
형태		동사원형+-ing	동사원형+-ed 또는 불규칙 과거분사형
쓰임	명사 수식	I am afraid of a barking dog. (분사와 명사가 능동 관계)	I like the play written by Shakespeare. (분사와 명사가 수동 관계)
	보어 역할	The dog sat barking up the tree. (주격 보어) I saw a dog barking fiercely. (목적격 보어)	Shakespeare remained written in history. (주격 보어) I found a letter written in code. (목적격 보어)
	동사적 성격	The dog is barking fiercely. (진행형)	He has written his first play. (완료형) The play was written by Shakespeare. (수동태)

개념 20 감정을 나타내는 분사

2 원인

현재분사(주어가 감정의 원인)	과거분사(주어가 감정을 느낌)
boring 지루한	bored 지루해하는
frustrating 좌절감을 주는	frustrated 좌절감을 느끼는
annoying 짜증스러운	annoyed 짜증이 난
surprising 놀라운	surprised 놀란
depressing 우울하게 만드는	depressed 우울한
embarrassing 당황하게 하는	embarrassed 당황한
confusing 혼란스러운	confused 혼란스러워 하는
disappointing 실망스러운	disappointed 실망한
frightening 무서운	frightened 겁먹은
satisfying 만족을 주는	satisfied 만족하는

바로 기본 확인 노트 개념 19–20 p. 93

A 01 challenging 02 flying
03 pulled 04 repaired
05 encouraged 06 injured
07 frightened 08 topped

B 01 (1) confusing (2) confused
02 (1) satisfied (2) satisfying
03 (1) depressed (2) depressing
04 (1) excited (2) exciting
05 (1) thrilling (2) thrilled

교과서에서 뽑은 405 문장 마스터하기 pp. 94–95

136 Look at the people wearing traditional Moroccan clothes.
137 There are many "fake" news articles published every day.
138 I think living in a jungle would be really exciting.

139 He told a complete stranger sitting beside him about his problem.
140 You will be amazed by the fantastic views.
141 Spinach can be used in a surprising way.
142 A diet containing a variety of foods keeps our bodies healthy.
143 Ants produce a chemical called a pheromone to communicate with one another.
144 They played instruments made out of garbage.
145 The girl waiting at the bus stop is my sister.
146 They are so shocked to lose their houses.
147 I could see the light swinging violently.
148 The judge was impressed by what she said.
149 Stores selling used things are always interesting.
150 Some of the writers' names are confusing.

개념 21 분사구문 p. 96

01 Arriving
02 Going
03 Taking
04 looking for
05 Running
06 Cleaning
07 Watching TV / TV를 보면서
08 Opening the door / 문을 열면
09 Not knowing what to do / 무엇을 할지 몰라서

개념 22 분사구문의 시제와 태 p. 97

01 Having eaten
02 Persuaded
03 Having visited
04 Disappointed
05 Not having taken
06 (Being) Built
07 Having watched

바로 개념 확인 노트 개념 21–22 p. 98

개념 21 분사구문

1 분사
3 will

분사구문 만드는 법	
As I entered the room, I switched the light on.	
~~As~~ I entered the room, ~	① 접속사 생략
~~I~~ entered the room, ~	② 부사절의 주어 생략 (주절의 주어와 같을 때)
Entering the room, ~	③ 동사를 현재분사로 바꾸기 (주절의 시제와 같을 때)

개념 22 분사구문의 시제와 태

1 having, 주절
2 과거분사

	단순 분사구문	완료 분사구문
능동	현재분사 ~	having+과거분사
수동	being+과거분사	having been+과거분사

바로 기본 확인 노트 개념 21–22 p. 99

A
01 Though he was forgiven by his sister
02 If you join our photography club
03 Because I stayed up all night
04 When I concentrated on mobile games
05 Before she went to bed

B
01 Having tried *kimchi*
02 (Being) Embarrassed by my mistakes
03 Having lived in Spain for 10 years
04 Not having made a reservation

교과서에서 뽑은 405 문장 마스터하기 pp. 100–101

151 Using various methods, experts analyze big data.
152 Looking for fantastic scenery, millions of tourists visit Mt. Halla.
153 Inspired by the video, Whitacre decided to make a virtual choir.
154 Being very powerful and dangerous, volcanoes do harm to people in many ways.
155 I did my math homework, listening to classical music.
156 He was excited, thinking about the bike he planned to buy.
157 Not knowing the news was false, many people panicked.
158 (When) Compared to other bicycles, his price was too high.
159 Start small, taking little steps.
160 Catching his breath, Nobel kept reading.
161 Being sick, I had to stay home all day.
162 Having changed coats, he doesn't have his wallet now.
163 (Being) Disappointed, Carter decided to leave Richmond High.
164 Feeling nervous, Jisu was studying her notes.
165 Hearing this, I felt really sorry for her.

개념 23 독립분사구문 p. 102

01 The rain beginning
02 Generally speaking
03 being
04 Judging from
05 being broken
06 Speaking of
07 It being
08 Strictly speaking
09 Judging from
10 Speaking of
11 being easy

개념 24 with + 명사(구) + 분사 p. 103

01 folded
02 turned on
03 shining
04 removed
05 running
06 broken
07 with the curtains closed
08 with her mouth full
09 with my legs shaking

바로 개념 확인 노트 개념 23–24 p. 104

개념 23 독립분사구문

1 분사 2 일반인

독립 분사구문	부사절 주어 ≠ 주절 주어	부사절의 주어를 생략하지 않고 분사 앞에 씀
비인칭 독립 분사구문	부사절 주어(일반인) ≠ 주절 주어	부사절의 주어 생략
	• frankly speaking (솔직히 말하면) • strictly speaking (엄밀히 말하면) • roughly speaking (대강 말하자면) • generally speaking (일반적으로 말하면) • speaking of (~ 이야기가 나와서 말인데) • judging from (~로 판단하건대) • considering ~ (~을 고려하면)	

개념 24 with + 명사(구) + 분사

1 동시 2 능동 3 수동 4 형용사

with+명사(구)+현재분사	~가 …하고 있는 채로	Mom fell asleep with the washing machine running. 엄마는 세탁기를 돌린 채로 잠이 들었다.
with+명사(구)+과거분사	~가 …하여진 채로	I took a rest with my eyes closed. 나는 눈을 감고 휴식을 취했다.

바로 기본 확인 노트 개념 23–24 p. 105

A 01 turned 02 being missing
03 being sold 04 flags waving
05 untied

B 01 Frankly speaking
02 Judging from
03 Generally speaking
04 Considering
05 Speaking of

교과서에서 뽑은 405 문장 마스터하기 pp. 106–107

166 Considering the limited technology in those days, it seemed impossible.
167 I found a small notebook with some words written on the cover.
168 The weather being fine, we went to the beach.
169 Jenny counted the stars with her finger pointing at each of them.
170 Strictly speaking, you are responsible for the accident.
171 Mr. White called time out with two minutes left on the clock.
172 It being cold, he put on a warm jacket.
173 Wormholes in space may contain two mouths, with a throat connecting the two.
174 Frankly speaking, I couldn't find the joke interesting.
175 Sit with your legs extended.
176 Speaking of ice cream, it was invented in China.
177 I started reading the book with my heart beating very fast.
178 Generally speaking, trains are faster than buses.
179 John's dog is running with John chasing after it.
180 Take the paper and fold it with the dots matched up.

REVIEW TEST pp. 108–110

01 ③ 02 ② 03 ④ 04 ③ 05 ②, ④
06 ④ 07 ③ 08 ③ 09 ⑤ 10 ④
11 ⑤ 12 ④ 13 ③ 14 ② 15 ③
16 ④ 17 ④ 18 ④

서술형 • 수행평가형

01 (1) There are a lot of people waiting outside the restaurant.
(2) She is playing the violin with her eyes closed.
02 (1) Not being invited to the party, she did not come.
(2) The concert being over, people went home.
03 (1) Visiting our website, you can get information
(2) Not living near my grandmother, I can't meet

01 ③ '1920년에 지어진 건물'이라는 수동의 의미로 과거분사 built를 써야 한다.
02 ② 소년이 '자신의 손을 들고 있는'이라는 능동의 의미이므로 현재분사 raising을 쓴다.
03 ① depressed ② surrounded ③ presented ⑤ satisfied
04 '나는 우울할 때 항상 베토벤이 작곡한 교향곡 9번을 듣는다.'는 의미로 the ninth Symphony composed by Beethoven이 알맞다.
05 <보기>는 대명사(those)를 뒤에서 수식하는 현재분사이고 ②, ④는 뒤에 있는 명사를 수식하는 현재분사이다. 나머지는 모두 동명사이다.
06 첫 번째 빈칸: '가족 앨범을 보면서'라는 의미로 Looking이 알맞다. 두 번째 빈칸: '독감에 걸려서'라는 의미로 Having이 알맞다.
07 보기와 ③은 이유를 나타내는 분사구문이다. ①, ④ 시간 ② 양보 ⑤ 조건

08 부사절과 주절의 주어와 시제가 같은 수동태 분사구문으로, Being written ~에서 Being은 생략이 가능하다.

09 부사절의 시제가 주절보다 앞선 시제이므로 완료 분사구문을 쓴다. 부정은 not을 「having+과거분사」 앞에 쓴다.

10 ④는 부사절의 시제가 주절의 시제보다 앞선 시제를 나타내는 완료 분사 구문으로 Having은 생략할 수 없다.

11 ⑤ Being이 생략된 수동태 분사구문으로 부사절로 바꾸면 When the rock is seen from far away, it looks like a horse.이다. 부사절과 주절의 주어를 바꿔 쓰는 것에 주의한다.
① As → (Al)Though ② Though → If ③ If → Because
④ If → Because

12 ④ 부사절의 시제가 주절보다 앞선 시제이므로 완료 분사구문인 Having been born이고, 이때 Having been은 생략이 가능하다.

13 수동태 분사구문으로 (Being) Moved by the novel이다. 부사절과 주절의 주어가 같을 때는 부사절의 주어를 생략한다.

14 ① ~로 판단하건대 ③ 대강 말하자면 ④ 엄밀히 말하면 ⑤ 일반적으로 말하면

15 부사절과 주절의 주어가 다를 때 부사절의 주어를 생략하지 않고 그대로 남겨두는데, 이때 주어는 분사 앞에 쓴다.

16 '행사는 모든 학생들이 의자에 앉은 채로 강당에서 열렸다.'는 의미로 명사구와 분사가 수동의 관계이므로 과거분사를 쓴다.

17 ④ '꼬리를 흔드는'이라는 능동의 의미이므로 wagged 대신 wagging을 쓴다.

18 with가 쓰인 분사구문에서 명사(구)와 분사가 능동의 관계이면 현재분사를 쓰고, 수동의 관계이면 과거분사를 쓴다. '다리를 꼰 채로'라는 수동의 의미이므로 과거분사 crossed를 쓴다.

서술형 • 수행평가형

01 (1) 식당 밖에 기다리는 사람들이 많이 있다. / 주어가 복수이므로 is를 are로 고치고, '기다리는 사람들'이라는 능동의 의미이므로 waited를 현재분사 waiting으로 쓴다.
(2) 그녀는 눈을 감은 채로 바이올린을 연주하는 중이다. / 현재 진행형은 「be동사+동사원형+-ing」이므로 played를 playing으로 고친다. 「with+명사구+분사」에서 명사구와 분사가 수동의 관계이므로 closed로 쓴다.

02 (1) 수동태 분사구문으로 부정어는 분사 앞에 쓴다.
(2) 부사절의 주어와 주절의 주어가 다른 독립분사구문으로 분사구문을 만들 때 부사절의 주어를 생략하지 않고 분사 앞에 둔다.

03 (2) 분사구문의 부정은 not을 분사 앞에 쓴다.

UNIT 07 수동태

개념 25 수동태의 의미와 형태, 시제 p. 112

01 be refilled
02 are watered
03 has been visited
04 be sent
05 were turned
06 must be caught
07 have been bought
08 was being driven
09 will have been completed

개념 26 4형식 문장의 수동태 p. 113

01 to
02 for
03 없음
04 to
05 of
06 was offered a cup of tea
07 was told to her
08 was sent the concert tickets
09 is going to be made for me

바로 개념 확인 노트 개념 25–26 p. 114

개념 25 수동태의 의미와 형태, 시제

시제	수동태 형태
현재	am/is/are + 과거분사
과거	was/were + 과거분사
미래	will be + 과거분사 / be동사 + going to be + 과거분사
진행	be동사 + being + 과거분사
완료	have/has/had/will have + been + 과거분사

조동사가 있을 때	조동사 + be + 과거분사

개념 26 4형식 문장의 수동태

1 직접목적어
2 to, for, of

<table>
<tr><td>4형식 문장의 형태</td><td colspan="2">주어 + 동사 + 간접목적어(A) + 직접목적어(B)</td></tr>
<tr><td>간접목적어가 주어가 될 때</td><td colspan="2">주어(A) + be동사 + 과거분사 + B + by + 행위자
(간접목적어) (직접목적어) (주어)</td></tr>
<tr><td rowspan="4">직접목적어가 주어가 될 때</td><td colspan="2">주어(B) + be동사 + 과거분사 + 전치사 + A + by + 행위자
(직접목적어) (간접목적어) (주어)</td></tr>
<tr><td>전치사 to를 쓰는 동사</td><td>give, teach, bring, send, show, tell, lend, sell, read, write, offer 등</td></tr>
<tr><td>전치사 for를 쓰는 동사</td><td>buy, choose, find, get, make, cook, do 등</td></tr>
<tr><td>전치사 of를 쓰는 동사</td><td>ask, request, inquire 등</td></tr>
</table>

바로 기본 확인 노트 개념 25–26 p. 115

A

01 will be
02 were
03 is used
04 has been
05 be
06 to be
07 is being
08 be
09 being

B

01 will be given some flowers
02 was read to me
03 was cooked for my family
04 were being told the news
05 was shown the new kitchen
06 was written to Mr. Hamilton
07 asked of you

교과서에서 뽑은 405 문장 마스터하기 pp. 116–117

181 His poems are loved by people of all ages.
182 He was attacked by wild animals.
183 Honey from ancient Egypt can be eaten today.
184 Satellites are being used in more and more fields.
185 I have no doubt that you will be elected.
186 Most of her money is spent on buying the new items.
187 This amazing shape has been created by rainfall.
188 Volcanoes should be studied and understood.
189 Many famous movies have been made in New Zealand.
190 The 3D printer will be used to print out food for astronauts.
191 The use of harmful chemicals on crops must be stopped.
192 The repairs will have been completed by the end of this week.
193 It read that she had been invited to the league's main tryouts in Chicago.
194 Before you complain, remember that you have been given a gift.
195 One of them was given to a 16-year-old girl in India.

개념 27 5형식 문장의 수동태 p. 118

01 Danny
02 to talk
03 to stay
04 playing
05 to keep
06 to complain [complaining]
07 happy
08 to go
09 to walk [walking]
10 Mary

개념 28 동사구의 수동태 p. 119

01 up by us
02 off by
03 with by
04 on at a time
05 forward to by
06 was made fun of
07 can be made use of
08 is looked up to
09 should be looked after

바로 개념 확인 노트 개념 27–28 p. 120

개념 27 5형식 문장의 수동태

2 to부정사
3 let, have

5형식 문장(주어 + 동사 + 목적어 + 목적격 보어)의 수동태	
대부분의 동사	주어(목적어) + be동사 + 과거분사 + 보어(목적격 보어) + by + 행위자(주어)
지각동사	목적격 보어가 동사원형일 때 → to부정사 주어(목적어) + be동사 + 과거분사 + to부정사(목적격 보어) + by + 행위자(주어) 목적격 보어가 현재분사일 때 → 현재분사 주어(목적어) + be동사 + 과거분사 + 현재분사(목적격 보어) + by + 행위자(주어)
사역동사	목적격 보어(동사원형) → to부정사 주어(목적어) + be동사 + 과거분사 + to부정사(목적격 보어) + by + 행위자(주어)

개념 28 동사구의 수동태

1 과거분사

바로 기본 확인 노트 개념 27–28 p. 121

A

01 ② 02 ① 03 ② 04 ②
05 ② 06 ② 07 ① 08 ②

B

01 made up by her
02 taken care of by Tom
03 made to help my sister by my parents
04 named Jack by the zookeeper
05 seen standing on the street by Ms. Skinner
06 looked forward to by baseball fans

교과서에서 뽑은 405 문장 마스터하기 pp. 122–123

196 New Zealanders are sometimes called Kiwis.
197 Minkyeong was asked out by a boy in her class.
198 Suddenly, a familiar song was heard coming from the German trenches.
199 The dog was named Kong by the children.

200 Spinach is considered one of the ten healthiest foods on the planet.

201 Have these animals been taken care of by her?

202 They tell us which light should be turned on.

203 When Mr. Boggis came back, the legs of the table had been cut off.

204 That story was probably made up by the royal family.

205 He was believed wise by his friends.

206 The report should be handed in on Tuesday.

207 The Nobel Prize was named after Alfred Nobel.

208 Everyone was allowed to use the grassland.

209 I was being made to wait.

210 She was seen to steal[stealing] the car by several people.

개념 29 by 이외의 전치사를 쓰는 수동태 p. 124

01 from 02 at 03 in
04 with 05 to 06 to
07 interested in 08 worried about
09 made of 10 satisfied with
11 crowded with 12 covered with

개념 30 that절을 목적어로 하는 문장의 수동태 p. 125

01 to 02 that
03 to 04 that
05 is said that 06 is expected to come
07 was believed that 08 are considered to

바로 개념 확인 노트 개념 29–30 p. 126

개념 29 by 이외의 전치사를 쓰는 수동태

be surprised at	~에 놀라다
be interested in	~에 관심이 있다
be tired of	~에 싫증나다
be worried about	~에 관해 걱정하다
be concerned about	~에 관해 염려하다
be involved in	~에 관련되다
be made of + 성질이 변하지 않는 재료	~으로 만들어지다
be made from + 성질이 변하는 재료	~으로 만들어지다
be covered with	~으로 덮여 있다
be filled with	~으로 가득 차다
be pleased with	~에 기뻐하다
be satisfied with	~에 만족하다
be crowded with	~으로 붐비다
be finished with	~을 끝내다
be accustomed to	~에 익숙하다
be related to	~에 관련이 있다

개념 30 that절을 목적어로 하는 문장의 수동태

1 it, 주어

목적어가 that절인 문장	주어 + 동사 + that절 (목적어)
가주어 it을 수동태 문장의 주어로 쓸 때	It (가주어) + be동사 + 과거분사 + that절 (진주어)
that절의 주어를 수동태 문장의 주어로 쓸 때	주어 (that절의 주어) + be동사 + 과거분사 + to부정사 ~ (that절의 동사)

바로 기본 확인 노트 개념 29–30 p. 127

A 01 are made of 02 am not accustomed to
03 Is, involved in 04 is not surprised at
05 was pleased with 06 is, crowded with

B 01 It, thought that 02 expected to win
03 said to be 04 believed that she has
05 Mr. Roland, reported, have been

교과서에서 뽑은 *405* 문장 마스터하기 pp. 128–129

211 The world is filled with millions of different colors.

212 I'm not satisfied with the steak.

213 Are you interested in drawing cartoons?

214 The thick walls are made of earth.

215 They're always worried about my grades.

216 It is always crowded with tourists from all over the world.

217 A lot of sea animals were covered with oil.

218 What you draw and how you draw it are related to your personality.

219 This simple drink is said to be good for a cold.

220 Gijisi *juldarigi* ropes are believed to help couples have a child.

221 The launch of new hydrogen cars is expected to help reduce air pollution.

222 It is said that he won the war only with twelve wooden ships.

223 She is considered to be the best singer on the team.

224 He was thought to have visited many places.

225 It is believed that the hamburger was invented in a small town in Texas, USA.

REVIEW TEST pp. 130–132

01 ① 02 ② 03 ② 04 ② 05 ⑤
06 ② 07 ③ 08 ① 09 ③ 10 ④
11 ① 12 ⑤ 13 ⑤ 14 ② 15 ④
16 ③ 17 ② 18 ④

서술형 • 수행평가형

01 (1) The plant has been used in medical treatment by many doctors.
(2) His old desk was always covered with dust.

02 (1) was sent a nice present by my grandfather, was sent to me by my grandfather
(2) was reported that the fire was four times the size of Manhattan by CNN, was reported to be four times the size of Manhattan by CNN

03 (1) it is not being cleaned by Susie
(2) Cookies are being made by Susie.
(3) The living room is being cleaned by them.

01 나무가 '잘리는' 것이므로 수동태로 써야 하며, 앞에 조동사 will이 있으므로 「be + 과거분사」를 써야 한다.

02 ② 조동사가 있는 수동태는 「조동사 + be + 과거분사」 형태로 써야 한다. should been treated → should be treated

03 부사구 'in 1443'으로 보아 과거 시제의 수동태를 써야 한다. 또한 주어가 단수이므로 be동사의 형태는 was가 알맞다.

04 ② 과거 시점을 나타내는 부사 yesterday가 있으므로 수동태도 과거 시제로 써야 한다. has been made → was made

05 have to 뒤에는 동사원형이 오므로 be동사의 원형 be를 쓰고 그 뒤에 과거분사를 쓴다.

06 ②의 빈칸에는 for를, 나머지 빈칸에는 to를 써야 한다.

07 ③ 사역동사 make가 쓰인 5형식 문장 'My sister made me wash the dishes.'를 수동태 문장으로 바꿔 쓴 것으로, 목적격 보어에 해당하는 동사원형은 to부정사로 바꿔야 한다. washing → to wash

08 4형식 문장 'Matt sent me the message.'를 각각 직접목적어와 간접목적어를 주어로 하여 수동태 문장으로 바꾼 것이다. 간접목적어를 주어로 할 때 직접목적어는 동사 뒤에 바로 쓴다.

09 ① of → to ② walk → to walk [walking] ④ by Ms. Anderson science → science by Ms. Anderson ⑤ to staying → to stay

10 동사구의 수동태를 쓸 때 동사 뒤의 전치사나 부사 등은 과거분사 바로 뒤에 쓴다.

11 동사구의 수동태를 쓸 때 동사 뒤의 전치사나 부사 등은 과거분사 바로 뒤에 쓴다. The form was filled out by the student. fill out: (양식을) 채우다

12 놀리다: make fun of

13 be concerned about: ~에 관해 염려하다, be worried about: ~에 관해 걱정하다

14 be accustomed to: ~에 익숙하다

15 • be finished with: ~을 끝내다 • be interested in: ~에 관심이 있다 • be made from: ~으로 만들어지다 (성질이 바뀌는 재료)

16 that절을 목적어로 하는 문장을 수동태 문장으로 쓸 때, that절의 주어를 문장의 주어로 쓰면 동사는 to부정사 형태로 쓴다.

17 명사절을 이끄는 접속사 that이 들어가는 것이 알맞다.

18 that절을 목적어로 하는 문장을 수동태 문장으로 쓸 때, that절의 주어를 문장의 주어로 쓰면 동사는 to부정사 형태로 쓴다. (← People think that the old man is very kind to his neighbors.)

서술형 • 수행평가형

01 (1) 식물이 '사용되는' 것이므로 수동태로 써야 한다. 현재완료의 수동태이므로 「has been + 과거분사」 형태이다.
(2) be covered with: ~으로 덮여 있다

02 (1) 4형식 문장을 수동태 문장으로 쓸 때 간접목적어와 직접목적어를 각각 주어로 하여 두 개의 문장을 쓸 수 있다.
(2) that절을 목적어로 하는 문장을 수동태 문장으로 쓸 때, 주어 자리에는 가주어 it을 쓰거나 that절의 주어를 쓸 수 있다.

03 (1) Susie는 거실 청소를 하고 있지 않으므로 부정으로 답한다.
(2) Susie가 만들고 있는 것은 쿠키이므로 쿠키를 주어로 한 수동태 문장으로 답한다.
(3) Tom과 Kyle에 의해 거실이 청소되고 있으므로 거실을 주어로 한 수동태 문장으로 답한다.

UNIT 08 관계사

개념 31 관계대명사_주격, 소유격, 목적격 p. 134

01 which 02 that 03 whom
04 who 05 who steals 06 which
07 who [that] won the gold medal
08 which [that] he showed to me
09 who(m) [that] Leo is talking with 또는 with whom Leo is talking

개념 32 관계대명사 what과 that p. 135

01 What 02 that 03 what
04 what 05 what 06 that
07 what 08 What 09 what
10 that 11 what 12 that

바로 개념 확인 노트 개념 31－32 p. 136

개념 31 관계대명사_주격, 소유격, 목적격

1 동사 2 명사

선행사	주격	소유격	목적격
사람	who	whose	who(m)
사물, 동물	which	whose / of which	which
사람, 사물, 동물	that	–	that

개념 32 관계대명사 what과 that

1 주어, 보어, 목적어, ~하는 것 3 who(m), which

관계대명사 what	관계대명사 that
명사절을 이끎	형용사절을 이끎
선행사 없음	선행사 있음
관계대명사 what + 불완전한 문장	관계대명사 that + 불완전한 문장

바로 기본 확인 노트 개념 31－32 p. 137

A 01 who [that]
02 which [that] 또는 삭제
03 which [that]
04 who [that] is 또는 삭제
05 in which 또는 where
06 suffer
07 which [that] 또는 삭제
08 everyone loves
09 whose
10 What

B 01 The police arrested the thief who broke into her store yesterday.
02 He is my new neighbor who(m) I talked about. [He is my new neighbor about whom I talked].
03 I met a woman whose hobby is rock-climbing.
04 This is one of the films which I'd like to watch.
05 Most people who(m) Kate invited to her house didn't show up.

교과서에서 뽑은 *405* 문장 마스터하기 pp. 138－139

226 The farmer visited a close friend who had four children.
227 Thulin wanted a sturdy, yet light bag which would last for ages.
228 It was written by a woman whose husband was far away.
229 He is one of the three gods who created humans.
230 This is the woman with whom I worked. 또는 This is the woman who(m) I worked with.
231 They decided to adopt the dog which they saw at the animal shelter.
232 Birbal came back with two pots whose necks were really narrow.
233 Ants live in colonies which have lots of residents living together.
234 I met a girl whose name is the same as mine.
235 Those who read the article carefully laughed out loud.
236 I entered a photo contest with the pictures I took in Iceland.
237 Can you imagine a building that looks like an egg?
238 I hope you like this poem which I wrote when I started high school.
239 What volcanoes do is not always bad for humans.
240 Is there any evidence that supports what the writer says?

개념 33 관계부사 p. 140

01 when 02 where
03 why 04 the way
05 which 06 which
07 when 08 where
09 why 10 how
11 when 12 where

개념 34 관계대명사의 계속적 용법 p. 141

01 which 02 who
03 which 04 which
05 all of whom 06 who died
07 who is 08 which is
09 which made

바로 개념 확인 노트 개념 33－34 p. 142

개념 33 관계부사

2 전치사, 관계대명사 3 how

	선행사	관계부사	전치사 + 관계대명사
시간	the day, the time, the week 등	when	in/at/on+which
장소	the place, the town, the city 등	where	in/at/on+which
이유	the reason	why	for which
방법	(the way)	how	in which

개념 34 관계대명사의 계속적 용법

2 콤마(,)　　3 that, what

제한적 용법	계속적 용법
선행사를 직접 수식함	선행사에 대한 보충 설명을 함
관계사 앞에 콤마(,)가 없음	관계사 앞에 콤마(,)가 있음
'~한, ~하는'으로 해석함	관계사 앞의 절부터 해석하고 and, but 등의 접속사를 넣어 관계사 뒤의 절을 해석함
He has two sons who are teachers. 그에게는 교사인 아들이 두 명 있다. (→ 아들이 둘 이상일 수 있음)	He has two sons, who(= and they) are teachers. 그에게는 아들이 둘 있고, 그들은 교사이다. (→ 아들이 둘 뿐임)

바로 기본 확인 노트 개념 33-34 p. 143

A
01 when, on which
02 where, in which
03 how, in which
04 why, for which

B
01 I have two close friends, who are very different from each other.
02 My teacher recommended this novel, which changed my life.
03 My favorite artist is Gustav Klimt, whose work is full of patterns and colors.
04 I met Sophia, who(m) I hadn't seen for ages.
05 The man said he didn't know Anne, which was a lie.

교과서에서 뽑은 405 문장 마스터하기 pp. 144-145

241 This is the day when my parents got married.
242 Turkey is a country where East meets West.
243 That's the reason why he hasn't finished the painting yet.
244 Calli should pick a time when her mom is ready to listen.
245 This letter shows how people got over these difficulties.
246 That is the place where my dog hides his food.
247 Sunmin's sister disliked how Sunmin had treated her.
248 Cancun is a city where 4.8 million tourists travel every year.
249 I share a room with my sister, who is two years older than me.
250 People use ROFL quite often, which means "Rolling On the Floor Laughing."
251 The book is about King Sejong, who invented Hangeul.
252 Most buildings need air conditioning, which uses a lot of energy.
253 Walnuts also have wrinkles, which the brain has too.
254 All the rules were explained by an old man in a suit, who sounded very serious and unkind.
255 Uncle Ben went on a trip to Africa, which was his lifelong dream.

개념 35 복합 관계대명사 p. 146

01 who　　02 whichever
03 whoever　　04 No matter who
05 whichever　　06 Whatever
07 Whatever　　08 Whoever
09 whatever　　10 Who(m)ever
11 whichever　　12 Whoever

개념 36 복합 관계부사 p. 147

01 Whenever　　02 when
03 However　　04 wherever
05 However tired you　　06 Wherever
07 wherever she goes
08 whenever you like
09 However hard the problem may be

바로 개념 확인 노트 개념 35-36 p. 148

개념 35 복합 관계대명사

1 관계대명사, -ever　　2 명사절

복합 관계대명사	명사절	양보의 부사절
whoever	anyone who ~하는 누구든지	no matter who 누가 ~하더라도
whomever	anyone whom ~하는 누구든지	no matter whom 누구를 ~하더라도
whichever	anything which ~하는 어느 것이든지	no matter which 어느 것이[을] ~하더라도
whatever	anything that ~하는 무엇이든지	no matter what 무엇이[을] ~하더라도

개념 36 복합 관계부사

1 관계부사, -ever 2 양보

3 however, 형용사/부사

복합 관계부사	시간, 장소의 부사절	양보의 부사절
whenever	at any time when ~할 때마다	no matter when 언제 ~하더라도
wherever	at any place where ~한 곳 어디에나	no matter where 어디에서 ~하더라도
however	–	no matter how 아무리 ~하더라도

바로 기본 확인 노트 개념 35–36 p. 149

A 01 Whoever breaks the law

02 Whatever you say

03 whenever I feel tired

04 However cold it is

B 01 whatever [whichever] you like

02 Whoever gets home first

03 However hard I tried

04 No matter what happens

05 anyone who passes

06 whenever anything goes wrong

07 Wherever she is

08 However loudly he might shout

교과서에서 뽑은 *405* 문장 마스터하기 pp. 150–151

256 Whenever I lose my temper, she tries to support me.

257 Whatever you do, you leave behind a digital footprint.

258 Whenever I do my best, they tell me I don't try hard enough.

259 We all know that people are the same wherever we go.

260 Whoever has a healthy mind is capable of reading other people's minds.

261 Please take whatever you want from the fridge.

262 Whenever he invented something, he experimented many times.

263 However difficult it is, I don't care.

264 Whenever a bat is struck, it vibrates in response.

265 Value yourself, whoever you are and whatever you do.

266 We will do whatever is necessary to help you.

267 Whoever comes to the party will be welcome.

268 The dog became very upset and depressed whenever she was left alone.

269 Whatever job I have in the future, I'll try to overcome the obstacles around me.

270 However serious the situation is, it is not hopeless.

REVIEW TEST pp. 152–154

01 ③	02 ⑤	03 ③	04 ①	05 ②
06 ⑤	07 ②	08 ⑤	09 ④	10 ③
11 ②	12 ①, ④	13 ③	14 ②	15 ②
16 ③	17 ④	18 ①	19 ④	20 ⑤

서술형 • 수행평가형

01 (1) what I did yesterday

(2) that she could do to win first prize

(3) which was a shame

(4) who has many fans worldwide

02 ⓑ → He explained everything (that [which]) he had experienced.

ⓓ → Venice is a city (which [that] is) located on the seacoast in the north of Italy.

03 (1) whose nickname is

(2) when Monica was born 또는 in which Monica was born [which Monica was born in]

(3) who is good at singing K-pop songs

01 첫 번째 빈칸에는 목적격 관계대명사가 필요하고 사람 선행사이므로 whom이 들어가야 한다. 두 번째 빈칸 다음에는 명사가 있으므로 소유격 관계대명사인 whose가 들어가야 한다.

02 관계대명사 that은 who(m), which와 바꿔 쓸 수 있다. 하지만 계속적 용법으로 쓰였을 때나 전치사가 앞에 있는 경우에는 관계대명사 that으로 바꿀 수 없다.

03 관계대명사 what은 선행사를 포함하며 '~하는 것'이라는 의미이다.

04 단어를 바르게 배열하면 which helps people who cannot see이다.

05 ② 앞에 선행사 something이 있으므로 that또는 which가 와야 한다. 나머지는 모두 선행사를 포함한 관계대명사 what이 알맞다.

06 관계대명사가 모두 계속적 용법으로 쓰였다. 첫 번째 빈칸에는 'to swim across the river'가 선행사이므로 관계대명사 which가 와야 한다. 두 번째 빈칸에는 사람 선행사이고 주어가 없으므로 who가 와야 한다.

07 선행사가 전치사의 목적어이므로 「전치사 + 관계대명사」의 형태로 써야 한다.

08 ⑤는 주격 관계대명사이고 나머지는 모두 목적격 관계대명사이다. 주격 관계대명사 다음에는 동사가 오고, 목적격 관계대명사 다음에는 「주어 + 동사」가 온다.

09 ④는 접속사 that이다. 접속사 that 앞에는 선행사가 없고 뒤에는 완전한 문장이 온다.

10 ③은 간접의문문에 쓰인 의문사로 '무엇'이라고 해석한다. 나머지는 모두 관계대명사(~하는 것)이다.

11 「주격 관계대명사 + be동사 + 분사」 구문에서 「주격 관계대명사 +

be동사」는 생략할 수 있다.

12 ① that이 주격 관계대명사로 쓰였으므로 생략할 수 없다. ④ 계속적 용법으로 쓰였을 때 관계대명사는 생략할 수 없다.

13 ③ 주격 관계대명사 다음에 분사만 남아 있으므로 「주격 관계대명사 + be동사」의 형태인 that was 또는 who was가 생략되었다고 볼 수 있다.

14 선행사 everyone 다음에 목적격 관계대명사인 that이 생략되어 있다.

15 빈칸에는 접속사와 부사 역할을 하는 관계부사가 필요하다. 선행사가 a place로 장소를 나타내므로 where가 와야 한다.

16 ③ 주어 역할을 하는 주격 관계대명사 which 또는 that이 와야 한다. 나머지는 모두 관계부사 when이 알맞다.

17 관계부사 how는 the way와 함께 쓰이지 않고 둘 중 하나는 생략해야 한다.

18 관계부사 why는 「for + 관계대명사 which」로 바꿔 쓸 수 있다.

19 however는 양보의 부사절을 이끌며 어순은 「however + 형용사/부사 + 주어 + 동사 ~」이다.

20 ⑤ 복합 관계대명사는 자체에 선행사를 포함하고 있으므로 Anyone 다음에는 who를 써야 한다. 또는 Anyone을 삭제한다.

서술형 • 수행평가형

01 (1) 선행사가 없으므로 관계대명사 what을 쓴다.
(2) 선행사에 all, the only, the same 등이 쓰이면 주로 관계대명사 that을 쓴다.
(3) 앞 문장 전체를 선행사로 받는 관계대명사 which를 써야 한다. 계속적 용법이므로 that은 쓸 수 없다.
(4) 선행사가 사람이므로 주격 관계대명사 who를 쓴다.

02 ⓑ 관계대명사 what은 선행사를 포함하고 있으므로 관계대명사 that 또는 which로 고쳐야 한다. 선행사가 -thing, -body, -one으로 끝나는 명사일 때는 주로 관계대명사 that을 쓴다. 목적격 관계대명사이므로 생략할 수 있다.
ⓓ 관계부사 where를 관계사절 안에서 주어 역할을 하는 관계대명사 which 또는 that으로 고쳐야 한다. 「주격 관계대명사 + be동사」를 생략할 수 있다.

03 (1) 'Monica는 별명이 Supergirl인 나의 가장 친한 친구이다'라는 의미가 되도록 소유격 관계대명사를 쓰고 명사를 쓴다.
(2) '8월은 Monica가 태어난 달이다'라는 의미가 되어야 하며, 선행사가 the month로 시간을 나타내므로 관계부사 when을 쓴다.
(3) '나는 Monica를 좋아하고, 그녀는 한국 대중가요를 잘 부른다'라는 의미가 되도록 관계대명사 who를 쓴다. 계속적 용법이므로 that은 쓸 수 없다.

UNIT 09 접속사

개념 37 상관접속사 p. 156

01 snow
02 nor
03 Max
04 is
05 as well as
06 Either, or
07 only, also
08 Not, but

개념 38 간접의문문 p. 157

01 what
02 how long
03 that
04 whether
05 why
06 if there is a bank near here
07 how I should take care of the puppies
08 do you guess the flight will take off

바로 개념 확인 노트 개념 37-38 p. 158

개념 37 상관접속사

2 동등한

상관접속사	의미	주어로 쓰일 때 동사의 수
both *A* and *B*	A와 B 둘 다	복수 취급
not only *A* but also *B*	A뿐만 아니라 B도	B에 맞춤
A as well as *B*	B뿐만 아니라 A도	A에 맞춤
not *A* but *B*	A가 아니라 B	B에 맞춤
either *A* or *B*	A 또는 B 둘 중 하나	B에 맞춤
neither *A* nor *B*	A도 B도 아닌	B에 맞춤

개념 38 간접의문문

2 의문사
3 if, whether

종류	형태
의문사가 있는 의문문	의문사 + 주어 + 동사 **주절의 동사가** think, believe, guess, suppose, imagine **등일 때**: 의문사 + do you think [believe, guess, ...] + 주어 + 동사 ...?
의문사가 없는 의문문	if + 주어 + 동사 / whether + 주어 + 동사

바로 기본 확인 노트 개념 37-38 p. 159

A
01 neither
02 not
03 but
04 and
05 nor
06 or
07 as, as
08 but also
09 either
10 not only

B
01 if [whether] you can bake a cake in an hour

02 do you guess they are going
03 if [whether] Julia will like the new school
04 how many people are in the hall
05 do you think Mr. Baron will get back to his hometown
06 who this woman in the photo is

교과서에서 뽑은 405 문장 마스터하기 pp. 160–161

271 He felt both happy and sad.
272 What they need is not tools, but cats.
273 She will buy either fish or meat.
274 He had no idea why he did it.
275 I wondered if I could do something for those girls.
276 He was neither a politician nor a soldier.
277 Not only Marie Curie but also her daughter was awarded the Nobel Prize.
278 Where do you think da Vinci's greatness came from?
279 You gave us courage as well as hope.
280 She could either stand up to give up her seat or stand up to injustice.
281 Nobody knows for sure how many volcanoes there are in the world.
282 You may wonder whether you can buy just a few flowers at the market.
283 What do you think I should do?
284 At first, I was not sure if he was telling the truth.
285 You will not only feel sure about yourself but also look confident to other people.

개념 39 부사절을 이끄는 접속사 p. 162

01 until
02 If
03 In case
04 When
05 As soon as
06 although [though]
07 so, that
08 If, not
09 in order to

개념 40 접속부사 p. 163

01 Thus
02 Otherwise
03 Nevertheless
04 However
05 Accordingly
06 Besides
07 Then
08 Moreover
09 However
10 on the other hand
11 Otherwise
12 As a result

바로 개념 확인 노트 개념 39–40 p. 164

개념 39 부사절을 이끄는 접속사

2 현재 시제

구분	접속사	의미
시간	when	~할 때
	while	~하는 동안
	as	~하면서
	until	~할 때까지
	as soon as	~하자마자
	since	~ 이후로
결과	so	그래서
	so ~ that	매우 ~해서 …하다
	so ~ that … can	매우 ~해서 …할 수 있다 (= ~ enough + to부정사)
	so ~ that … can't	너무 ~해서 …할 수 없다 (= too ~ to 부정사)

구분	접속사	의미
이유	because	~ 때문에
	as	~ 때문에
	since	~ 때문에
조건	if	만일 ~라면
	unless	만일 ~ 아니라면 (= if ~ not)
	in case (that)	~할 경우에는 (= in case of + 명사)
목적	so that … *can, in order that … *can	~하기 위해 (= in order + to부정사 / to부정사) *조동사 may, will 등도 쓰임
양보	though, although, even though	비록 ~이지만, ~에도 불구하고 (= in spite of/ despite + 명사)

개념 40 접속부사

구분	접속부사	의미
양보, 대조	however	하지만
	nevertheless	그럼에도 불구하고
	on the other hand	반면에
첨가	also	또한
	furthermore	더욱이
	besides	더욱이
	in addition	게다가
	moreover	게다가

구분	접속부사	의미
결과	therefore	그러므로
	thus	그러므로
	accordingly	따라서
	consequently	결과적으로
	as a result	결과적으로
기타	then	그러고 나서
	otherwise	그 외에는, 그렇지 않으면

바로 기본 확인 노트 개념 39–40 p. 165

A
01 I have learned English since I was 10.
02 As soon as the movie ended, they ran out of the theater. / As soon as they ran out of the theater, the movie ended.
03 I was late for school because the bus had a flat tire.
04 It was so cold that I couldn't stay out anymore.
05 In case you are lost, install the map application on your phone.

B
01 Otherwise
02 Even though
03 that, couldn't
04 If
05 so that
06 As a result
07 Nevertheless [However]
08 In addition
09 in order
10 On the other hand

교과서에서 뽑은 405 문장 마스터하기 pp. 166–167

286 As a result, most of his constructions use curved stones.

287 I have blue eyes. On the other hand, my brother has brown eyes.

288 Mr. Boggis was so shocked that he couldn't say anything.

289 As soon as I arrived in Beijing, I met my host family.

290 In case you get thirsty between meals, you can carry a water bottle with you.

291 When she's so stressed that her life looks gloomy, she cleans her room.

292 It is raining too hard. Therefore, we should stay at home.

293 Although we started small, we are making a big difference.

294 Don't stop dreaming until your dreams come true.

295 While he was drinking his coffee, a headline caught his eye.

296 Negative thoughts are so harmful that they can damage your brain.

297 We have to tidy up the garden. In addition, we have to prepare for the party.

298 They made up this fake article so that they could draw the readers' attention.

299 If this kind of data is analyzed wisely, the spread of the flu can be predicted.

300 Children cannot enter the theater unless they are with their parents [if they are not with their parents].

REVIEW TEST pp. 168–170

01 ④ 02 ③ 03 ④ 04 ③ 05 ①, ②
06 ② 07 ① 08 ④ 09 ④ 10 ①
11 ② 12 ⑤ 13 ②, ⑤ 14 ① 15 too weak 16 smart enough 17 ⑤ 18 ②
19 ③ 20 ⑤

서술형 • 수행평가형

01 (1) I'm not sure if [whether] we can get there on time.
(2) Where do you guess he went during the vacation?
(3) Tell me how many books I can check out at the library.

02 (1) I arrived at the restaurant so late that I could not order dinner.
(2) The man was so strong that he could lift the heavy box.

03 (1) In addition (2) On the other hand
(3) because (4) In case

01 *A* as well as *B*: B뿐만 아니라 A도

02 ③ 「both *A* and *B*」가 주어로 쓰이면 항상 복수 취급한다. likes → like

03 ④ 상관접속사는 문법적으로 동등한 어구를 연결하므로, not과 but이 명사 desserts와 동사구 take a walk를 연결하는 것은 어색하다.

04 간접의문문을 사용하여 바르게 영어로 옮긴 것은 ③이다.

05 ① 간접의문문이 바르게 사용되었다. ② 접속사 that이 동사의 목적어 역할을 하는 명사절을 이끌고 있다. ③ 주절의 동사가 guess, think 등일 때 간접의문문의 의문사는 문장 맨 앞에 쓴다. → What do you guess my nickname is? ④ 간접의문문의 어순은 「의문사 + 주어 + 동사」이다. when was the boy found → when the boy was found ⑤ 간접의문문의 「의문사 + 주어 + 동사」에서 의문사가 문장 맨 앞으로 이동한 형태이다. did John deceive us → John deceived us

06 ②의 빈칸에는 접속사 that이 알맞다.

07 두 문장의 관계로 보아 '그 반에서 아무도 모르기 때문에 수줍어했다'는 것이 자연스럽다. 따라서 이유를 나타내는 접속사 as가 빈칸에 알맞다.

08 '선생님이 너를 부르지 않는다면 답을 말하지 마라.'라고 해석하는 것이 자연스럽다. 따라서 '만일 ~ 아니라면'이라는 의미의 unless가 빈칸에 알맞다.

09 '내가 휴가에서 돌아올 때까지 그가 나 대신 개를 돌봐주길 바란다.'라고 해석하는 것이 자연스럽다. 따라서 '~할 때까지'라는 의미의 until이 알맞다.

10 조건을 나타내는 부사절에서는 현재 시제로 미래를 나타내므로 is가 알맞다.

11 ② unless는 '만일 ~ 아니라면'이라는 의미의 접속사이므로 이 문장에서는 '만일 ~라면'이라는 의미의 if로 바꾸는 것이 자연스럽다.

12 「so ~ that ...」은 '매우 ~해서 …하다'라는 뜻이다.

13 접속사 so that은 '~하기 위해서'라는 의미로 「(in order +) to부정사구」로 바꿔 쓸 수 있다.

14 빈칸에는 부사 so가 꾸밀 수 있는 말이면서 주어 The food의 보어가 될 수 있는 말이 와야 한다. 따라서 형용사가 들어가는 것이 알맞으며 명사 salt는 들어갈 수 없다.

15 so ~ that ... can't = too ~ to부정사

16 so ~ that ... can = ~ enough + to부정사

17 thus는 '그러므로'라는 의미이므로, 서로 상반되는 내용의 두 문장을 연결하기에는 어울리지 않는다.

18 '그럼에도 불구하고'라는 의미의 though와 비슷한 뜻의 접속부사를 찾는다. '그러나'라는 의미의 however가 가장 적절하다.

19 빈칸에는 '그렇지 않으면'이라는 의미의 otherwise가 들어가는 것이 알맞다.

20 빈칸에는 둘 다 '게다가, 더군다나'의 의미를 갖는 접속부사가 들어가는 것이 어울린다.

서술형 • 수행평가형

01 (1) 의문사가 없는 의문문을 간접의문문으로 쓸 때에는 if 또는 whether를 쓰고 그 뒤에 주어와 동사 순으로 쓴다.

(2) 주절의 동사가 think, guess 등일 때에는 간접의문문의 의문사를 문장의 맨 앞에 쓰고 나머지를 주어와 동사 순으로 쓴다.

(3) 간접의문문을 쓸 때 의문문은 「의문사 + 주어 + 동사」의 어순으로 바꾸어 넣는다.

02 (1) 「too ~ to부정사」는 「so ~ that … can't」 구조의 문장으로 바꿔 쓸 수 있다.

(2) 「~ enough + to부정사」는 「so ~ that … can」 구조의 문장으로 바꿔 쓸 수 있다.

03 (1) 뒤에 있는 문장은 앞 문장의 내용에 추가되는 것이므로 '게다가'라는 의미의 in addition이 빈칸에 어울린다.

(2) 뒤에 있는 문장이 앞의 내용과 상반되므로 '반면에'라는 의미의 on the other hand가 빈칸에 어울린다.

(3) 빈칸 뒤의 내용이 앞 내용의 이유이므로 빈칸에는 because가 어울린다.

(4) 빈칸에는 '~할 경우에는'이라는 의미로 조건을 나타내는 접속사가 어울리므로 in case가 알맞다.

해석 대부분의 사람들은 다양한 호불호가 있다. 나 또한 내가 좋아하는 일과 좋아하지 않는 일이 있다. 예를 들어 나는 늘 TV 보는 것과 독서를 즐긴다. 또한 드럼 연주하는 것과 영화 보러 가는 것을 좋아한다. 반면에 물을 무서워하기 때문에 수영하러 가는 것은 싫어한다. 수영장에 갈 경우에는 대부분의 시간을 수영장 가장자리에 앉아 있다.

UNIT 10 비교 구문

개념 41 원급 비교 p. 172

01 as **02** can **03** so
04 twice **05** as **06** long
07 as solid as it looks
08 not so expensive as her car
09 half as fast as the old one
10 as beautifully as we can
11 as quickly as you can
12 three times as bright as the other one

개념 42 여러 가지 비교급 표현 p. 173

01 happier **02** and **03** a little
04 less **05** the fewer
06 a lot bigger than mine
07 getting colder and colder
08 the sleepier you will get
09 even stronger than they predicted

바로 개념 확인 노트 개념 41–42 p. 174

개념 41 원급 비교

1 원급 2 three times, four times

원급 비교	*A* ~ as + 원급 + as + *B* 의미: A가 B만큼 ~하다
can을 활용한 원급 비교	as + 원급 + as + 주어 + can (= as + 원급 + as possible) 의미: …가 할 수 있는 한 ~한/하게
배수 표현을 사용한 비교	*A* ~ 배수 표현 + as + 원급 + as + *B* 의미: A는 B보다 …배만큼 ~하다

개념 42 여러 가지 비교급 표현

1 than 2 강조

비교급 구문	의미
비교급 + than	…보다 더 ~한
much / a lot / far / even + 비교급	훨씬 더 ~한
a little / a bit / slightly + 비교급	약간 더 ~한
less + 원급 + than	…보다 덜 ~한
비교급 + and + 비교급	점점 더 ~한
the + 비교급 ~, the + 비교급 ...	더 ~할수록 더 …하다

바로 기본 확인 노트 개념 41–42 p. 175

A
01 big **02** louder
03 old **04** more
05 heavier **06** can
07 popular **08** longer, longer

B
01 as tall as
02 much [a lot, far, even] sweeter than
03 three times as big as
04 a little [a bit, slightly] better
05 as slowly as she could
06 The more difficult, the more students

교과서에서 뽑은 405 문장 마스터하기 pp. 176–177

301 Mina can play the guitar as well as Joan.
302 Chicken is much tastier than sandwiches.
303 This is three times as long as that.
304 They fought harder and harder.
305 Try to get as much information as you can.
306 The harder you dig, the faster you'll finish.
307 This restaurant is not so nice as we expected.
308 This chair is less comfortable than that sofa.
309 The more books we share, the more we learn.
310 Drawing on a wall was much harder than drawing on paper.
311 My old bike is almost as good as a new one.

312 I hid the slippers behind me as quickly and naturally as I could.

313 More and more people are using reusable bags.

314 We made our neighborhood a little brighter and happier.

315 The more sincere your apology is, the better it will be received.

개념 43 여러 가지 최상급 표현 p. 178

01 of
02 longest
03 the funniest
04 of
05 the smartest
06 artists
07 the shortest
08 the youngest of
09 the fastest, in
10 the kindest, ever met

개념 44 원급과 비교급을 이용한 최상급 표현 p. 179

01 than
02 No
03 as
04 more creative
05 all
06 more exciting than, more exciting than, No movie, exciting as this movie
07 smaller than, than this island

바로 개념 확인 노트 개념 43-44 p. 180

개념 43 여러 가지 최상급 표현

1 the

최상급 구문	의미
the + 최상급 ~ + in + 장소/집단	…에서 가장 ~한
the + 최상급 ~ of + 복수 명사	… 중에서 가장 ~한
one of the + 최상급 + 복수 명사	가장 ~한 … 중 하나
the + 최상급 + 명사 (+ that) + 주어 + have ever + 과거분사	지금까지 …한 것 중 가장 ~한

개념 44 원급과 비교급을 이용한 최상급 표현

원급과 비교급을 이용한 최상급 표현	의미
비교급 + than + any other + 단수 명사	다른 어떤 …보다 ~한
비교급 + than + all the other + 복수 명사	다른 모든 …보다 ~한
No (other) + 명사 ~ + 비교급 + than	어떤 -도 …보다 ~하지 않다
No (other) + 명사 ~ + as [so] + 원급 + as	어떤 -도 …만큼 ~하지 않다

바로 기본 확인 노트 개념 43-44 p. 181

A
01 the oldest in
02 more important than
03 the youngest teacher of
04 have ever seen
05 one of the highest mountains
06 earlier than any other student in

B
01 No (other) actor is more talented
02 as important for life
03 faster than
04 more wonderful than

교과서에서 뽑은 *405* 문장 마스터하기 pp. 182-183

316 Mt. Everest is higher than any other mountain in the world.

317 The Sagrada Familia is one of the most famous churches in the world.

318 It will be the most embarrassing day of my life.

319 This is the most amazing book that I have ever seen.

320 No one can play the guitar as fast as Joe (can).

321 I can be the richest farmer in this village.

322 Popcorn is one of the most popular snacks around the world.

323 They performed much better than any other team.

324 The Netherlands has the largest flower market in the world.

325 This is the best beef I've ever tasted!

326 What do you think is the most important skill a game designer needs?

327 Leonardo da Vinci is known as one of the greatest painters of all time.

328 No other thing is more urgent than solving this problem.

329 This is better than any other jam I've ever had.

330 In the queen's mind, the kitten was worth far more than all the jewels in the world.

REVIEW TEST pp. 184-186

01 ② 02 ① 03 ④ 04 ② 05 ②
06 ⑤ 07 ③ 08 ② 09 ①, ②, ③
10 ④ 11 ⑤ 12 ③ 13 ④ 14 ③
15 ④ 16 ④ 17 ② 18 ②

서술형 • 수행평가형

01 (1) no writer is better than Ms. Brett
(2) Sometimes price is less important than comfort.

02 (1) Christine is the fastest of all.
(2) Anita is the tallest of all.
(3) Lindsay is younger than Christine.

03 [예시답] (1) I run faster than Suyeong and Minjae.
(2) I get up earlier than my brother.
(3) I have the most books in my class.
(4) I have the most friends in my school.
(5) I am more popular than any other student in my class.

01 as + 원급 + as: …만큼 ~한
02 원급 비교의 부정은 「not so [as] + 원급 + as」로 쓴다.
03 주어진 문장이 '내 방이 네 방의 절반 크기이다.'라는 의미이므로 ④ '네 방은 내 방의 두 배만큼 크다.'라는 의미의 문장과 뜻이 통한다.
04 as + 원급 + as + 주어 + can: …가 할 수 있는 한 ~하게, 주절의 시제에 맞춰 can을 과거형 could로 써야 한다.
05 not은 원급 비교의 부정을 나타낼 때 쓰고, 배수 표현인 twice, half, three times는 원급 비교 구문 앞에 써서 '~배만큼 …한'의 의미를 나타낼 수 있다. so는 원급 비교의 부정을 나타낼 때 앞의 as 대신 쓸 수 있는 말이므로 빈칸에는 어울리지 않는다.
06 '더 ~할수록 더 …하다'라는 의미의 「the + 비교급 ~, the + 비교급 …」 형태가 되어야 한다.
07 ③ less 뒤에는 원급이 와서 '덜 ~한'의 의미를 나타낸다.
08 than 앞에는 비교급이 와야 한다. much는 비교급을 강조하는 부사로 쓰였다.
09 ① pale and pale → paler and paler ② more healthier → healthier ③ your → yours
10 「the + 비교급 ~, the + 비교급 …」 형태가 되어야 하므로 The more와 the wiser가 알맞다.
11 ⑤ even은 비교급을 강조하는 표현이며, than 앞에는 비교급이 와야 한다. even outgoing than → even more outgoing than
12 ① → the fastest one
② → the most in this album
④ → the longest movie that
⑤ → one of the biggest animals
13 ④ '이것은 공원에서 가장 오래된 나무이다.' ≠ '이것은 공원에서 가장 오래된 나무 중 하나이다.'
14 late(늦은)의 최상급 latest는 '최신의, 가장 나중의'라는 의미이다.
15 ④를 제외한 나머지는 모두 '이 조각상이 가장 큰 조각상이다.'라는 의미이다. ④는 '이 조각상은 가장 큰 조각상들 중 하나이다.'라는 의미로 쓰였다.
16 주어진 문장은 비교급을 사용하여 최상급의 의미를 나타낸 문장이다. 바꿔 쓸 수 있는 문장으로는 마찬가지로 비교급을 사용하여 최상급의 의미를 나타내는 ④가 알맞다.
17 첫 번째 문장은 비교급을 사용하여 최상급의 의미를 나타낸 문장이다. 두 번째 문장의 빈칸에 「as + 원급 + as」를 넣어 같은 의미를 나타낼 수 있다.
18 ② 「No + 명사 ~ + as + 원급 + as」 구문이므로 비교급 friendlier를 원급 friendly로 고쳐야 한다.

서술형 • 수행평가형

01 (1) 「No + 명사 ~ + 비교급 + than …」으로 최상급 의미를 나타낼 수 있다.
(2) less + 원급 + than: …보다 덜 ~한
02 질문의 내용을 파악한 뒤 가장 빠른 사람, 가장 키가 큰 사람, Christine보다 어린 사람을 표를 보고 찾아 답한다.
03 최상급과 비교급을 사용하여 자기 자신에 대해 설명하는 문장을 자유롭게 쓴다.

UNIT 11 가정법

개념 45 가정법 과거와 과거완료 p. 188

01 could exercise
02 moved
03 would have listened
04 would
05 hadn't worn
06 had started
07 were, would make
08 had, could build
09 had gotten, would not have been

개념 46 혼합 가정법 p. 189

01 would be
02 wouldn't be
03 had checked
04 wouldn't have
05 had followed
06 had closed, would be
07 had not broken, could go
08 had not walked, would not have

바로 개념 확인 노트 개념 45-46 p. 190

개념 45 가정법 과거와 과거완료

1 가정법 과거 2 가정법 과거완료 3 콤마(,)

		if절	주절
가정법 과거	현재 사실의 반대	If+주어+were 또는 동사의 과거형 ~,	주어+조동사 과거형 (would, could, might)+동사원형 ~.
가정법 과거완료	과거 사실의 반대	If+주어+had+과거분사 ~,	주어+조동사 과거형 (would, could, might)+have+과거분사 ~.

개념 46 혼합 가정법

1 과거완료, 과거 2 과거, 현재

		if절(가정법 과거완료)	주절(가정법 과거)
혼합 가정법	과거에 실현되지 못한 일이 현재까지 영향을 줄 때	If+주어+had+과거분사 ~,	주어+조동사 과거형(would, could, might)+동사원형 ~.

바로 기본 확인 노트 개념 45–46 p. 191

A 01 would drive 02 would believe
03 ate 04 had caught
05 hadn't broken 06 would be
07 had been fine

B 01 had, could take
02 had napped, would not be
03 had not made, could have won
04 had not left, could buy
05 were not afraid, could get
06 had seen, would not have hit

교과서에서 뽑은 *405* 문장 마스터하기 pp. 192–193

331 If he knew my address, he would send me a letter.
332 If the wind had not been so strong, we could have had tea outside.
333 The water inside would quickly boil over if the lid did not have that hole.
334 If I had apologized to her, we would be friends now.
335 I would have died if you hadn't saved my life.
336 If I had enough eggs, I could bake bread for my family.
337 I would not have received a passing grade if you had not helped me.
338 If I had had enough sleep last night, I would not be tired today.
339 If I were an astronaut, I would walk in space.
340 If I got a letter from you, I would be very happy.
341 If we had no smartphones, our lives would be more difficult.
342 If I were you, I would not spend too much time online.
343 If my phone battery had not died, I would have called you earlier.
344 If he had fixed his air conditioner, he could take a good rest now.
345 If the store had been open, I would have bought them.

개념 47 I wish 가정법 / as if 가정법 p. 194

01 were 02 had been
03 had not 04 were
05 had let 06 were
07 I wish I had
08 as if she had heard
09 I wish you had traveled
10 as if he were

개념 48 Without 가정법 p. 195

01 would fail 02 would have been
03 couldn't get 04 could have been
05 it were not for air
06 it were not for the map
07 it had not been for my parents

바로 개념 확인 노트 개념 47–48 p. 196

개념 47 I wish 가정법 / as if 가정법

1 현재 2 과거

I wish 가정법	과거	~라면 좋을 텐데	I wish + 주어 + were 또는 동사의 과거형
	과거완료	~했더라면 좋을 텐데	I wish + 주어 + had + 과거분사
as if 가정법	과거	마치 ~인 것처럼	as if + 주어 + were 또는 동사의 과거형
	과거완료	마치 ~이었던 것처럼	as if + 주어 + had + 과거분사

개념 48 Without 가정법

1 But for, were not 2 had not been

Without 가정법	과거	~이 없다면, …할 것이다	Without + 명사(구), 주어 + 조동사 과거형 + 동사원형 ~.
	과거완료	~이 없었다면, …했을 것이다	Without + 명사(구), 주어 + 조동사 과거형 + have+과거분사 ~.

바로 기본 확인 노트 개념 47–48 p. 197

A 01 had been 02 had not slept
03 But 또는 If it had not been
04 had not trusted 05 were
06 it were not for 07 lived
08 knew

B 01 it were not for bees 02 I wish there were
03 Without [But for] him 04 as if he got
05 I wish I had bought 06 as if she had not taken
07 I could not have entered

교과서에서 뽑은 405 문장 마스터하기 pp. 198–199

346 I wish I had more time.
내게 시간이 더 있다면 좋을 텐데.

347 Live every day as if it were your last.
매일을 마치 너의 마지막 날인 것처럼 살아라.

348 Without the hat, we wouldn't have recognized her.
모자가 없었다면, 우리는 그녀를 알아보지 못했을 것이다.

349 I wish I could float around like an astronaut.
내가 우주 비행사처럼 떠다닐 수 있다면 좋을 텐데.

350 He talks as if he had been there.
그는 마치 거기 있었던 것처럼 말한다.

351 Without the support of my family, I would be in real trouble.
우리 가족의 지원이 없다면, 나는 정말 난처할 것이다.

352 It looked as if the lights were slowly dancing to the music.
그것은 마치 불빛들이 음악에 맞춰 천천히 춤을 추고 있는 것처럼 보였다.

353 I wish you had met him earlier.
네가 그를 더 일찍 만났더라면 좋았을 텐데.

354 I wish I could live in space.

355 Without this little hole, airplane windows might break in an emergency.

356 I felt as if I were in Giant Land in *Gulliver's Travels*.

357 Without their efforts, the *Sillok* might have been lost forever.

358 I wish you had been kinder to my friends.

359 I often acted as if I were the kind of person they wanted me to be.

360 It looked as if white paint had been spilled everywhere.

REVIEW TEST pp. 200–202

01 ③	**02** ④	**03** ④	**04** ⑤	**05** ③
06 ①	**07** ④	**08** ③	**09** ④	**10** ④
11 ③	**12** ②	**13** ⑤	**14** ②	**15** ①
16 didn't read		**17** ④	**18** ②, ⑤	

서술형 • 수행평가형

01 (1) If I had enough strawberries, I could make strawberry jam.
(2) If we had not been wearing seatbelts, we would have been seriously injured.
(3) I wish our classroom had an air conditioner.

02 (1) He nodded his head as if he had understood everything.
(2) Without my family, I would be nothing.

03 I wish I had studied, sleeping

01 가정법 과거의 주절에 be동사가 있으면 주어의 인칭과 수에 관계없이 were를 쓴다.

02 '그가 바빠서 나는 그를 만나지 못했다.'는 의미의 직설법은 '그가 바쁘지 않았더라면 나는 그를 만났을 텐데.'라는 가정법 과거완료로 나타낼 수 있다.

03 '늦잠을 자지 않았더라면 공항에 제시간에 갈 수 있었을 텐데.'라는 의미로 과거 사실의 반대를 나타내는 가정법 과거완료이다.

04 가정법 과거완료는 과거 사실의 반대를 나타내므로 비가 너무 많이 와서 비행기가 연착되었다는 직설법 문장으로 바꿔 쓸 수 있다.

05 ③은 단순 조건문에 쓰인 if이고, 나머지는 모두 가정법 과거에 쓰인 if이다.

06 '어제 병원에 갔더라면, 오늘 아프지 않을 텐데.'라는 의미를 나타내는 혼합 가정법이다. 혼합 가정법의 주절에는 가정법 과거를 쓴다.

07 혼합 가정법으로 주절에는 가정법 과거를 쓴다. would not have been → would not be

08 ③은 were를 쓰고, 나머지는 모두 had를 쓴다.

09 과거 사실과 반대되는 일을 소망하고 있으므로 I wish 가정법 과거완료를 쓴다.

10 ①, ②, ③, ⑤는 모두 영화를 보지 않은 것에 대한 유감을 표시하고 있다. 반면 ④의 「should + have + 과거분사」는 과거 일에 대한 후회를 나타내며 '영화를 보지 말았어야 했다'는 의미이다.

11 현재 실현 가능성이 매우 희박한 소망은 I wish 가정법 과거를 쓴다.

12 과거의 일에 대한 아쉬움을 나타내는 I wish 가정법 과거완료 문장으로 「had+과거분사」로 나타낸다.

13 '마치 ~했던 것처럼'은 「as if + 가정법 과거완료」로 나타낸다.

14 「as if+가정법 과거」는 현재 사실의 반대를 가정할 때 쓴다.

15 ⓒ 가정법 과거완료는 「If+주어+had+과거분사 ~, 주어+조동사 과거형+have+과거분사 ~.」의 형태이다.

16 'Julia는 그 책을 읽은 것처럼 행동하지만 사실 그것을 읽지 않았다'는 의미이다.

17 「Without+가정법 과거」 문장으로 Without 대신 But for를 쓰거나 또는 If it were not for를 쓸 수 있다.

18 「Without+가정법 과거완료」에서 Without 대신 But for를 쓰거나 또는 If it had not been for를 쓸 수 있다.

서술형 • 수행평가형

01 (1) 딸기가 충분히 없어서, 딸기잼을 만들 수 없다. / 현재 사실과 반대되는 일을 가정하는 가정법 과거 문장으로 나타낸다.
(2) 안전벨트를 하고 있었기 때문에 우리는 심하게 다치지 않았다. / 과거 사실과 반대되는 일을 가정하는 가정법 과거완료 문장으로 나타낸다.

(3) 우리 교실에 에어컨이 없어서 유감이다. / 현재 이룰 수 없는 소망을 나타내는 I wish 가정법 과거로 나타낸다.

02 (1) '마치 ~이었던 것처럼'은 as if 가정법 과거완료로 쓴다.

(2) But for my family, I would be nothing. / It it were not for my family, I would be nothing.으로도 바꿔 쓸 수 있다.

03 어젯밤에 공부를 하다가 잠이 들어서 시험을 망친 상황이다. instead of 뒤에는 동명사를 쓴다.

UNIT 12 일치, 화법, 특수 구문

개념 49 수 일치 p. 204

01 look 02 are 03 know
04 are 05 is 06 is
07 was 08 have 09 is
10 was 11 is 12 were

개념 50 시제 일치 p. 205

01 had happened 02 broke
03 sets 04 does
05 every cloud has a silver lining
06 we had done our best
07 I could go with him
08 what he had been looking for

바로 개념 확인 노트 개념 49-50 p. 206

개념 49 수 일치

1 수

주어의 종류	수	예
every / each + 명사	단수 취급	Every girl has ...
나라, 작품, 학문 이름		The United States makes ...
시간, 거리, 금액, 무게		One hundred kilometers is ...
the number of + 복수 명사		The number of stars is ...
분수, 부분 표현 + 단수 명사		Two-fifths of the cake was ...
단일 개념의 「A and B」		Curry and rice is ...
a number of + 복수 명사	복수 취급	A number of people gather ...
the + 형용사 (복수의 의미)		The young are ...
분수, 부분 표현 + 복수 명사		Three-fifths of the apples are ...
both (A and B)		Both a cat and a dog are ...
항상 복수형인 명사		Those socks were ...

개념 50 시제 일치

1 주절 2 과거, 과거완료

시제 일치의 예외인 경우	종속절의 시제	예
불변의 진리, 속담, 현재의 사실, 습관 등	항상 현재	We learned that the sun sets in the west.
역사적 사실	항상 과거	I learned that Edison invented the light bulb.
가정법이 쓰인 종속절, 비교 구문 등	주절에 영향 받지 않음	He looked healthier last year than he does now.

바로 기본 확인 노트 개념 49-50 p. 207

A
01 wants → want
02 will move → would move
03 그대로 04 그대로
05 그대로 06 were → was
07 was → were 08 그대로
09 has → have
10 has scratched → had scratched

B
01 Each day is 02 Two hours is
03 I had bought 04 invented
05 had gone to bed 06 were sent

교과서에서 뽑은 405 문장 마스터하기 pp. 208-209

361 Every language is hard at first.
362 Most of the signs on the stores were red.
363 He realized what he had done wrong.
364 The Netherlands means "low lands."
365 I knew that he had got[gotten] up late that day.
366 Half of the money was stolen.
367 Two-thirds of the country is covered with forest.
368 Both teams were fighting for the football.
369 About a third of the bee population dies every year.
370 I found that I had left my ticket at home.
371 Six hundred dollars is enough for five days in Tokyo.
372 They wondered when the Tower of London was built.
373 The article said that he had become rich from the deaths of others.
374 One of the most impressive rooms was the Four Doors Room.
375 Did you know that the sun never sets in Norway during summer?

개념 51 평서문의 화법 전환 p. 210

01 told, suited me
02 told, her, before
03 it will be
04 couldn't remember, had said
05 had moved there
06 was going, then
07 she would go

개념 52 의문문과 명령문의 화법 전환 p. 211

01 if
02 had bought
03 to
04 how, knew
05 not to wait for him
06 if Joe was okay
07 how the weather had been that day

바로 개념 확인 노트 개념 51-52 p. 212

개념 51 평서문의 화법 전환

1 직접, 간접

평서문의 화법 전환			
동사 전환	• say는 그대로 • say to → tell	주절과 피전달문 연결	접속사 that으로 연결 (인용 부호, 콤마 등 생략)
피전달문 나머지 부분 일치시키기	• 주절의 동사가 과거일 때 시제 일치: 현재 → 과거 / 과거 → 과거완료 • 대명사와 부사(구): 내용과 주절의 시점에 맞춰 전환 this → that here → there now → then ago → before today → that day yesterday → the day before		

개념 52 의문문과 명령문의 화법 전환

	의문문의 화법 전환	명령문의 화법 전환
동사 전환	ask	• 지시: tell • 충고: advise • 부탁, 요청: ask • 명령: order
주절과 피전달문 연결	• 의문사 또는 if [whether]로 연결 • 피전달문 어순: 의문사/if [whether] + 주어 + 동사	• 긍정명령문: → to부정사 • 부정명령문: → not + to부정사
피전달문 나머지 부분 일치시키기	• 시제 일치 • 대명사와 부사(구) 일치시키기	

바로 기본 확인 노트 개념 51-52 p. 213

01 she hadn't visited
02 meet him the next day
03 whom he had recommended
04 to taste those cookies
05 not to make noise there
06 to go to bed early
07 how he could get to Lincoln Park
08 what movie she wanted to see
09 why I had been late
10 she hadn't liked his idea
11 if she liked playing basketball
12 she will buy something nice for me

교과서에서 뽑은 405 문장 마스터하기 pp. 214-215

376 She told him that she was very happy to meet him.
377 Lisa asked me if she had a problem.
378 Yena advised me to log on to the school website.
379 Ann said that her knife didn't cut well.
380 He told me that he had already seen the movie.
381 My father told me that the dog had appeared in the town two days before.
382 I asked her if she would help me with my experiments.
383 They said that they were going to climb the mountain that day.
384 He told people that he was a furniture dealer.
385 I said to them, "I want to show your culture to the world."
386 The teacher told Corky to stand against a pole.
387 My mother said to me, "I have to work late."
388 He said that he was ready to present his work.
389 Emily told him not to bring his cat to the library.
390 She asked me what I wanted to buy.

개념 53 강조 p. 216

01 that
02 who
03 do
04 believe
05 in the least
06 the very
07 that [who]
08 that [when]
09 at all
10 did
11 that
12 very

개념 54 도치 p. 217

01 did they fight
02 So did I.
03 was the statue
04 could I breathe
05 Here are some examples of his theory.
06 Seldom does Mr. Hardy take off his hat
07 Down came the rain
08 Never have we met again

바로 개념 확인 노트 개념 53–54 p. 218

개념 53 강조

강조 구문	It + be동사 + 강조할 말 + that ~ └ 주어, 목적어, 부사구 * 강조되는 말에 따라 that 대신 who, whom, when, where 등 사용 가능
동사 강조	do [does/did] + 동사원형
명사 강조	the very + 명사
부정어 강조	not ~ at all / not ~ in the least

개념 54 도치

1 바뀌는
2 맨 앞

문장의 앞에 오는 어구	문장 구조	예
부정어	부정어 + 조동사 + 주어 + 동사	Rarely did they fight with other groups.
only를 포함한 부사구	부사구 + 조동사 + 주어 + 동사	Only then did we understand the problem.
장소·방향의 부사구	부사구 + 동사 + 주어 * 주어가 대명사일 때: 부사구 + 주어 + 동사	On the platform stood a young boy.
there / here	There + be동사 + 주어 (…이 있다) Here + 동사 + 주어 * 주어가 대명사일 때: Here + 주어 + 동사	Here comes the bus!
so / neither	So / Neither + (조)동사 + 주어 (…도 역시 그렇다)	Neither do I.

바로 기본 확인 노트 개념 53–54 p. 219

A
01 at noon that [when] Dana called Maggie
02 did understand what you said
03 the very part I wanted to tell
04 take care of the dogs at all [in the least]
05 a good result for me at all [in the least]
06 Miguel that [who] noticed the error in the article
07 at the park that [where] my class is going to have a picnic

B
01 Never have I lied to my mom.
02 So did I.
03 On the hill stood the small school.
04 Scarcely did they have breakfast.
05 In front of the house was a big apple tree.

교과서에서 뽑은 405 문장 마스터하기 pp. 220–221

391 It was literature that he loved most.
392 The very writer who gave life to Frodo was British.
393 This one doesn't look scary at all.
394 It is we who are the finest smiths.
395 Never did I expect that you would come here.
396 In the center appears a man.
397 Spinach does have a lot of nutrients.
398 It was in 1969 that Apollo 11 landed on the moon.
399 It is calcium that builds strong bones and teeth.
400 There are many clubs and activities waiting for you.
401 Hardly did I hear Howard say bad words to others.
402 Right in front of the hotel was Market Square.
403 It is a guitar that I want to get for my birthday gift.
404 It was six years ago that I met the little prince in the Sahara Desert.
405 That is the very photo that the reporter took during the war.

REVIEW TEST pp. 222–224

01 ④	02 ④	03 ①	04 ⑤	05 ⑤
06 ③	07 ②	08 ②	09 ⑤	10 ④
11 ④	12 ③	13 ④	14 ③	15 ④
16 ④	17 ②	18 ⑤	19 ②	20 ①

서술형 • 수행평가형

01 (1) It was on the bus that he heard the news.
(2) It was Daniel that was being interviewed then.
02 (1) Nancy not to disturb him while he was studying
(2) me how I had been
(3) my sister if I could borrow her backpack the next day
03 why she hadn't told me the news, she hadn't known it then, had she lied to me

01 ④「a number of + 복수 명사」가 주어일 때 동사는 복수형으로 쓴다. is → are

02 「분수 표현 + of + 명사」가 주어일 때 동사의 수는 명사의 수에 맞춘다.

03 「neither *A* nor *B*」가 주어일 때 동사는 B에 맞춘다. 따라서 첫 번째 문장에서는 he와 일치하는 is를 써야 한다. 두 번째 문장의 주어는 This car이고 together with those cars는 This car를 꾸미는 말이므로 동사는 단수형 belongs를 써야 한다.

04 ⑤「부분 표현 + of + 명사」가 주어일 때 동사의 수는 명사의 수에 맞추므로 the apples에 맞춰 are가 되어야 한다.

05 간접의문문의 주어는 whose socks와 수가 같아야 하므로 복수형 these로 쓰는 것이 알맞다. 따라서 동사도 복수형 are로 써야 한다.

06 ③「the + 형용사」는 복수 보통명사처럼 쓰이므로 빈칸에는 are가 알맞다. (the old = old people)

07 ② 주절의 시제가 과거이고, 뒤에 이전 시점을 나타내는 부사 before가 있으므로 종속절의 시제는 과거완료가 되어야 한다. tell a lie → had told a lie

08 주절의 시제가 과거가 되면 종속절의 시제도 과거 또는 과거완료로 쓴다. 여기에서는 주절과 종속절의 시제가 같으므로 종속절의 시제를 과거로 쓰는 것이 알맞다.

09 ⑤ 역사적 사실은 주절의 시제와 상관없이 과거형으로 쓴다.

10 ④ that이 이끄는 절에 이전 시점을 나타내는 부사구인 the day before가 쓰였으므로 종속절의 시제가 주절의 시제인 과거보다 앞서야 한다. came → had come

11 평서문의 화법을 전환할 때에는 say to를 tell로 바꾸고 전달할 말을 that절로 바꿔 쓰되 주절의 시제와 일치시키고, 대명사와 부사구 등을 알맞게 고쳐 쓴다.

12 화법을 전환할 때 전달할 말의 인칭대명사는 상황에 맞게 바꾸어야 한다. 이 문장에서 말하는 사람은 she이므로 전달할 말의 I를 she로, your는 듣는 사람인 I에 맞게 my로 고쳐 쓴다.

13 ① was she → she was ② not me to open → me not to open ③ will → would ⑤ can → could

14 ① will → would ② said me → said to me ④ that go → to go ⑤ was the bread → the bread was

15 종속절의 시제가 주절과 같으므로, 직접 화법일 때에는 현재 시제로 써야 한다는 것에 유의한다.

16 주어진 문장의 밑줄 친 did는 동사를 강조하기 위해 쓰였다. 쓰임이 같은 것은 ④이다. ① 부정문을 만드는 조동사 ② 의문문을 만드는 조동사 ③ 일반동사 ⑤ 일반동사

17 ② 부정어가 문장의 앞에 쓰이면 주어와 동사는 도치된다. I have → have I

18 ⑤ hardly는 부정어로, 문장의 앞에 쓰이면 주어와 동사를 도치해야 한다. 일반동사가 쓰였으면 do를 이용해 도치하고 일반동사는 원형으로 쓴다. Hardly realized I → Hardly did I realize

19 첫 번째 문장의 빈칸에는 동격의 that이 들어간다. 두 번째 문장은「It ~ that」 강조 구문이므로 빈칸에 that이 들어가는 것이 알맞다.

20 ① 장소를 나타내는 부사가 문장의 앞에 쓰일 때 주어와 동사의 위치를 바꿔야 하지만, 주어가 대명사일 때에는 바꾸지 않는다. ② → Here comes the bus. ③ Little did I know about him. ④ Down the hill ran the truck. ⑤ He didn't come, and neither did she.

서술형 • 수행평가형

01 「It ~ that」 강조 구문에서 강조할 말은 'It + be동사'와 that 사이에 쓴다.

02 (1) 명령문을 포함한 문장을 간접 화법으로 전환할 때 to부정사를 활용한다. 부정 명령문일 때에는 to부정사 앞에 not을 쓴다.

(2) 의문문을 포함한 문장을 간접 화법으로 전환할 때 동사를 ask로 쓰고, 의문문은「의문사 + 주어 + 동사」의 어순으로 고쳐 쓴다.

(3) 의문사가 없는 의문문을 포함한 문장을 간접 화법으로 전환할 때 동사 ask를 쓰고, 의문문은「if/whether + 주어 + 동사」의 어순으로 고쳐 쓴다.

03 첫 번째 문장과 두 번째 문장은 직접 화법의 문장을 간접 화법으로 전환해야 하고, 세 번째 문장은 부정어를 강조하여 주어와 동사를 도치시켜야 한다.

해석 (A) 나는 Judy에게 "왜 어제 나에게 그 소식을 말하지 않았니?"라고 말했다. 그녀는 나에게 "난 그때 그것을 몰랐어."라고 말했다. 그녀는 그때까지 내게 거짓말을 한 적이 없어서 나는 그녀의 말을 믿었다.

memo

memo

문장 바로 쓰는 문법

LEVEL 3

핵심 개념노트

✓ 1등하는 공부 습관

1. 개념노트 항상 가지고 다니기
2. 수업 전, 후에 한 번씩 살펴보기
3. 개념 표를 만들어 스스로 채워보기

CHUNJAE
EDUCATION, INC.

CONTENTS

BACKGROUND KNOWLEDGE

01 12시제

시간 관계를 나타내는 문법 범주를 시제(tense)라고 하며, 영어의 시제에는 크게 과거, 현재, 미래가 있다. 그리고 이를 다시 진행형, 완료형과 결합시켜 12시제로 쓸 수 있다.

UNIT 01 문장의 형식

개념 01 5형식 1

1 5형식은 「주어 + 동사 + 목적어 + 목적격 보어」의 형태로 쓰며, 목적격 보어는 목적어의 성질이나 상태를 보충 설명한다.

2 목적격 보어가 명사나 형용사일 때 목적어와 목적격 보어는 의미상 주어와 서술어의 관계이며, 목적격 보어로 부사는 쓸 수 없다.

3 목적격 보어가 to부정사일 때 목적격 보어는 목적어가 하는 동작을 나타내며, 부정은 「not+to부정사」로 나타낸다.

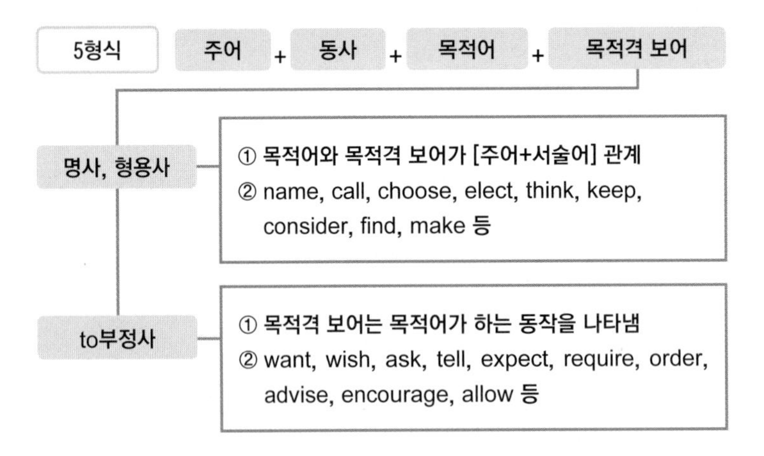

개념 02 5형식 2

1 지각동사(see, watch, feel, smell, hear, listen to 등)는 목적격 보어로 동사원형과 분사를 쓴다.
2 사역동사(make, have, let 등)는 목적격 보어로 동사원형과 과거분사를 쓴다. 단, let은 과거분사를 쓸 수 없다.
3 get은 '~에게 …하도록 시키다'라는 사역의 의미일 때 목적격 보어로 to부정사와 과거분사를 쓴다.
4 help는 목적격 보어로 동사원형 또는 to부정사를 둘 다 쓸 수 있고, 이때 의미는 동일하다.

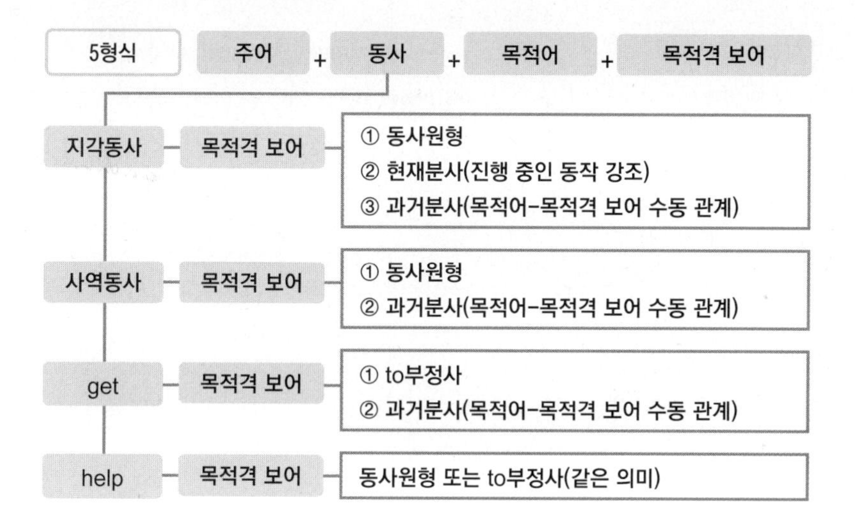

UNIT 02 시제

개념 03 현재완료 1_완료, 경험

1 현재완료는 「have [has]+과거분사」의 형태로, 과거에 일어난 일이 현재까지 영향을 줄 때 사용한다.

2 부정문은 「주어+have [has]+not+과거분사 ~.」이고, 의문문은 「(의문사+)Have [Has]+주어+과거분사 ~?」이다.

3 현재완료는 현재와 관련 있는 어떤 과거의 일을 나타내며, 과거 시제는 현재와 전혀 관련 없는 과거의 일을 나타낸다.

4 과거를 나타내는 부사(구)인 ago, last, yesterday, just now, then 등과 when은 현재완료와 함께 쓸 수 없다.

쓰임	의미	함께 자주 쓰이는 표현
완료	(과거에 시작한 일이 현재) 막 ~했다, 이미 ~했다	already, just, yet, still 등
경험	(과거부터 현재까지) ~한 적이 있다	ever, never, once, twice, ~ times, before, 최상급 등

개념 04 현재완료 2_계속, 결과

1 전치사 for 뒤에는 a week, two hours처럼 시간의 길이를 나타내는 표현을 쓴다.

2 전치사 since 뒤에는 yesterday, last week처럼 특정한 시점을 나타내는 표현을 쓴다. 접속사 since가 이끄는 부사절에는 과거 시제를 쓴다.

3 have gone to는 '~에 가 버렸다'는 결과를 나타내고, have been to는 '~에 가 본 적이 있다'는 경험을 나타낸다.

4 have got은 현재완료형이지만 구어체에서는 보통 have(소유하다)의 의미로 쓰인다.

쓰임	의미	함께 자주 쓰이는 표현
계속	(과거부터 현재까지) 계속 ~해 왔다	since(~부터), for(~ 동안), so far, how long 등
결과	(과거에) ~한 결과 (현재는) …이다	go, lose, grow, buy, leave 등

개념 05 과거완료 / 미래완료

1 과거완료는 「had+과거분사」의 형태로, 과거 특정 시점보다 더 이전에 일어난 일이 특정 시점까지 영향을 줄 때 사용한다. 이때 먼저 일어난 일을 과거완료형으로 나타내며 이를 대과거라고 한다.

2 미래완료는 「will have+과거분사」의 형태로, 현재부터 미래의 또 다른 어느 시점까지 영향을 주는 일을 나타낸다. 함께 자주 쓰이는 표현은 until, 「by+미래년도」, 「by the time+미래 시점」 등이 있다.

	과거완료	미래완료
긍정문	주어 + had + 과거분사 ~.	주어 + will have + 과거분사 ~.
부정문	주어 + had not + 과거분사 ~.	주어 + will not have + 과거분사 ~.
의문문	(의문사+) Had + 주어 + 과거분사 ~?	(의문사+) Will + 주어 + have + 과거분사 ~?

개념 06 완료 진행

1 과거완료 진행형은 「had been+현재분사」의 형태로, 과거의 특정 시점보다 더 이전에 일어난 일이 특정 시점까지 계속 진행되었다는 것을 나타낼 때 쓴다.

2 현재완료 진행형은 「have [has] been+현재분사」의 형태로, 과거의 일이 현재까지 계속 진행되고 있다는 것을 강조할 때 쓴다. 함께 자주 쓰이는 표현은 for, since, all day [week] 등이 있다.

3 현재완료는 이전에 시작한 동작이 완료된 결과를 말하고, 현재완료 진행형은 현재까지도 계속되고 있는 것을 말한다.

	과거완료 진행	현재완료 진행
긍정문	주어 + had been + 현재분사 ~.	주어 + have [has] been + 현재분사 ~.
부정문	주어 + had not been + 현재분사 ~.	주어 + have [has] not been + 현재분사 ~.
의문문	(의문사+) Had + 주어 + been + 현재분사 ~?	(의문사+) Have [Has] + 주어 + been + 현재분사 ~?

UNIT 03 조동사

개념 07 had better / would rather / used to / would

1 조동사 구문을 이용하여 충고, 선호, 과거의 습관 · 상태 등을 나타낼 수 있다.

2 used to와 would는 둘 다 과거의 습관을 나타낼 때 쓸 수 있지만 상태동사(be, have, like 등)와 함께 과거의 상태를 나타낼 때는 used to만 가능하고 would는 쓸 수 없다.

조동사 구문	의미		
had better + 동사원형	충고 · 경고	~하는 게 좋겠다	부정: had better not
would rather + 동사원형[A] (+than + 동사원형[B])	선호	(B하기 보다는 차라리) A하겠다	부정: would rather not
used to + 동사원형	현재는 지속되지 않는 과거의 습관 · 상태	~하곤 했다, ~이었다	부정: used not to / 부정: didn't use(d) to
would + 동사원형	과거의 습관	~하곤 했다	

cf. 「be [get] used to + 동명사」: ~하는 데 익숙하다 [익숙해지다]
「be used to + 동사원형」: ~하는 데 이용되다

개념 08 조동사 + have + p.p.

1 「조동사 + have + p.p.」는 과거에 대한 추측, 후회나 유감 등을 나타내는 표현이다.

2 「should have p.p.」: ~했어야 했다 (과거에 하지 못한 일에 대한 후회)
「shouldn't have p.p.」: ~하지 말았어야 했다 (과거에 했던 일에 대한 후회)

should have p.p.	과거의 일에 대한 후회나 유감	~했어야 했다
must have p.p.	과거의 일에 대한 강한 추측	~이었음에 틀림없다
may [might] have p.p.	과거의 일에 대한 약한 추측	~했을지도 모른다
cannot have p.p.	과거의 일에 대한 강한 의심	~이었을 리가 없다
could have p.p.	과거의 일에 대한 가능성	~할 수도 있었다

UNIT 04 to부정사

개념 09 명사적 용법

1 to부정사는 「to + 동사원형」의 형태로 명사처럼 문장의 주어, 보어, 목적어 역할을 할 수 있으며 '~하는 것, ~하기'라고 해석한다.

2 「의문사 + to부정사」는 명사처럼 쓰이며 「의문사 + 주어 + should + 동사원형」으로 바꿔 쓸 수 있다.

3 to부정사의 부정은 「not [never] + to부정사」의 형태이다.

to부정사를 목적어로 쓰는 동사				
want	hope	wish	expect	plan
need	choose	decide	learn	agree
promise	refuse	manage	pretend	would like

의문사 + to부정사	
what + to부정사	무엇을 ~할지
when + to부정사	언제 ~할지
where + to부정사	어디로 ~할지
how + to부정사	어떻게 ~할지, ~하는 방법
which + to부정사	어느 것을 ~할지
who(m) + to부정사	누가 [누구를] ~할지

개념 10 가주어, 의미상 주어, 가목적어, It takes ~ to

1 to부정사가 주어로 쓰일 때 주로 가주어 it을 주어 자리에 쓰고 to부정사(구)는 뒤로 보낸다. 가주어 it은 해석하지 않는다.

2 to부정사의 행위의 주체가 문장의 주어와 다를 때 to부정사 앞에 「for / of + 목적격」을 써서 의미상 주어를 나타낸다.

3 to부정사가 목적어로 쓰일 때 가목적어 it을 목적어 자리에 쓰고 to부정사(구)는 뒤로 보낸다. 가목적어 it은 해석하지 않는다.

4 「It takes + 목적격 + 시간 + to부정사」는 '~가 …하는 데 시간이 걸리다'라는 의미이다.

가주어	「가주어 it ~ to부정사」	
의미상 주어	「for + 목적격」	일반적인 to부정사의 의미상 주어
	「of + 목적격」	사람의 성격을 나타내는 형용사가 보어로 쓰였을 때 *kind, rude, polite, generous, wise, foolish, careful 등
가목적어	「주어 + 동사 + 가목적어 it + 목적격 보어(형용사/명사) + 진목적어」(← 5형식) * 가목적어를 주로 쓰는 동사: think, believe, find, make, consider 등	

UNIT 04 to부정사

개념 11 형용사적 용법

1 to부정사는 형용사처럼 명사 또는 대명사를 뒤에서 수식하는 역할을 할 수 있고, 이때 to부정사는 '~할, ~하는'이라는 의미이다.

2 -thing, -one, -body로 끝나는 대명사가 쓰일 때 「-thing, -one, -body (+형용사)+to부정사」의 어순이다.

3 to부정사의 수식을 받는 명사가 전치사의 목적어일 때 to부정사 뒤에 전치사를 쓴다.

4 「be+to부정사」는 예정, 의무, 가능, 운명, 의지 등의 의미를 나타낸다.

명사·대명사 수식 (~할, ~하는)	명사·대명사+to부정사	
	-thing, -one, -body (+형용사)+to부정사	
	(대)명사+to부정사+전치사	
be+to부정사	예정	~할 예정이다
	의무	~해야 한다
	가능	~할 수 있다
	운명	~할 운명이다
	의지	~할 작정이다

개념 12 부사적 용법

1 to부정사는 부사처럼 동사, 형용사, 부사를 수식할 수 있다.

2 부사적 용법의 to부정사는 목적, 감정의 원인, 판단의 근거, 결과 등을 나타낸다.

3 「(in order / so as) not to+동사원형」은 '~하지 않도록'이라는 의미이다.

목적	~하기 위해서	= in order to [so as to]
감정의 원인	~해서, ~하니	감정을 나타내는 형용사를 뒤에서 수식 *glad, surprised, excited, shocked, disappointed 등
판단의 근거	~하다니	주로 함께 쓰는 표현: cannot, must 등
결과	…해서 (결국) ~하다	주로 함께 쓰는 표현: live, grow up, awake, wake up 등
형용사 수식	~하기에	to부정사가 형용사를 뒤에서 수식

개념 13 too ~ to / enough to

1 「too ~ to」는 '…하기에 너무 ~한/하게'라는 부정의 의미를 나타낸다.

2 「enough to」는 '…할 만큼 충분히 ~한/하게'라는 긍정의 의미를 나타낸다.

3 「too ~ to」와 「enough to」를 「so ... that ~」을 이용하여 바꿔 쓸 때 주어와 시제 일치, that절에 동사의 목적어가 필요한 경우 등에 유의한다.

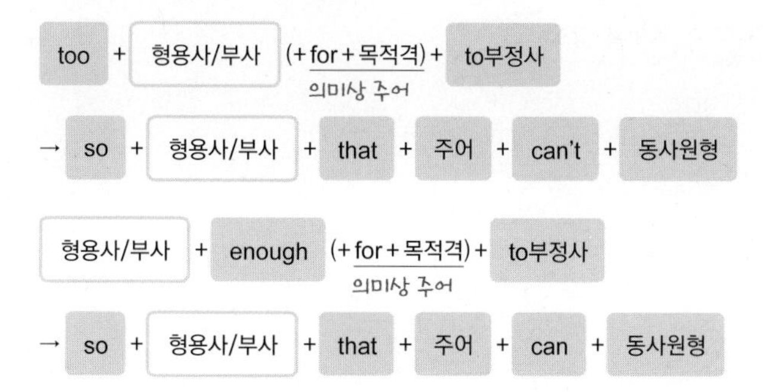

개념 14 seem to

1 「seem to + 동사원형」은 '~인 것 같다'라는 의미이다.

2 「주어 + seem(s) to + 동사원형」은 「It seems that + 주어 + 동사 ~」로 바꿔 쓸 수 있다.

3 to부정사의 행위가 본동사의 시제보다 이전에 일어났을 때는 「주어 + seem(s) to + have + p.p.」로 나타낸다.

단순부정사	「to + 동사원형」	to부정사의 시제가 본동사의 시제와 일치하거나 미래일 때
완료부정사	「to + have + p.p.」	to부정사의 시제가 본동사보다 앞선 시제일 때

UNIT 05 동명사

개념 15 동명사의 역할

1 동명사는 「동사원형+-ing」의 형태로, 문장 내에서 명사 역할(주어, 보어, 목적어)을 하며 '~하는 것, ~하기'라는 의미이다.

2 동명사의 부정은 「not [never]+동명사」의 형태이다.

3 현재분사는 '~하는, ~하고 있는'의 의미로 진행형을 만들거나 명사 앞에서 명사를 수식한다.

동명사를 목적어로 쓰는 동사			
enjoy	finish	keep	stop
quit	mind	avoid	admit
deny	recommend	practice	imagine
consider	dislike	give up	put off

cf. stop+to부정사: '~하기 위해 멈추다'라는 의미임 〈to부정사의 부사적 용법〉

개념 16 동명사의 의미상 주어와 시제

1 동명사의 의미상 주어가 일반인이거나, 문장의 주어·목적어와 일치할 때는 이를 생략할 수 있다.

2 동명사의 행위를 하는 주체가 문장의 주어와 다를 때 동명사 앞에 소유격을 써서 의미상 주어를 나타낸다. 구어체에서는 주로 목적격의 형태로 쓰기도 한다.

3 동명사가 문장의 시제보다 앞서 일어난 일을 나타낼 때는 「having+p.p.」로 쓴다.

동명사의 의미상 주어	소유격 [목적격]+동명사 *의미상 주어가 all, both, this[these], that[those], 또는 무생물일 때는 목적격을 씀
단순동명사(동사원형+-ing)	본동사의 시제와 같거나 미래일 때
완료동명사(having+p.p.)	본동사의 시제보다 이전일 때

개념 17 동명사와 to부정사

동명사를 목적어로 쓰는 동사	enjoy, finish, keep, stop, quit, mind, avoid, admit, deny, recommend, practice, imagine, consider, dislike, give up, put off 등
to부정사를 목적어로 쓰는 동사	want, hope, wish, expect, plan, need, choose, decide, learn, agree, promise, refuse, manage, pretend, would like 등
의미의 차이 없이 동명사와 to부정사를 모두 목적어로 쓰는 동사	start, begin, like, love, hate, prefer, continue 등
동명사와 to부정사를 모두 목적어로 쓸 수 있지만 의미가 달라지는 동사	forget, remember, regret, try 등

forget	+동명사	(과거에) ~했던 것을 잊다
	+to부정사	(앞으로) ~할 것을 잊다
remember	+동명사	(과거에) ~했던 것을 기억하다
	+to부정사	(앞으로) ~할 것을 기억하다
regret	+동명사	(과거에) ~했던 것을 후회하다
	+to부정사	(현재 · 미래에) ~하게 되어 유감이다
try	+동명사	시험 삼아 (한번) ~해 보다
	+to부정사	~하려고 노력하다

개념 18 관용적 표현

go -ing	~하러 가다	be busy -ing	~하느라 바쁘다
on [upon] -ing (= as soon as + 주어 + 동사)	~하자마자	be used to -ing	~하는 데 익숙하다
keep (on) -ing	계속 ~하다	How [What] about -ing?	~하는 게 어때?
be worth -ing	~할 만한 가치가 있다	look forward to -ing	~하기를 고대하다
feel like -ing (= would like to + 동사원형)	~하고 싶다	make a point of -ing (= make it a rule to + 동사원형)	~하는 것을 규칙으로 하다
far from -ing	전혀 ~이 아닌	on the point of -ing (= be about to + 동사원형)	막 ~하려고 하는
spend + 시간/돈 + -ing	~하느라 시간/돈을 쓰다	It is no use -ing	~해도 소용없다
not [never] ... without -ing	…하면 꼭 ~하다	keep [prevent] ... from -ing	…가 ~하지 못하게 막다
cannot help -ing (= cannot help but + 동사원형)	~하지 않을 수 없다	have trouble [difficulty] (in) -ing	~하는 데 어려움이 있다

UNIT 06 분사와 분사구문

개념 19 현재분사와 과거분사

1 분사는 동사의 형태를 바꿔 형용사처럼 쓰는 것으로, 명사를 수식하는 한정적 용법과 보어로 쓰이는 서술적 용법이 있다.

2 분사가 단독으로 명사를 수식할 때는 분사를 명사 앞에 쓰고, 목적어나 수식어구가 붙어 있는 경우 명사 뒤에 쓴다.

3 분사는 「be동사+ 현재분사」의 진행형과 「have+ 과거분사」의 완료형, 그리고 「be동사+ 과거분사」의 수동태를 만든다.

4 「현재분사+명사」에서 현재분사는 명사의 동작이나 상태를 나타내고, 「동명사+명사」에서 동명사는 명사의 용도를 나타낸다.

		현재분사 (진행/능동의 의미)	과거분사 (수동/완료의 의미)
형태		동사원형+-ing	동사원형+-ed 또는 불규칙 과거분사형
쓰임	명사 수식	I am afraid of a barking dog. (분사와 명사가 능동 관계)	I like the play written by Shakespeare. (분사와 명사가 수동 관계)
	보어 역할	The dog sat barking up the tree. (주격 보어) I saw a dog barking fiercely. (목적격 보어)	Shakespeare remained written in history. (주격 보어) I found a letter written in code. (목적격 보어)
	동사적 성격	The dog is barking fiercely. (진행형)	He has written his first play. (완료형) The play was written by Shakespeare. (수동태)

개념 20 감정을 나타내는 분사

1 감정을 나타내는 분사는 현재분사나 과거분사가 형용사처럼 쓰이는 것이다.

2 현재분사는 주어가 감정의 원인이 되는 것으로 주로 사물이 주어이거나 사물을 수식할 때 쓴다.

3 과거분사는 주어가 감정을 느끼는 것으로 주로 사람이 주어이거나 사람을 수식할 때 쓰이지만, 항상 그런 것은 아니다.
(e.g.) He is bored.(그는 지루하다.) He is boring. (그는 지루한 사람이다.)

현재분사 (주어가 감정의 원인)	과거분사 (주어가 감정을 느낌)
boring 지루한	bored 지루해하는
embarrassing 당황하게 하는	embarrassed 당황한
frustrating 좌절감을 주는	frustrated 좌절감을 느끼는
confusing 혼란스러운	confused 혼란스러워 하는
annoying 짜증스러운	annoyed 짜증이 난
disappointing 실망스러운	disappointed 실망한
surprising 놀라운	surprised 놀란
frightening 무서운	frightened 겁먹은
depressing 우울하게 만드는	depressed 우울한
satisfying 만족을 주는	satisfied 만족하는

UNIT 06 분사와 분사구문

개념 21 분사구문

1 분사구문은 부사절에서 접속사와 주어를 없애고 동사를 현재분사로 바꿔 부사구로 만든 것이다.
부정은 분사 앞에 not 또는 never를 쓴다.

2 분사구문은 부사절의 접속사에 따라 시간, 이유, 동시동작, 연속동작, 조건, 양보 등의 다양한 의미를 가지며, 분사구문의 의미를 명확하게 나타내기 위해 접속사를 생략하지 않고 남겨 두기도 한다.

3 조건을 나타내는 경우에는 주절에 보통 will, can, may 등이 있다.

분사구문 만드는 법	
As I entered the room, I switched the light on.	
~~As~~ **I entered the room**, I switched the light on.	① 접속사 생략
~~I~~ **entered the room**, I switched the light on.	② 부사절의 주어 생략 (주절의 주어와 같을 때)
Entering the room, I switched the light on.	③ 동사를 현재분사로 바꾸기 (주절의 시제와 같을 때)

개념 22 분사구문의 시제와 태

1 완료형의 분사구문은 「having + 과거분사」의 형태로 부사절의 시제가 주절보다 한 시제 앞선 시제일 때 쓴다.
부정은 「not [never] + having + 과거분사」의 형태로 쓴다.

2 수동태의 분사구문에서는 보통 Being 또는 Having been을 생략하고 과거분사로 시작한다.

3 현재완료가 쓰인 부사절도 완료 분사구문으로 바꿔 쓸 수 있다.

	단순 분사구문	완료 분사구문
능동	현재분사 ~	having + 과거분사
수동	being + 과거분사	having been + 과거분사

개념 23 독립분사구문

1 독립분사구문은 부사절과 주절의 주어가 서로 다를 때, 부사절의 주어를 생략하지 않고 분사 앞에 남겨 둔 것이다.

2 비인칭 독립분사구문은 부사절의 주어가 we, you, people처럼 막연한 일반인일 때 주절의 주어와 다르더라도 생략하고 관용어처럼 쓰는 것이다.

독립분사구문	부사절 주어 ≠ 주절 주어	부사절의 주어를 생략하지 않고 분사 앞에 씀
비인칭 독립분사구문	부사절 주어(일반인) ≠ 주절 주어	부사절의 주어 생략
	• frankly speaking (솔직히 말하면) • strictly speaking (엄밀히 말하면) • roughly speaking (대강 말하자면) • generally speaking (일반적으로 말하면) • speaking of (~ 이야기가 나와서 말인데) • judging from (~로 판단하건대) • considering ~ (~을 고려하면)	

개념 24 with + 명사(구) + 분사

1 「with+명사(구)+분사」는 '~한 채로, ~하면서'라는 의미로 동시에 일어나는 두 가지 상황을 나타낼 때 쓴다.

2 「with+명사(구)+현재분사」는 '~가 …하고 있는 채로'의 의미로 명사(구)와 분사가 능동의 관계이다.

3 「with+명사(구)+과거분사」는 '~가 …하여진 채로'의 의미로 명사(구)와 분사가 수동의 관계이다.

4 분사 대신 형용사나 부사(구)를 쓸 수도 있다.

with+명사(구)+현재분사	~가 …하고 있는 채로	Mom fell asleep with the washing machine running. 엄마는 세탁기를 돌린 채로 잠이 들었다.
with+명사(구)+과거분사	~가 …하여진 채로	I took a rest with my eyes closed. 나는 눈을 감고 휴식을 취했다.

UNIT 07 수동태

개념 25 수동태의 의미와 형태, 시제

1 수동태는 행위의 대상을 주어로 하는 동사의 형태로, 「be동사 + 과거분사」로 쓴다. 행위의 주체는 「by + 행위자」로 나타낸다.

2 수동태의 시제는 be동사의 형태 변화로 나타낸다.

3 조동사가 있을 때 수동태는 be동사를 원형으로 쓴다.

시제	수동태 형태
현재	am/is/are + 과거분사
과거	was/were + 과거분사
미래	will be + 과거분사 / be동사 + going to be + 과거분사
진행	be동사 + being + 과거분사
완료	have/has/had/will have + been + 과거분사
조동사가 있을 때	조동사 + be + 과거분사

개념 26 4형식 문장의 수동태

1 4형식 문장의 수동태는 간접목적어를 주어로 쓸 수도 있고, 직접목적어를 주어로 쓸 수도 있다. 단, 동사가 buy, make, cook, sell, read, write, choose 등이면 직접목적어만 주어로 쓸 수 있다.

2 4형식 문장의 직접목적어를 주어로 하는 수동태 문장을 쓸 때, 간접목적어였던 명사 앞에 동사에 따라 전치사 to, for, of를 쓴다.

4형식 문장의 형태	주어 + 동사 + 간접목적어(A) + 직접목적어(B)	
간접목적어가 주어가 될 때	주어(A) + be동사 + 과거분사 + B + by + 행위자 (간접목적어) (직접목적어) (주어)	
직접목적어가 주어가 될 때	주어(B) + be동사 + 과거분사 + 전치사 + A + by + 행위자 (직접목적어) (간접목적어) (주어)	
	전치사 to를 쓰는 동사	give, teach, bring, send, show, tell, lend, sell, read, write, offer 등
	전치사 for를 쓰는 동사	buy, choose, find, get, make, cook, do 등
	전치사 of를 쓰는 동사	ask, request, inquire 등

UNIT 07 수동태

개념 27 5형식 문장의 수동태

1 5형식 문장을 수동태 문장으로 바꿀 때 목적어를 수동태 문장의 주어로 쓰고 목적격 보어는 동사 바로 뒤에 쓴다.

2 5형식 문장의 동사가 지각동사나 사역동사일 때 목적격 보어인 동사원형은 수동태 문장에서 to부정사로 고쳐 쓴다. 지각동사의 목적격 보어가 현재분사면 그대로 동사 뒤에 쓴다.

3 사역동사 let과 have는 수동태로 쓰지 않으므로 주의한다.

5형식 문장(주어 + 동사 + 목적어 + 목적격 보어)의 수동태	
대부분의 동사	주어(목적어) + be동사 + 과거분사 + 보어(목적격 보어) + by + 행위자(주어)
지각동사	목적격 보어가 동사원형일 때 → to부정사 주어(목적어) + be동사 + 과거분사 + to부정사(목적격 보어) + by + 행위자(주어)
	목적격 보어가 현재분사일 때 → 현재분사 주어(목적어) + be동사 + 과거분사 + 현재분사(목적격 보어) + by + 행위자(주어)
사역동사	목적격 보어 (동사원형) → to부정사 주어(목적어) + be동사 + 과거분사 + to부정사(목적격 보어) + by + 행위자

개념 28 동사구의 수동태

1 '동사+전치사/부사'가 하나의 동사 역할을 할 때, 수동태는 '동사 + 전치사/부사'를 한 덩어리로 취급하여 만든다. 따라서 전치사 또는 부사를 'be동사 + 과거분사' 바로 뒤에 쓴다.

능동태	주어 + 동사 + 전치사/부사 + 목적어
수동태	주어 + be동사 + 과거분사 + 전치사/부사 + by + 행위자

개념 29 by 이외의 전치사를 쓰는 수동태

be surprised at	~에 놀라다	be covered with	~으로 덮여 있다
be interested in	~에 관심이 있다	be filled with	~으로 가득 차다
be tired of	~에 싫증나다	be pleased with	~에 기뻐하다
be worried about	~에 관해 걱정하다	be satisfied with	~에 만족하다
be concerned about	~에 관해 염려하다	be crowded with	~으로 붐비다
be involved in	~에 관련되다	be finished with	~을 끝내다
be made of + 성질이 변하지 않는 재료	~으로 만들어지다	be accustomed to	~에 익숙하다
be made from + 성질이 변하는 재료	~으로 만들어지다	be related to	~에 관련이 있다

개념 30 that절을 목적어로 하는 문장의 수동태

1 that절을 목적어로 하는 문장의 수동태는 가주어 it을 사용하거나, that절의 주어를 수동태 문장의 주어로 하여 쓸 수 있다.

2 주로 say, report, believe, consider, expect, think 등 전달, 사고와 관련된 동사가 쓰인다.

목적어가 that절인 문장	주어 + 동사 + that절(목적어)
가주어 it을 수동태 문장의 주어로 쓸 때	It(가주어) + be동사 + 과거분사 + that절(진주어)
that절의 주어를 수동태 문장의 주어로 쓸 때	주어(that절의 주어) + be동사 + 과거분사 + to부정사(that절의 동사) ~

UNIT 08 관계사

개념 31 관계대명사_주격, 소유격, 목적격

1 주격 관계대명사는 관계사절 안에서 주어 역할을 한다. 바로 뒤에는 동사가 오며 동사의 수는 선행사에 일치시킨다.

2 소유격 관계대명사는 관계사절 안에서 소유격 역할을 한다. 소유격 관계대명사 뒤에는 명사가 온다.

3 목적격 관계대명사는 관계사절 안에서 목적어 역할을 한다. 목적격 관계대명사 뒤에는 「주어 + 동사」를 쓴다.

4 선행사가 전치사의 목적어일 때 「전치사 + 관계대명사」의 형태로 쓰거나 전치사를 관계사절 끝에 쓴다.

선행사	주격	소유격	목적격
사람	who	whose	who(m)
사물, 동물	which	whose / of which	which
사람, 사물, 동물	that	–	that

관계대명사의 생략	① 「주격 관계대명사 + be동사 + 분사(형용사)」 구문에서 「주격 관계대명사 + be동사」는 생략 가능 ② 목적격 관계대명사는 생략 가능
관계대명사 that을 쓸 수 없는 경우	① 앞에 전치사가 있을 때 쓸 수 없음 ② 소유격 관계대명사 대신 쓸 수 없음

개념 32 관계대명사 what과 that

1 관계대명사 what은 명사처럼 쓰여 주어, 보어, 목적어 역할을 하며 '~하는 것'이라는 의미이다.

2 관계대명사 what은 선행사를 포함하므로 앞에 선행사가 없고, the thing(s) which [that]와 바꿔 쓸 수 있다.

3 관계대명사 that은 주격 · 목적격 관계대명사 who(m), which 대신 쓸 수 있으며 that 앞에는 선행사가 있다.

4 선행사에 「사람+사물」, 「사람+동물」, all, the only, -thing, -body, -one, 최상급, 서수가 있으면 주로 관계대명사 that을 쓴다.

관계대명사 what	관계대명사 that
명사절을 이끎	형용사절을 이끎
선행사 없음	선행사 있음
관계대명사 what + 불완전한 문장	관계대명사 that + 불완전한 문장

개념 33 관계부사

1 관계부사는 시간, 장소, 이유, 방법을 나타내는 선행사를 수식하는 절을 이끌며 접속사와 부사의 역할을 한다.

2 관계부사는 「전치사 + 관계대명사」와 바꿔 쓸 수 있다.

3 관계부사 how와 the way는 함께 쓰일 수 없으므로 둘 중 하나는 생략해야 한다.

	선행사	관계부사	전치사 + 관계대명사
시간	the day, the time, the week 등	when	in / at / on + which
장소	the place, the town, the city 등	where	in / at / on + which
이유	the reason	why	for which
방법	(the way)	how	in which

개념 34 관계대명사의 계속적 용법

1 관계대명사의 계속적 용법은 선행사에 대한 부가적인 정보를 제공할 때 쓰인다.

2 관계대명사가 계속적 용법으로 쓰일 때 관계사 앞에 콤마(,)를 쓰며, 명사뿐만 아니라 구나 절도 선행사가 될 수 있다.

3 계속적 용법으로 쓰인 관계대명사는 생략할 수 없고, 관계대명사 that과 what은 계속적 용법으로 쓰일 수 없다.

제한적 용법	계속적 용법
선행사를 직접 수식함	선행사에 대한 보충 설명을 함
관계사 앞에 콤마(,)가 없음	관계사 앞에 콤마(,)가 있음
'~한, ~하는'으로 해석함	관계사 앞의 절부터 해석하고 and, but 등의 접속사를 넣어 관계사 뒤의 절을 해석함
He has two sons who are teachers. 그에게는 교사인 아들이 두 명 있다. (→ 아들이 둘 이상일 수 있음)	He has two sons, who(= and they) are teachers. 그에게는 아들이 둘 있고, 그들은 교사이다. (→ 아들이 둘 뿐임)

UNIT 08 관계사

개념 35 복합 관계대명사

1 복합 관계대명사는 「관계대명사 + -ever」의 형태로 자체에 선행사를 포함하고 있다.

2 복합 관계대명사는 문장 내에서 주어 또는 목적어 역할을 하는 명사절이나 양보의 부사절을 이끈다.

3 복합 관계대명사가 주어일 때는 단수 동사를 쓴다.

복합 관계대명사	명사절	양보의 부사절
whoever	anyone who ~하는 누구든지	no matter who 누가 ~하더라도
whomever	anyone whom ~하는 누구든지	no matter whom 누구를 ~하더라도
whichever	anything which ~하는 어느 것이든지	no matter which 어느 것이[을] ~하더라도
whatever	anything that ~하는 무엇이든지	no matter what 무엇이[을] ~하더라도

개념 36 복합 관계부사

1 복합 관계부사는 「관계부사 + -ever」의 형태로 자체에 선행사를 포함하고 있다.

2 복합 관계부사는 시간, 장소의 부사절이나 양보의 부사절을 이끈다.

3 however는 양보의 부사절만 이끌며 어순은 대개 「however + 형용사/부사 + 주어 + 동사 ~」이다.

복합 관계부사	시간, 장소의 부사절	양보의 부사절
whenever	at any time when ~할 때마다	no matter when 언제 ~하더라도
wherever	at any place where ~한 곳 어디에나	no matter where 어디에서 ~하더라도
however	–	no matter how 아무리 ~하더라도

UNIT 09 접속사

개념 37 상관접속사

1 상관접속사는 두 개 이상의 단어가 짝을 이루는 접속사이다.

2 상관접속사는 문법적으로 동등한 요소를 연결한다.

3 상관접속사가 연결하는 말이 주어로 쓰일 때 동사의 수에 유의한다.

상관접속사	의미	주어로 쓰일 때 동사의 수
both *A* and *B*	A와 B 둘 다	복수 취급
not only *A* but also *B*	A뿐만 아니라 B도	B에 맞춤
A as well as *B*	B뿐만 아니라 A도	A에 맞춤
not *A* but *B*	A가 아니라 B	B에 맞춤
either *A* or *B*	A 또는 B 둘 중 하나	B에 맞춤
neither *A* nor *B*	A도 B도 아닌	B에 맞춤

개념 38 간접의문문

1 간접의문문은 의문문이 다른 문장의 일부로 쓰인 것을 말하고, 주어, 목적어, 보어 역할을 한다.

2 의문사가 있는 의문문은 간접의문문이 될 때 「의문사+주어+동사 ...」 형태로 쓴다. 주절의 동사가 think, believe, guess, suppose, imagine 등일 때에는 의문사를 문장 맨 앞에 쓴다.

3 의문사가 없는 의문문은 접속사 if 또는 whether가 이끄는 절로 쓴다.

종류	형태
의문사가 있는 의문문	의문사 + 주어 + 동사
	주절의 동사가 think, believe, guess, suppose, imagine 등일 때: 의문사 + do you think [believe, guess, ...] + 주어 + 동사 ...?
의문사가 없는 의문문	if + 주어 + 동사 / whether + 주어 + 동사

UNIT 09 접속사

개념 39 부사절을 이끄는 접속사

1 부사절은 시간, 이유, 조건, 양보, 결과, 목적 등의 의미를 나타내며 주절의 앞이나 뒤에 쓰일 수 있다.

2 시간이나 조건을 나타내는 부사절에서는 미래를 나타낼 때 현재 시제를 쓴다.

구분	접속사	의미
시간	when	~할 때
	while	~하는 동안
	as	~하면서
	until	~할 때까지
	as soon as	~하자마자
	since	~ 이후로
결과	so	그래서
	so ~ that	매우 ~해서 …하다
	so ~ that ... can	매우 ~해서 …할 수 있다 (= ~ enough + to부정사)
	so ~ that ... can't	너무 ~해서 …할 수 없다 (= too ~ to부정사)

구분	접속사	의미
이유	because as since	~ 때문에
조건	if	만일 ~라면
	unless	만일 ~ 아니라면 (= if ~ not)
	in case (that)	~할 경우에는 (= in case of + 명사)
목적	so that ... *can, in order that ... *can	~하기 위해 (= in order + to부정사 / to부정사) *조동사 may, will 등도 쓰임
양보	though, although, even though	비록 ~이지만, ~에도 불구하고 (= in spite of / despite + 명사)

개념 40 접속부사

구분	접속부사	의미
양보, 대조	however	하지만
	nevertheless	그럼에도 불구하고
	on the other hand	반면에
첨가	also	또한
	furthermore	더욱이
	besides	
	in addition	게다가
	moreover	

구분	접속부사	의미
결과	therefore	그러므로
	thus	그러므로
	accordingly	따라서
	consequently	결과적으로
	as a result	결과적으로

구분	접속부사	의미
기타	then	그러고 나서
	otherwise	그 외에는, 그렇지 않으면

UNIT 10 비교 구문

개념 41 원급 비교

1 비교되는 두 대상의 성질 또는 수량이 같을 때 형용사와 부사의 원급을 이용하여 '…만큼 ~하다'라는 원급 비교의 의미를 나타낼 수 있다.

2 '몇 배'를 나타내는 배수 표현을 원급 비교 구문과 함께 써서 '…배만큼 ~하다'라는 의미를 나타낼 수 있다. 배수 표현은 half(절반), twice(두 번), three times(세 번), four times(네 번) 등으로 나타낸다.

원급 비교	*A* ~ as + 원급 + as + *B*
	의미: A가 B만큼 ~하다
can을 활용한 원급 비교	as + 원급 + as + 주어 + can (= as + 원급 + as possible)
	의미: …가 할 수 있는 한 ~한/하게
배수 표현을 사용한 비교	*A* ~ 배수 표현 + as + 원급 + as + *B*
	의미: A는 B보다 …배만큼 ~하다

개념 42 여러 가지 비교급 표현

1 비교급을 사용해 두 대상을 비교할 때 비교 대상 앞에 than을 쓴다.

2 비교급을 강조할 때 비교급 앞에 much, a lot, far, even 등을 쓴다.

3 비교급을 활용하여 다양한 비교 구문을 쓸 수 있다.

비교급 구문	의미
비교급 + than	…보다 더 ~한
much / a lot / far / even + 비교급	훨씬 더 ~한
a little / a bit / slightly + 비교급	약간 더 ~한
less + 원급 + than	…보다 덜 ~한
비교급 + and + 비교급	점점 더 ~한
the + 비교급 ~, the + 비교급 ...	더 ~할수록 더 …하다

개념 43 여러 가지 최상급 표현

1 최상급 앞에는 대개 the를 쓴다.

2 최상급 표현 뒤에 비교 범위를 나타내는 부사구가 오는 경우가 많다.

최상급 구문	의미
the + 최상급 ~ + in + 장소/집단	…에서 가장 ~한
the + 최상급 ~ + of + 복수 명사	… 중에서 가장 ~한
one of the + 최상급 + 복수 명사	가장 ~한 … 중 하나
the + 최상급 + 명사 (+ that) + 주어 + have ever + 과거분사	지금까지 …한 것 중 가장 ~한

개념 44 원급과 비교급을 이용한 최상급 표현

원급 또는 비교급을 이용한 최상급 표현	의미
비교급 + than + any other + 단수 명사	다른 어떤 …보다 ~한
비교급 + than + all the other + 복수 명사	다른 모든 …보다 ~한
No (other) + 명사 ~ + 비교급 + than	어떤 –도 …보다 ~하지 않다
No (other) + 명사 ~ + as [so] + 원급 + as	어떤 –도 …만큼 ~하지 않다

UNIT 11 가정법

개념 45 가정법 과거와 과거완료

1 가정법 과거는 '(만약) ~한다면, …할 텐데[것이다]'라는 의미로 현재 사실과 반대되거나 실제로 일어날 가능성이 거의 없는 일을 가정할 때 쓴다. if절의 동사가 be동사인 경우 주어의 인칭과 수에 관계없이 were를 쓴다.

2 가정법 과거완료는 '(만약) ~했다면, …했을 텐데[것이다]'라는 의미로 과거 사실과 반대되는 일을 가정할 때 쓴다.

3 if절과 주절의 위치는 바꿀 수 있으며, 주절이 앞에 있을 때는 주절 뒤에 콤마(,)를 쓰지 않는다.

		if절	주절
가정법 과거	현재 사실의 반대	If + 주어 + were 또는 동사의 과거형 ~,	주어 + 조동사 과거형(would, could, might) + 동사원형 ~.
가정법 과거완료	과거 사실의 반대	If + 주어 + had + 과거분사 ~,	주어 + 조동사 과거형(would, could, might) + have + 과거분사 ~.

개념 46 혼합 가정법

1 혼합 가정법은 if절에 가정법 과거완료를, 주절에 가정법 과거를 쓴 것으로 '(만약) ~했다면, …할 텐데'라는 의미이다. 과거에 실현되지 못한 일이 현재까지 영향을 줄 때 사용한다.

2 if절에는 주로 과거를 나타내는 부사(구)를 쓰고, 주절에는 현재를 나타내는 부사(구)를 쓴다.

		if절 (가정법 과거완료)	주절 (가정법 과거)
혼합 가정법	과거에 실현되지 못한 일이 현재까지 영향을 줄 때	If + 주어 + had + 과거분사 ~,	주어 + 조동사 과거형(would, could, might) + 동사원형 ~.

개념 47 I wish 가정법 / as if 가정법

1 I wish 가정법 과거는 현재 이루기 힘든 소망이나 현실에 대한 아쉬움을 나타낸다.

2 I wish 가정법 과거완료는 과거 이루지 못한 일에 대한 아쉬움을 나타낸다.

3 as if 가정법 과거는 주절과 같은 시점의 사실과 반대되는 상황을 가정할 때 쓴다.

4 as if 가정법 과거완료는 주절보다 앞선 시점의 사실과 반대되는 상황을 가정할 때 쓴다.

I wish 가정법	과거	~라면 좋을 텐데	I wish + 주어 + were 또는 동사의 과거형
	과거완료	~했더라면 좋을 텐데	I wish + 주어 + had + 과거분사
as if 가정법	과거	마치 ~인 것처럼	as if + 주어 + were 또는 동사의 과거형
	과거완료	마치 ~이었던 것처럼	as if + 주어 + had + 과거분사

개념 48 Without 가정법

1 「Without + 명사(구), 가정법 과거」는 현재 있는 것이 없다고 가정할 때 쓴다. Without 대신 But for나 If it were not for로 바꿔 쓸 수도 있다.

2 「Without + 명사(구), 가정법 과거완료」는 과거에 있었던 것이 없었다고 가정할 때 쓴다. Without 대신 But for나 If it had not been for로 바꿔 쓸 수도 있다.

Without 가정법	과거	~이 없다면, …할 것이다	Without + 명사(구), 주어 + 조동사 과거형 + 동사원형 ~.
	과거완료	~이 없었다면, …했을 것이다	Without + 명사(구), 주어 + 조동사 과거형 + have + 과거분사 ~.

UNIT 12 일치, 화법, 특수 구문

개념 49 수 일치

1 동사의 형태는 주어의 수와 인칭에 일치시킨다.

주어의 종류	수	예
every / each + 명사	단수 취급	Every girl has ...
나라, 작품, 학문 이름		The United States makes ...
시간, 거리, 금액, 무게		One hundred kilometers is ...
the number of + 복수 명사		The number of stars is ...
분수, 부분 표현 + 단수 명사		Two-fifths of the cake was ...
단일 개념의 「*A* and *B*」		Curry and rice is ...
a number of + 복수 명사	복수 취급	A number of people gather ...
the + 형용사 (복수의 의미)		The young are ...
분수, 부분 표현 + 복수 명사		Three-fifths of the apples are ...
both (*A* and *B*)		Both a cat and a dog are ...
항상 복수형인 명사 (e.g. socks)		Those socks were ...

개념 50 시제 일치

1 영어 문장에서 종속절의 시제는 주절의 시제에 맞춘다. 그러나 항상 현재 시제 또는 과거 시제로 쓰이는 예외의 경우도 있다.

2 주절의 시제가 현재일 때 종속절의 시제는 어느 것이나 쓸 수 있지만, 주절의 시제가 과거일 때에는 종속절의 시제를 과거 또는 과거완료로 쓴다.

시제 일치의 예외인 경우	종속절의 시제	예
불변의 진리, 속담, 현재의 사실, 습관 등	항상 현재	We learned that the sun sets in the west.
역사적 사실	항상 과거	I learned that Edison invented the light bulb.
가정법이 쓰인 종속절, 비교 구문 등	주절에 영향 받지 않음	He looked healthier last year than he does now.

개념 51 평서문의 화법 전환

1 다른 사람이 한 말을 그대로 전하는 것이 직접 화법이고, 이것을 전달하는 사람의 입장에서 바꿔 말하는 간접 화법으로 전환하여 쓸 수 있다.

2 직접 화법을 간접 화법으로 전환할 때, 주어와 주절의 시점에 유의하여 시제와 대명사, 부사구 등을 전환한다.

평서문의 화법 전환			
동사 전환	• say는 그대로 • say to → tell	주절과 피전달문 연결	접속사 that으로 연결 (인용 부호, 콤마 등 생략)
피전달문 나머지 부분 일치시키기	• 주절의 동사가 과거일 때 시제 일치: 현재 → 과거 / 과거 → 과거완료 • 대명사와 부사(구): 내용과 주절의 시점에 맞춰 전환 this → that here → there now → then ago → before today → that day yesterday → the day before		

개념 52 의문문과 명령문의 화법 전환

	의문문의 화법 전환	명령문의 화법 전환
동사 전환	ask	• 지시: tell • 충고: advise • 부탁, 요청: ask • 명령: order
주절과 피전달문 연결	• 의문사 또는 if [whether]로 연결 • 피전달문 어순: 의문사 / if [whether] + 주어 + 동사	• 긍정명령문: → to부정사 • 부정명령문: → not + to부정사
피전달문 나머지 부분 일치시키기	• 시제 일치 • 대명사와 부사(구) 일치시키기	

UNIT 12 일치, 화법, 특수 구문

개념 53 강조

「It ~ that」 강조 구문	It + be동사 + 강조할 말 + that ~ └→ 주어, 목적어, 부사구 * 강조되는 말에 따라 that 대신 who, whom, when, where 등 사용 가능
동사 강조	do [does/did] + 동사원형
명사 강조	the very + 명사
부정어 강조	not ~ at all / not ~ in the least

개념 54 도치

1 주어와 동사의 위치가 바뀌는 것을 도치라고 한다.

2 주로 부정어나 부사구 등을 강조하기 위해 문장의 맨 앞에 쓸 때 도치가 일어난다.

문장의 앞에 오는 어구	문장 구조	예
부정어	부정어 + 조동사 + 주어 + 동사 부정어 not, no, never, little, hardly, rarely, seldom, scarcely ...	Rarely did they fight with other groups.
only를 포함한 부사구	부사구 + 조동사 + 주어 + 동사	Only then did we understand the problem.
장소 · 방향의 부사구	부사구 + 동사 + 주어 * 주어가 대명사일 때: 부사구 + 주어 + 동사	On the platform stood a young boy.
there / here	There + be동사 + 주어 (…이 있다) Here + 동사 + 주어 * 주어가 대명사일 때: Here + 주어 + 동사	Here comes the bus!
so / neither	So / Neither + (조)동사 + 주어 (…도 역시 그렇다)	Neither do I.

문장

바로 쓰는 문법

핵심은
이안에
있지 !